DISCOURSES ON LIVY

NICCOLÒ MACHIAVELLI was born in Florence in 1469. Very little is known of his life until his entrance into the Florentine chancery in 1498, where he served his mentor, the Florentine standard-bearer Piero Soderini, until the return of the Medici in 1512 overthrew Soderini's republic and brought Machiavelli both the loss of his position and even brief imprisonment for his republican sympathies. Retiring to his farm outside Florence, Machiavelli wrote *The Prince* in 1513 (first posthumously published in 1532) and began the *Discourses on Livy* (first published posthumously in 1531). In addition to these major political works treating respectively the nature of the ruler and republican government (the latter always Machiavelli's preference in spite of his evil reputation as a counsellor of tyrants), the Florentine writer also wrote lyric poetry, a novella, numerous brief essays and diplomatic narratives, a large and important body of private and public correspondence, *The Art of War*, *The History of Florence*, and the masterpiece of Italian Renaissance comedy, *The Mandrake Root*. Machiavelli died in 1527.

JULIA CONAWAY BONDANELLA is Associate Professor of French and Italian and Associate Director of the Honors Division at Indiana University. She is the author of *Petrarch's Visions and Their Renaissance Analogues* and *Rousseau's Political Works* and she is editor with Peter Bondanella of the *Cassell Dictionary of Italian Literature*. For the World's Classics series she has translated and edited Giorgio Vasari's *Lives of the Most Famous Artists*, and a new translation and critical edition of Benvenuto Cellini's *Autobiography* with Peter Bondanella, is in progress.

PETER BONDANELLA is Distinguished Professor of Comparative Literature and Professor of Film Studies, Italian, and West European Studies at Indiana University, where he serves as Chairman of the Department of West European Studies. He is author of works on Machiavelli, Umberto Eco and Italian cinema (including individual works on Fellini and Rossellini). For the World's Classics series he has translated and edited Machiavelli's *The Prince*.

THE WORLD'S CLASSICS

NICCOLÒ MACHIAVELLI

Discourses on Livy

Translated with an Introduction and Notes by
JULIA CONAWAY BONDANELLA
and
PETER BONDANELLA

Oxford   New York
OXFORD UNIVERSITY PRESS
1997

Oxford University Press, Great Clarendon Street, Oxford OX2 6DP

Oxford New York

Athens Auckland Bangkok Bogota Bombay Buenos Aires
Calcutta Cape Town Dar es Salaam Delhi Florence Hong Kong Istanbul
Karachi Kuala Lumpur Madras Madrid Melbourne Mexico City
Nairobi Paris Singapore Taipei Tokyo Toronto Warsaw
and associated companies in
Berlin Ibadan

Oxford is a trade mark of Oxford University Press

British Library Cataloguing in Publication Data
Data available

Library of Congress Cataloging in Publication Data
Data available
ISBN 0-19-282945-9

1 3 5 7 9 10 8 6 4 2

Typeset by Jayvee, Trivandrum, India
Printed in Great Britain by
Caledonian International Book Manufacturing Ltd.
Glasgow

CONTENTS

For Livia Emilia Della Rovere *in memoriam*

INTRODUCTION

Niccolò di Bernardo Machiavelli was born on 3 May 1469 into a middle-class Florentine family from the Oltrarno section of the city. Although his ancestors had filled a number of posts in the city's government, the family was certainly not a major patrician clan equal in wealth or prestige to the more important families of the times. Not a great deal is known about Machiavelli's early life. It is evident that his father must have instilled in him a love for Latin language and ancient history. He owned a copy of the *Historarum ab inclinatione romani imperii decades* (1452–53, *The Decades*) by Flavio Biondo (1392–1463), an important Latin historical work in thirty-two books that narrated the history of Italy from the invasion of the Goths and the destruction of Rome in AD 410 down to Biondo's own times. Biondo was one of the Florentine humanists who imitated the historical works of the Roman writer Titus Livius or Livy (59 BC–AD 17) and who were responsible for making Livy the major historical model during the entire European Renaissance. Machiavelli's father considered one of his prize possessions an edition of Livy's history of republican Rome, which he obtained from the printer in return for the laborious task of compiling an index of Livy's place-names. When Machiavelli entered the Florentine chancery in 1498, shortly after the execution of Girolamo Savonarola in the Piazza della Signoria, he entered an atmosphere imbued with the humanist spirit where Petrarch and Petrarch's favourite literary models (Cicero and Livy) provided models for the writing of eloquent governmental correspondence as well as historiography in Latin.

When Machiavelli was exiled from active political life in 1513 and retired to his country home in Sant'Andrea in Percussina outside Florence, he began work on his commentary upon Livy's history of Rome. Around the same time (scholars are still debating exactly when and how), he also wrote one of the most famous of all political treatises, *The Prince*, first published posthumously in 1532, a year after the posthumous publication of his *Discourses on Livy*. A classic of modern social thought, *The Prince* continues to arouse heated debate and controversy for its sometimes shockingly realistic treatment of the relationship between politics and ethics. The immediate practical purpose of *The Prince*—embodied in an exhortation by its author in the book's concluding chapter to the Medici family to lead a crusade against foreign invaders of Italy—was superseded within a decade of its composition, but Machiavelli's radically original treatment of crucial philosophical and political issues in *The Prince* has held the attention of fascinated readers for centuries.

Machiavelli's writings all reflect one of the most characteristic features of Italian Renaissance culture—the rebirth of classical antiquity. Where other Renaissance artists eagerly drew on classical motifs, copied ancient statues, and attempted to emulate and eventually surpass the classical image of the human figure in art and sculpture and the classical heritage in architecture, Machiavelli believed that the ancient Romans and, to a much lesser extent, the ancient Greeks had, in their major historical works, laid down a number of fundamental rules for the understanding of human behaviour, particularly in the realm of politics. His *Discourses on Livy* is filled with citations or references to numerous classical authors: primarily Livy, of course, but also Aristotle, Cicero, Diodorus Siculus, Tacitus, Procopius, Sallust, Xenophon, Thucydides, Virgil, Juvenal, Q. Curtius Rufus, and Herodian. He most likely relied on other unnamed classical authors, such as Herodotus, Justin, Lucian, Suetonius, and Valerius Maximus. In sharp contrast, Machiavelli cites or mentions only three Italian writers: Dante, Lorenzo de' Medici, and Flavio Biondo (who wrote in Latin, not the vernacular). Roman antiquity represented for the Florentine writer a repository of special wisdom that had great relevance for the present.

The juxtaposition of classical examples with those from his own times, a concept fundamental not only to *Discourses on Livy* but to all of Machiavelli's work, seems to have been an automatic reflex in his thinking. We know, for example, that between 1502 and 1503, when Machiavelli was sent to Urbino, Rome, and Imola on diplomatic missions for the Florentine republic at the court of Cesare Borgia, the warrior son of Pope Alexander VI who would soon become the controversial ideal model of the ruler in *The Prince*, he asked a close friend, Biagio Buonaccorsi, for a copy of Plutarch's *Lives*. Not content to have before him the flesh-and-blood embodiment of the modern prince, Machiavelli wanted to measure this contemporary *exemplum* against other heroic figures from the ancient past. An important early political essay written in 1503 and based upon the political lessons Machiavelli learned during his dramatic encounter with Borgia—*Del modo di trattare i popoli della Valdichiana ribellati* (*On the Method of Dealing with the Rebellious Peoples of the Valdichiana*)—contrasts Livy's description of the Romans' effective method of subduing an uprising with the disastrous errors of the Florentine republic on a similar occasion. This method of comparing the practice of the ancient Romans to that of his contemporaries would provide Machiavelli with a consistent point of view in all his literary, political, historical, and diplomatic works. It was based upon a commonly held supposition during the Italian Renaissance that ancient Rome had reached the pinnacle of human achievement in a number of fields—art, architecture, politics, historiography, warfare—and that contemporary Italians should base their actions upon models found in the distant past of antiquity if they wished to emulate ancient perfection.

The Renaissance Myth of Roman Antiquity and the Livian Model

The myth of classical antiquity, or more accurately, the myth of Roman antiquity, occupies a key place in Renaissance culture. Petrarch (1304–74), the father of Renaissance humanism, once asked: 'what else, then, is all history, if not the praise of Rome?'[1] His question was a rhetorical one which assumed agreement with Petrarch's bold assertion. Petrarch's humanist followers inside the Florentine chancery before Machiavelli—Coluccio Salutati (1331–1406), Leonardo Bruni (1369–1444), and Poggio Bracciolini (1380–1459)—would all have concurred with this

---

[1] Cited by Theodor E. Mommsen in 'Petrarch's Conception of the Dark Ages', in *Medieval and Renaissance Studies*, ed. Eugene F. Rice (Ithaca: Cornell University Press, 1969), 122. The citation comes from Petrarch's Latin work *Apologia contra cuiusdam anonymi Galli calumnias*.

statement, particularly since Petrarch's historical model, Livy, wrote in praise of a republican form of government to which the Florentines liked to compare themselves. In the only political or historical work he published during his lifetime, *L'arte della guerra* (1519, *The Art of War*), Machiavelli declared that he would never advise deviating, in any human endeavour, from the venerable model provided by 'his' Romans (Book I). In what is perhaps the most famous single letter from the Italian Renaissance, Machiavelli paid tribute to the ancient Romans in a description of an intellectual kinship with them that surpassed all other ties he felt:

When evening comes, I return to my home, and I go into my study; and on the threshold, I take off my everyday clothes, which are covered with mud and mire, and I put on regal and curial robes; and dressed in a more appropriate manner I enter into the ancient courts of ancient men and am welcomed by them kindly, and there I taste the food that alone is mine, and for which I was born; and there I am not ashamed to speak to them, to ask them the reasons for their actions; and they, in their humanity, answer me; and for four hours I feel no boredom, I dismiss every affliction, I no longer fear poverty nor do I tremble at the thought of death: I become completely part of them.[2]

Livy's history of republican Rome, in the hands of what has since become identified by modern scholarship as the 'civic humanist' movement, constituted a special mythical world, a form of secular religion, a realm of superhuman affairs where ordinary street-clothes were insufficiently elegant for Rome, the metropolis of the mind.[3] At the core of the myth of Rome are two diametrically opposed models of political and ethical behaviour: a virtuous Roman republic defended by stalwart

---

[2] See *The Portable Machiavelli*, ed. and trans. Peter Bondanella and Mark Musa (New York: Penguin, 1979), 69.

[3] The fundamental text linking the civic humanism of the Quattrocento to Machiavelli's works and subsequent republican theory in England and America is J. G. Pocock, *The Machiavellian Moment: Florentine Political Thought and the Atlantic Republican Tradition* (Princeton: Princeton University Press, 1975). A recent book dedicated to Italy's impact upon the formation of American political and cultural traditions, *La virtù e la libertà: Ideali e civiltà nella formazione degli Stati Uniti*, ed. Marcello Pacini (Turin: Edizioni della Fondazione Giovanni Agnelli, 1995), contains a number of important essays that discuss the Pocock thesis and affirm Machiavelli's relevance to contemporary republican theory.

citizen-soldiers and ever-vigilant guardians of public liberty, on the one hand; and a corrupted empire, on the other, whose citizens were occupied by an overpowering lust for power and wealth (and sometimes merely lust, pure and simple). The basic materials for this Roman mythology, this historical morality play, derive from a number of sources. But the primary ideas for the republican model were provided by Livy, while Tacitus became the major source for its imperial counterpart. The republican model was advocated not only by the humanist republican scribes in the Florentine chancery, but it was also transmitted throughout Renaissance culture through a series of eloquent and moving artistic images. For example, in the Palazzo Pubblico in Siena, Taddeo di Bartolo (c.1362–1422) was commissioned in 1422 to complete a fresco cycle depicting Roman republican heroes. A central inscription on the wall reads in Italian: 'Take Rome as your example if you wish to rule a thousand years; follow the common good, and not selfish ends; and give just counsel like these men.'[4] Many of the other city-states of the Italian peninsula employed similar imagery in their public buildings and monuments to underline the actual or imagined continuity between their republics and that of ancient Rome.

In Florence, between 1495 and 1504—and therefore, squarely in the middle of the period of Florentine republicanism during which time Machiavelli served in the chancery—Sandro Botticelli created a pair of Livian panel paintings, *The Tragedy of Lucretia* and *The Tragedy of Verginia* (whose deaths form the subject of key episodes in Livy's history), that celebrated the defence of the Roman republic against its tyrannical opponents. Other important figures in Roman mythology played a key role in the political vocabulary employed during Machiavelli's times. Marcus Junius Brutus, the heroic figure depicted by Plutarch and immortalized by Shakespeare, known as the 'second' Brutus because of his role in the assassination of Julius Caesar, the destroyer of Roman republican liberty, was frequently invoked as a noble defender of freedom. When the Medici family

[4] Cited from Peter Bondanella, *The Eternal City: Roman Images in the Modern World* (Chapel Hill: University of North Carolina Press, 1987), 42.

returned to power in 1513 and sent Machiavelli into exile and enforced retirement from politics, one of the conspirators against their return, Paolo Boscoli, was condemned for his part in an anti-Medici conspiracy that falsely implicated Machiavelli and caused him several turns on the rack. As Boscoli was about to be executed, he called out to a friend: 'Ah! Luca, pluck Brutus from my mind, that I may pass from the world a perfect Christian!'[5] When Lorenzino de' Medici murdered his cousin, Duke Alessandro, in 1537, in a futile attempt to prevent Medici tyranny, he was hailed by anti-Medici forces as the 'Tuscan Brutus'. Shortly after Machiavelli's death in 1527, Domenico Beccafumi was commissioned to add additional republican frescos to the Hall of the Consistory in Siena's Palazzo Pubblico. Between 1529 and 1535 Beccafumi provided the republican government of that city opposed to Medici absolutism in Tuscany with a number of brilliant images of the ignominious fates that would befall those, like Spurius Cassius or Marcus Manlius Capitolinus—two of Livy's most memorable villains—who betrayed the Sienese Republic. Even after the Medici family had firmly reestablished its hegemony over Machiavelli's beloved Florence, Michelangelo (who always held strong republican convictions in spite of his years of service to the Medici) created one of the most powerful of all republican images, his marble bust of *Brutus*, persuaded to do so between 1539 and 1540 by the staunch Medici opponent Donato Giannotti, the last republican secretary of the Florentine government and the aide of Cardinal Ridolfi, an anti-Medici exile from Florence. The republican sentiment that these and many other important works of art reflected during the sixteenth century underscores the importance of such ideas in Italian Renaissance culture. In an age when political absolutism was increasingly the norm, Machiavelli's republican theories would become a dangerous ideology until they were revived abroad in England and America during subsequent periods of republican sentiment. Even works of art, such

⁵ Cited from D. J. Gordon, 'Giannotti, Michelangelo and the Cult of Brutus', in *The Renaissance Imagination: Essays and Lectures by D. J. Gordon*, ed. Stephen Orgel (Berkeley: University of California Press, 1975), 235 (Gordon's translation).

as Michelangelo's bust of Brutus, had to be reinterpreted to soften their political purpose. When Francesco, Grand Duke of Tuscany, acquired the bust between 1574 and 1575, he added a Latin inscription to its base which advanced the improbable thesis that Michelangelo left the work incomplete because he realized that the actions of a tyrannicide were reprehensible!

Livy's History of Rome as Exemplary History

The ideas contained in Livy's works were, therefore, not mere academic topics of calm discussion. They represented a major political idiom of the times, a language of both images and ideas interpreted by Machiavelli and other Renaissance artists and thinkers for their concrete relevance to the practical world of Italian politics. Livy had lived during the last days of the Roman republic, survived the reign of the Emperor Augustus, and died during the reign of Tiberius. His major work, *Ab urbe condita* (From the Foundation of the City), may well be said to constitute the single most important historical work in Western culture. Originally containing 142 books, of which only 35 are extant, Livy's masterful historical narrative espoused a view of history as a source of models of behaviour that the Italian Renaissance embraced. As Livy put it, history was full of 'fine things to take as models, base things, rotten through and through, to avoid'.[6] Livy's narrative covered the period stretching from the foundation of Rome (traditionally dated as 753 BC) through the city's rise to power in the Mediterranean world after its triumph over rival Carthage in the Punic Wars. Most particularly in the first five surviving books of his history, which cover the heroic early period between 753 BC and the temporary occupation of Rome by the Gauls in 386 BC, Livy firmly established in the Western imagination the image of a virtuous, noble republic composed of selfless citizen-soldiers who believed in death before dishonour. He thus created a cast of characters that has since influenced Western political thought, literature, and art: Lucius Junius Brutus (the 'first' Brutus), who avenged the

---

[6] Cited from Livy, *The Early History of Rome*, trans. Aubrey De Selincourt (New York: Penguin, 1979), 34.

death of Lucretia, exiled the Tarquin tyrants responsible for such an outrage, and established the first Roman republic, later executing his sons when they proved to be traitors; Mucius Scaevola, who burned his hand when it failed to carry out the assassination of Lars Porsenna, a defender of the Tarquin tyrants; Horatius Cocles (the famous 'Horatio at the bridge'), who defended the River Tiber against a host of invaders; Lucius Quinctius Cincinnatus, the republican dictator who left his humble farm to save Rome and then, in an amazing display of selflessness that was later to be followed by George Washington (to whom he was frequently compared), abandoned power and returned to his farm; and Titus Manlius Torquatus, who followed Brutus and executed his son when he disobeyed the republic's orders. These and numerous other figures from Livy, as well as from Plutarch and other Latin writers, constituted a republican tradition that would appeal not only to the humanist and political scientist in Machiavelli but also to the masterful literary stylist, who understood very clearly that the rhetorical impact of a superhuman hero's gallant deeds upon a reader's imagination was, on occasion, superior to the force of logic or the persuasive power of historical precedent.

Machiavelli: Theorist of the Principality or the Republic?

Machiavelli's reputation as a republican thinker has been overshadowed for centuries by the negative image he gained as a result of his discussion of politics and morality in his brief treatise, *The Prince.* Much scholarly effort during the last few decades has been spent upon trying to resolve the apparent paradox scholars believe they detect in the contradictory image of Machiavelli, the author of a treatise on absolute rulers, and Machiavelli, the progressive republican theorist. Apparent inconsistencies in Machiavelli's works, in particular his views on the republic and the principality, must not be taken as proof of mental confusion, insincerity, or cynicism. There is no doubt about which political system Machiavelli preferred under the best of circumstances—a republican form of self-government for his native Florence or any similar city-state. Given the rapidly changing political situation in sixteenth-century Italy, marked by foreign invasions and a balance of power on the Italian peninsula that was constantly shifting, Machiavelli had to remain flexible and intellectually alert to rapid political and social change. To pigeon-hole Machiavelli as either the counsellor of tyrants or the republican theorist simply obscures the concern central to any political system he ever proposed. And that concern, an overriding concern, was to maximize Florentine and Italian liberty—that is, external independence and internal self-government, whenever possible, whenever practical, in an imperfect world.

Indeed, it is much more profitable for readers of the *Discourses on Livy* to bear in mind crucial similarities between Machiavelli's two greatest and most seminal works of political theory rather than to concentrate upon their differences. In the first place, *The Prince* was most probably written for a specific historical opportunity that quickly faded away—the chance to combine Medici control of the papacy with Medici control of a central Italian state around Florence. Such a unique opportunity might well, Machiavelli fervently believed, provide the nucleus of a new nation-state that could have driven foreign invaders out of Italy. When that unique possibility vanished by 1519 with the deaths of the Medici pope Leo X and the two Medici princes to whom he had dedicated his treatise on principalities, Machiavelli felt free to turn (or to return, according to some scholars) to the completion (or the composition, according to other scholars) of his more comprehensive work on republics.[7] The *succès de scandale* that launched Machiavelli's fame as the author of *The Prince* immediately after its posthumous publication in 1532 (one year after the posthumous publication of the *Discourses on Livy*) has most certainly clouded understanding of his importance as an original republican thinker.

The Discourses on Livy certainly began as a simple commentary upon Livy's history, but Machiavelli expanded the traditional genre of academic textual commentary on a classical author, so typical of erudite writing in the Italian

---

[7] For a more detailed discussion of the relationship of *The Prince* and the *Discourses on Livy*, see the Introduction to the World's Classics edition of Machiavelli, *The Prince*, ed. Peter Bondanella (Oxford: Oxford University Press, 1984).

Renaissance, into the most important discussion of republican government since the classical period. The key concept in *The Prince* is that of *virtù*—usually translated as 'ability', 'talent', 'strength', 'power', 'skill', 'ingenuity', and only rarely as 'virtue'. Whatever the translation, Machiavellian *virtù* is primarily a masculine quality found in very rare individuals, heroic figures who managed to found states or civic institutions by establishing *ordini* or 'institutions'. In the *Discourses on Livy*, Machiavelli continues to argue for the fundamentally important role such a unique individual has to play in the foundation of republics. A single man alone is usually required to found a state or to reform a corrupted body politic. But such political ability cannot sustain its accomplishments through historical time without the assistance of the people. The founder's personal *virtù* must take on *ordini* to endure; and just as a single prince or ruler is best suited to create such civic institutions, the people in a republican form of government are best suited to protect such institutions after they are created. Thus, the goals of *The Prince* and the *Discourses on Livy* are not so far apart as too many readers of Machiavelli have traditionally believed. The personal ability of a prince or ruler (the focus of *The Prince*) must be transformed or institutionalized into public institutions (the focus of the *Discourses on Livy*) before any independent, self-governing republican state can function properly.

The Originality of Machiavelli's Republican Thought

Politics and Morality

Machiavelli's political thought is unfortunately too often identified with the phrase 'the end justifies the means', a statement erroneously attributed to him by his detractors and unskilful translators. Even in the infamous pages of *The Prince*, the careful reader will note that, in chapter VIII of that treatise, Machiavelli makes a clear distinction between actions that increase the ruler's power and those that increase his glory: 'Still, it cannot be called ingenuity [*virtù*] to kill one's fellow citizens, to betray friends, to be without faith, without mercy, without religion; by these means one can acquire power but not glory.'[8] The clearest discussion of the relationship between political means and ends appears in a crucial passage of the *Discourses on Livy* (i. 9) where Machiavelli discusses the murder of Remus by his brother Romulus and the founding of Rome. On this specific and momentous historical occasion, Machiavelli accepts violence as a regrettably necessary means of pursuing an important political goal: 'It is truly appropriate that while the act accuses him, the result excuses him, and when the result is good, like that of Romulus, it will always excuse him, because one should reproach a man who is violent in order to ruin things, not one who is so in order to set them aright.' Note that Machiavelli stops here, as elsewhere, far short of justifying all political ends. On the contrary, he praises an admittedly violent but unavoidable action because it was performed in the public interest and not for private advantage. Moreover, it resulted in a specific and historically laudable result—the establishment of the most durable and powerful republican government in human history. Only the foundation of a republican form of government and the maintenance of its external independence through historical time constitute for Machiavelli an end important enough to justify real political violence.

The Immutability of Human Nature

The doctrine of imitation is not original with Machiavelli. As we have already seen, Renaissance artists were clearly engaged in imitation of the classical past which they juxtaposed as a superior model to corrupt present practices even before the sixteenth century. Machiavelli, however, held a far more pessimistic view of human nature than was typical of his humanist predecessors from the Quattrocento, such as Giovanni Pico della Mirandola or Leon Battista Alberti. Rather than believing that his fellow human beings were, as Pico put it, only a little lower than the angels and were capable, like Proteus, of changing their essence to become almost godlike, Machiavelli returned to a more traditionally Christian view of man as a selfish, egotistical animal

---

[8] *The Prince*, 30.

controlled by an insatiable desire for material gain and moved only by self-interest. Easily fooled by appearances, man is not to be trusted unless such trust is based upon fear rather than love. This negative, pessimistic assessment of mankind, outlined brilliantly in the most famous passages of *The Prince* and never rejected in the *Discourses on Livy*, nevertheless paradoxically yields positive and optimistic conclusions in Machiavelli's thought. If human nature is fundamentally that evil state which has been fixed since the Fall of Man, the actions of mankind are also somewhat predictable and repetitious like the nature these actions reflect. As such actions occur over historical time, the careful observer may organize, study, and employ them as a guide to contemporary practice. This doctrine of imitation, so fundamental to Machiavelli and the entire range of Italian Renaissance culture, thus yields a primitive form of empirical political science based upon the concept of history as a vast reservoir of didactic models and guides. And the greatest of models could only be found, for a republican theorist, in the works of Livy.

Politics as Conflict and Conflict as Beneficial to the Body Politic

An advantage of the essentially cynical and negative view of human nature Machiavelli held is that the Florentine writer had no interest in concentrating his attention upon ideal or utopian schemes designed to deny or eliminate political conflict. Instead, in the *Discourses on Livy* Machiavelli advances what is perhaps his most original and controversial view of politics. Classical political theory, such as Plato's *Republic*, tends to de-legitimize political conflict and violence. When everyone in the Platonic utopia fulfils his or her proper role, political conflict disappears. Medieval political theory continued the utopian brand of theory which defined the king or prince as the shepherd of his flock (the people). According to most medieval theorists, the ruler as good shepherd will safeguard, rather than fleece, his charges. Machiavelli will have none of such naïve thinking about political behaviour. His conception of politics accepts social strife as a fact of life, the irreducible reality of his subject-matter. In fact, his discussion of conspiracies (iii. 6) is the longest and most sophisticated treatment of this archetypal political upheaval in all of political theory up to his day. But Machiavelli goes a step further to an even more revolutionary affirmation, based upon the historical evidence he found in Livy. For he maintains that such political conflict, properly channelled and managed, may well be a beneficial force in society. While the direction of history was rapidly moving against Machiavellian republicanism in the sixteenth century, since political power was being gradually consolidated in Europe in the hands of dynastic monarchies, principalities, or duchies (with the notable exception of the Republic of Venice and several city-states in Tuscany), Machiavelli advanced eloquent arguments against a prejudice inherited from classical and medieval political theory—the belief that republican government was inherently unstable and potentially anarchic.

Political Stability and the Cycle of Governments

Machiavelli argues in the *Discourses on Livy* that all governments—the three good forms (principality, aristocracy, and democracy) and their three corrupted counterparts (tyranny, oligarchy, and anarchy)—undergo inevitable change. He thus accepts the theory advanced by Polybius, the Greek historian of Rome, that a mixed form of government, embodying elements of the three good forms of government, provides the greatest possible political stability. But unlike other thinkers who attempt to create stability by denying the existence of change or conflict, Machiavelli's close analysis of Livy's Rome led him to believe that a healthy body politic was characterized by social friction and conflict, not rigid stability. Roman liberty and a republican form of government maintaining its external independence over many centuries not only survived but flourished as long as the class conflict between plebeians and patricians was properly managed. Thus, unlike Plato's ideal republic, Machiavelli's model republic was characterized by a dynamic equilibrium between opposing forces rather than the suppression of one interest group or class in order to maintain a façade of domestic tranquillity.

Civic Corruption and the Citizen-Soldier

Once a republican form of government was established, Machiavelli worried most about its destruction through internal corruption, since his cyclic view of history, derived primarily from Polybius, convinced him that all governments, both good and bad, eventually decayed and collapsed. Rome's republic endured for many centuries, and Machiavelli's analysis of Livy discerns a number of reasons for its relative lack of corruption. One primary cause was the preservation of a strong sense of religion among pagan republicans. Romans admired courage and valour, not a Christian humility, and the Roman republic would never have permitted a religion to become a secular government as the Catholic church was to be in Italy, substituting its moral authority for secular force. Another source of civic corruption in Rome was excessive wealth or power in the hands of private individuals. Concentrated wealth or power was a threat to a republican form of government because it provided an easy means of transforming potentially beneficial social conflicts into dangerous struggles between factions or partisans. So long as Rome's social conflicts were between plebeians and aristocrats and were carried on without regard to excessive private interest, they proved to be a means of protecting republican liberty. When private citizens acquired inordinate power, wealth, and influence and employed these resources to further purely personal goals, the supporters of such powerful individuals were transformed from citizens into partisans, since private goals undermined the bedrock of the republican *polis*—the shared community of values and goals within a commonwealth.

Machiavelli's views on citizen-soldiers are explained in great detail in *The Art of War*, but even in the *Discourses on Livy* it is clear from the praise he bestows upon such figures as Cincinnatus and Scipio Africanus that he admires non-professional soldiers whose feats of arms were carried out for the good of the republic and not for mere private gain. In his works there is a clear understanding that a fundamental link exists between republican self-government and a militia of citizen-soldiers, since citizens (as opposed to subjects) fight for the common good and will oppose any move to a tyrannical form of government within the republic.

The Machiavellian Legacy in Republican Theory

Machiavelli's posthumous reputation owes a great deal to the scandalized reactions aroused by *The Prince*. Moralists, particularly in France and England, assailed that treatise as a collection of cynical maxims for evil tyrants. In 1559 the Catholic church placed Machiavelli's works on the Index of Prohibited Books, the Counter Reformation institution that attempted to censor published works in Catholic countries. No amount of censorship, however, was able to prevent the creation of numerous 'Machiavellian' characters in Elizabeth literature. In some 400 references to Machiavelli, the Elizabethans introduced the derogatory terms 'Machiavellian' and 'Machiavellianism' into the English language, and since the Florentine's writings were also assumed to be atheist in inspiration, Niccolò Machiavelli came to be associated with an already-popular term for the devil: 'Old Nick'. Machiavelli appears in the prologue of Marlowe's *The Jew of Malta* (1589), and remarks: 'I count religion but a childish toy | And hold there is no sin but ignorance.' Other 'Machiavellian' characters in this period are Shakespeare's Iago in *Othello* and the young duke of Gloucester, the future Richard III, in *Henry VI*, who speaks of changing 'shapes with Proteus for advantage' and setting 'the murderous Machiavel to school'.

This aspect of Machiavelli's literary reputation has, of course, guaranteed an audience for his work over many centuries, but it is precisely the kind of obstacle that makes understanding his republican theories difficult. In the late seventeenth and eighteenth centuries (a period of republican upheaval in England, France, and America), a more positive image of Machiavelli as republican theorist began to emerge to counter the scandalous image of 'Old Nick'. James Harrington, author of the *Commonwealth of Oceana* (1656), called Machiavelli 'the prince of politicians'. Rousseau rejected the idea that Machiavelli had been a teacher of tyrants and used his republican writings to great advantage in his works. Risorgimento Italians emphasized Machiavelli's nationalism and saw him as the intellectual precursor of a republican movement toward national independence. The fact that Italian fascist dictator Benito Mussolini wrote a preface to an edition of *The Prince* and frequently cited Machiavelli in his speeches did Machiavelli's reputation little good among liberal democrats. On the other hand, it is difficult to call Machiavelli a proto-fascist, since the Marxist thinker Antonio Gramsci relied extensively upon his ideas in the same treatise to produce *The Modern Prince*, which demonstrated the relevance of Machiavelli's political thinking for Marxist philosophy.

The best recent scholarship has emphasized Machiavelli's contributions to the history of republican theory in the *Discourses on Livy* without neglecting the impact or the philosophical importance of *The Prince*. The centuries-old debate on the meaning of Machiavelli's work promises to continue without any easy resolution. This should come as no surprise, for the complex ideas of truly great political theorists raise different questions for each generation of new readers.

TRANSLATORS' NOTE

A good translator often feels caught between two competing goals: the first is to translate the original with accuracy and a sensitivity for the style and intention of the author; the second is to render it in an idiom that is equally understandable in the translator's own language. In translating texts from the past, even with a writer like Machiavelli whose language and syntax are essentially modern, it is necessary to remain aware that some differences exist between current and Renaissance usage. In our effort to create an English version that is as readable, idiomatic, and clear as the original, we have still attempted to remain faithful to the sense and style of the original. We have tried to avoid paraphrasing what we thought Machiavelli was attempting to say, and we have also tried to avoid using archaic syntax or diction to achieve a Renaissance 'flavour'.

In translating Machiavelli's *Discourses on Livy*, we have tried to follow the path of moderation in rendering Machiavelli's style and thoughts. Where the normal contemporary usage of a word does not make sense in a particular context, we have tried to express Machiavelli's meaning. For example, where Machiavelli refers to the ancient Gauls as 'the French' and the Etruscans as 'the Tuscans', we have omitted the anachronism to avoid confusion and made the proper distinction between the ancient and modern peoples. In other cases, we have not always translated certain terms or expressions literally. For example, the term *civiltà* (iii. 49) often means civility or civilization, but is often translated, as it is here, as citizenship, civic life, or civic body. *Peccato* (i. 31; iii. 29) normally means sin, fault, or error, but the word clearly refers, in this instance, to an act damaging to the body politic, such as a crime. *Esterni* (i. 14), which normally means exteriors, refers here to foreigners. *Scandoli* (i. 17, etc.) probably refers to disorders, 'discords', or 'disagreements' rather than scandals in most cases where it is used. *Grazia* (i. 18) often means grace or favour, but 'popularity' seems more appropriate in this context. *Coniettura* (i. 31), which means speculation or conjecture, is occasionally translated as impression or judgement. On rare occasions Machiavelli uses terms which are obsolete, such as *ossidione* (instead of *assedio*) for siege. In all such cases we considered etymologies, philological evidence, and consulted annotations in the critical editions, such as those listed below.

Likewise, in selecting a vocabulary to express key concepts, we aimed for consistency by translating them with a common term or a common group of terms, depending on their context. Among these key phrases, terms, or groups of interrelated terms, those that follow recur throughout the *Discourses on Livy*, and our translations reflect the separate contexts in which they occur: *virtù* has been rendered as 'exceptional skill', 'ability', 'talent', 'valour', 'excellence', or 'ingenuity', and occasionally as 'strength', or 'power'; *ordini* usually as 'institutions', but occasionally as 'regulations', 'battle formations', or 'systems'; *ordinato* as 'arranged', 'organized', 'established', or 'ordered'; *ordinatori* as 'founders', or 'organizers'; *animo* as 'mind', 'heart', 'courage', or 'inner strength'; *esempli* as 'worthy actions', 'exemplary acts', or 'examples'; *fine* as 'aim', 'goal', or 'end'; *modo del procedere* as 'mode of conduct', or 'method of proceeding'; *patria* as 'native land', 'native country', or 'native city'; *tumulti* as 'disturbances', 'upheaval', or 'strife'; *utile* or *utilità* as 'gain', 'profit', or 'benefit'; *vivere civile* as 'civic life', 'civic body', or 'civic state'; *vivere politico* as 'body politic'; *vivere libero* as 'a free way of life', or 'free society'; *vivere commune* as 'community', or 'social body'; *omori* as 'humours' (a Renaissance medical term).

In dealing with Machiavelli's rhetorical devices, we have tried to find solutions that would not distort the original. Nevertheless, they pose some distinct challenges for the translator. Machiavelli often uses *e, perchè, talchè, donde, dove* at the beginning of sentences. Normally, we have followed English style in finding an appropriate adverb. Furthermore, he often uses *e* or *perchè* to begin and to connect a series of dependent or independent clauses, to give them rhetorical symmetry, to lengthen his Latinate periods, and to elaborate complex ideas. Unlike some previous translators, we have tried to avoid chopping up his sentences and inserting periods where he clearly intended the extension of an argument or the elaboration of a thought, even if he begins a new sentence with *e* or *perchè*. For example, in iii. 3, we tried to find an acceptable way of expressing the connections among the four long sentences joined by *e*. In English it seemed appropriate either to drop the conjunction or to find another way to make the connection, such as using a demonstrative pronoun and an active verb.

Occasionally, Machiavelli uses language in a colloquial fashion that would not be considered acceptable in formal writing. He is sometimes inconsistent in his use of pronouns, shifting from an impersonal expression in the third person to the familiar form of 'you', as if to personalize the abstract political questions being raised. For example, he writes:

Talché si vede certo che di quel che si dica uno popolo circa la buona o mala disposizione sua, si debba tenere non gran conto, quando tu sia ordinato in modo da poterlo mantenere s'egli è bene disposto; s'egli è male disposto, da potere provedere che non ti offenda. (i. 57)

In order to give the flavour of the original, we have avoided mixing the impersonal and personal pronouns, but we have chosen to translate these passages with the personal pronoun 'you', even though it is less acceptable in formal English:

Thus, it is clearly evident that you should not give much consideration to what the people say concerning their good or bad inclinations as long as you are organized in such a way as to be able to maintain the people's goodwill, if they are well disposed, or, if they are ill disposed, to make provisions so that they cannot harm you.

In other cases, where Machiavelli uses either a singular or a plural verb with collective nouns (the people, the plebeians, the army, the nobility), we have slightly modified what he wrote to make it correct in English, since we feel that such stylistic peculiarities are of interest mainly to specialists, who will be able to read the original Italian. Also, where it is not possible to express an appropriate antecedent with a pronoun in English, we have generally substituted a noun or some appropriate phrase.

In rendering such general nouns and verbs as *cosa* or *prendere*, we have sometimes chosen to translate them with an English verb of greater precision, depending on the context. We have considered the range of meanings possible for Italian vocabulary, both in Renaissance and modern Italian, and we have chosen English equivalents which best express the idea in its context. For example, *infiniti* could be translated as infinite or countless, without clouding Machiavelli's meaning. On the other hand, the context sometimes determines the meaning of a word. In ii. 2, the reference to the *punta d'Italia* is not to the 'point' of Italy but to the 'tip', that is, the 'toe'.

For the Italian text, we have followed Giorgio Inglese's excellent recent edition, *Discorsi sopra la prima deca di Tito Livio* (Milan: Rizzoli, 1984), while consulting the only complete manuscript of the *Discorsi* (London, British Museum, ms. Harleian 3533) and the 1531 editions of the work published in Rome and Florence. For the variants, we have also checked old standards, including the editions of Mario Casella (1930), Federico Chabod (1944), Leslie J. Walker (1950), Sergio Bertelli (1960), Mario Puppo (1969), and Ezio Raimondi (1969). In translating Machiavelli's many citations from classical authors, we decided that it would be less confusing to cite from the currently available editions rather than providing our own new translations. Our annotations are intended to resolve textual difficulties, clarify key concepts, and explain the important historical references, both ancient and modern.

Our sincere thanks go to Judith Luna and Joanna Rabiger, who waited and waited for this edition. And our special gratitude goes to Jeff New, a truly intelligent and superb copyeditor—no translation could have received more careful and critical attention than he provided.

SELECT BIBLIOGRAPHY

ITALIAN EDITIONS Italian editions of Machiavelli's individual or collected works are numerous. A critical edition used for decades by scholars is *Tutte le opere storiche e letterarie* (Florence: G. Barbara, 1929), edited by Guido Mazzoni and Mario Casella. The most useful and accessible edition of Machiavelli's complete works is *Tutte le opere* (Florence: Sansoni, 1972), edited by Mario Martelli. A more recent and de-luxe complete edition is *Niccolò Machiavelli: Opera omnia* (Verona: Edizioni Valdonega, 1968–80), edited by Sergio Bertelli in eleven volumes. The specific critical edition upon which the present translation is based is *Discorsi sopra la prima deca di Tito Livio*, introduction by Gennaro Sasso with preface and notes by Giorgio Inglese (Milan: Biblioteca Universale Rizzoli, 1984).

ENGLISH TRANSLATIONS There are several major anthologies of Machiavelli's works in English. *The Historical, Political, and Diplomatic Works of Niccolò Machiavelli*, 4 vols. (Boston: James R. Osgood, 1882), translated by Christian E. Detmold, is still worth consulting and contains a complete version of *Discourses on Livy*. Another complete English version containing extensive critical commentary is Leslie J. Walker's *The Discourses of Niccolò Machiavelli*, 2 vols. (New Haven: Yale University Press, 1950). A more recent anthology of Machiavelli's major works in English, translated by Allan Gilbert, *Machiavelli: The Chief Works and Others*, 3 vols. (Durham: Duke University Press, 1965), contains the entire text but very little commentary. The Detmold translation is reprinted in *The Prince and The Discourses*, ed. Max Lerner (New York: Random House, 1950). The Walker translation, partially revised by Brian Richardson, is reprinted in *The Discourses*, ed. Bernard Crick (New York: Penguin, 1974). Finally, the most recent translation of the work is *Discourses on Livy*, translated by Harvey C. Mansfield and Nathan Tarcov (Chicago: University of Chicago Press, 1996). Major sections of *Discourses on Livy*, as well as a selection from Machiavelli's other political, historical, and literary works (including private letters) may also be found in *The Portable Machiavelli* (New York: Penguin, 1979), edited by Peter Bondanella and Mark Musa.

MACHIAVELLI'S LIFE AND TIMES An indispensable guide through the mass of critical literature devoted to Machiavelli is provided in Silvia Ruffo Fiore, *Niccolò Machiavelli: An Annotated Bibliography of*

Modern Criticism and Scholarship (New York: Greenwood Press, 1990), which covers the period 1939–88. The classic Italian treatment of Machiavelli's life and career is Roberto Ridolfi's biography, which has found an English translation as *The Life of Niccolò Machiavelli* (Chicago: University of Chicago Press, 1963). An unusual intellectual biography of Machiavelli, Sebastian de Grazia's *Machiavelli in Hell* (Princeton: Princeton University Press, 1989), may be read to complement Ridolfi's more traditional approach. Machiavelli's personal correspondence provides an invaluable insight into his intellectual milieu. For a recent fresh translation of his letters, see *Machiavelli and His Friends: Their Personal Correspondence*, translated and edited by James B. Atkinson and David Sices (Dekalb: Northern Illinois University Press, 1996). A number of these letters are discussed in John M. Najemy, *Between Friends: Discourses of Power and Desire in the Machiavelli–Vettori Letters of 1513–1515* (Princeton: Princeton University Press, 1993).

Among the many books that the reader will find useful on Machiavelli's times are: Felix Gilbert, *Machiavelli and Guicciardini: Politics and History in Sixteenth-Century Florence* (Princeton: Princeton University Press, 1965); Rudolf von Albertini, *Firenze dalla repubblica al principato* (Turin: Einaudi, 1970); Quentin Skinner, *The Foundations of Modern Political Thought*, 2 vols. (Cambridge: Cambridge University Press, 1978); Gennaro Sasso, *Niccolò Machiavelli: Storia del suo pensiero politico* (Bologna: Il Mulino, 1980); and Roger D. Masters, *Machiavelli, Leonardo, and the Science of Power* (Notre Dame: University of Notre Dame Press, 1996).

MACHIAVELLI AS REPUBLICAN THEORIST Studies emphasizing Machiavelli's contributions to the history of republican thought have become more numerous of late, reflecting the growing critical consensus about Machiavelli's many positive contributions to republican theory in the *Discourses on Livy*. Harvey Mansfield, Jr., *Machiavelli's New Modes and Orders* (Ithaca: Cornell University Press, 1979), provides a close commentary on each book and chapter of the work. Mansfield is indebted to the approach to Machiavelli identified with Leo Strauss, whose *Thoughts on Machiavelli* (Seattle: University of Washington Press, 1967) still continues to provoke debate. A series of important essays on the composition of the *Discourses on Livy* by Felix Gilbert may be found in his *History: Choice and Commitment* (Cambridge, Mass.: Harvard University Press, 1977). Mark Hulliung's *Citizen Machiavelli* (Princeton: Princeton University Press, 1988) and Anthony J. Parel's *The Machiavellian Cosmos* (New Haven: Yale University Press, 1992) both make important contributions to the discussion of Machiavelli's views on citizenship and the state. J. G. A. Pocock's *The Machiavellian Moment: Florentine Political Thought and the Atlantic Republican Tradition* (Princeton: Princeton University Press, 1975), represents the most important study of Machiavelli's place within republican theory. The most recent consideration of the impact of Italy (including Machiavelli) upon the formation of American political and cultural traditions, with special reference to the Pocock thesis, is *La virtù e la libertà: Ideali e civiltà nella formazione degli Stati Uniti*, ed. Marcello Pacini (Turin: Edizioni della Fondazione Giovanni Agnelli, 1995), which contains essays by Gordon S. Wood, Edward Countryman, John Patrick Diggins, Vickie Sullivan, Peter Bondanella, and others. Essays by different hands on Machiavelli's republicanism are edited by Gisela Bock, Quentin Skinner, and Maurizio Viroli in *Machiavelli and Republicanism* (Cambridge: Cambridge University Press, 1990). For a general consideration of the place of Machiavelli in the development of republican theory or in the growth of Roman mythology from the Renaissance to the present, see respectively William R. Everdell, *The End of Kings: A History of Republics and Republicans* (New York: The Free Press, 1983), Peter Bondanella, *The Eternal City: Roman Images in the Modern World* (Chapel Hill: University of North Carolina Press, 1987), and Vickie B. Sullivan, *Machiavelli's Three Romes: Religion, Human Liberty, and Politics Reformed* (Dekalb: Northern Illinois University Press, 1996).

MACHIAVELLI AS A STYLIST Machiavelli's development as a historical writer from the early diplomatic correspondence to the mature historical and political works is traced by Peter Bondanella in *Machiavelli and the Art of Renaissance History* (Detroit: Wayne State University Press, 1973). Wayne A. Rebhorn's *Foxes and Lions: Machiavelli's Confidence Men* (Ithaca: Cornell University Press, 1988), discusses how literary tradition informs all of Machiavelli's writings. Hanna Fenichel Pitkin's *Fortune is a Woman: Gender and Politics in The Thought of Niccolò Machiavelli* (Berkeley: University of California Press, 1984), offers a feminist reading of Machiavelli's political theory. In *Machiavelli and the Discourse of Literature* (Ithaca: Cornell University Press, 1993), edited by Albert Ascoli and Victoria Kahn, eleven contributors discuss Machiavelli's relationship to the literature of his time.

MACHIAVELLI'S INFLUENCE The impact of Machiavelli's work upon subsequent generations of writers, philosophers, historians, and politicians may be traced in a number of works: James Burnham, *The Machiavellians: Defenders of Freedom* (New York: John Day, 1943); Friedrich Meinecke, *Machiavellism: The Doctrine of Raison d'État and*

Its Place in Modern History (London: Routledge & Kegan Paul, 1957); Mario Praz, *The Flaming Heart* (New York: Norton, 1973); Felix Raab, *The English Face of Machiavelli: A Changing Interpretation 1500–1700* (London: Routledge & Kegan Paul, 1964); Josef Macek, *Machiavelli e il Machiavellismo* (Florence: La Nuova Italia, 1980); and Giuliano Procacci, *Machiavelli nella cultura europea dell'età moderna* (Rome: Laterza, 1995). Machiavelli's ideas have given rise to an empirical psychological test measuring 'Machiavellianism' defined as the degree of success a subject enjoys in manipulating competitors—see Richard Christie and Florence L. Geis, *Studies in Machiavellianism* (New York: Academic Press, 1970). A best-seller on management, Anthony Jay's *Management and Machiavelli: An Inquiry into the Politics of Corporate Life* (New York: Ballantine, 1968), is inspired by a reading of Machiavelli. More recently, Machiavelli's works have served as the inspiration for a computer game on CD-ROM entitled *Machiavelli the Prince* (Hunt Valley, Md: MicroProse Software, 1995), where winning, according to the game's instructions, 'is a matter of strength, shrewdness, and clever deception'.

A CHRONOLOGY OF NICCOLÒ MACHIAVELLI

1469   Born in Florence, Italy.

1492   Rodrigo Borgia elected to the papacy as Alessandro VI; Lorenzo de' Medici dies.

1494   King Charles VIII of France invades Italy; Piero de' Medici is driven out of Florence and a republic coloured by the political theories of Girolamo Savonarola is instituted in Florence.

1498   Louis XII assumes the French throne; Savonarola burned at the stake in the Piazza della Signoria in Florence; Machiavelli elected Secretary of the Florentine Republic's Second Chancery (19 June); additional responsibilities with the Dieci di Balìa (one of the republican government's many magistracies) are added shortly thereafter (14 July).

1499   Louis XII occupies Milan.

1500   Machiavelli completes his first diplomatic mission to France, where he encounters Louis XII and Georges d'Amboise, Cardinal of Rouen.

1502   Piero Soderini is elected *gonfaloniere* (standard-bearer) of the Florentine republic for life.

1502–3   Machiavelli completes diplomatic missions to Cesare Borgia in the Romagna and Rome, witnessing Borgia's fall from power after the death of his father, Pope Alexander VI (18 August 1503); election of Cardinal Della Rovere to papacy as Julius II (31 October).

1504   Returns to France on a diplomatic mission.

1506   Sent to the court of Pope Julius II.

1506–7   Undertakes his first diplomatic mission to Emperor Maximilian; assumes additional responsibilities as chancellor to the Nove Ufficiali dell'Ordinanza e Milizia Fiorentina; deals with the newly formed Florentine militia (12 January 1507).

1512   Soderini's republic is overthrown (31 August) and the Medici return to power (16 September); Machiavelli is sacked from his position in the chancery of the Florentine republic (7 November).

1513   After arrest and torture as a suspected accomplice in a con-
            spiracy against the Medici (12 February), upon the election
            of Cardinal Giovanni de' Medici to the papacy as Leo X
            (11 March) Machiavelli receives a pardon and retires to his
            country estate in Sant'Andrea in Percussina, where he com-
            poses *The Prince* (the exact dates are still a matter of
            dispute).

1513–17   Composition of *Discourses on Livy* (the exact dates are still
            a matter of dispute).

1515–16(?) *The Art of War* is completed.

1516–17   Frequents the republican circle at the Orti Oricellari in
            Florence.

1518(?)   Composes *The Mandrake Root*, his greatest comedy.

1519(?)   Publication of *The Mandrake Root*.

1520   After completing *The Life of Castruccio Castracani*,
            Machiavelli is asked to write a history of Florence.

1521   Publication of *The Art of War* (the only one of his political
            or historical works to appear in print during his lifetime);
            Pope Leo X dies (1 December).

1523   Election of Giulio de' Medici as Pope Clement VII
            (18 November).

1525   Another comedy (*Clizia*) is staged; Machiavelli probably
            composed his *Discourse or Dialogue on Language* at this
            time, although his authorship of the work is disputed by
            some scholars; presents *The History of Florence* to Pope
            Clement VII.

1527   The Sack of Rome begins (6 May); the Medici are expelled
            from Florence (16 May); Machiavelli dies (21 June) and is
            buried in Santa Croce in Florence.

1531   Posthumous publication of *Discourses on Livy*.

1532   Posthumous publication of *The Prince*.

1559   Machiavelli's works are placed on the Index of Prohibited
            Books.

DISCOURSES ON LIVY

CONTENTS

Book I

Contents

Contents

Book II

Book III

Contents

BOOK I

NICCOLÒ MACHIAVELLI TO ZANOBI BUONDELMONTI* AND COSIMO RUCELLAI,* GREETINGS

I am sending you a present which, though it may not meet my obligations to you, is of such a kind that it is, without a doubt, the best gift Niccolò Machiavelli could send to you, for in it I have conveyed as much as I know and as much as I have learned of worldly affairs through long experience and continuous study. And since neither you nor anyone else could desire more of me, you cannot complain if I have not given you more. The poverty of my wit may displease you, if by chance these narratives of mine are weak, and so may the failures of my judgement, if I am often mistaken in my arguments. This being true, I do not know which of us should be less obligated to the other: whether I should be so to you, who have forced me to write what I never would have written for my own sake, or you to me, when in writing, I may not have satisfied you. Take this, therefore, in the way in which all things are taken from friends, where one gives greater consideration to the intentions of the sender than to the quality of the gift being sent. Please believe that in all of this, I have but a single consolation when I think that although I might be mistaken in many of its details, in this one matter I know I have not erred—to have chosen you to whom, above all others, I direct these discourses of mine, both because in doing this, it seems to me that I have shown some gratitude for favours received, and because I think that I have deviated from the common custom of writers who usually address their works to some prince, and blinded by ambition and avarice, praise him for all his virtuous qualities when they ought to blame him for every vile one. Thus, in order not to fall into this error, I have chosen not those who are princes but those who, by reason of their countless good qualities, deserve to be, not those who could

load me down with ranks, honours, and riches but those who
would do so if they could, because men, when they wish to judge
accurately, have to consider those who are generous, not those
who are able to be so, and, likewise, they have to consider those
who know how to rule a kingdom, not those who, without
knowing how, are allowed to do so. Writers praise Hiero of
Syracuse* more when he was a private citizen than Perseus of
Macedonia* when he was king, because Hiero lacked nothing
but a kingdom to be a prince, while the latter possessed no
kingly attributes except a kingdom. Enjoy, therefore, this good
thing or this bad thing you yourselves have insisted on, and if
you persist in the erroneous opinion that these beliefs of mine
bring you pleasure, I shall not fail to follow this up with the rest
of the history, as I promised you in the beginning.* Farewell.

PREFACE TO AUTOGRAPH MANUSCRIPT*

Although the envious nature of men has always made it no less perilous to discover new methods and institutions* than to search for unknown lands and seas,* since men are more ready to blame than to praise the actions of others, nevertheless, driven by that natural desire I have always felt to do without hesitation those things I believe may bring common benefits to everyone, I have resolved to enter upon a path still untrodden, which, though it may bring me distress and difficulty, could also bring me rewards from those who will kindly consider the goal of these labours of mine. Even if my feeble intellect, my meagre experience in current affairs, and my weak knowledge of ancient ones render this effort of mine defective and of little use, it may at least open the way for someone who with more ability, more eloquence, and more judgement will be able to carry out this plan of mine, which, if it does not earn me praise, should not bring me blame.

Considering, therefore, how much honour is attributed to antiquity, and how many times (leaving aside countless other examples) someone has purchased a fragment from an ancient statue at a great price just to have it near him, to decorate his home, and to have it imitated by those who delight in that art, and also how those artists then with great diligence strive to represent it in all their works; and, on the other hand, seeing that the most virtuous enterprises the histories show us to have been accomplished in ancient kingdoms and republics by kings, generals, citizens, lawgivers, and others who have laboured for their native lands, are admired rather than imitated (indeed are avoided by everyone in every minute detail to the extent that no trace of that ancient ability has survived), I cannot be but both amazed and saddened. And even more so when I see that in the civil disputes that arise among citizens, or in the illnesses that afflict men, we always have recourse to those judgements or remedies that have been pronounced or prescribed by the ancients, since civil laws are nothing other than the decisions delivered by the jurists of antiquity which, organized into a body of laws, teach the jurists of our own times how to render judgements, nor again is medicine anything other than the experiments performed by the doctors of antiquity upon which today's doctors and their diagnoses rely. Nevertheless, in organizing republics, maintaining states, governing kingdoms, in instituting a militia and conducting a war, in executing legal decisions among subjects, and in expanding an empire, no prince, republic, or military leader can be found who has recourse to the examples of the ancients. I believe this arises not so much from the state of weakness into which today's religion* has led the world, or from the harm done to many Christian provinces and cities by an ambitious idleness, as from not possessing a true understanding of the histories, so that in reading them, we fail to draw out of them that sense or to taste that flavour they intrinsically possess. As a result, it happens that countless people who read them take pleasure in hearing about the variety of incidents they contain without otherwise thinking about imitating them, since they believe that imitation is not only difficult but impossible, as if the sky, the sun, the elements, or human beings had changed in their motions, order, and power from what they were in antiquity. Wishing, therefore, to extricate men from this error, I have deemed it necessary to write about all the books by Livy* that have not been taken from us by the hostility of time, what, according to my understanding of ancient and modern affairs, I judge necessary for a greater understanding of them, so that those who will read these comments of mine may more easily derive from them that practical knowledge one must seek from a familiarity with the histories. And although this undertaking may be difficult, nevertheless, assisted by those who have encouraged me to take on this burden, I believe I can carry it forward in such a manner that only a short path will remain for another to bring it to its destined goal.

PREFACE TO 1531 ROMAN EDITION

Considering how much honour is attributed to antiquity, and how many times (leaving aside many other examples) someone has purchased a fragment of an ancient statue at a great price to have it near him, to decorate his home, and to have it imitated by those who delight in that art, and how those artists with every diligence then strive in all their works to represent it, and, on the other hand, seeing that the most virtuous enterprises the histories show us to have been carried out in ancient kingdoms and republics by kings, generals, citizens, lawgivers, and others who have laboured for their native lands are praised with astonishment rather than imitated (indeed, are avoided by everyone in every way, to the extent that no trace of that ancient ability has survived), I cannot be but both amazed and saddened. And I am even more so when I see that in the civil disputes that arise among citizens, or in the illnesses that afflict men, we always have recourse to those remedies or those judgements that have been pronounced or prescribed by the ancients, since civil laws are nothing other than the decisions delivered by the jurists of antiquity which, organized into a body of laws, teach our contemporary jurists how to render judgements, nor again is medicine anything other than the experiments performed by the doctors of antiquity upon which today's doctors and their diagnoses rely. Nevertheless, in organizing republics, maintaining states, governing kingdoms, in instituting a militia and administering a war, in executing legal decisions among subjects, and in expanding an empire, no prince, republic, military leader, or citizen can be found who has recourse to the examples of the ancients. I am persuaded that this arises not so much from the state of weakness into which today's education* has led the world, or from the harm an ambitious idleness has done to many Christian provinces and cities, as from not possessing a true understanding of the histories, so that in reading them, we fail to draw out of them that sense or to taste that flavour they intrinsically possess. As a result, it happens that the countless people who read may take pleasure in hearing about the variety of incidents they contain without otherwise thinking about imitating them, since they believe that such imitation is not only difficult but impossible, as if the sky, the sun, the elements, or human beings had changed in their motion, order, and power from what they were in antiquity. Wishing, then, to extricate men from this error, I have deemed it necessary to write about all those books by Livy that have not been taken from us by the hostility of time, what, according to my understanding of ancient and modern affairs, I judge necessary for a greater understanding of them, so that those who will read these discourses of mine may more easily derive from them that practical knowledge one must seek from a familiarity with the histories. And although this undertaking may be difficult, nevertheless, assisted by those who have encouraged me to assume this burden, I believe I can carry it forward in such a manner that only a short path will remain for another to bring it to its destined goal.

BOOK I

CHAPTER I

What the Beginnings of Cities Have Always Been, and What the Beginnings of Rome Were Like

Those who read about the beginnings of the city of Rome, about its lawgivers, and how it was organized will not be surprised that so much ability was preserved there over so many centuries, nor that afterwards it gave rise to the imperial power which that republic attained. In wishing first to discuss its birth, I must say that all cities are built either by men who are natives of the place where they are built or by foreigners. The first situation comes about when the inhabitants, scattered in many small groups, feel they are not living in security, since each group on its own, because of both its location and its small size, cannot resist the onslaught of anyone who may attack it, and in uniting for their defence when the enemy comes, they are either not in time, or even if they are, they are forced to abandon many of their strongholds, and in this way come to be ready prey to their enemies. Hence, to escape these dangers, moved either by themselves or by someone among them of greater authority, they draw closer to each other to settle in a place they have chosen which is more convenient to live in and easier to defend.

Among many others, Athens and Venice were cities of this type. The first, under the authority of Theseus, was built for similar reasons by scattered inhabitants; as for the second, once many peoples took refuge upon certain small islands that stood at the end of the Adriatic Sea to escape those wars that arose in Italy every day because of the arrival of new barbarians after the decline of the Roman empire, they began, without any particular ruler to give them orders, to live under those laws that they felt were most apt to sustain them. This turned out happily for them because of the long peace that the site afforded them; the sea had no harbour and the peoples tormenting Italy did not possess ships with which to harass them, with the result that this meagre beginning enabled them to reach the level of greatness they presently enjoy.

The second situation comes about when a city is built by foreigners and is born either of free men or of those who depend on others, such as the colonies sent either by a republic or by a prince to relieve their lands of inhabitants, or to defend newly acquired territory which they wish to maintain securely and without expense (the Roman people built many of these cities throughout its empire); or they may be built by a prince not as a place to live but to his own glory, as the city of Alexandria was built by Alexander. And since these cities do not have free origins, it rarely happens that they make great advances and can be numbered among the chief cities of kingdoms. The building of Florence was like this, for (either built by the soldiers of Sulla or perhaps by the inhabitants of the mountains of Fiesole who, trusting in the long peace that arose in the world under Octavius, came to dwell on the plain above the Arno), Florence was built under the Roman empire, and it could not in its beginnings undergo any growth except that which the generosity of its prince allowed it.

The builders of cities are free when any people, either under a prince or on its own, is forced by disease, famine, or war to abandon its native land and seek a new home: such peoples as these either settle in the cities they discover in the lands they acquire, as Moses did, or they build new cities, as Aeneas did. In this case, we recognize the ability of the builder and the fortune of what he has built: this is more or less remarkable according to whether he who has been its founder is more or less able. His ability is recognized in two ways: the first is in his selection of a site, and the other is in his organization of the laws. Moreover, because men act either out of necessity or by choice, and since ability is greater where choice has less authority, it must be considered whether, for the building of cities, it is preferable to select barren sites, so that men, forced to work industriously and less occupied in idle pursuits will live more united, having less reason for disagreements because of the poverty of the site, as happened in Ragusa* and many other cities built in similar places; such a choice would no doubt be wiser and more useful if men were content to live on their own resources and did not insist on seeking others. Nevertheless, since men cannot live in security without power, they must avoid such barrenness in a country and situate themselves in the most fertile regions, where, since the richness of the site allows them to expand, they can defend themselves from those who attack them and subdue anyone who opposes their greatness. As for the idleness that the site brings to the city, it is essential to organize things in such a way that the laws force upon the city those necessities that the site does not impose, and to imitate those who have been wise and have lived in the most pleasant and most fertile countries, those more apt to produce idle men unfit for any useful activity, where in order to avoid the harm the pleasant nature of the country might have caused due to idle pursuits, the people made training compulsory for those who were to become soldiers, so that as a result of this regulation, they became better soldiers than men in those countries which were naturally harsh and barren. Among countries such as these was the kingdom of the Egyptians, where although the country was very pleasant, the necessity imposed by the laws was so powerful that they produced the most excellent men, and if their names had not been erased by the passing of the ages, we would see that they would deserve more praise than Alexander the Great and many others of whom memory is still fresh. And whoever might have considered the kingdom of the Sultan and the organization of the Mamelukes* and that of their militia before Selim, the Grand Turk, had destroyed it, would have seen in it many such exercises for the soldiers and would have, in fact, recognized how much they feared that idleness that the beneficence of the land could have brought upon them, had they not prevented this with the strictest laws.

Let me say, therefore, that it is more prudent to select a fertile site when this fertility can be kept within proper bounds by the laws. When he wished to construct a city to his glory, the architect Dinocrates* came to Alexander the Great and showed him how he could build a city on the top of Mount Athos, a location which, besides being a fortified position, could be shaped in such a fashion that the city would take on a human form, something which would be an astonishing and rare thing, worthy of his greatness. When Alexander asked him what the inhabitants would live on, Dinocrates answered that he had not thought about it: Alexander laughed at this, and, abandoning that mountain, built Alexandria, where its inhabitants willingly lived because of the richness of the land and the convenience of the sea and the Nile.

Anyone, therefore, who examines the founding of Rome, if he takes Aeneas as its first father, will consider it as one of the cities built by foreigners; if he takes Romulus as Rome's first father, he will consider it as one of the cities built by men who are natives of the place; and in any case, he will see it as having had a free beginning without depending upon anyone; and, as will be discussed below, he will also see how many necessities were imposed upon this city by Romulus, Numa, and the others, so that the fertility of the site, the convenience of the sea, the frequent victories, and the great size of its empire were unable to corrupt it for centuries, and these laws kept it full of as much exceptional ability as ever adorned any other city or republic.

And because the deeds performed by this city, and celebrated by Livy, came about either through public or private consultation, either within or outside the city, I shall begin to discuss those matters which occurred within the city through public assemblies which I judge to be most worthy of comment, adding to them everything that depended upon them: this first book, or rather this first part, will end with these commentaries.

CHAPTER 2

How Many Kinds of Republics There Are, and What Kind the Roman Republic Was

I wish to set aside an examination of those cities that had their beginnings while subject to others, and I shall speak of those cities that had their beginnings far removed from any kind of external servitude and were immediately governed by their own will either as republics or as principalities, that have had different laws and institutions just as they have had different beginnings. For some of them, either at their origin or after a short time, were given laws all at once by one person alone, like those given by Lycurgus to the Spartans; others received their laws by chance, on different occasions, and according to unforeseen circumstances, as did Rome. That republic may be called fortunate if it produces a man so prudent that he gives it laws organized in such a fashion that it can live safely under them without needing to reform them. We can see that Sparta observed its laws for more than 800 years without corrupting them or without any dangerous strife and that, on the contrary, that city remains to some degree unfortunate when it has not happened upon a prudent founder and is forced to reorganize itself. Of these cities, the one furthest from order is still more unfortunate, and the city furthest from it is the one in which the institutions have gone completely off the straight path that can lead it to the perfect and true goal, since it is almost impossible for cities in this condition to set themselves aright through some unexpected turn of events; those other cities that, although lacking a perfect order, have given themselves good beginnings and have taken actions to become even better, can become perfect through an unforeseen turn of events. But it is certainly true that they will never reorganize themselves without risk, for most men will never agree to a new law that concerns a new order in a city unless a certain necessity shows them it is required, and since this necessity cannot arise without risk, it is an easy thing for that republic to be ruined before it can be brought to perfection in its organization. The republic of Florence testifies to this, for it was reorganized on account of what happened in Arezzo in 1502, and, on account of what happened in Prato in 1512, its institutions were destroyed.*

Since I wish, therefore, to discuss the institutions of the city of Rome and the unforeseen events which brought them to perfection, let me say that some of those who have written about republics declare that in each of them is one of the three forms of government, which they call principality, aristocracy, and democracy, and they say that those who organize a city must turn to one of these types, whichever, in their view, seems most suitable. Some other and, in the opinion of many, wiser men hold the opinion that there are six kinds of governments: three of these are very bad; three others are good in themselves but so easily corruptible that they also come to be pernicious.* Those which are good are the three mentioned above; those which are bad are three others which depend upon the first three, and each of them is in a way similar to its counterpart, so that they all easily jump from one form to the other: the principality easily becomes tyrannical; aristocracy quite easily becomes the government of the few; and democracy without difficulty turns into anarchy. For this reason, if the founder of a republic organizes one of these three governments in a city, he organizes it there for a brief time, because no remedy can prevent it from slipping into its contrary due to the similarity that exists, in this case, between the virtue and the vice.

These variations in governments arise among men by chance, for in the beginning of the world, when its inhabitants were few, they lived for a time scattered like the beasts; then as the generations multiplied they gathered together, and in order better to defend themselves, they began to consider carefully who among them was stronger and braver, and they made him their leader and obeyed him. From this arose knowledge of things honourable and good as opposed to those which are pernicious and evil, for noticing that when someone did harm to his benefactor it aroused hatred and compassion among men, since they condemned the ungrateful and honoured those who showed gratitude, and thinking that the same injuries could also be inflicted upon themselves, they set about making laws in order to avoid similar evils and ordained punishments for whoever violated them: from this arose knowledge of justice. The result was that later when they had to elect a prince, they did not support the boldest but, instead, the man who was most prudent and just. Yet later when they began creating princes through hereditary succession and not by election, the heirs immediately began to degenerate from their ancestors, and abandoning acts of special worth, they thought princes had nothing to do but surpass others in luxury and lasciviousness and all other forms of licentiousness, so that as the prince came to be hated, then became afraid on account of this hatred, and quickly passed from fear to harmful acts, tyranny immediately arose. Subsequently, this gave rise to the beginning of the collapse and the conspiracies and plots against princes, executed not by those who were either timid or weak but by those who surpassed others in generosity, greatness of soul, wealth, and nobility; such men as these could not endure the dishonourable life of such a prince. The masses, following the authority of these powerful men, therefore, took up arms against the prince, and once he had been eliminated, obeyed them as their liberators. And since these men hated the very idea of a single leader, they constituted a government among themselves, and in the beginning, mindful of past tyranny, they governed themselves according to the laws they had instituted, subordinating their own interests to the common good, and with the greatest care they managed and maintained both their private and public affairs. This administration later passed to their sons, who did not understand the changeability of fortune since they had never experienced evil, and unwilling to remain content with civic equality, they turned to avarice, ambition, and the unlawful seizure of women, causing a government of aristocrats to become a government of the few, without regard for civic bonds of any kind, so that in a brief time what happened to the tyrant happened to them, because, disgusted by this system of government, the multitude became the instrument of anyone who designed any kind of plan to attack these rulers, and someone thus soon rose up, who, with the aid of the multitude, destroyed them. Furthermore, since the memory of the prince and the injuries he inflicted was still fresh, after having destroyed the government of the few and unwilling to re-establish that of a prince, the people turned to democratic government, and they organized it in such a way that neither the few powerful men nor a single prince would ever have any authority whatsoever. Since all governments receive some respect in the beginning, this democratic government was maintained for a while but not for long, at the most until the generation that had founded it passed away, for it immediately fell into a state of undisciplined liberty, where neither private citizens nor public officials were feared; as a result, with each person living according to his own wishes, a thousand injuries were inflicted every day, so that, forced by necessity or by the suggestion of some good man, in order to flee such permissiveness they returned once again to the principality, and from that, step by step, they returned towards a state of undisciplined liberty in the ways and for the reasons given.

And this is the cycle* through which all states that have governed themselves or that now govern themselves pass, but rarely do they return to the same forms of government, because almost no republic can be so full of life that it may pass through these mutations many times and remain standing. But it may well happen that in the course of its troubles, a republic ever lacking in counsel and strength becomes subject to a nearby state that is better organized; but if this were not to occur, a republic would be apt to circle about endlessly through these types of government.

Let me say, therefore, that all the forms of governments mentioned above are defective, because of the brief duration of the three good ones, and because of the evil nature of the three bad ones. Thus, since those men who were prudent in establishing laws recognized this defect, they avoided each of these forms by itself alone and chose a form of government that combined them all, judging such a government steadier and more stable, for when in the same city there is a principality, an aristocracy, and a democracy, one keeps watch over the other.

Among those who have deserved most praise for such constitutions is Lycurgus, who organized his laws in Sparta in such a way that, allocating to the kings, the aristocrats, and the people their respective roles, he created a state that lasted for more than 800 years, resulting in the highest praise for him and in tranquillity for that city.* The opposite happened to Solon, who organized the laws in Athens, and who by instituting only a democratic form of government there gave it such a brief existence that, before he died, he saw the tyranny of Pisistratus arise, and although after forty years the heirs of Pisistratus were driven out and Athens regained its freedom, since a democratic form of government was re-established following Solon's laws, it did not last more than 100 years, even though to preserve it many constitutions were devised to repress the insolence of the upper class and the abuse of freedom on the part of the populace, laws which were unforeseen by Solon. Nevertheless, since Solon did not mix a popular form of government with the power of the principality and that of the aristocrats, Athens endured a very brief time in comparison to Sparta.

But let us turn to Rome where, despite the fact that this city never had a Lycurgus to organize it at the beginning in such a way that it might live in freedom for a long period of time, so many special circumstances nevertheless arose from the conflict that existed between the plebeians and the senate that what a founder had not done was brought about by chance. If Rome was not allotted the first arrangement, it was allotted the second, for its early institutions, even if defective, did not, none the less, deviate from the straight path which could lead them to perfection. In fact, Romulus and all the other kings passed many good laws suitable to living in liberty, but because their goal was to found a kingdom and not a republic, when that city became free it lacked many public institutions which should have been organized in a manner favourable to liberty, institutions which had not been established by those kings. Even though its kings lost their empire for the reasons and in the ways already discussed, those who drove them out, having immediately established two consuls who took the place of the kings, nevertheless drove out of Rome only the title of king and not kingly power, so that, since that republic had only the consuls and the senate, it came to be nothing more than a mixture of two of the three elements mentioned above, that is, the principality and the aristocracy. It remained only for the city to give way to popular government: once the Roman nobility became insolent for reasons to be related below, the people rose up against it, so that in order not to lose everything, the nobility was forced to concede to the people its share of power, but for their part, the senate and the consuls still retained so much authority that they were able to preserve their rank in that republic. In this manner the creation of the tribunes of the plebeians came about, after which the condition of the republic became more stable, since all three forms of government had their roles. And fortune was so favourable to Rome that although this city passed from a government of kings and aristocrats to a government of the people, through the same steps and for the same reasons that were discussed above, the kingly authority none the less was never entirely abolished to give authority to the aristocrats, nor was the authority of the aristocrats completely diminished in order to give it to the people, but since this authority remained mixed, it created a perfect republic, and Rome came to this perfection through the discord between the plebeians and the senate,* as will be demonstrated at greater length in the following two chapters.

CHAPTER 3

The Circumstances that Caused the Creation of the Tribunes of the Plebeians, Making the Republic More Perfect

As is demonstrated by all those who discuss civic life—and every history is filled with such examples—it is necessary for anyone who organizes a republic and establishes laws in it to take for granted that all men are evil and that they will always act according to the wickedness of their nature whenever they have the opportunity, and when any wickedness remains hidden for a time, it arises from a hidden cause that is not recognized by those who lack experience of its contrary, but time, which people say is the father of every truth, will eventually uncover it.

An absolute harmony appeared to exist between the plebeians and the senate in Rome after the expulsion of the Tarquins, and the nobles, appearing to have put aside their pride and to have become democratic in spirit, were tolerated by everyone, even the most humble. This deception remained hidden, nor was the motive for it clear as long as the Tarquins, whom the nobles feared, were alive, and fearing that the plebeians, if mistreated, would draw closer to the Tarquins, they conducted themselves humanely with them, but when the Tarquins were dead and the nobles had lost their fear, they began to pour out upon the plebeians all the venom they had held within their breasts, and in every way they could they offended them. This fact testifies to what I said above, that men never do good except out of necessity, but where choices are abundant and unlimited freedom is the norm, everything immediately becomes confused and disorderly. Hence, it is said that hunger and poverty make men industrious and laws make them good, and where something works well by itself without the law, the law is unnecessary, but when that good custom is lacking, the law is immediately necessary. Thus, after the Tarquins were gone, fear of whom had kept the nobility in check, it was necessary to consider a new institution that would produce the same effect that the Tarquins produced while they were alive. In this way, after many disorders, disturbances, and the danger of disagreements that arose between the plebeians and the nobility, the creation of the tribunes came about for the security of the plebeians, and these tribunes were established with such power and prestige that they could always thereafter act as intermediaries between the plebeians and the senate and could curb the insolence of the nobles.

CHAPTER 4

How the Division Between the Plebeians and the Roman Senate Made That Republic Free and Powerful

I must not fail to discuss the disturbances that persisted in Rome from the death of the Tarquins to the creation of the tribunes and, afterwards, certain other matters to counter the opinion of those who declare that Rome was a disorderly republic, full of so much turmoil that if good fortune and exceptional military ability had not made up for its defects, the city would have been inferior to every other republic. I cannot deny that fortune and their military were reasons for Roman dominance, but it seems clear to me that these thinkers fail to realize that where there is good military organization, there must also be good institutions, and only rarely does this occur where there is not also good fortune. But let us move on to other details concerning this city. I must say that it appears to me that those who condemn the disturbances between the nobles and the plebeians condemn those very things that were the primary cause of Roman liberty, and that they give more consideration to the noises and cries arising from such disturbances than to the good effects they produced; nor do they consider that in every republic there are two different tendencies, that of the people and that of the upper class, and that all of the laws which are passed in favour of liberty are born from the rift between the two, as can easily be seen from what happened in Rome, since from the time of the Tarquins to that of the Gracchi, a period of more than 300 years, the disturbances in Rome rarely led to exile and even more rarely to bloodshed. It is not possible, therefore, to judge these disturbances to be harmful or such a republic to be divided, since over such a long period of time its strife sent no more than eight or ten citizens into exile, killed very few of them, and condemned not many more to pay fines. Nor can one in any way reasonably call a republic disorganized where so many examples of exceptional ability occur, for good examples arise from good training, good training from good laws, and good laws from those disturbances that many people thoughtlessly condemn, and anyone who carefully examines the goal of these laws will find that they did not lead to exile or to violence against the common good, but instead brought forth laws and institutions for the benefit of civic liberty. And suppose someone were to say: the means were extraordinary and almost barbarous—see how all the people are crying out against the senate, the senate against the people; how they are running wildly through the streets, closing the shops; and how all the plebeians of Rome are leaving the city together—events which terrify even those who read about them; I will respond that every city must possess its own methods for allowing the people to express their ambitions, especially those cities that intend to make use of the people in important affairs. Among these cities, the city of Rome had such a method, for when the people wanted a new law, either they did some of the things mentioned above, or they refused to sign up to go to war, so that to placate them it was necessary to give them some measure of satisfaction. The desires of free peoples are rarely harmful to liberty, because they arise either from oppression or from the suspicion that they will be oppressed. Clearly, should these opinions prove to be in error, there is the remedy of public assemblies where some worthy man may arise and, making a speech, demonstrate to the people that they are mistaken, for as Cicero declares,* the people, although ignorant, can grasp the truth, and they readily yield when they are told the truth by a trustworthy man.

One should, therefore, criticize Roman government more sparingly and consider that the many good effects that came out of that republic were produced only by the best causes. If these disturbances were the cause for the creation of the tribunes, they deserve the highest praise, because besides giving to the people its role in democratic administration, the tribunes were established as the guardians of Roman liberty, as will be demonstrated in the following chapter.

CHAPTER 5

Whether the Guardianship of Liberty May Be More Securely Lodged in the People or in the Upper Classes; and Who Has More Reason to Create an Uprising, He Who Wishes to Acquire or He Who Wishes to Maintain

Among the most necessary things established by those who have founded a republic in a prudent fashion is a safeguard for liberty, and according to whether it is well established or not, that free way of life is more or less enduring. Because in every republic there are men of prominence and men of the people, some doubt has arisen over whose hands into which this guardianship would best be placed. Among the Spartans and, in our own times, among the Venetians, it was placed in the hands of the nobles, but among the Romans it was placed in the hands of the plebeians.

For this reason, it is necessary to examine which of these republics made the best choice. If we were to explore the reasons, something could be said for both sides, but if we examine the results, we would choose the side of the nobles, since the liberty of Sparta and Venice endured longer than that of Rome. Turning to the causes, let me say, while first taking the side of the Romans, that the guardianship must be given to those who have less of an appetite to usurp it. No doubt, if we consider the goal of the nobles and that of the common people, we shall see in the former a strong desire to dominate and in the latter only the desire not to be dominated, and, as a consequence, a stronger will to live in liberty, since they have less hope of usurping it than men of prominence; just so, since the common people are set up as guardians of this liberty, it is reasonable to think that they will take better care of it, and, being incapable of appropriating it for themselves, they will not permit others to do so. On the other hand, those who defend the organization of Sparta and Venice declare that those who place the guardianship in the hands of the powerful accomplish two good things: first, they better satisfy their ambition, and since they have a larger part to play in the republic with this club in their hands, they have more reason to be content; second, they remove a kind of authority from the restless minds of the plebeians that is the cause of countless conflicts and disagreements in any republic and is likely to drive the nobility to despair, which, in the passing of time, will produce harmful consequences. As an example they offer Rome itself, where, once the tribunes of the people had this authority in their hands, they did not consider it sufficient to have one plebeian consul and wanted two of them.* After this, they wanted the censorship,* the praetorship,* and all the other positions of power in the city; nor did this suffice, for led by this same consuming desire, they then began in time to idolize those men they saw capable of beating down the nobility; and from this arose the power of Marius and the ruin of Rome.* Truly, anyone who properly considers one side or the other could remain in doubt about which of the two should be chosen as the guardian of such liberty, not knowing which human disposition is more harmful in a republic: either that which wishes to preserve honour already acquired, or that which wishes to acquire honour yet to be possessed.

In the end, anyone who examines everything closely will draw this conclusion: either you discuss a republic that wishes to create an empire, like Rome, or you discuss one that is satisfied to maintain itself. In the first case, it is necessary to do everything as Rome did; in the second case, it is possible to imitate Venice or Sparta for reasons to be explained in the following chapter.

But to turn to a discussion of what kinds of men are most harmful to a republic—either those who wish to acquire something, or those who fear losing what they have acquired—let me say that Marcus Menenius and Marcus Fulvius,* both plebeians, had been made respectively dictator and master of the horse in order to investigate certain conspiracies which were being plotted in Capua against Rome, and the people afterwards also granted them authority to seek out anyone in Rome who, through ambition and extraordinary means, might contrive to obtain the consulate and the other offices of the city. Furthermore, the nobility, feeling that such authority was given to the dictator to oppose them, spread the rumour throughout Rome that it was not they who sought the offices out of ambition and through extraordinary means but was, instead, the commoners, who, lacking confidence in their own blood and ability, were seeking through extraordinary measures to rise to these ranks, and in particular they blamed the dictator. This accusation had such force that, having delivered a speech and having complained about the false accusations lodged against him by the nobles, Menenius renounced the dictatorship and submitted himself to the judgement that would be pronounced upon him by the people, and later, when his case had been examined, he was absolved, whereupon it was widely debated as to who was more ambitious, either a man who wishes to keep something or a man who wishes to acquire it, since one or the other can easily become the cause of the greatest disturbances. At any rate, in most cases such disturbances are caused by those who possess something, since the fear of losing it generates in them the same desires as exist in those who wish to acquire something, because men do not believe they truly possess what they own if they do not acquire still more from others. In addition, those who possess a great deal can with greater power and speed bring about change, and still more, their improper and ambitious conduct kindles in the breasts of those who possess nothing the desire to possess something, either in order to gain revenge upon the rich by despoiling them, or in order to be able themselves to come into that wealth and those offices that they see so badly used by others.

CHAPTER 6

Whether in Rome It Was Possible to Organize a Government that Could Do Away with the Enmities Between the People and the Senate

We have discussed above the effects of the controversies between the people and the senate. Now, since these controversies continued down to the time of the Gracchi, when they were the cause of the ruin of a free way of life, someone might wish that Rome could have achieved the great results that the city realized without there being such enmities within it. It seems to me a matter worthy of consideration, therefore, to see if in Rome it might have been possible to organize a government that could have done away with these same disputes, and in wishing to examine this matter, it is necessary to refer to those republics which, without such enmities and disturbances, remained free for a long period of time and to see what kind of government they possessed and whether it could have been introduced in Rome. As an example, among the ancients there is Sparta, and among the moderns Venice, both of which I mentioned above. Sparta created a king with a small senate* to govern itself; Venice did not distinguish the parts of its government by specific names, but all those who might hold an administrative post were called gentlemen under a single title. This system was given to them more by chance than by the prudence of those who gave them their laws, since, having taken shelter upon those islands where their city now stands for the reasons mentioned above, the inhabitants who had increased in such numbers that they had to create laws if they wished to live together, established a form of government; they frequently met together in their councils to deliberate about the city, and when they felt their numbers were sufficient to form a body politic, they closed the avenue to participation* to all those who might come there to live in the future; and in time, when a considerable number of the inhabitants in that city found themselves outside the government, they enhanced the reputation of those who governed by calling the latter gentlemen and the others commoners. It was possible for this system to arise and maintain itself without any disturbance, because when it was born, whoever then lived in Venice was made part of the government, so that no one could complain; those who later came there to live found the government fixed and limited, but they had no motive or opportunity to cause a disturbance. There was no motive, because nothing of theirs had been taken away; there was no opportunity, because those who ruled kept them in check and did not use them in matters through which they might acquire authority. Moreover, those who later came to live in Venice were not many or of a sufficient number to create a disproportion between those who govern and those who are governed,* for the number of gentlemen was either equal to or superior to their number, so that for these reasons Venice was able to establish that kind of government and keep it united.

Sparta, as I said, was governed by a king and a senate of limited size. It was able to sustain itself for such a long time because it had few inhabitants and access to participation had been taken away from those who came there to live, and once the laws of Lycurgus, the observance of which removed all causes for strife, were adopted to good effect, the Spartans were able to live in unity over a long period of time. With his laws, Lycurgus created in Sparta greater equality of property and less equality of rank, so that there was an equality of poverty there, and the plebeians were less ambitious since the high ranks of the city, extended to few citizens, were denied to them; nor did the nobles ever give the plebeians any desire to obtain these ranks by mistreating them. This was due to the Spartan kings, who, being set up in that principality and placed in the midst of that nobility, had no better way to secure their office than to protect the plebeians from every injury; this meant that the plebeians did not fear nor did they desire power, and neither possessing power nor fearing it, the competition they might have had with the nobility and the cause of such disturbances were eliminated, and they were able to live in unity for a long period of time. But there were two principal causes for this unity: first, the fact that Sparta had few inhabitants and could therefore be governed by few men; second, the fact that by not accepting foreigners into their republic, they did not have the opportunity either to become corrupt or to grow to such an extent that the city became an intolerable burden for the few who governed it.

Hence, taking into consideration all these things, one sees that Rome's legislators had to do one of two things if they wanted Rome to remain as peaceful as the two republics mentioned above: either they could avoid using the plebeians in warfare, as the Venetians did, or they could avoid giving open access to foreigners, as the Spartans did. The Romans did both the one and the other: this gave the plebeians strength and an increase in their numbers, as well as countless opportunities to create disturb-ances. But had the Roman state become more peaceful, another disadvantage that would have arisen is that it would have also been weaker, because it would have cut itself off from the path to realizing the greatness it attained, so that, had Rome wished to eliminate the causes of her disturbances, she would also have eliminated the causes for her expansion. And in all human affairs, anyone who examines them closely will see that one can never cancel one disadvantage without another arising from it. Consequently, if you wish to create a numerous and well-armed people, in order to build a great empire, you create it with such qualities that you cannot then manage it as you wish, and if you keep it either small or disarmed in order to manage it, once you acquire territory you cannot hold it, or you become so helpless that you are easy prey to anyone who attacks you. Thus, in all our deliberations, we must consider where the fewest draw-backs lie and take that as the best alternative, because an option that is completely clear and completely without uncertainty cannot ever be found. Rome like Sparta could, therefore, have created a prince for life and a small senate, but she could not, like Sparta, have avoided increasing the number of her citizens if she wished to establish a great empire; this means that having a king for life and a small number in the senate would have been of little benefit in so far as her unity was concerned.

If anyone wishes, therefore, to organize an entirely new republic, he should examine whether he would like it to expand in size and power like Rome, or to remain within narrow limits. In the first case, it is necessary to organize it like Rome and make room for the disturbances and widespread disagreements as best one can, because without a large number of well-armed men, no republic will ever be able to grow or, if it does so, to maintain itself. In the second case, you can organize it like Sparta or Venice, but since expansion is the poison of such republics, any-one who organizes them must, in all the ways possible, prevent them from acquiring territory, for such acquisitions built upon a weak republic constitute its complete ruin. This came about in Sparta and in Venice: the former, having subjugated almost all of Greece, demonstrated her fragile foundations in a minor inci-dent, because when the rebellion of Thebes brought on by

Pelopidas persisted, other cities rebelled, and that brought about the complete ruin of the republic.* In like manner, after Venice had occupied a large part of Italy, in the main with money and cleverness rather than war, she had to test her strength, and lost everything in a single day.* I should think that the way to create a republic that could endure for a long period of time would be to organize it internally like Sparta or Venice, and to place it in a strong location with such power that no one would believe he could suddenly subjugate it, although the republic should not be so large that it seems formidable to its neighbours; and in this fashion the city could enjoy its form of government over a long period of time. Hence, there are two reasons to wage war upon a republic: first, to become its ruler; second, for fear it will take possession of your own. The above-mentioned method almost entirely eliminates these two reasons, because if the republic is difficult to destroy, as I assume it will be, since it is well organized for defence, rarely or never will any-one try to develop a plan to seize it. If it remains within its own boundaries, and experience shows that it lacks ambition, no one will ever have to wage war against it out of fear, and this would be even more likely if it had a constitution or laws which pro-hibited expansion. I believe, without any doubt, that if such an entity could be held in balance this way, the result would be a true body politic and true tranquillity in a city. But since all human affairs are in continual motion and cannot remain fixed, they must either rise or fall, and reason does not always lead you to the many things to which necessity leads you, so that if a republic were to be capable of maintaining itself without expan-sion, and necessity forced it to expand, its foundations would be demolished and it would be brought to ruin very quickly. Thus, on the other hand, even if heaven were so kind that it never had to wage war, it might happen that idleness would make it either weak or divided, and these two things together, or each one in itself, would be the cause of its ruin. Consequently, being unable, in my opinion, to find a balance in this matter or strictly to maintain this middle way, it is necessary in the organization of a republic to consider the most honourable elements and to organize them in such a way that even when necessity forces it to expand, the republic may conserve what it has acquired. To return to my first argument, I believe it is necessary to follow the political organization of Rome and not that of other republics, because I cannot believe it is possible to find a middle way between the one alternative and the other, and it is necessary to tolerate those enmities that arose between the people and the senate, taking them as a disadvantage necessary to attain Roman greatness. Thus, besides the other reasons I have set forth, where I demonstrated the authority of the tribunes to have been necessary for the protection of liberty, it is easy to observe the benefit republics derive from the right to make public accusations, which was among the other powers granted to the tribunes, as will be discussed in the following chapter.

CHAPTER 7

To What Degree Public Indictments Are Necessary in a Republic to Maintain Its Liberty

Those who are set up in a city as the guardians of its liberty cannot receive a more useful and necessary authority than the power to indict citizens before the people or some magistrate or council when they commit any kind of offence against free government. This institution has two extremely useful effects upon a republic. The first is that, for fear of being accused, the citizens do not engage in attempts upon the government, and if they do make such attempts, they are immediately suppressed without respect for who they are. The second is that it provides a release for those humours* that arise within cities in one way or another against certain citizens, for when these humours have no legal form of release, they resort to illegal means that bring about the ruin of the whole republic. Thus, there is nothing that makes a republic so stable and steady as organizing it in such a way that the variability of those humours that agitate the republic has a means of release that is instituted by the laws. This can be demonstrated through many examples, and especially through the one Livy cites concerning Coriolanus, where he says that at a moment when the Roman nobility was irritated with the plebeians, because they believed the plebeians had too much power as a result of the creation of the tribunes who used to defend them, and Rome, as it happened, was suffering from a great scarcity of food, causing the senate to send for grain from Sicily, Coriolanus, enemy of the popular faction, advised that the time had come to punish the plebeians and to take away the authority they enjoyed at the expense of the nobility by keeping them hungry and by not distributing the grain to them; when his advice reached the ears of the people, they were so indignant against Coriolanus that they would have murdered him in a riot at the exit of the senate if the tribunes had not summoned him to appear and to plead his case.* Concerning this incident, what was said above should be noted, that is, how useful and necessary it is for republics to provide through their laws a means of venting the anger the multitude feels toward an individual citizen, because when such legal means are not available, they will resort to illegal ones, and without any doubt the latter produce much worse effects than the former.

For this reason, when a citizen is oppressed by legal means, even if this does injury to him, little or no disorder in the republic follows, because the enforcement is not accomplished with private or foreign forces which are the ones that ruin free societies, but it is done with public forces and institutions which have their specific limits, nor do they go far beyond them to anything that would ruin the republic. With respect to corroborating this opinion with examples, I think it will suffice for me to mention that of Coriolanus from the ancients, from which anyone can judge how much evil would have befallen the Roman republic had he been put to death in a riot, because this would have given rise to a case of individuals harming individuals, the kind of injury that generates fear; fear seeks protection, for which partisans are procured; out of partisans factions are born in cities, from which arises their destruction. But since the affair was handled by those who had the authority to do so, all those evils that could have arisen from handling it with private authority were avoided.

We have seen in our own times what changes occurred in the republic of Florence when the multitude was unable to vent its animosity in a legal fashion against one of its citizens, as happened when Francesco Valori,* who was like the prince of the city, came to be considered by many as ambitious and as a man who wished with his audacity and courage to rise above the laws of civil society, and in the absence of any way to resist him in that republic except by a sect* contrary to his own, it came about that since he feared only extraordinary measures, he began to cultivate supporters who would defend him; on the other hand, those who opposed Valori, lacking a legal method of repressing him, thought about employing illegal means to the point that they turned to arms. Thus, where he might have been opposed through legal means and his power destroyed with damage to him alone, they were obliged to destroy it by illegal means, which resulted in damage not only to him but also to many other noble citizens.

In support of the above conclusion, it is also possible to cite an incident that likewise occurred in Florence in connection with Piero Soderini,* which came about entirely because that republic lacked any method of bringing an indictment against the ambition of powerful citizens. It is not sufficient to indict a powerful citizen before eight judges* in a republic; judges must be many in number, because the few always act in the interest of the few. Hence, if such methods had existed in Florence, either the citizens would have brought an indictment against Soderini had his conduct been bad, and through this means without bringing in the Spanish army, they would have given vent to their animosity, or, had his conduct not been bad, they would never have dared to work against him for fear of being charged themselves, and in either case the appetite that was the reason for the conflict would thus have disappeared. Hence, it is possible to conclude this much: that whenever we see foreign forces called in by a faction of men who live in a city, we can believe that this situation finds its origins in that city's bad institutions, since it does not possess within its walls any institution that permits the venting of the malignant humours born in men without resorting to illegal means; full provision is made for this by instituting a system of public indictments before a large number of judges and by giving these indictments sufficient status. These measures were so well organized in Rome that during the many conflicts between the plebeians and the senate, neither the senate nor the plebeians nor any private citizen sought to avail themselves of outside forces, because by having a remedy at home, there was no need to seek it outside. Although the examples above are more than sufficient to demonstrate this, I nevertheless want to cite another, related by Livy in his history.* He reports that in Chiusi, a most noble city of Etruria in those times, a certain Lucumo raped the sister of Arruns, and when Arruns was unable to avenge himself because of the rapist's power, he went off to find the Gauls, who then ruled the area today called Lombardy, and urged them to come armed to Chiusi, showing them how with profit to themselves they could compensate him for the injury he had received: if Arruns had seen that he could avenge himself through the city's institutions, he would not have sought out the barbarian forces.* But just as these public indictments are useful in a republic, so false accusations are useless and harmful, as we shall discuss in the following chapter.

CHAPTER 8

False Accusations Are As Harmful to Republics As Public Indictments Are Useful

Notwithstanding the fact that the ability of Furius Camillus, after he had freed Rome from the oppression of the Gauls, made all of the Roman citizens defer to him without causing them to feel that they had lost reputation or rank, Manlius Capitolinus could not, all the same, endure the fact that so much honour and glory was attributed to him, since it seemed to him that in so far as the salvation of Rome was concerned, he deserved as much deference as Camillus for having saved the Capitol, and that in so far as praiseworthy feats of military valour were concerned, he was not inferior to him.* Thus, so full of envy that he could not restrain himself on account of the other's glory, and realizing that he could not sow discord among the senators, he turned to the plebeians, spreading various sinister rumours among them. Among the other things he said was that the treasure collected to give to the Gauls, but which was then not given to them, had been usurped by private citizens, and that if it could be recovered it could be converted to the public benefit, by relieving the plebeians either of their taxes or of some private debt. These words were quite persuasive with the plebeians, with the result that they began to hold meetings and, as they wished, to create a number of disturbances in the city; this displeased the senate, and since they considered it a significant and dangerous situation, they created a dictator* to examine the matter and to hold Manlius' impetuosity in check. As a result, the dictator quickly summoned Manlius and brought him before the public, the one man confronting the other, the dictator amidst the nobles and Manlius amidst the plebeians. Manlius was told he must reveal who held this treasure about which he spoke, because the senate was as anxious to hear about it as the plebeians; Manlius did not respond to this in detail but evaded the issue, saying that it was not necessary to tell them something they already knew, so that the dictator had him put in prison.

It is to be noted from this text how detestable false accusations are in free cities, as well as in any other form of civil society, and how, in order to repress them, one must not ignore any institution which might do so. Nor is there a better method for eliminating them than to provide many open avenues for indictments, because public indictments bring as many benefits to republics as false accusations bring them harm, and there is this difference between them, that false accusations need neither witnesses nor any other particular corroboration to prove them, so that anyone can be slandered by anyone else, but not everyone can be publicly indicted, since indictments require true corroboration and circumstances which demonstrate the truth of the charges. Men are publicly indicted before the magistrates, the people, and the councils; they are falsely accused in the public squares and under the porticoes. False accusations are most often employed where there are fewer public indictments and wherever cities are less well organized to receive them. Nevertheless, the organizer of a republic must find an arrangement which allows charges to be made against any citizen in the republic without fear and without respect to the individual's position, and after a charge has been made and thoroughly examined, he must severely punish those making false accusations, who cannot complain when they are punished, since the avenues were open to hear the charges against those whom they falsely chose to accuse under the porticoes. Wherever this element is not well organized, great disorders always follow, because false accusations irritate but do not punish the citizens, and those who are irritated think about proving their worth by hating rather than fearing the things that are said against them.

This element, as was mentioned, was well organized in Rome, and it has always been poorly organized in our city of Florence. And just as in Rome this institution did much good, so in Florence the lack of such an institution caused much harm. Anyone reading the histories of this latter city will see how many false accusations were lodged in every era against citizens who were actively involved in the city's most important affairs. Of one they said that he had robbed funds from the city government; of another, that he had not succeeded in some undertaking because he was bribed; and of yet another, that because of his ambition, he had committed this or that impropriety. As a consequence of this hatred arose on every side, which led to deep disagreements, from deep disagreements to sects, and from sects to ruin.* If in Florence there had been an institution for making public indictments against citizens and for punishing those who made false accusations, the endless disorders that resulted would not have come about: those citizens, both the condemned and the acquitted, would not have been able to harm the city, and there would have been fewer men publicly indicted than falsely accused, since, as I have stated, it is not as easy to make public indictments as to make false accusations. Among the other means a citizen has employed to prove his worth and become great, there have been these false accusations; used against powerful citizens opposed to his appetite for power, these methods are very effective, because by taking the side of the people and confirming their low opinion of his opponents, he can make the people his friend. Although one could cite many examples of this, I shall be satisfied to cite only one. The Florentine army was in the field at Lucca under the command of Messer Giovanni Guicciardini, its commissioner.* Whether because of his bad leadership or his bad fortune, the destruction of that city did not come about. Still, whatever the case may have been, Messer Giovanni was blamed for it, since it was said that he had been bribed by the people of Lucca; this false accusation was supported by his enemies and almost drove Messer Giovanni to complete despair. Although in order to vindicate himself he wished to be placed into the hands of the Captain [of the People],* none the less he could never clear himself, since no means of doing so existed in that republic. As a result, great indignation arose among Messer Giovanni's friends, who were for the most part powerful men, and among them some who wished to make changes in Florence.* Both as a result of this affair and for other reasons, the problem grew to such an extent that it brought about the ruin of that republic.*

Manlius Capitolinus was, therefore, a false accuser and not a lawful one, and in this case the Romans demonstrated exactly how false accusers must be punished. Indeed, they must be turned into public accusers, and when the public indictment is found true, either reward them or avoid punishing them, but when it is found false, punish them as Manlius was punished.

CHAPTER 9

That a Man Must Be Alone If He Wishes to Organize a New Republic or Completely to Reform Its Ancient Institutions

Perhaps someone will think that I have gone through too much Roman history without yet having mentioned the founders of that republic or those institutions that concern religion and the profession of arms. Not wishing, therefore, to keep the minds of those who would like to hear something on this subject in suspense any longer, I must say that many are likely to judge it a bad example for the founder of a body politic, as Romulus was, to have first murdered his brother and later to have consented to the execution of Titus Tatius, the Sabine, elected by him as his companion in the kingdom,* concluding that citizens, out of ambition and a desire to rule, could, after the example of their leader, attack those opposed to their authority. This opinion would be true, if we were not to consider the goal which led Romulus to commit such a homicide.

Also, this must be taken as a general rule: that never or rarely does it happen that a republic or a kingdom is organized well from the beginning or is completely reformed apart from its old institutions, unless it is organized by one man alone; or rather, it is necessary for a single man to be the one who gives it shape, and from whose mind any such organization derives. Thus, the prudent founder of a republic, one who has this courageous desire to serve not his own interests but the common good, and not his own heirs but rather everyone in their native land, must strive to assume sole authority; nor will a wise mind ever reproach anyone for some illegal action that he might have undertaken to organize a kingdom or to constitute a republic. It is truly appropriate that while the act accuses him, the result excuses him, and when the result is good, like that of Romulus, it will always excuse him, because one should reproach a man who is violent in order to ruin things, not one who is so in order to set them aright.* He must, however, be so prudent and able that he will not bequeath the authority he has taken for himself to another as an inheritance, because men are more prone to evil than to good, and his successor might use in an ambitious fashion the power that he himself had used with skill. Besides this, although one man alone is capable of instituting a government, what he has instituted will not long endure if it rests upon the shoulders of a single man, but it endures when it remains a matter of concern to many and when it is the task of many to maintain it. Thus, just as the many are not capable of instituting anything, being unable to recognize its goodness, because of the diversity of opinions that exist among them, so in like manner, once they realize they have it, they will not agree to abandon it. That Romulus was among those who deserve to be excused for the death of his brother and his companion, and that what he did was for the common good and not for private ambition, is shown by the fact that he immediately established a senate with which he consulted and according to whose opinions he made decisions. Anyone who will carefully examine the authority that Romulus reserved for himself will see that he reserved nothing more for himself than the authority to command the armies when war was declared and to convene the senate. This became evident later when Rome became free because of the expulsion of the Tarquins, and not a single ancient institution was altered, except that in place of a king for life they created two consuls chosen annually; this testifies to the fact that all the original institutions of that city were more suitable to a free civil state than to one that was absolutist and tyrannical.*

Countless examples in support of what I have written above could be set forth, such as Moses, Lycurgus, Solon, and other founders of kingdoms and republics who were able to create laws for the common good, because they had assumed for themselves sole authority, but I wish to pass over them, since they are well known.

I shall set forth only one such example, not so famous but one to be considered by those who wish to be the creators of good laws: that is, when Agis, king of Sparta, wished to lead the Spartans back inside the boundaries within which the laws of Lycurgus had enclosed them, being of the opinion that by having deviated from them in part, his city had lost a great deal of its ancient ability and, as a result, much of its strength and its empire, he was murdered during his initial undertakings by the Spartan Ephors as a man who wanted to establish a tyranny.* But when Cleomenes succeeded him on the throne, and the same desire was born in him through his discovery of Agis' memoirs and writings, which made Agis' thoughts and intentions evident, he realized that he could not do this good for his native city if he did not become the sole authority, believing that because of human ambition, he could not help the many against the will of the few, and taking advantage of the right opportunity, he had all the Ephors murdered and anyone else who could oppose him; he then restored in their entirety the laws of Lycurgus. This decision would have been enough to give new life to Sparta and to give Cleomenes the same reputation enjoyed by Lycurgus had it not been for the power of the Macedonians and the weakness of the other Greek republics. After that reorganization Cleomenes was attacked by the Macedonians, and when he found himself weaker in force and had no one from whom to seek help, he was defeated, and this plan of his, no matter how just and praiseworthy it was, remained incomplete.

Having therefore considered all these matters, I conclude that in organizing a republic it is necessary to be alone, and that for the deaths of Remus and Titus Tatius, Romulus deserves to be excused and not blamed.

CHAPTER 10

The Founders of a Republic or a Kingdom Deserve As Much Praise As Those Who Found a Tyranny Deserve Blame

Among all men who are praised, the most highly praised are those who have been leaders and founders of religions. Close afterwards come those who have founded either republics or kingdoms. After them the most celebrated men are those who, placed at the head of armies, have enlarged either their own realm or that of their native country. To these may be added men of letters, who, being of many types, are each celebrated according to his level of accomplishment. To other men, infinite in number, some portion of praise may be attributed, on the basis of their profession or its practice. On the contrary, infamous and detestable are those men who have been destroyers of religions, wasters of kingdoms and republics, enemies of the virtues, of letters, and of every other profession that brings honour and advantage to the human race, such as the impious, the violent, the ignorant, the worthless, the lazy, and the cowardly. And no one will ever be so foolish or so wise, so bad or so good, that, faced with the choice between these two kinds of men, he will not praise what is to be praised and blame what is to be blamed. None the less, in the end almost all men, deceived by a false good and a false glory, allow themselves, either willingly or through ignorance, to pass into the ranks of those who deserve more blame than praise, and having the capacity to create, to their everlasting honour, either a republic or a kingdom, they turn to tyranny, failing to realize how much fame, how much glory, how much honour, security, tranquillity, and peace of mind they are losing through this choice, and how much infamy, disgrace, blame, danger, and anxiety they incur.

If they read the histories and made good capital out of the records of ancient affairs, it would be impossible for those living as private citizens in a republic, even if they have become its princes through fortune or exceptional ability, not to want to live in their native land as Scipio rather than Caesar, if they are private citizens, and as Agesilauses, Timoleons, and Dions, rather than Nabises, Phalarises, and Dionysiuses, if they are princes, because they would see that the latter were strongly condemned, while the former were extravagantly praised.* They would also see that Timoleon and the others possessed no less authority in their countries than Dionysius and Phalaris, and that they had greater security over a long period of time.

Nor should anyone be deceived by Caesar's glory, hearing him celebrated with the highest praise by the ancient writers, because those who praise him are seduced by his good fortune and terrified by the duration of the empire which was ruled under his name and did not permit writers to speak freely about him.* But anyone who wishes to know what writers, when free, would say about him should see what they say about Catiline.* Caesar is all the more detestable, just like the man who is to be blamed more for committing an evil deed than for wishing to do so. Also, let the reader see how they celebrate Brutus with so much praise, to the extent that, unable to blame Caesar because of his power, they celebrate his enemy.*

Furthermore, let any man who has become a prince in a republic consider how much more deserving of praise were those emperors who lived under the laws and as good princes after Rome became an empire than those who lived in a contrary fashion, and he will see that Titus, Nerva, Trajan, Hadrian, Antoninus, and Marcus had no need of praetorian guards or a multitude of legions to defend them, because their habits, the goodwill of the people, and the love of the senate defended them. Such a prince will also observe that for Caligula, Nero, Vitellius, and so many other villainous emperors the eastern and western armies were insufficient to save them from the enemies that their evil habits and their wicked lives had created for them. If the history of these men were carefully examined, it would be a sufficient lesson to demonstrate to any prince the path to glory or to blame, and to security or to fear. Of the twenty-six emperors that existed from Caesar to Maximinus, sixteen of them were murdered and ten died natural deaths; and if among those who were murdered there were several good ones, such as Galba and Pertinax, they were killed by the corruption their predecessors had left behind in the soldiers; and if among those who died natural deaths there was one wicked man, such as Severus, it came about as the result of his very great fortune and ability,* two qualities found together in few men. A prince will also see through the reading of this history how one can organize a good kingdom: all the emperors who took the imperial throne through hereditary succession, with the exception of Titus, were bad; those who did so through adoption were all good, as were those five from Nerva to Marcus; and when the empire lapsed into hereditary succession, it came again to ruin.

Let a prince, therefore, carefully consider the times from Nerva to Marcus, let him compare them with the times that came before and afterward, and then let him choose the period in which he would like to be born or in which he would like to be put in charge.* In those times governed by good emperors, he will see a ruler secure in the midst of secure citizens, and the world full of peace and justice; he will see the senate with its authority, the magistrates with their honours, the wealthy citizens enjoying their wealth, nobility and talent exalted; he will see every kind of tranquillity and well-being, and, on the other hand, the elimination of every kind of rancour, licence, corruption, and ambition; he will see a golden age where each person can hold and defend the opinions that he wishes. He will see, in conclusion, the world in triumph, its prince in possession of respect and glory, its peoples of love and security. If he will next consider in close detail the times of the other emperors, he will see them filled with atrocities on account of the wars, filled with dissension on account of sedition, cruel both in times of peace and in times of war; he will see so many princes dead by the sword, so many civil wars, so many foreign wars; and he will see Italy afflicted and full of new disasters,* her cities devastated and sacked. He will see Rome burned, the Capitol destroyed by her own citizens, the ancient temples desolate, their rites corrupted, the cities filled with adulteries; he will see the sea covered with exiles, the shores with blood. He will see countless cruelties committed in Rome, and he will see nobility, wealth, past honours, and, above all, exceptional ability judged to be capital sins.

He will see false accusers rewarded, servants corrupted to turn against their masters and freedmen against their [former] owners, and those who lack enemies oppressed by their friends. He will then understand very well what a debt Rome, Italy, and the world owe to Caesar.

And without doubt, if he is of human birth, the prince will be dismayed by any imitation of evil times and will burn with a powerful desire to follow the good ones. Truly, if a prince seeks earthly glory, he should have the desire to possess a corrupt city, not to ruin it completely, as Caesar did, but to reorganize it, as Romulus did, for the heavens cannot bestow upon men a greater opportunity for glory, nor can men wish for a greater one. If it were necessary to abandon a city in order to reorganize it properly, a man who failed to do so in order to avoid losing his rank might deserve some excuse, but were he able both to retain the principality and to reorganize it, he would deserve no excuse whatsoever. In conclusion, let those to whom the heavens grant such opportunities consider that there are two paths open before them: one enables them to live in security and, after their death, renders them illustrious; the other causes them to live in continuous anxiety and, after their death, to leave behind an eternal legacy of infamy.

CHAPTER II

On the Religion of the Romans

Although Rome had Romulus as its first organizer, and, like a daughter, had to recognize that she owed her birth and upbringing to him, since the heavens judged that Romulus' institutions would not suffice for so great an empire, they inspired the Roman senate to elect Numa Pompilius as his successor,* so that the matters left undone by Romulus were organized by Numa. Having found a very fierce people and wishing to bring them to civil obedience with the arts of peace, he turned to religion as something absolutely necessary for maintaining a civilized society, and he established it in such a way that for many centuries there was never more fear of God than in that republic; this greatly facilitated any enterprise the senate or those great men of Rome ever planned to undertake. Anyone who examines the countless deeds of the Roman people as a whole and of many individual Roman citizens will see that they feared breaking an oath more than breaking the laws, like people who respected the power of God more than that of men: this is clearly revealed in the examples of Scipio and of Manlius Torquatus. After Hannibal's rout of the Romans at Cannae,* many citizens had gathered together, and, terrified for their native city, they agreed to abandon Italy and to go to Sicily, but when Scipio heard about this he went to find them and, with his bare sword in his hand, he forced them to swear not to abandon their native land. Lucius Manlius, the father of Titus Manlius (who was later called Torquatus), was indicted by Marcus Pomponius, tribune of the plebeians, but before the day for his trial arrived Titus went to Marcus and, by threatening to kill him if he did not swear to withdraw the accusation against his father, he forced him to take an oath, and once Marcus had sworn an oath out of fear, he withdrew the charge. Thus, those citizens, whose love for their native land or its laws could not keep them in Italy, were kept there by the oath they were forced to take, and that tribune set aside the hatred he felt for the father and the injury inflicted upon him by the son, as well as his own honour, to obey the oath he had sworn; this arose from nothing other than the religion Numa had introduced into that city. Furthermore, it will be evident to anyone who carefully examines Roman history how useful religion was in controlling the armies, in giving courage to the plebeians, in keeping men good, and in shaming the wicked. Accordingly, if one had to debate the question of which of these princes Rome was more indebted to— either Romulus or Numa—I believe that Numa would sooner be ranked first, for where there is religion, arms can easily be introduced, but where there are arms but no religion, the latter can be introduced only with difficulty. It is evident that Romulus did not find God's authority necessary to organize the senate or to create many other civil and military institutions, but it was necessary for Numa, who pretended to have a close relationship with a nymph* who advised him about how he should advise the people; all of this came about because Numa wanted to establish new and unusual institutions in that city, and he doubted that his own authority was sufficient. In truth, no maker of extraordinary laws who did not have recourse to God has ever existed in any society, because these laws would not otherwise be accepted, and because although the good things known to a prudent man are many, these things in themselves lack the self-evident qualities that can persuade others. Wise men who wish, therefore, to avoid this difficulty have recourse to God. Lycurgus did so, as did Solon, and many others who had their same goal. Thus, marvelling in Numa's goodness and prudence, the Roman people yielded to his every decision. Of course, it is true that those times were very religious and those men with whom he had to work were ignorant, and this fact made it easier to pursue his plans, since he could simply imprint them with any new form whatsoever.* Without doubt, anyone wishing to establish a republic at present would find it easier among mountain people, where there is no civil society, than among men who are used to living in cities, where civil society is corrupt; a sculptor will more easily extract a beautiful statue from a rough piece of marble than he can from one badly blocked out by others.

Having, therefore, considered everything, I conclude that the religion introduced by Numa was among the principal reasons for the happiness of that city, because it produced good institutions, the good institutions created good fortune, and from good fortune arose the happy successes of their undertakings. Just as the observance of divine worship is the cause of the greatness of republics, so the disregard of divine worship is the cause of their ruin, because where fear of God is lacking, that kingdom must either come to ruin or be sustained through fear of a prince who makes up for the shortcomings in its religion. Since princes are short-lived, such a kingdom must quickly fail when it loses his exceptional ability. Hence, it happens that kingdoms which depend only upon the exceptional ability of a single man are not long enduring, because such talent disappears with the life of the man, and rarely does it happen to be restored in his successor, as Dante prudently declares:

> Not often does the sap of virtue
> descend to all its branches. This is His own gift,
> and we can only beg that He bestow it.*

The salvation of a republic or a kingdom is not, therefore, merely to have a prince who governs prudently while he lives, but rather one who organizes the government in such a way that after his death it can be maintained. Although uncultivated men are more easily persuaded to adopt a new institution or opinion, it is still not impossible for that reason to persuade civilized men or men who do not consider themselves uncultivated to do the same. The people of Florence did not consider themselves to be either ignorant or uncultivated; they were nevertheless persuaded by Brother Girolamo Savonarola that he spoke with God.* I do not wish to judge whether this was true or not, since one must speak of such a man with reverence, but I must say that countless people believed him without ever having seen anything extraordinary to make them believe him, because his life, his doctrine, and the [sermon] topics he chose were sufficient to persuade them to put their faith in him. No one, therefore, should be dismayed if he cannot achieve what others have achieved, because men, as was stated in our preface, are always born, live, and die in the same way.

CHAPTER 12

How Important It Is to Take Account of Religion, and How Italy, Lacking in Religion Thanks to the Roman Church, Has Been Ruined

Those princes or republics that wish to maintain their integrity must, above all else, maintain the integrity of their religious ceremonies, and must always hold them in veneration, because there can be no greater indication of the ruin of a state than to see a disregard for its divine worship. This is easy to understand if one knows how the religion in the place where a man is born has been founded, because the life of every religion has its foundations in one of its principal institutions. The existence of the pagan religion* was founded upon the responses of the oracles and the sect of diviners and soothsayers; all the other ceremonies, sacrifices, and rites depended upon them, because they simply believed that the god who could predict your future good or evil could also grant it to you. From this belief arose the temples, from this the sacrifices, from this the supplications and every other ceremony devoted to their veneration; from this, the oracle of Delphi, the temple of Jupiter Ammon, and other famous oracles, which filled the world with wonder and devotion. Later, as these oracles began to speak in a way similar to that of the powerful and their falsity was discovered by the peoples, men became disbelievers and capable of undermining every good institution. The rulers of a republic or a kingdom must, therefore, uphold the foundations of the religion they profess; and having done this, they will find it an easy matter for them to maintain a devout republic and, as a consequence, one that is good and united. They must also encourage and support all those things that arise in favour of this religion, even those they judge to be false, and the more they have to do so, the more prudent they are and the more knowledgeable about natural phenomena. Because this method has been followed by wise men, there has arisen a belief in miracles that are celebrated even by false religions; thus, prudent men magnify their importance, no matter the principle from which they originate, and through the authority of these miracles they gain everyone's confidence. There were many such miracles in Rome: among them was the one that occurred while Roman soldiers were sacking the city of Veii, when a number of them entered the temple of Juno and, drawing close to the goddess's image, asked it 'Do you wish to come to Rome?', and it seemed to some that she nodded her head and to others that she said 'yes'. Since these men were steeped in religion (something Livy demonstrates, for upon entering the temple they came inside without making any disturbance, all devout and full of reverence), they seemed to hear a response to their question that they might by chance have expected; their opinion and credulity was strongly encouraged and supported by Camillus and the other rulers of the city. If this kind of religion had been maintained by the clergy of Christian republics just as it had been instituted by its founder, Christian states and Christian republics would be more united and more happy than they are now. Nor can there be another, better basis for speculating about its decline than to see that those peoples who are nearer the Roman church, the head of our religion, have less religion. Anyone who studies its fundamental principles and sees how different present practice is from them would judge it to be, without any doubt, very near either ruin or punishment.*

Since many are of the opinion that the well-being of the Italian cities arises from the Roman church, I want to discuss the arguments that occur to me against this opinion, and I shall cite as evidence two very powerful ones which, in my view, cannot be refuted. The first is that because of the evil examples set by this court, this land has lost all piety and religion; this brings with it countless disadvantages and countless disorders, because just as we take for granted every good thing where religion exists, so, where it is lacking, we take for granted the contrary. We Italians have, therefore, this initial debt to the church and to the priests, that we have become irreligious and wicked, but we have an even greater debt to them, which is the second cause of our ruin: that is, the church has kept and still keeps this land divided, and truly, no land is ever united or happy unless it comes completely under the obedience of a single republic or a single prince, as has occurred in France and Spain. The reason why Italy is not in that same condition and why it, too, does not have either a single republic or a single prince to govern it lies solely with the church, because although the church has its place of residence in Italy and has held temporal power there, it has not been so powerful nor has it possessed enough skill to be able to occupy the remaining parts of Italy and make itself ruler of this country, and, on the other hand, it has not been so weak that, for fear of losing control over its temporal affairs, it has been unable to bring in someone powerful* to defend it against anyone in Italy who had become too powerful: this is seen to have happened in ancient times through a number of examples, as when with Charlemagne's assistance, the Lombards, already kings of almost all of Italy, were driven out, and when in our own times the church took power away from the Venetians with the aid of France and then chased out the French with the aid of the Swiss.* Since it has not, therefore, been powerful enough to take possession of all of Italy, nor has it permitted anyone else to do so, the church has been the reason why Italy has been unable to unite under a single leader and has remained under a number of princes and lords, who have produced so much disunity and weakness that it has come to be easy prey not only to powerful barbarians* but to anyone who might attack it. For this we Italians are indebted to the church and to no one else. Anyone who might wish to see this truth more clearly through actual experience needs to possess sufficient power to send the Roman court, with all the authority it possesses in Italy, to live in the lands of the Swiss, who are today the only people who live, with respect to religion and military institutions, as the ancients did, and he would observe that in a brief time the wicked customs of that court would create more disorder in that land than any other event that could at any time take place there.

CHAPTER 13

How the Romans Made Use of Religion to Reorganize Their City, to Carry Out Their Enterprises, and to Quell Disturbances

I do not think it beside the point to set forth some examples in which the Romans employed religion to reorganize their city and to carry out their enterprises, and although there are many of them in Livy, I nevertheless wish to be satisfied with these. After the Roman people had created tribunes with consular powers, who, with one exception, were all plebeians, and after plague and famine had occurred that year and certain portentous signs had appeared, the nobles took the occasion of the new creation of the tribunes to declare that the gods were angry because Rome had misused the majesty of her empire and that there was no other remedy to placate the gods than to return the election of the tribunes to its former system; the result was that the plebeians, terrified by this use of religion, created tribunes who were all nobles. It can also be seen how, in the conquest of the city of Veii, the leaders of the armies employed religion to keep their armies resolute in their undertaking: since Lake Albanus had miraculously increased in size that year, and the Roman soldiers were weary of the long siege and wanted to return to Rome, the Romans discovered that Apollo* and certain other soothsayers were saying that the city of Veii would be defeated during the year in which Lake Albanus overflowed its banks; this made the soldiers endure the hardships of the siege, in their hope of taking the city by storm, and they remained content to continue the campaign until Camillus was made dictator and captured the city after the ten years during which it had been under siege. Thus, the careful use of religion helped both in the capture of that city and in the return of the tribunate to the nobility, without which it would have been difficult to carry out either enterprise.

I do not want to fail to add another example on this topic. Many disturbances arose in Rome because of Terentillus the tribune,* who wished to propose a certain law for reasons that will be stated below in the proper place, and among the first remedies that the nobility employed in this case was religion, which they made use of in two ways. First, they had the Sibylline Books consulted and the response given that, because of sedition, the city was threatened with the loss of her liberty that year; although the tribunes exposed this scheme, it nevertheless inspired so much terror in the hearts of the plebeians that their desire to follow the tribunes cooled off. The other way was this: a certain Appius Herdonius,* with a crowd of exiles and slaves numbering 4,000 men, occupied the Capitol by night, so that everyone would fear that had the Aequi and the Volscians, perpetual enemies of Rome, come to the city, they would have taken it. Since the tribunes did not, on this account, abandon their persistence in proposing the law of Terentillus, declaring that the possibility of attack was fabricated, not real, a certain Publius Ruberius,* a dignified citizen of authority, came out of the senate with words that were partly friendly and partly menacing, demonstrating to the plebeians the dangers to the city and the untimeliness of their demand; in this way, he constrained the plebeians to swear not to depart from the wishes of the consul, with the result that the compliant plebeians retook the Capitoline Hill by force. But since Publius Valerius the consul was killed in this assault, Titus Quinctius was immediately re-elected consul.* In order to avoid allowing the plebeians to rest or to have time to think about the law of Terentillus, he ordered them to leave Rome to move against the Volscians, declaring that they were obliged to follow him because of the oath they had taken not to abandon the consul: the tribunes opposed this order, saying that the oath had been sworn to the dead consul and not to him. Nevertheless, Livy demonstrates how through fear of their religion the plebeians preferred to obey the consul rather than to believe the tribunes, writing the following words in favour of the ancient religion: 'there was as yet no sign of our modern scepticism which interprets solemn compacts, such as those embodied in an oath or a law, to suit its own convenience'.* Because of this, the tribunes, fearing they would lose all their prestige, reached an agreement with the consul that they would yield to him, and that for a year they would not discuss the law of Terentillus, while the consuls could not, for a year, lead the plebeians outside the city walls to war. Thus, religion enabled the senate to overcome the difficulties they could never have overcome without it.

CHAPTER 14

The Romans Interpreted the Auspices According to Necessity, and They Prudently Made a Show of Observing Religion Even When They Were Forced Not to Observe It; and If Anyone Dared to Disparage It, They Punished Him

As was discussed above, the auguries were not only in large part the foundation of the ancient religion of the pagans, but they were also the cause of the well-being of the Roman republic. For this reason, the Romans had greater concern for them than for any other institution, and they employed them in their consular elections, in beginning their undertakings, in leading forth their armies, in fighting their battles, and in every important activity, either civil or military; nor would they ever have gone on an expedition without first having persuaded their soldiers that the gods had promised them a victory. Among other auspices, they had in their armies a certain order of soothsayers they called *pullarii,** and whenever the Romans decided to engage the enemy in battle, they wanted the *pullarii* to take the auspices; when the chickens pecked, the Romans fought with a good augury; when they did not peck, the Romans abstained from any encounter. None the less, when reason showed the Romans that something had to be done, they undertook it, notwithstanding the fact that the auspices were unfavourable, but they gave them a different meaning with such suitable words and methods that they did not appear to be doing so with any disrespect to religion.

Such methods were employed by the consul Papirius* in a very important military encounter with the Samnites, which left the Samnites in all respects weak and in distress. When Papirius was encamped facing the Samnites, believing that victory in the battle was assured and desiring, therefore, to engage the enemy, he ordered the *pullarii* to take their auspices, but since the chickens refused to peck and the leader of the *pullarii* saw the great readiness of the army for combat, as well as the commander's belief, shared with his men, that they would be victorious, he reported to the consul that the auspices were favourable in order not to deprive the army of an occasion for a good operation. While Papirius was ordering his squadrons to draw themselves into formation, some *pullarii* told certain soldiers that the chickens had not pecked, who reported the conversation to Spurius Papirius, nephew of the consul, and when he told the consul, Papirius immediately replied that he expected him to carry out his duties properly: that as for him and his army, the auspices were favourable, and if the *pullarius* had told any lies they would be detrimental to him alone. So that the result would correspond to his prediction, he ordered his legates to place the *pullarii* in the front lines of the battle. Hence, it happened that as they advanced against the enemy, one of the Roman soldiers shot an arrow and accidentally killed the leader of the *pullarii*; when the consul learned of this, he declared that everything was going according to plan and with the favour of the gods, because, with the death of this liar, the army had been excused for any blame and any wrath the gods might have directed against it. Thus, with the knowledge of exactly how to accommodate his plans to the auspices, he made the decision to enter into battle without the army

realizing that he had in any way disregarded the institutions of
their religion.

Appius Pulcher in the First Punic War did just the opposite in
Sicily: since he wanted to engage the Carthaginian army he had
the *pullarii* take the auspices, and when they reported to him
that the chickens were not pecking, he declared: 'Let's see if they
will drink!' and had them thrown into the ocean.* For whatever
cause, after engaging in combat he lost the battle, and for this he
was condemned in Rome, while Papirius was honoured, not so
much because the latter had won and the former had lost but
rather because one man had acted prudently against the auspices
while the other had done so recklessly. Nor did this means of
taking the auspices serve any purpose other than sending the
soldiers confidently into battle, for from such confidence victory almost always results. This stratagem was used not only by
the Romans but by foreigners, and I think it appropriate to provide an example of it in the next chapter.

CHAPTER 15

The Samnites Turned to Religion
As a Last Resort in Times of Misfortune

After the Samnites had suffered numerous defeats by the
Romans and had finally been destroyed in Etruria, with their
armies and leaders killed and their allies, such as the Etruscans,
the Gauls, and the Umbrians conquered, 'they could carry on no
longer, either with their own resources or with outside support,
yet they would not abstain from war—so far were they from tir-
ing of freedom even though they had not succeeded in defending
it, preferring to be defeated rather than not to try for victory'.*
They resolved, therefore, to make one last effort, and since they
knew that to create the desire to win it was necessary to instil
determination into the minds of their soldiers, and that there was
no better means of doing so than religion, they thought they
would repeat one of their ancient sacrificial rites, with the help of
their priest Ovius Paccius. They organized this sacrifice in this
way: once they had made the solemn sacrifice, between the dead

victims and the lighted altars, they made all the leaders of the army swear never to abandon the battle, and they called forward the soldiers one by one, and between the altars and in the midst of a number of centurions with their drawn swords in hand, they made the soldiers swear first that they would never repeat what they had seen or heard; then, with curses and verses full of fear, they made the men promise the gods they would go swiftly wherever their commanders sent them and would never flee from battle and would kill anyone they saw fleeing: if this oath were not observed, it would come back upon the heads of their families and tribes. When some of the men became terrified and unwilling to swear their oaths, they were immediately put to death by their centurions; as a result all the others that followed, frightened by the ferocity of the spectacle, then swore their oaths. Moreover, in order to make their gathering more magnificent, since they numbered 40,000 men, they dressed half of them in white uniforms with crests and plumes upon their helmets, and organized in this manner, they took their position near Aquilonia. Coming to face them, Papirius, urging on his soldiers, declared: 'crested helmets dealt no wounds, and Roman javelins could pierce shields which were painted and gilded'.* In order to weaken his soldiers' opinion of the enemy on account of the oath they had taken, Papirius declared that the oath was based on their fear rather than on their strength, because at the same time they were in fear of their fellow citizens, the gods, and their enemies. Once they joined in the conflict the Samnites were overcome, for Roman ability* and the fear engendered by past defeats overcame whatever determination the Samnites might have been able to derive from the strength of their religion and the oath they had sworn. Nevertheless, it is evident that they did not feel they had any other alternative, nor that they could make any other attempt to regain the hope of recovering their lost valour. This clearly testifies to how much confidence can be acquired through religion when it is properly used.* And although this section may perhaps require that it be placed in the discussion of foreign affairs,* since it nevertheless depends upon one of the most important institutions of the republic of Rome, I felt I should place it in this section in order to avoid dividing this subject-matter and having to return to it several times.

CHAPTER 16

A People Accustomed to Living Under a Prince Maintains Its Freedom With Difficulty If, by Some Accident, It Becomes Free

How difficult it is for a people accustomed to living under a prince to preserve its freedom if, by some accident, it has acquired freedom, as the Romans did once they drove out the Tarquins, is demonstrated by countless examples that can be read in the annals of ancient history. Such difficulty is understandable, because that people is no more than a brutish animal which, while still ferocious and wild by nature, has always been kept imprisoned and enslaved, and then, left by chance in an open field, unaccustomed to feeding itself and not knowing the spots where it might seek refuge, becomes prey to the first person who seeks to put it back into chains.*

The same things happen to a people accustomed to living under the government of others, since not knowing how to reason about either public defence or offence, and not understanding princes or being understood by them, it swiftly returns under a yoke which is, in most instances, heavier than the one that only a short while earlier had been lifted from its neck, and it finds itself in these difficulties even though its substance is not corrupted.* In fact, a people which has become completely corrupted cannot live free even for a brief time, not even a moment, as will be discussed below, and our inquiries, therefore, concern those peoples where corruption has not spread too widely and there remains more of the good than the tainted.

Another difficulty to be added to the one mentioned above is that a state that becomes free creates for itself enemies rather than friends.* All those who took advantage of the tyrannical government and who fed off the wealth of the prince become hostile members; having lost the possibility of privilege, they can no longer live content, and each of them is forced to try to retrieve the tyranny in order to return to his former authority. Nor will such a state, as I have said, acquire friendly members, because free government confers honours and prizes for honest and specific reasons, and beyond them confers no honours or prizes whatsoever, and when a man possesses those honours and advantages he feels he deserves, he does not admit an obligation to those who have rewarded him. Besides this, the common benefit derived from a free government is recognized by no one while it is possessed, that is, to be able freely to enjoy one's possessions without worry, to feel no fear for the honour of one's women and children, and to feel no fear for one's own safety, because no one ever admits owing an obligation to someone who does not harm him.

Yet, as I said above, the state that is free and newly established comes to acquire enemies and not friends. In the desire to remedy these disadvantages and the disorders which the aforementioned difficulties bring along with them, there is no more powerful remedy, nor one more valid, safe, and necessary than to kill the sons of Brutus, who, as history demonstrates, were led to conspire together with other young Romans against their native city* for no other reason than that they were unable to enjoy the extraordinary privileges under the consuls that they had enjoyed under the king, so that it seemed to them that the liberty of the people had become their slavery. Anyone who undertakes governing a multitude of people, either under a free system or under a principality, and does not protect himself from the people who are hostile to the new order, creates a state of short duration. It is true that I judge those princes unfortunate who, having the multitude as their enemy, must have recourse to extraordinary means to protect their state, because the ruler who has the few as his enemy can protect himself easily and without much discord, but the man who has the general population as his enemy can never protect himself, and the more cruelty he employs, the weaker his principality becomes. Thus, the best remedy he has is to try to make the people friendly to him.*

Although this commentary may diverge from what I have written above, since I speak here of a prince and there of a republic, nevertheless, in order not to have to return to this topic later, I wish to discuss it briefly now. If a prince wishes, therefore, to win over a people that has been hostile to him (I am speaking of those princes who have become rulers in their native lands), let me say that he must first examine what the people want, and he will always discover that they want two things: first, to take revenge against those who were the cause of their being enslaved, and second, to regain their liberty. The prince can satisfy the first desire completely but the second only in part. For the first, there is an appropriate example.* When Clearchus, tyrant of Heraclea, was in exile, it happened that a dispute arose between the people and the aristocrats of Heraclea; the aristocrats, realizing they were weaker, turned to support Clearchus, and conspiring with him, they placed him in power against popular opinion in Heraclea and took away the people's freedom. As a result, when Clearchus found himself caught between the insolence of the aristocrats, whom he could neither satisfy nor punish in any way, and the anger of the people, who could not bear having lost their freedom, he decided to free himself from the annoyance of the patricians and to win over the people to his side in a single stroke. Taking advantage of a suitable occasion for this, he cut all the aristocrats into pieces to the greatest satisfaction of the people.* Thus, Clearchus satisfied one of the wishes all peoples have, that is, to take revenge. But as for their other desire, to regain their liberty, since a prince cannot satisfy that he must examine the causes that make them wish to be free, and he will discover that a small part of the people wish to be free in order to command, but all the others, who are countless, desire liberty in order to live in safety. In all republics, no matter how they are organized, no more than forty or fifty citizens ever reach the ranks of command, and since this is a small number, it is an easy task to protect oneself from them, either by eliminating them or by bestowing upon them so many honours that, according to their standing, they will for the most part be content. The others for whom it is enough to live in safety can be easily satisfied by establishing institutions and passing laws which provide for both the prince's personal power and the public safety. When a prince does this and the people realize that under no circumstances will he break these laws, they will begin in a short time to live in security and contentment. An example of this is the Kingdom of France, which lives in security for no other reason than the fact that its kings are constrained by countless laws which also provide for the security of all its people. The person who organized that state wanted the kings to do as they wished in military affairs and in financial affairs, but to dispose of every other matter as the laws ordained. Thus, that prince or that republic which has not made itself secure at the beginning of its rule must do so at the first opportunity, just as the Romans did. Anyone who allows the occasion to pass will repent too late for not having done what he should have done.

Since the Roman people were therefore not yet corrupt at the time they recovered their liberty, they were able to maintain it, once the sons of Brutus were dead and the Tarquins done away with, employing all those means and institutions we have previously discussed. But if that people had been corrupt, sound remedies capable of sustaining that liberty would not have been found either in Rome or elsewhere, as will be shown in the following chapter.

CHAPTER 17

A Corrupt People Which Becomes Free Can Remain So Only With the Greatest Difficulty

I believe it was necessary either for the kings in Rome to die off or for Rome to have become weak and of little worth in a very short time, because considering the degree of corruption into which these kings fell, if two or three successive reigns had followed in the same manner, so that the corruption which was within them had begun to spread throughout the members, once the members had become corrupted it would have been impossible ever to reform the city. But since the head was lost while the body was still intact, the Romans were easily able to bring themselves back to living a free and well-ordered existence. It must be taken as absolutely true that a corrupt city living under a prince can never regain its liberty, even if a prince and his entire family are done away with, indeed, even if one prince does away with the other, and without the creation of a new ruler, the city will never be at rest until the goodness of a single man, along with his exceptional ability, keeps it free. Yet this liberty will endure only as long as his own life, as happened in Syracuse with Dion and Timoleon, whose exceptional ability at different times kept that city free as long as they lived; once they were dead, the city returned to its long-standing tyranny.* But no more powerful example can be found than that of Rome, for, once the Tarquins were driven out, it was immediately able to seize and maintain its liberty; still, after Caesar, Gaius Caligula, and Nero died, and Caesar's race was extinguished,* not only could Rome never maintain its freedom but it could never even give it a beginning. Such dissimilar results in the same city arose from nothing other than the fact that in the time of the Tarquins the Roman people were still uncorrupted, while in those later times they were extremely corrupt. In that former time, in order to make the people steadfast and willing to avoid kings, it was enough merely to make them swear that they would never agree to the reign of another king in Rome, while in these later days, the authority and severity of Brutus plus all the eastern legions were not sufficient to make the people willing to maintain the liberty that he, like the first Brutus,* had restored to them. This arose from the corruption that the factions of Marius had established among the people; as the leader of these factions, Caesar was able to blind the multitude so that they did not recognize the yoke that they themselves were placing upon their own necks.

Although this example from Rome is preferable to any other, nevertheless, on this subject I want to bring forward examples of peoples known in our own times. Let me say, therefore, that no event, though it might be serious or violent, could ever have restored freedom to Milan or Naples, since their members were completely corrupt. This can be seen after the death of Filippo Visconti,* when Milan, desiring to restore its liberty, was not able, nor did the city know how, to maintain it. Thus, it was Rome's greatest good fortune that its kings quickly became corrupt, so that they were driven out, and long before their corruption had passed into the heart of the city; this lack of corruption was the reason why the countless disturbances that took place in Rome never caused any harm but, rather, benefited the republic, given that those men had good aims.

Hence, one can draw this conclusion: that where the material is not corrupt, disturbances and other disorders can do no harm, and where the material is corrupt, carefully enacted laws do no good, unless they are initiated by a man who, with enormous power, causes them to be observed in such a way that the material becomes good. Whether this has ever occurred, or whether it might ever possibly occur, I do not know, because it is evident, as I declared above, that once a city has begun to decline through the corruption of its substance, if it ever manages to rise again, this occurs through the exceptional ability of a single man who is alive at the time and not through the exceptional ability of the people as a whole who support good institutions, and as soon as that man is dead the city returns to its former habits, just as in Thebes, which, through the exceptional skill of Epaminondas, was able to maintain the republican form of government and an empire while he was living but once he was dead returned to its former disorders.* The reason is that no single man can live long enough to train well a city long accustomed to bad habits. If one man with an extraordinarily long life, or one skilful ruler succeeded by another, does not set it back in order, the lack of such men, as I have said above, brings it to ruin, unless they have, at the risk of much danger and bloodshed, brought about its rebirth. Thus, such corruption and so little aptitude for living in freedom arise from an inequality that exists in the city, and if one wishes to bring the city back to a state of equality, it is necessary to employ extraordinary measures, which few know how or wish to employ, as will be discussed in another place in greater detail.*

CHAPTER 18

How a Free Government Can Be Maintained in Corrupt Cities If One Already Exists, or, If One Does Not Already Exist, How to Establish It

I do not consider it out of place or in conflict with the commentary above to consider whether or not it is possible to maintain a free government in a corrupt city if one already exists; or whether or not, if one does not already exist, it can be established there. On this subject, let me say how very difficult it is to accomplish either the one or the other, and although it is almost impossible to supply a rule for the problem, since it would be necessary to proceed according to the extent of the corruption, nevertheless I do not want to omit this, since it is always good to discuss everything. I shall assume that the city in question is extremely corrupt, which will further increase this difficulty, because neither laws nor institutions will be found in it sufficient to check universal corruption. Thus, just as good customs require laws in order to be maintained, so laws require good customs in order to be observed. Besides this, institutions and laws established in a republic at the time of its birth, when men were good, are no longer suitable later, once men have become evil, and if the laws vary in a city according to circumstances, its institutions never or rarely ever change: this means that new laws are insufficient, because the institutions that remain in place corrupt them.

In order to clarify this matter further, let me say that in Rome there was the arrangement of the government, or rather, the state, and later on the laws that along with the magistrates kept the citizens in check. The order of the state encompassed the authority of the people, the senate, the tribunes, and the consuls, the means of proposing and appointing magistrates, and the method of making the laws. These institutions changed little or not at all according to circumstances. The laws holding citizens in check varied—as occurred with the law against adultery, the sumptuary law, the one against ambition, and many others—according to the way in which the citizens, in turn, became corrupt, one by one. But since the institutions of the state, which were no longer good amidst the corruption, remained fixed, these laws, which were renewed were not sufficient to keep men good, but they would have been very useful if, along with the innovations in the laws, the institutions had been changed once again.

That such institutions in a corrupt city were not good is clearly evident, especially in two principal cases, that is, in appointing magistrates and instituting laws. The Roman people did not give the consulate or the other key positions in the city to anyone except those who sought them. This institution was good at the beginning, because no one asked for these offices except those citizens who deemed themselves worthy, and to be refused was disgraceful; as a result, in order to be deemed worthy of them everyone behaved well. This system later became extremely harmful in the corrupt city, because those with the most power rather than those who possessed the most ability asked for the magistracies, and those lacking power, no matter how able, refrained from asking for them out of fear. Rome did not arrive at this disadvantageous situation all at once, but rather by degrees, just as one falls into all the other kinds of difficulties, because once the Romans had conquered Africa and Asia and had brought almost all of Greece under their control, they became secure in their freedom and did not feel they had any other enemies capable of making them afraid. This sense of security, along with the weakness of their adversaries, caused the Roman people, in granting the consulate, to take charm rather than ability into consideration, raising to that rank those men who knew best how to please others rather than those who knew best how to conquer their enemies, and then, from those who had greater charm, they descended to giving it to men with more power, so that good men, through the defect in this institution, remained completely excluded from such offices. A tribune or any other citizen could propose a law to the people, and every citizen could speak either in favour or against it before the law was enacted. This was a good institution while the citizens were good, because it has always been proper for anyone who understood the commonweal to be able to propose a law, and it is right for anyone to be able to express his opinion of it, so that the people, after hearing them all, is then able to select the best. But once the citizens became wicked this institution became very harmful, because only the powerful proposed laws, not in the name of a common freedom but for the benefit of their own authority, and against them no one could speak for fear of reprisal, so that the people came to be either deceived or forced into deciding upon their own destruction.

It was therefore necessary, if Rome wished to remain free amid the corruption, that just as the city had created new laws in the course of its existence, it should also have created new institutions, because different institutions and ways of life must be established for a subject who is evil rather than good, nor can

similar forms exist in completely different substances. But since all
these institutions must either be reformed all in a single stroke as
soon as it is discovered they are no longer good, or little by little
before everyone recognizes they are bad, let me say that both of
these two alternatives are almost impossible. The wish to reform
them little by little requires a prudent man to come forward who
sees this problem from some distance and in its initial stages. It is
very likely that an individual of this type may never emerge in a
city, and even if one were to emerge, he might not be able to persuade others of what he himself has come to understand, because
men used to living in one way do not wish to change, and all the
more so when they do not see the evil for themselves but must
have it demonstrated to them through abstract arguments. As for
changing these institutions all at once, when everyone realizes
they are no longer good, let me say that this ineffectiveness,
though easily recognized, is difficult to correct, because to do so
ordinary practices are no longer sufficient, once ordinary
methods have become wicked, and it is necessary to turn to extraordinary methods, such as violence or arms, and to become,
above all else, prince of the city and able to arrange it as one
wishes. Furthermore, since the reorganization of a city into a
body politic* presupposes a good man, whereas becoming the
prince of a republic through violent means presupposes an evil
one, we will discover, for this reason, that only on the rarest
occasions will a good man wish to become prince through evil
means, even though his goal might be a good one; we will also discover that equally rarely will an evil man who has become prince
wish to govern well, or that it would ever enter his mind to use
properly the authority he has acquired in a wicked fashion.

From all the above-mentioned factors arises the difficulty or
impossibility of maintaining a republic in corrupt cities or of
establishing a new one in them, and even if one had to be established or maintained there, it would be necessary to lead it more
towards a monarchical than towards a popular government, so
that those insolent men who cannot be improved [by the laws]
would be held in check by an authority which is almost kingly.
To try to make them become good by other means would be
either a most cruel undertaking or completely impossible, as I
said above concerning what Cleomenes did:* if Cleomenes

murdered the ephors in order to rule alone, and if Romulus killed his brother and Titus Tatius the Sabine for the same reasons, and afterwards they employed this authority of theirs well, we must remind ourselves, nevertheless, that neither the one nor the other had a subject stained by the corruption we have been discussing in this chapter, and they were, therefore, able to try and, trying, to put their plan into effect.

CHAPTER 19

After an Excellent Prince, a Weak Prince Can Maintain Himself; but After a Weak Prince, No Kingdom Can Be Maintained With Another Weak One

Considering the exceptional ability and the modes of conduct characteristic of Romulus, Numa, and Tullus, the first three kings of Rome, one may see that Rome enjoyed extremely good fortune, having a first king who was extremely fierce and warlike, a second peaceful and religious, and a third similar in ferocity to Romulus and more a lover of war than of peace. In Rome it was necessary for a founder of its civic institutions to arise during its earliest beginnings, but afterwards it was likewise necessary for the other kings to reclaim the ability of Romulus, since that city would otherwise have become effeminate and prey to its neighbours. From this fact, it can be noted that a successor who possesses less ability than the first ruler can maintain a state through the ability of the man who governed it before him, and can enjoy the fruits of his labours, but if it happens either that this successor has a long life or that after him no other arises who reclaims the ability of the first ruler, that kingdom must, by necessity, come to ruin. Thus, on the contrary, if two rulers, one after the other, possess extraordinary ability, it is often observed that they accomplish the greatest deeds and that their fame reaches as far as the heavens.

David was undoubtedly a man of the greatest excellence in arms, religion, and judgement; his ability was so exceptional that after he had conquered and overcome all his neighbours, he left to his son Solomon a peaceful kingdom, which Solomon was able to preserve with the arts of peace and not those of war; and Solomon was happily able to enjoy the fruits of his father's ability. But he was unable to leave the kingdom to his son Rehoboam, who, lacking his grandfather's ability and his father's good fortune, remained heir to a sixth part of the kingdom only with great effort.* Bajazet, sultan of the Turks,* although a man who was more a lover of peace than of war, was able to enjoy the fruits of his father Mahomet's labours;* his father, like David, having beaten down his neighbours, left his son a secure kingdom that could easily be maintained with the arts of peace. But if the present ruler, his son Selim,* had resembled his father and not his grandfather, that kingdom would have come to ruin, and it is evident that Selim is about to surpass the glory of his grandfather. Let me say with these examples, therefore, that after an excellent prince it is possible to maintain a weak prince, but after a weak prince, it is impossible to maintain any kingdom with another weak prince, unless it were like France, where the kingdom's ancient institutions would maintain the state: weak princes are those who are not engaged in preparing for war.

I conclude, then, with this argument: the ability of Romulus was so great that it made room for Numa Pompilius, who was able to rule Rome for many years with the arts of peace, but after Numa followed Tullus, whose reputation for ferocity reflected that of Romulus, and after him came Ancus,* who was endowed by nature in such a way that he was able both to employ the arts of peace and to cope with war. He first tried to hold to the way of peace, but he quickly realized that his neighbours, having judged him effeminate, held him in little esteem, and so much so he decided that in order to try to save Rome, he would have to turn to war and to be like Romulus rather than Numa.

All princes who have a state should take this as an example: that is, anyone who is like Numa will either keep or will not keep his state according to the cycle of time and fortune under which he lives, but anyone who is like Romulus and who is armed both with prudence and with weapons will keep his state in any event, unless it is taken from him by some persistent and extraordinary force. Certainly it can be assumed that if it had been Rome's lot to have had, as its third king, a man who did not know how to restore the city's reputation with the force of arms, it would never—or only with the greatest difficulty—have been able to gain a firm foothold later on, or to have had the impact that it had. Thus, while Rome lived under the kings it ran the risk of being ruined under the rule of either a weak or an evil king.

CHAPTER 20

Two Continuous Successions of Able Princes Produce Great Results; and Since Well-Organized Republics Necessarily Have a Succession of Able Rulers, Their Acquisitions and Growth Are Also Great

After Rome had driven out its kings, the dangers threatening the city, which we have described above as resulting in the succession of a king who was either weak or evil, disappeared, because the supreme authority resided in the consuls, who came to hold that authority not through heredity or trickery or violent ambition, but rather through the free votes of the people, and they were always the most excellent men. Since Rome enjoyed the exceptional ability and good fortune of men such as these, the city was eventually able to reach its pinnacle of greatness in the same number of years it spent under the rule of the kings.* Thus, it is evident that two continuous successions of able princes, such as Philip of Macedonia and Alexander the Great, are sufficient to conquer the world.* A republic ought to be able to accomplish even more, since it possesses through its method of election not only two successions but an infinite number of the most able princes who may succeed each other: this kind of skilful succession should always exist in every well-organized republic.

CHAPTER 21

How Much Blame a Prince or a Republic Which Lacks Its Own Armed Forces Deserves

Contemporary princes and modern republics who lack their own troops for either defence or offence should be ashamed of themselves, and they should consider, on the basis of Tullus' example,* that such a defect is due not to a lack of men capable of military service, but rather to a defect of their own, since they have not known how to make soldiers out of their own men. When Tullus succeeded to the throne after Rome had been at peace for forty years, he did not find a single man who had ever been to war; nevertheless, while planning to wage war he did not think of using either the Samnites or the Etruscans or any other people accustomed to serving in armed forces, but he resolved, as the extremely prudent man he was, to use his own subjects. His skill was so exceptional that under his rule he was quickly able to create extremely fine soldiers. And it is more true than any other truth that wherever men are not soldiers, this arises from the fault of the prince and not from any defect either of the site or of nature.

Of this a very recent example can be found. Everyone knows how in recent times the king of England attacked the kingdom of France and took no other troops than his own subjects, and since that kingdom had spent more than thirty years without waging war, it possessed no soldiers nor any commander who had ever served in the military; nevertheless, he was not afraid to attack with such soldiers a kingdom full of commanders and good troops who had continuously been at arms during the Italian wars.* All this derives from the fact that the king was a prudent man with a well-organized kingdom, who in peacetime did not neglect the institutions of war.

The Thebans Pelopidas and Epaminondas, after having freed Thebes and having led her away from the servitude of Spartan rule, found themselves in a city accustomed to domination and amidst a people that had become soft, but so great was this people's ability, that Pelopidas and Epaminondas did not fear arming the Thebans and, with them, taking the field against the Spartan armies and conquering them; the historian who writes about this feat* declares that in a short time these two men demonstrated that warriors were born not only in Lacedemonia but wherever men existed, if only one could find a man who knew how to train them for military service, as Tullus obviously knew how to train the Romans. And Virgil could not express this opinion better, nor could he show in any other words that he shared it, than where he says: 'And Tullus restored his shiftless men to arms.'*

CHAPTER 22

What Is Notable in the Case of the Three Roman Horatii and the Three Alban Curiatii

Tullus, king of Rome, and Mettius, king of Alba, agreed that the people whose above-mentioned three warriors were victorious would rule the other. All three of the Curiatii were killed and one of the Roman Horatii remained alive, and for this reason Mettius, the Alban king, along with his people became subjected to the Romans.* When the victorious Horatius returned to Rome, he met one of his sisters, who, married to one of the three Curiatii, was weeping over the death of her husband, and he killed her. For this offence Horatius was brought to judgement, and after much debate he was released, more through his father's prayers than his own merits. There are three things to be noted here: first, that one should never risk one's entire fortune with only part of one's forces; second, that in a well-organized city a man's merits never compensate for his faults; and third, that agreements are never wise if their observance should or might be doubtful. In truth, the fact of being subservient is so important to a city that one must never believe that any king or people would ever remain satisfied when three of their citizens have left them in servitude, as is evident in what Mettius tried to do. Although immediately after the victory of the Romans Mettius declared himself vanquished and promised his obedience to Tullus, nevertheless, during the very first expedition that he had to organize against the Veientes, it is evident that he tried to deceive Tullus, like a man who had realized only too late the recklessness of the decision he took.* And since we have spoken sufficiently about this third important point, we shall discuss the other two in the following two chapters.

CHAPTER 23

That One Should Not Jeopardize All of One's Fortune or All of One's Forces; and, for This Reason, Defending Passes Is Often Dangerous

It has never been judged a wise course of action to endanger your entire fortune without committing all of your forces. This can be done in several ways. One way is to do as Tullus and Mettius did, when they entrusted the entire fortune of their native cities and the skill of so many men, as many as both had in their respective armies, to the skill and fortune of three of their fellow citizens, who constituted only a very small part of each ruler's forces. Nor did they realize that in adopting such a course of action, all the labour their predecessors endured in organizing the republic in order to make it live long in freedom and to make its citizens the defenders of their own liberty had been rendered almost vain, since it was in the power of so few to lose it. Nothing could have been more ill-considered than what those kings did.

The same kind of trouble almost always befalls those who, just as the enemy arrives, plan to hold difficult positions and to guard passes, because this decision will almost always be harmful unless you are comfortably able to keep all of your forces in this difficult position. In this case such a decision should be taken, but if the position is so rugged that you cannot keep all your forces there, the decision is dangerous. I am led to think this way by the example of those who, having been attacked by a powerful enemy in their own country, which is surrounded by mountains and alpine terrain, have never attempted to engage the enemy on the passes and on the mountain slopes but have instead gone forth to meet the enemy elsewhere, or when they have not wished to do this, have awaited the enemy's attack within these mountains but in favourable locations rather than in mountainous ones. The explanation for this is the one mentioned above: that is, it is impossible to utilize many men in guarding mountainous positions, both for the reason that it is impossible to live there for a lengthy period of time and for the reason that, in narrow positions capable of containing only a few troops, you cannot hold out against an enemy who comes to attack you in great numbers, and it is easy for the enemy to attack in great numbers, because his intention is to pass and not to stop, while the defender awaiting the attack cannot wait with a large force, since he must camp there for a longer period of time in places which are, as I have said, constricted and barren, not knowing when the enemy might want to pass through. Thus, once you have lost the pass you have decided to hold and in which your people and your army had placed their trust, in most instances your people and your remaining troops are seized with such terror that without being able to test their skill, you remain the loser; and thus, you come to the point of having lost your entire fortune with only part of your forces.

Everyone knows the difficulty with which Hannibal crossed the Alps dividing Lombardy from France and with what difficulty he crossed those dividing Lombardy from Tuscany; the Romans nevertheless waited for him first on the Ticino River and then in the plains of Arezzo, preferring that their army be destroyed by the enemy in positions where it might also have a chance of victory rather than to lead it over the Alps to be destroyed as the result of an unfavourable site.

Anyone who reads all the history books in a sensible way will discover very few able commanders who have attempted to hold similar passes, for the reasons previously stated, and for the reason that it is impossible to close them all, since mountains are like open country, having not only familiar and often-frequented roads but many others which, if unknown to foreigners, are well known to the people of the area, with whose assistance you will always be guided to any location against the will of the one who opposes you. Of this a very recent example can be cited: in 1515, when Francis, king of France, planned to pass into Italy to recover control of Lombardy, the major objection raised by those who were opposed to his enterprise was that the Swiss would hold him back in the mountains. As experience later demonstrated, their objection was raised in vain, because by avoiding the two or three positions defended by the Swiss that king came by another unknown route,* and was in Italy and approaching the enemy before they realized it. Thus, their terrified troops retreated to Milan, and all the peoples of Lombardy went over to the French side, having given up the opinion that the French would be held back in the mountains.

CHAPTER 24

Well-Organized Republics Establish Rewards and Punishments for Their Citizens but Never Compensate One With the Other

The merits of Horatius were very great, since with his skill he had overcome the Curiatii; his offence was atrocious, since he murdered his sister. The Romans, nevertheless, were so angered by this homicide that they put him on trial for his life despite the fact that his merits were so great and new. Such a thing, to anyone considering the event superficially, would appear to be an example of popular ingratitude: anyone who examines the matter more closely and with greater reflection into which institutions republics ought to have will, nevertheless, blame the people for having absolved Horatius rather than for having wished to condemn him. The reason for this is that no well-organized republic ever cancels the demerits of its citizens with their merits, but after having instituted rewards for a good deed and punishments for an evil one, and after rewarding a man for having acted well, if that same individual later acts badly it punishes him without any regard whatsoever for his good deeds. When such regulations are well observed a city lives in freedom for a long period of time; otherwise it will always come to ruin very quickly, because if a citizen who has rendered some distinguished service to his city adds to the reputation his deed has brought him additional audacity and the confidence that he will be able to undertake without fear of punishment some action that is not good, he will become in a brief time so insolent that every element of civic life will disappear.

It is certainly necessary, if one wishes penalties for evil deeds to be upheld, to provide rewards for good ones, as we see was done in Rome. Although a republic may be poor and may give very little, it should not hold back from giving that small amount, because every little gift bestowed upon anyone as a reward for doing something good, no matter how great, will always be esteemed by the receiver as honourable and extremely grand. The stories of Horatius Cocles and Mucius Scaevola are well known: how the one held off the enemy over a bridge while it was being cut down, and how the other burned his hand for having erred in the attempt to kill Porsenna, the king of the Etruscans. For these two remarkable actions the public gave two pieces of land to each of these men. The story of Manlius Capitolinus is also well known. After he had saved the Capitol from the Gauls who had encamped there, he was given a small measure of flour by the citizens who had been besieged with him. This reward, according to the fortunes of the Romans at that time, was large and of such a kind that later, when Manlius, moved either by envy or his evil nature to create sedition in Rome, tried to win the favour of the people, he was thrown headlong without any respect whatsoever for his merits from the very Capitol he had earlier saved with such great honour.

CHAPTER 25

Whoever Wishes to Reform a Long-Established State in a Free City Should Retain At Least the Appearance of Its Ancient Ways

Anyone who desires or tries to reform the government of a city in a way that is acceptable and capable of maintaining it to everyone's satisfaction will find it necessary to retain at least the semblance of its ancient customs, so that it will not seem to the people that its institutions have changed, though in fact the new institutions may be completely dissimilar from those of the past, because men in general live as much by appearances as by realities: indeed, they are often moved more by things as they appear than by things as they really are. For this reason the Romans, recognizing this necessity at the beginning of their free way of life, created two consuls instead of a single king but wanted them to have no more than twelve lictors to avoid surpassing the number of those who attended the king. Besides this, an annual sacrifice was made in Rome that could be offered only by the king in person, and since the Romans did not wish the people to go wanting for any of their ancient customs in the absence of a king, they created a leader for this sacrifice whom they called the king of the sacrifice, and they placed him under the authority of the high priest, so that in this way the people came to be satisfied with that sacrifice and never had reason, for lack of it, to desire the return of the kings. This should be observed by all those who wish to abolish an ancient way of life in a city and guide it to a new and free way of life: since what is new may change men's minds, you must arrange it so that these alterations retain as much of the ancient ways as possible, and if the number, authority, and terms of office of the magistracies differ from those of the ancient ones, they should at least retain their titles. And as I have said, anyone who wishes to institute a body politic, whether a republic or a kingdom, should observe this, but anyone who wishes to create an absolute authority, a form the authors called tyranny, must create everything anew, as will be explained in the following chapter.

CHAPTER 26

A New Prince, in a City or Province He Has Seized, Must Create Everything Anew

Anyone who becomes a prince either of a city or a state, especially when his foundations are weak and he does not wish to give either a republican or a monarchical form to civil life, will find that the best remedy he possesses for holding on to that principality is, if he is a new prince, to create everything in that state anew; that is, in the cities he must create new governments with new names, new authorities, and new men; he must make the rich poor and the poor rich, as David did when he became king, who 'filled the hungry with good things, and sent the rich away empty';* he must build new cities, destroy those already built, move the inhabitants from one place to another, and, in short, leave nothing in that province intact, no rank, order, position, or wealth that is not acknowledged by the one who possesses it as coming from you; and he must take as his model

Philip of Macedonia, the father of Alexander the Great, who with these means rose from petty king to ruler of Greece. Those who write of him declare that he moved men from province to province, just as shepherds move their flocks about. These are extremely cruel methods and inimical to every way of life, not only Christian but human, and every man should avoid them and prefer to live as a private citizen rather than as a king with so much damage to other men; anyone who does not wish to take this first good course of action must nevertheless take this evil one if he wishes to maintain himself. But men take certain middle courses of action which are extremely damaging, because they do not know how to be entirely good or entirely bad, as the following chapter will demonstrate through an example.

CHAPTER 27
Men Very Rarely Know How to Be Entirely Good or Entirely Bad

When he went to Bologna in 1505 to expel from that state the Bentivogli family which had held the principality of that city for a hundred years, Pope Julius II* also wanted to remove Giovampagolo Baglioni* from Perugia, where he was ruler, just as the pope had conspired against all those rulers who held lands belonging to the church. And having arrived in the vicinity of Perugia with this purpose and intention, which were known to everyone, Julius did not wait for his own army, which was protecting him, but entered the city unarmed, notwithstanding the fact that Giovampagolo was inside with many of the people he had gathered around him for his defence. Thus, carried away by that wild enthusiasm with which he governed all his affairs, Julius placed himself with no one other than his bodyguard in the hands of his enemy whom he then led away with him, leaving a governor in that city to render justice in the name of the church. The prudent men* who were with the pope noted the audacity of Julius and the cowardice of Giovampagolo, and they could not understand why Giovampagolo had not in a single stroke crushed his enemy, thereby gaining everlasting fame, and enriched himself with his wealthy prey, since all the cardinals and their luxurious belongings were with the pope. Nor were they able to believe that he had refrained from doing so either out of goodness or scruples that held him back, because in the heart of such a vicious man who kept his sister as his mistress and had his cousins and nephews put to death in order to rule, no pious concern could be aroused, but they concluded that men clearly do not know how to be honourably bad or perfectly good, and that when an evil deed contains in itself some grandeur or some generosity, they do not know how to carry it out.

Thus, Giovampagolo, who felt no concern about being guilty of incest or public parricide, did not know how, or to put it better, did not dare—having the perfect opportunity for doing so—to perform a feat for which everyone would have admired his courage and which would have secured him eternal renown as being the first man to have shown these priests how little there is to value in those who live and rule as they do, and he would have performed a deed the greatness of which would have surpassed all the infamy and all the danger that could possibly have come from it.

CHAPTER 28

Why the Romans Were Less Ungrateful to Their Citizens Than the Athenians

Anyone who reads about the deeds of republics will find in all of them a bit of ingratitude against their own citizens, but he will find less in Rome than in Athens and perhaps than in any other republic. In seeking the reason for this, while speaking of Rome and Athens, I believe this came about because the Romans had less reason to suspect their citizens than did the Athenians. In Rome, considering the time from the expulsion of the kings down to the age of Sulla and Marius, the city was never deprived of its liberty by any of its citizens, so that there was no great reason to suspect them or, consequently, to offend them in a thoughtless way. The very opposite happened in Athens, for, after Pisistratus had taken away its liberty at the moment of its greatest prosperity under the guise of doing good, Athens later became free as before, and the city, remembering the injuries received and its past servitude, became a most ready avenger not only of the errors but even of the appearance of errors on the part of its citizens. Thus came about the exile and the death of so many excellent men; thus arose the practice of ostracism and every other kind of violence used against the city's aristocrats at various times. What writers on civic life say is very true—that once it has recovered its liberty, a people bites more ferociously than when it has only managed to preserve it. Anyone considering, therefore, all that has been said will not criticize Athens or praise Rome in this matter, but he will blame necessity alone for the variety of events which arose in these two cities. Anyone who considers these matters closely will observe that if Rome had lost its liberty as Athens had, it would not have been more indulgent toward its citizens than Athens was. It is possible to speculate with some accuracy about what happened to Collatinus and Publius Valerius after the expulsion of the kings: the former* was sent into exile for no other reason than that he bore the name of the Tarquins, although he had helped to free Rome, while the latter was made an exile after having no more than aroused suspicion by building a home on the Caelian Hill.* Thus, having seen how suspicious and severe Rome was in these two instances, one can conclude that this city would have shown the same ingratitude as Athens if it, like Athens, in its beginnings and before its growth, had been injured by its own citizens. And so as not to be obliged to return to this topic of ingratitude, I shall say what needs to be said about it in the following chapter.

CHAPTER 29
Who Is More Ungrateful, a People or a Prince?

In reference to the subject treated above, it seems appropriate to me to discuss whether more striking examples of this ingratitude are displayed by a people or a prince, and in order better to debate this matter, let me say that this vice of ingratitude is born either from avarice or from suspicion. When a people or a prince has sent forth one of its military leaders on an important expedition, and this commander through being victorious acquires great glory, that prince or that people is bound to reward him upon his return, and if instead of rewarding him and, motivated by avarice, it dishonours or injures him, restrained by its own greed from giving him his due, it commits an error which allows no excuse and, on the contrary, brings with it eternal infamy. Yet many princes can be found who commit this error, and Cornelius Tacitus states the reason in this sentence: 'Men are more inclined to repay injury than kindness: the truth is that gratitude is irksome, while vengeance is accounted gain.'* But when they fail to reward or, to tell the truth, to offend, motivated not by avarice but by suspicion, then either the people or the prince deserve some excuse. We read about many such acts of ingratitude displayed for just such a reason, because the commander who has skilfully acquired an empire for his lord by overcoming his enemies and, showering himself with glory and his troops with riches, necessarily acquires among his own soldiers and his enemies and among the subjects of his prince such renown that his victory cannot prove other than distasteful to the very lord who sent him forth. Furthermore, because human nature is ambitious, suspicious, and incapable of setting limits to a man's fortunes, it is impossible for the suspicion immediately aroused in the prince after his commander's victory not to be increased by some arrogant action or display of words on the commander's part. Thus, the prince is unable to think of anything other than securing himself against his commander, and to accomplish this he considers either having him executed or taking away the reputation he has acquired with his army and among his peoples, and with every means possible he demonstrates that victory has come about not because of the commander's ability but, instead, because of good fortune or the cowardice of the enemy or the prudence of the other leaders who were with him in that action.

When Vespasian was in Judaea, he was proclaimed emperor by his army, and Antonius Primus, who found himself with another army in Illyria, took his side and entered Italy with him against Vitellius, who was reigning in Rome, and with a great show of skill, he defeated two of Vitellius' armies and occupied

Rome, so that Mucianus, who had been sent by Vespasian, discovered that because of Antonius' exceptional skill everything had been taken and every difficulty overcome. The reward Antonius received for this service was that Mucianus immediately took away his command of the army and, little by little, reduced him to a state of no authority in Rome, so that when Antonius went to see Vespasian, who was still in Asia, he was received by him in such a way that in a short time he was reduced to no rank whatsoever and, almost in despair, he died. Our histories are full of such examples. In our own times, everyone presently alive knows with what industry and skill Gonsalvo Ferrante, fighting in the Kingdom of Naples against the French for King Ferdinand of Aragon, conquered and vanquished that kingdom, and that the reward he received for his victory was that Ferdinand left Aragon and, having come to Naples, he first took away Gonsalvo's command of the army; later he took away his fortresses; and then he took him to Spain, where a short time after he died in obscurity. This suspicion is so natural to princes that it cannot be avoided, and it is impossible for them to show gratitude to those whose victories have brought about great conquests under their banners.

It is no wonder that a prince cannot defend himself against this ingratitude, nor is it even noteworthy that a people cannot defend itself from it as well, because a city which lives in freedom has two goals, the first to acquire territory, the other to keep itself free, and it is likely to err in the pursuit of both of these goals through excessive love. As for the errors committed in acquiring territory, they will be discussed in the proper place. As for the errors committed in keeping itself free, there are, among others, the following: to injure citizens who should be rewarded; to be suspicious of those who should be trusted. Although these methods in a republic given over to corruption are the cause of great evils and quite often actually lead it to tyranny, as occurred in Rome with Caesar, who seized by force what ingratitude had denied him, they are nevertheless the cause of great benefits in an uncorrupted republic, and they cause it to live longer in liberty, since the fear of punishment makes men better and less ambitious. It is true that among all the peoples who ever possessed an empire, Rome was the least ungrateful for the reasons outlined above, because it can be said that there is no other example of her ingratitude than the case of Scipio, since Coriolanus and Camillus were exiled because of the harm each had inflicted upon the plebeians. The former was never pardoned, for he always harboured hostility in his heart against the people; the latter not only was recalled but he was adored as if he were a prince throughout the rest of his life. But the ingratitude shown to Scipio arose from a suspicion that the citizens began to have about him and which they did not feel about the others: a suspicion which arose from the grandeur of the enemy Scipio had vanquished; the fame which the victory in such a long and dangerous war had given him; the swiftness of this victory; and the favours which his youth, prudence, and other memorable virtues were acquiring for him. These things were so numerous that even the magistrates of Rome feared his authority, something which was displeasing to wise men since it was so unusual in Rome. His way of life seemed so unusual that Cato the Elder, reputed to be a saintly man, was the first to criticize him and to declare that a city could not call itself free when there was a citizen who was feared by the magistrates. Thus, if the people of Rome followed the opinion of Cato in this case, they deserve the excuse, as I stated above, that those peoples and princes deserve who are ungrateful out of suspicion. In bringing this discourse to a conclusion, then, let me say that the vice of ingratitude is displayed as a result of either avarice or suspicion, and it will be seen that the people never display it out of avarice, and that they resort to it out of suspicion much less often than princes do, since they have less cause to be suspicious, as will be explained below.

CHAPTER 30

What Means a Prince or a Republic May Employ to Avoid the Vice of Ingratitude; and What Means a Commander or a Citizen May Employ in Order to Avoid Being Overcome by It

To avoid the necessity of having to live with suspicion or to be ungrateful, a prince should personally accompany his military expeditions, as the Roman emperors did in the beginning, as the Turk does in our own times, and as all able leaders have done and still do. When such leaders are victorious, the glory and the territory acquired belong entirely to them; when they are not present, since the glory belongs to others, they feel they cannot make use of the acquired territory without destroying in these others the glory they did not know how to win for themselves, and they become ungrateful and unjust; their loss is, without any doubt, greater than their gain. But when, either on account of negligence or on account of lack of prudence, they remain idly at home and send forth a military commander, I have no other precept to offer them except one they will learn for themselves. But let me say to this commander that since I believe him incapable of avoiding the sting of ingratitude, he should do one of two things: either let him abandon the army and place himself again in the hands of his prince immediately after his victory, taking care to avoid every insolent or ambitious act, so that when his prince has been deprived of every suspicion, he will have reason either to reward him or to refrain from injuring him; or, when this does not seem the proper thing to do, let him boldly take the opposite course of action and consider all the reasons for which he should believe the acquired territory to be his own and not that of his prince, making his troops and subjects well-disposed towards him, making new alliances with his neighbours, occupying all the fortresses with his soldiers, bribing the commanders of his army, and securing himself against those whom he cannot corrupt, and through these means he should seek to punish his lord for the ingratitude that he is likely to show him. No other way exists, but as was explained above, men do not know how to be either entirely wicked or entirely good. It always happens that, immediately after a victory, commanders do not want to abandon their army; they are incapable of comporting themselves with modesty; they do not know how to employ violent measures which are honourable in themselves; and, as a result, remaining undecided, between their own indecision and their ambiguity they are eliminated.

As for a republic, if it wishes to avoid the vice of ingratitude, it cannot employ the same remedy as a prince: that is, that it command in person and avoid sending forth military expeditions, since it is compelled to send one of its citizens. It is, however, proper for me to offer as a remedy the idea that a republic should adopt the same means used by the Roman republic to be less ungrateful than other republics. These arose from the practices of its government: since the entire city, both the aristocrats and the plebeians, took part in warfare, in every era there always arose in Rome so many able men decorated in various victories that the people, who were many in number and kept an eye on each other, never had reason to doubt any one of them. Furthermore, they maintained their integrity so well and were so careful to avoid showing even the slightest trace of ambition, or to give the people reason to harm them because of their ambition, that when any of them reached the rank of the dictatorship, they gained greater glory the sooner they gave that office up. Thus, since such behaviour could not generate suspicion, it did not generate ingratitude. For this reason, a republic that wishes to avoid having any reason for ingratitude must govern itself as Rome did, and a citizen who wishes to avoid the sting of ingratitude should observe the limits observed by Roman citizens.

CHAPTER 31

Why Roman Commanders Were Never Excessively Punished for Errors They Committed, Nor Were They Ever Punished When Their Ignorance or Poor Decisions Resulted in Harm to the Republic

The Romans, as we explained above, were not only less ungrateful than other republics but also more compassionate and respectful in the punishments of their army commanders than any other republic. Even if a commander's error was committed out of malice, they punished him humanely, and if it was committed out of ignorance, they not only avoided punishing him but they rewarded and honoured him. This method of proceeding was carefully thought out by them, because they judged it to be of such great importance for those who commanded their armies to possess a free and ready mind, unhindered by irrelevant matters in making decisions, that they did not wish to add to something already difficult and dangerous in itself new difficulties and dangers, believing that if they did so, no commander would ever be able to take skilful action. For instance, suppose they sent an army into Greece against Philip of Macedonia or into Italy against Hannibal or against those peoples whom they had conquered earlier: the commander placed in charge of such an expedition was distressed by all the concerns that such enterprises involve, concerns that are serious and extremely important. Now if to those concerns were added additional examples of Roman commanders who had been crucified or otherwise put to death when they had lost a day's battles, it would be impossible for that commander, beset by so many suspicions, to make courageous decisions. Judging, therefore, that the disgrace of having lost was more than enough punishment, the Romans did not want to demoralize their commanders with other penalties.

Here is one example of an error that was not committed out of ignorance. Sergius and Virginius were encamped at Veii, each in charge of one part of the army; Sergius was situated so that he might encounter the Etruscans and Virginius was on the other side. It happened that when Sergius was attacked by the Faliscans and other tribes, he allowed himself to be routed and driven away before sending to Virginius for assistance. On the other hand, since Virginius was waiting for Sergius to humiliate himself, he preferred to see his native city dishonoured and that army ruined rather than march to its aid. This is certainly a very wicked case, one likely to be remembered, and to leave a bad impression of the Roman republic if one or the other of the commanders had not been punished. It is certainly true that where another republic would have imposed capital punishment on them, Rome punished them with monetary fines. This came about not because their sins did not deserve greater punishment but rather because in this case the Romans wanted, for the reasons already given, to maintain their ancient customs. As for errors committed out of ignorance, there is no finer example of this than Varro, whose rashness caused the destruction of the Romans by Hannibal at Cannae which endangered that republic's liberty, but because it was a matter of ignorance and not malice, they not only avoided punishing Varro but they honoured him, and the entire order of the senate went out to greet him upon his return to Rome, and since they could not congratulate him on the outcome of the battle, they thanked him for having returned to Rome and for not having despaired of the republic's affairs. When Papirius Cursor wanted to put Fabius to death for having engaged in battle with the Samnites against his orders, among other arguments Fabius' father set forth against the dictator's obstinacy was that, after their losses, the Roman people had never treated their commanders as Papirius wanted to do after a victory.

CHAPTER 32

A Republic or a Prince Should Not Delay in Rewarding Men Even in Situations of Necessity

The Romans happily succeeded in being generous to the populace once danger arose, and when Porsenna came to attack Rome to restore the Tarquins, (even though the senate, suspecting that the plebeians preferred to accept the kings rather than to sustain a war, relieved them of the duty on salt and all other taxes to secure their favour, stating that the poor did enough to benefit the public by feeding their children), the plebeians exposed themselves to enduring siege, famine, and war in order to gain these benefits. But let no one, relying upon this example, defer winning popular support during periods of danger; what worked for the Romans will never work for you, because people in general will decide that they gained this favour not from you but from your adversaries, and since they must fear that after the danger has passed you will take back from them what you have been forced to give them, they will feel no obligation to you whatsoever. This policy succeeded for the Romans because their government was new and not yet stabilized; the people had seen how earlier laws were passed for their benefit, such as the right of appeal to the plebeians, and they could therefore persuade themselves that this benefit had been bestowed upon them not so much because of the enemy's arrival but rather because of the senate's inclination to help them. Besides this, their memory of the kings by whom they had been scorned and abused in many ways was still fresh. Because similar circumstances rarely occur, it will rarely occur that similar remedies are of much use. Any type of state, therefore, whether a republic or a principality, must consider in advance what kinds of adverse times are likely to befall it and what kinds of men it is likely to need in adverse times, and then it must live with them in the way it deems necessary no matter what occurs. Any state, whether republic or principality but especially a principality, that acts otherwise and really believes it can win men back with benefits the instant danger arises deceives itself, because not only will this fail to make the state secure, but it will accelerate its own ruin.

CHAPTER 33

When a Problem Has Arisen Either Within a State or Outside It, It Is Safer To Delay Dealing With It Than to Attack It

While the Roman republic was growing in reputation, strength, and dominion, its neighbours, who at first had not thought about how much damage this new republic might inflict upon them, began too late to recognize their error; and since they wished to remedy what they had not remedied earlier, some forty peoples formed an alliance against the Romans. Hence, the Romans, among the other customary remedies taken during times of urgent danger, decided to create a dictator, that is, to give power to a man who might make decisions without any consultation whatsoever and who, without any right of appeal, might execute his decisions. Thus, this remedy, which was useful at the time, and was the reason why the Romans overcame the above-mentioned dangers, always remained extremely useful in all those circumstances which arose at different times to hinder the republic's efforts to expand its empire.

Regarding this matter, there is this to be said: first, that when a problem arises either inside or outside a republic, brought about by internal or external causes, and has become so serious that it has begun to terrify everyone, the safest policy is to put off dealing with it rather than trying to eliminate it, because almost always those who eliminate it only increase its strength and hasten the harm that is expected from it. Circumstances of this kind arise in a republic more often for internal rather than for external reasons: it often happens that either a citizen is allowed to acquire more power than is reasonable, or that a law which is the nerve and life of a free government begins to become corrupted, and this error is allowed to go on until it becomes a more dangerous policy to attempt a remedy than to allow it to continue. Moreover, it is even more difficult to recognize these problems when they arise, since it always seems more natural for men to approve the beginnings of things: and such approval is more likely for undertakings that seem to possess some merit and which are the work of young men than for anything else. If a young nobleman who possesses some extraordinary ability emerges in a republic, the eyes of all the citizens begin to turn toward him and they race without any concern to honour him, so that if in that man there exists an iota of ambition, through a combination of the favours nature grants him and these circumstances, he quickly assumes such a rank that when the citizens come to realize their error they have few remedies to employ, and if they wish to employ those remedies they possess, they do nothing but accelerate his rise to power.

One could set forth many examples of this, but I only wish to give one from our own city. Cosimo de' Medici, to whom the Medici family owed the origin of its greatness in our city, acquired so much renown as a result of the favour that his prudence and the ignorance of other citizens had earned for him that he began to arouse the fear of the government, to the extent that other citizens considered attacking him to be dangerous and leaving him as he was even more dangerous. But living in those times there was a certain Niccolò da Uzzano, who was held to be a man of great expertise in civic affairs, and while he had committed the first error of not recognizing the dangers arising from Cosimo's reputation, as long as he lived, he never permitted himself to commit the second error—that is, of trying to do away with him, considering such an attempt to entail the complete ruin of the government; this was seen to be true after his death, for the citizens who were left did not follow his advice and they joined forces against Cosimo and chased him out of Florence. Thus, it came about that Cosimo's faction, feeling resentment for this injury, shortly afterwards recalled Cosimo and made him prince of the republic, a rank he never would have reached without this open opposition.*

The same thing happened in Rome to Caesar, whose exceptional ability won him the favour of Pompey and others, but shortly thereafter this favour turned into fear, to which Cicero testifies when he declares that Pompey began to fear Caesar too late.* This fear caused them to seek remedies, and the remedies they adopted hastened the downfall of their republic.

Let me say, therefore, that since it is difficult to recognize these evils when they arise—a difficulty caused by the way in which these matters deceive you at the beginning—it is a wiser policy to put off dealing with them when they are recognized rather than to combat them, because when you put off dealing with them, they either fade away by themselves or at least the evil is postponed for a longer time. In all such affairs, princes who plan on eliminating these difficulties or opposing them impetuously with force should keep their eyes open to avoid increasing them in a harmful way, thinking that they are pushing something away by dragging it behind them—as one might drown a plant by watering it. But the strength of the disease must be carefully considered, and if you are capable of curing it, put yourself to doing so without hesitation; otherwise, leave it alone and make no attempt to do anything, because what happened to Rome's neighbours, as was mentioned above, would happen to you. Since Rome had grown so powerful, it would have been far safer for them to placate the city and hold it back by peaceful means than to force it by warlike means to consider new institutions and new defences, because their conspiracy accomplished nothing other than to make the Romans more united, more courageous, and intent upon finding new ways to expand their power in a shorter period of time. One of these methods was the creation of the office of a dictator, a new institution which not only overcame present dangers but also prevented countless evils which that republic would have incurred without such a remedy.

CHAPTER 34

Dictatorial Authority Did Good, Not Harm, to the Roman Republic; and How Authority Citizens Take for Themselves, Not That Which Is Granted Them Through Free Elections, Is Harmful to Civic Life

Some writers have condemned those Romans who found a way to create a dictator in their city as if it had, with the passage of time, brought a tyranny to Rome, alleging that the first tyrant to exist in that city ruled it under the title of dictator, and stating that if this title had not existed, Caesar would never have been able to disguise his tyranny under some public title. This matter was not carefully explored by those who hold this opinion, however, and it was accepted without good reason, because it was neither the title nor the rank of dictator that enslaved Rome but rather the authority taken from its citizens by the length of his dominion, and if in Rome the title of dictator had not existed, they would have chosen another, because power easily acquires titles but titles do not acquire power. Moreover, we can see that the dictatorship, as long as it was bestowed in accord with public laws and not by private authority, always benefited the city, because it is the creation of magistrates and the granting of power by extraordinary means which harm republics, not those which are created by ordinary means: this is clear from what happened in Rome over a long period of time during which no dictator ever did anything but good for the republic.

There are some very obvious explanations for this. First, if a citizen is able to commit an offence and to seize for himself extraordinary authority, it is necessary for him to have many qualities that in an uncorrupted republic he can never possess, for he must be extremely wealthy and have many supporters and followers, whom he cannot have wherever the laws are observed, and even if he were to have them, men of this kind are so formidable that free elections never favour them. Besides this, the dictator was named for a fixed period and not in perpetuity, and only to deal with the problem that caused him to be appointed; the dictator's authority included the power to decide by himself on the remedies against that urgent danger, to undertake everything without consultations, and to punish anyone without appeal, but he could do nothing to curtail the government, such as taking authority away from the senate or from the people, or abolishing the city's old institutions and creating new ones. Thus, in combination, the brief duration of the dictator's appointment, his limited authority, and the fact that the Roman people was uncorrupted made it impossible for the dictator to go beyond his limitations and to harm the city, and experience shows the dictatorship was always a useful institution.

Among all the other Roman institutions, this one truly deserves to be considered and numbered among those which were the source of the greatness of such an empire, because without a similar system cities survive extraordinary circumstances only with difficulty. The usual institutions in republics are slow to move, since no council nor any magistrate can undertake anything alone, for in many instances they need to consult one another; and, since time is wasted in coming to an agreement, the remedies for republics are very dangerous when they must find one for a problem that cannot wait. Republics must therefore have among their laws a procedure like the following: the Venetian Republic, which among modern republics is most excellent, has reserved to a small number of citizens the authority to deliberate on matters of urgent need without consulting anyone else, if they are in complete agreement. When a republic lacks such a procedure, it must necessarily come to ruin by obeying its laws or break them in order to avoid its own ruin. But in a republic, it is not good for anything to happen which requires governing by extraordinary measures. Although extraordinary measures may be beneficial at a certain moment, the example nevertheless causes harm, because if one establishes the habit of breaking the laws for good reasons, later on, under the same pretext, one can break them for bad reasons. Thus, no republic will ever be perfect unless its laws contain a provision for everything and establish a remedy for every circumstance and set up a means for dealing with it. In conclusion, then, I would say that those republics which have no recourse during the most pressing dangers either to a dictator or to some similar authority will always come to ruin during serious misfortunes.

It is to be noted, in connection with this new institution, how wisely the Romans provided for the method of electing the dictator. Since the creation of the dictator brought some shame to the consuls, who from being the rulers of the city were reduced to obedience like everyone else, and since they assumed this would create contempt toward them among the citizens, the Romans decided that the power to elect the dictator would remain with the consuls, believing that when the circumstance came about and Rome needed this royal authority, they would do it willingly, and since they did it themselves, it would be less painful. The wounds and all the other evils that men inflict upon themselves voluntarily are far less painful than those which are inflicted upon them by others. Yet, afterwards in the later periods, the Romans were accustomed to granting such dictatorial authority to the consul, instead of a dictator, with these words: 'that the consul shall see to it that the state takes no harm.'* But to return to our subject, let me conclude that Rome's neighbours, in seeking to conquer the city, caused it to create institutions that not only enabled it to defend itself but also to attack its neighbours with greater strength, better advice, and more authority.

CHAPTER 35

The Reason Why the Creation of the Decemvirate in Rome Was Harmful to the Liberty of That Republic, Notwithstanding the Fact that It Was Created by Free and Public Elections

The election of ten citizens invented by the Roman people to make laws in Rome may seem to contradict what was said above (that authority seized by violent means, not authority given by means of free elections, is harmful to republics): these men in time became tyrants and without any respect whatsoever deprived Rome of its liberty.* At this point, we must consider the means of conferring authority and the period of time for which it is conferred, for when unlimited authority is conferred for a lengthy period of time—calling one year or more a long time—it will always be dangerous, and its effects will be good or evil according to how evil or good those are to whom it is given. If we consider the authority held by the decemvirs and that by the dictators, we will see that the power of the decemvirs was without any comparison greater. Once the dictator was created, the tribunes, the consuls, and the senate with their respective powers remained, nor could the dictator take them away, and even if he could have deprived a man of the consulate or another of his senatorial rank, he could not dissolve the senatorial order or create new laws. In this manner, the senate, the consuls, and the tribunes, remaining with their authority, came to be like his guardian to keep him from straying from the straight path. But the exact opposite occurred in the creation of the decemvirs, because the consuls and tribunes were annulled, and the decemvirs given authority to create laws and to act in every way as if they were the Roman people. Thus, finding themselves alone, without consuls, without tribunes, without appeals to the people, and as a consequence, having no one to watch over them, during their second year they were able, moved by the ambition of Appius, to become insolent. For this reason, it should be noted that when it is said that an authority conferred by free elections never injures a republic, it is presumed that a people can never be led to confer it except under proper circumstances and for proper periods of time, but when, blinded either by deception or some other cause, a republic is led to confer such authority imprudently and in the manner in which the Roman people conferred it upon the decemvirs, then the same thing that happened to the Roman people will always happen to it. This can be easily proved if we consider the reasons that kept the dictators good and those which made the decemvirs bad, and if we consider, in addition, the actions of those republics that have maintained good institutions while conferring authority for long periods of time, as the Spartans did upon their kings or the Venetians upon their doges, for in both instances it will be seen that safeguards were put in place to make them unable to abuse their authority. Nor is it of any advantage in such a case to have material that is not corrupt;* for an absolute authority corrupts the material in the shortest time and creates friends and partisans.* Nor is it any disadvantage to be poor or to lack family ties, for wealth and every other favour quickly pursue authority, as we shall discuss in a detailed manner with respect to the creation of these previously mentioned decemvirs.*

CHAPTER 36

Citizens Who Have Held the Highest Offices Should Not Disdain the Lesser Ones

The Romans had made Marcus Fabius and G. Manlius consuls and had won a most glorious victory over the Veientes and the Etruscans, during which Quintus Fabius, brother of the consul, who had served as consul the year before, died. At this point, it should be observed how capable that city's institutions were of making it great and how mistaken other republics are that depart from its practices. Even though the Romans were great lovers of glory, they nevertheless did not deem it dishonourable to obey someone today who on other occasions they had commanded, or to find themselves serving in an army in which they had formerly been commanders. This custom is contrary to the opinion, institutions, and practices of citizens of our times: in Venice they still make the mistake of allowing a citizen who once obtained a high rank and is ashamed of accepting a lower one, to step aside. Although such a course may be honourable for a private citizen, it has no benefits whatsoever for the public, because a republic should have more hope and place more confidence in a citizen who from a high rank descends to hold a lower one than in a citizen who rises from a lower rank to hold a greater one, for it is not reasonable to believe in the latter, unless he is surrounded by men of such authority or exceptional ability that his inexperience may be moderated by their counsel and authority. If the same custom had existed in Rome as in Venice and other modern republics and kingdoms, that whoever had been consul on one occasion would never agree to enter the army unless he were consul, countless events inimical to a free way of life would have arisen, both because of the errors

that inexperienced men would have committed and because of
the ambition that they would have been better able to display,
lacking men around them in whose presence they would fear to
go astray, and thus they would have come to be more unrestrained, which would have been entirely to the detriment of the
public.

CHAPTER 37

What Discord Arose in Rome From the Agrarian Laws; and How Absolutely Outrageous It Is for a Republic to Pass a Retroactive Law Which Is Contrary to an Ancient Custom of the City

It is a saying of ancient writers* that men usually inflict evil
upon themselves and become bored with the good, and that
both of these attitudes give rise to the same effects, because
whenever the necessity for fighting is taken away from them,
they fight for the sake of ambition, which is so powerful a passion in the human breast that, no matter the rank to which a man
may rise, he never abandons it. The reason is that nature has created men in such a way that they can desire everything but are
unable to obtain everything, so that their desire is always greater
than their power of acquisition, and discontent with what they
possess and lack of satisfaction are the result. This situation
gives rise to variations in fortune, for since some men desire to
possess more and others fear to lose what they have acquired,
enmities and wars are the result, from which comes the ruin of
one province and the exaltation of another.* I have written this
discourse because it was not enough for the Roman plebeians,
who were driven to this desire by necessity, to secure themselves against the nobles by creating the tribunes; immediately
after having obtained the creation of the tribunes, they began to
quarrel with the nobles out of ambition and the desire to share
with them honours and possessions, as the things most prized
by men. From this conflict arose the disease that gave birth to
the struggle over the agrarian law, which was finally the cause of

the destruction of the republic. Since well-organized republics have to keep the public treasury rich but their citizens poor, some defect must have existed in this law in the city of Rome: it was either not created at the beginning in such a way that it did not require daily amendments, or its creation was so long deferred that it became outrageous applied retroactively; or it was well instituted at the beginning but was then corrupted in its application, so that, whichever way it may have been, this law was never discussed in Rome without the city being thrown into turmoil.

This law had two principal provisions.* The one provided that no citizen could possess more than so many *jugers* of land; the other provided that lands taken from the enemy were to be divided among the Roman people. It harmed the nobility, however, in two respects: those who possessed more land than the law allowed (and the greatest number of these were nobles) had to be deprived of this surplus, and dividing lands taken from the enemy among the plebeians deprived the nobles of the means of enriching themselves. Thus, as these laws came to offend powerful men who considered opposing them to be defending the public interest, whenever this issue was brought up the entire city, as was mentioned, was thrown into turmoil, and the nobles with patience and skill delayed action on it, either by calling out an army or by putting the tribune who proposed the law in opposition to another tribune, or sometimes by yielding in part, or even by sending a colony to the place where the lands were to be distributed, as occurred with the region around Antium, where, once this controversy about the law arose, they sent a colony drawn from Rome to which this region was assigned. In this regard, Livy makes a noteworthy remark, declaring that it was difficult to find anyone in Rome willing to give his name to go to that colony, so much more ready were the plebeians to insist on property in Rome than to go and take possession of it in Antium.* Dissatisfaction with this law thus went on causing trouble for a long time until the Romans began to send their armies to the far corners of Italy or outside of Italy, after which it seemed to die down. This happened because the lands possessed by Rome's enemies, which were far from the eyes of the plebeians and in places where cultivation was not easy, came to be less desirable than other lands; in like manner the Romans were also less harsh in punishing their enemies, and even when they plundered some of their lands, they sent colonies there. Hence, for these reasons this law remained dormant up to the time of the Gracchi, and once revived, it completely destroyed Roman liberty, because the power of the opponents was twice as great, and in this way the law ignited such hatred between the plebeians and the senate that it led to armed conflict and bloodshed beyond every civil usage and practice. Since the public magistrates were unable to find a remedy for this and none of the factions had any more faith in them, they therefore had recourse to private remedies, and each of the factions began to look for a leader who would defend it. Anticipating this disgrace and disorder, the plebeians turned their favour to Marius, and they did so in such a manner that they made him consul four times, and his consulate lasted with few intervals for such a length of time that he was able to have himself named consul on three other occasions.* Having no remedy against this plague, the nobility turned to favour Sulla,* and once he had been made leader of their faction, the civil wars broke out, and after much bloodshed and many changes of fortune, the nobility retained the upper hand. Later these animosities again arose in the time of Caesar and Pompey, for after Caesar had become leader of Marius' party and Pompey head of Sulla's, they came to blows and Caesar came out the winner:* he was the first tyrant of Rome, after which the city was never again free.

Such was the beginning and the end of the agrarian law. Although we have elsewhere demonstrated how enmities between the senate and the plebeians kept Rome free, since they gave rise to laws in favour of liberty, and the result of this agrarian law may therefore seem to contradict this conclusion, I must say that I shall not persist in this opinion on the matter, because the ambition of the prominent is so great that if it is not resisted in various ways and by various means in a city, it will soon reduce that city to ruin. Thus, if the controversy over the agrarian law caused conflict for 300 years before enslaving Rome, the city would certainly have been much more quickly reduced to servitude if the plebeians had not constantly checked the ambition of the nobility with this law and other expressions of its desires. It is also clear from this that men value their property more than honours, for the Roman nobility always gave way to the plebeians without extraordinary strife in matters concerning honours, but when it came to property, their stubbornness in defending it was so great that in order to satisfy their own desires, the plebeians had recourse to those extraordinary methods that have been discussed above. The Gracchi, whose intentions were more praiseworthy than their prudence, were the chief instigators of these disorders, because to seek an end to a disorder that has arisen in a republic and to do so by passing a law to be applied retroactively is a badly conceived policy, and as we explained at length above, this does nothing other than accelerate the evil to which that disorder has brought you, but by putting it off, the evil will either occur later, or, with the passage of time, extinguish itself on its own before reaching its end.

CHAPTER 38

Weak Republics Are Indecisive and Do Not Know How to Reach Decisions; If They Ever Do Take Sides, This Arises More by Necessity Than by Choice

With a very serious plague in Rome, it seemed to the Volscians and the Aequi that the time had come to attack Rome, and after these two peoples had raised an enormous army, they attacked the Latins and the Hernici, and after laying waste to their lands, they forced the Latins and the Hernici to make Rome aware of this and to beg the Romans to defend them: the Romans, afflicted by the plague, responded that they should decide to defend themselves with their own forces, since the Romans could not defend them. This shows the generosity and the prudence of the Roman senate, and how it always insisted, no matter the circumstances, on being the ultimate authority in any decisions that its allies might have to take, but it was never ashamed to make a decision contrary to its usual procedures or to other decisions it had taken, when necessity required it.

I say this because, on other occasions, the same senate had prohibited these same peoples from taking up arms and defending themselves, and a less prudent senate than this one would have considered its reputation to have been diminished had it conceded them this possibility to defend themselves. But the senate always judged things as they ought to be judged, and it always selected the less harmful decision as the best one; as much as it displeased the senate to be unable to defend its subjects, and as much as it displeased them to allow their subjects to take up arms without their support, for reasons already mentioned and for many others that are obvious, nevertheless, recognizing that their allies would have had to arm themselves in any case, since they had the enemy at their gates, it chose the honourable course of action and insisted that they do what they were forced to do with their permission, so that in disobeying out of necessity, they should not become accustomed to disobeying by choice. Although this seems to be a decision that every republic ought to make, nevertheless, weak and poorly advised republics do not know how to make them, nor do they understand how to behave honourably in such situations of necessity. Duke Valentino* had taken Faenza* and had forced Bologna to come to terms with him.* Then, wishing to return to Rome through Tuscany, Borgia sent one of his men to Florence to request passage for himself and his army. In Florence they conferred over how to manage the situation, but no one ever advised granting him this request. In this matter, Florence did not follow the Roman practice: since the duke was heavily armed and the Florentines were insufficiently armed to prevent his passage, it was a much more honourable course of action for them to make it seem that he passed with their permission rather than by force, and whereas the entire matter resulted in their disgrace, had they managed the situation differently it would have been a minor matter. But the worst defect weak republics can have is to be indecisive, so that all their decisions are taken out of necessity, and if any good comes to them, it comes through force of circumstance rather than through their own prudence.

I wish to cite two other examples of this which occurred during our own times in the government of our city. In 1500, after

King Louis XII of France had retaken Milan, he wished to give
Pisa back to Florence in return for the 50,000 ducats the city had
promised for such a restitution, and he sent his armies towards
Pisa, commanded by Monsignor de Beaumont, who, although a
Frenchman, was, nevertheless, a man in whom the Florentines
had great confidence. The army and this commander marched
between Cascina and Pisa in order to attack the city's walls, and
while they remained there for several days to ready the siege,
Pisan ambassadors came to Beaumont and offered to surrender
the city to the French army under these conditions: that in the
king's name he would promise not to place the city in the hands
of the Florentines before four months had passed. This proposal was completely rejected by the Florentines, with the
result that they continued marching into the field and then left
in disgrace.* This proposal was refused for no other reason than
distrust of the king's word on the part of those who, as a result
of the weakness of their planning, had been forced to place
themselves in his hands and who, on the other hand, were
unable to trust him: they failed to see how much better it was for
the king to restore Pisa to them once he was inside the city, or, if
he did not restore it, to reveal his intentions, than for him to
promise it to them when he did not yet have it, and to force them
to pay for his promises. Thus, it would have been much more
profitable for them to have agreed that Beaumont could take the
city for any promise whatsoever: experience made this clear
later on in 1502 when, after the rebellion of Arezzo, Monsignor
Imbault, sent by the king of France with French troops, came to
the aid of the Florentines; once he had approached Arezzo he
began after a brief time to negotiate with the Aretines, who
under certain conditions wished to surrender the city as the
Pisans had wanted to do. This proposal was refused by the Florentines; once he saw this and realized that the Florentines had
little understanding of the matter, Monsignor Imbault began to
work out the details of the agreement by himself without the
participation of the Florentine commissioners: he concluded
the agreement in his own way, and under those terms he entered
Arezzo with his troops, making the Florentines understand that
he thought they were crazy and understood nothing of worldly
affairs, and that if they wanted Arezzo they should make it clear

to the king, since he could give it to them much more easily with his troops inside the city rather than outside it. There was no end in Florence to the backbiting and abuse heaped upon this Imbault, nor did they stop until they finally realized that if Beaumont had acted like Imbault, they would have had Pisa as well as Arezzo.

And so, to return to our topic, indecisive republics never choose beneficial policies except by force of circumstance, because their weakness never allows them to make decisions where any doubt exists; if that doubt is not erased by some violent act that drives them on, they remain forever in a state of indecision.

CHAPTER 39
The Same Circumstances Are Often Seen Among Different Peoples

Anyone who studies current and ancient affairs will easily recognize that the same desires and humours exist and have always existed in all cities and among all peoples. Thus, it is an easy matter for anyone who examines past events carefully to foresee future events in every republic and to apply the remedies that the ancients employed, or if old remedies cannot be found, to think of new ones based upon the similarity of circumstances. But since these considerations are ignored or misunderstood by those who read, or they are understood but are not recognized by those who govern, it always follows that the same conflicts arise in every era.

After 1494 when the city of Florence lost part of its empire, such as Pisa and other regions, it was forced to wage war against those who had occupied them. Since those who occupied them were powerful, it followed that a great deal was spent on war, which bore little fruit: these expenditures produced a great many heavy taxes, and heavy taxes produced countless squabbles among the people; and since this war was administrated by a magistracy of ten citizens, called the Ten of War, the masses began to hold them in contempt, as if they had been the cause of both the war and its cost, and they began to convince themselves that if they removed that magistracy the war would end, so that when it was time to select new members, instead of making new appointments they allowed the magistracy to lapse and entrusted their affairs to the Signoria.* This decision was so disastrous that it not only failed to end the war, as the masses were persuaded it would, but once it removed the very men who had been administering the war with prudence, so much disorder followed that, besides Pisa, they lost Arezzo and other places, so that after the people had realized their mistake and saw that the cause of the disease was the fever and not the physician, they re-established the magistracy of the Ten.* This same dissatisfaction arose in Rome against the institution of the consuls, for when the people saw that one war followed another, allowing them no rest, they ought to have realized that this sprang from the ambition of Rome's neighbours who wished to overcome them but, instead, they believed that this sprang from the ambition of the nobles, who wished to take the people outside Rome under the leadership of the consuls in order to oppress them where they had no one to defend them, since inside the city the nobles were unable to punish the plebeians, who were defended there by the authority of the tribunes. For this reason, they thought it necessary either to abolish the consuls or to regulate their power in such a way that they would have no authority over the people either inside or outside the city. The first to attempt to pass such a law was a certain Terentillus, a tribune:* he proposed that five men should be appointed to study the consuls' power and to limit it. This greatly angered the nobility, who felt that the majesty of their authority was in complete decline, to the extent that the nobility no longer held any rank at all in the republic. Nevertheless, the stubbornness of the tribunes was such that the consular title was abolished, and after some other laws had been passed, the people were finally satisfied with the appointment of tribunes with consular powers rather than consuls, so much greater was the people's hatred of the consuls' title than of their actual authority. And so they went on in this way for a long period of time, but finally they recognized their error, and just as the Florentines went back to the Ten, so they re-created the consuls.*

CHAPTER 40

The Creation of the Decemvirate in Rome and
What Is Noteworthy About It; Including, Among
Many Other Matters, the Consideration of
How the Same Circumstances May Either Save or
Destroy a Republic

Since I wish to discuss in detail the circumstances that arose in
Rome with the creation of the decemvirate, it does not seem
superfluous to recount, first, all the similar creations that followed and, then, to discuss those elements that are worthy of
note in these actions, which are numerous and of great significance, both for those who wish to maintain a free republic and
for those who are planning to take one over. In such a discussion
we shall observe the many errors committed by the senate and
by the plebeians that were detrimental to liberty, as well as the
many errors committed by Appius, leader of the decemvirate,
that were detrimental to the tyranny he had planned to establish
in Rome.

After the many quarrels and disputes that occurred between
the people and the nobility, in order to establish new laws in
Rome which would strongly reinforce the liberty of that government, they both agreed to send Spurius Postumius with two
other citizens to Athens for copies of the laws that Solon gave to
that city in order that they might base Roman laws upon them.*
After they had gone and returned, the men who were to examine and decide on these laws were then chosen, and they
appointed ten citizens for the period of a year, among whom was
Appius Claudius, a shrewd but restless man.* Because these men
were able to create such laws without any constraints, all the
other magistrates of Rome, and in particular the tribunes and
the consuls, were eliminated, as was the right of appeal to the
people, with the result that this magistracy came to be the
absolute ruler of Rome. Through the favour Appius gained with
the plebeians, all the authority of his other associates came to be
concentrated in his hands, for he had made himself so popular
through his behaviour that it seemed amazing for him so

quickly to have acquired a new character and a new talent, having previously been considered a cruel persecutor of the plebeians.

These decemvirs governed without resorting to tyrannical methods, never keeping more than twelve lictors who marched before the man they had chosen as their leader.* Although they enjoyed absolute authority, nevertheless, when they had to punish a Roman citizen for homicide they would summon him forth to appear before the people and had the people judge him. They wrote their laws on ten tablets, and before confirming them they placed them on public view, so that everyone could read and discuss them, and so that they would know if some defect were found in them, in order to amend them before they were confirmed. Regarding these tablets, Appius had a rumour spread throughout Rome that if to these ten tablets another two were added, they would be complete, and this opinion gave the people an opportunity to reappoint the decemvirs for another year; they agreed to do this willingly, whether because the consuls would not be reappointed or because they thought they could do without tribunes, given the fact that they were acting as judges in trials, as was said above. After they had made the decision to reappoint the decemvirs, all of the nobility, therefore, made an effort to obtain this office, and among the foremost was Appius, and he showed such humanity toward the plebeians in asking for support that he began to arouse the suspicions of his associates: 'such excessive affability to inferiors could hardly be without some ulterior motive.'* Hesitant to oppose him directly, they resolved to do so with cunning, and although he was the youngest of them all, they gave him the power of proposing future decemvirs to the people, believing he would observe the custom that others had observed by not nominating himself, since in Rome this was considered an unthinkable and disreputable practice. 'He then proceeded to turn his disability to his own advantage', and he named himself among the first, to the amazement and displeasure of all the nobles: he then nominated nine other men to suit himself. This new reappointment, made for another year, began to show the people and the nobility how they had erred. Immediately 'Appius threw off his mask' and began to show his inborn arrogance, and in a few days

time he passed his own habits on to his associates. And in order
to terrify the people and the senate, instead of twelve lictors he
appointed 120.

Both sides were equally afraid for several days, but the
decemvirs then began to engage in discussions with the senate
and to oppress the plebeians, and if anyone who was treated
badly by one of the decemvirs made an appeal to another, he was
treated worse in the appeal than in the original sentence. Thus,
once the plebeians had recognized their mistake, full of distress,
they began to look to the nobles, 'hoping to catch some breath of
liberty even from their one-time enemies and dreaded masters,
by terror of whose tyranny they had brought the country to its
present pass'. This distress of theirs was pleasing to the nobility,
'till in utter desperation they came to wish the old days back
again, with two consuls'. The days that marked the end of the
year arrived: the two tablets of laws were drawn up but not made
public. In this way the decemvirs took the opportunity of continuing their magistracy, and they began to hold on to the government with violence and to make themselves some supporters
out of the young nobles, to whom they gave the property of
those they condemned: 'with such gifts the young men were
corrupted, preferring as they did the licence granted them to liberty for all.'* At this time, it happened that the Sabines and the
Volscians* began to wage war against the Romans, and in their
fear the decemvirs began to recognize the weakness of their situation, because without the senate they could not prepare for
war, and they thought they would lose the state by calling the
senate into session. Driven by necessity, however, they chose
this second alternative, and once the senators assembled many
of them, in particular Valerius and Horatius,* spoke out against
the arrogance of the decemvirs; and their authority would have
been completely extinguished had the senate, out of animosity
towards the plebeians, not wished to demonstrate its own
authority, believing that if the decemvirs renounced their
authority voluntarily, it might happen that the tribunes of the
plebeians would not be reappointed. They decided, therefore,
upon going to war; two armies set out, led by some of these same
decemvirs; Appius remained to govern the city. And so, it
happened that he fell in love with Virginia, and that her father,

Virginius, discovering that he wished to take her by force, killed her in order to free her; whence followed disturbances in Rome and inside the armies: the armies joined together with the remainder of the Roman plebeians and they marched to the Mons Sacer,* where they remained until the decemvirs relinquished their magistracy and the tribunes and the consuls were appointed, and Rome was restored to the form of its ancient liberty.

It is therefore to be noted from this text that, in the first place, the disadvantage involved in creating this tyranny arose in Rome from the same causes that give rise to most tyrannies in cities: that is, from an excessive desire on the part of the people to be free, and from an excessive desire on the part of the nobles to rule; and when they do not agree to establish a law that favours liberty but, instead, one of the parties rushes to support a single man, it is then that tyranny quickly arises. The people and the nobles of Rome agreed to establish the decemvirs and to establish them with so much authority on account of the desires of each faction—one hoped to abolish the office of consul and the other to abolish the tribunate. Once the decemvirs were established, the people, believing Appius had become their supporter and would oppress the nobility, turned to support him. When a people is led to commit the error of respecting a man because he might oppose those they despise, and when this man is shrewd, it will always happen that he will become tyrant of that city, because he will wait for the support of the people to destroy the nobility, and he will never turn to oppress the people before he has destroyed it: at the point where the people realize that they have been enslaved, they will have nowhere to take refuge. All those who have founded tyrannies in republics have employed this method. If Appius had employed this method, this tyranny of his would have had a longer life, and it would not have so quickly come to an end, but he did exactly the opposite. Nor could he have acted more imprudently, for in order to maintain his tyranny he made himself the enemy of those who had given it to him and who could have saved it for him, as well as the friend of those who had not joined forces to give it to him and who would not have been able to save it for him; and he lost those who were his friends while he sought to have as his friends those who could not become his friends.

Whereas the nobles may wish to play the tyrant, the part of the nobility excluded from the tyranny is always unfriendly to the tyrant: the tyrant can never win them over completely because of their great ambition and greed, and the tyrant can never possess enough wealth or honours to satisfy them all. And so, when Appius abandoned the people and drew closer to the nobles he committed a very obvious error, for the reasons outlined above and also because in wishing to hold something by force, the one who uses coercion must be more powerful than the one who is being coerced. Whence it happens that those tyrants who have the masses as their friends and the nobles as their enemies are more secure, since their power is upheld by greater forces than the power of those who have the people as their enemy and the nobility as their friend. With this kind of support, internal forces are sufficient for survival, just as they sufficed for Nabis, tyrant of Sparta,* when all of Greece and the Roman people attacked him; once Nabis had assured himself of the support of a few nobles, having the people as his friend, he defended himself with the people's support, something he could not have done had they been his enemy. In that other situation, since few friends remain within, internal forces are insufficient, and it is useful to seek them outside. And this assistance must be of three kinds: first, hiring foreign henchmen to serve as bodyguards; second, arming the countryside, which will assume the duties the plebeians would have performed; and third, allying yourself with powerful neighbours who will defend you. Anyone who follows these methods and observes them well, even if he has the people as his enemy, could save himself in one way or another. But Appius was not able to use this method of winning over the countryside, since the countryside and Rome were one and the same thing, and whatever he was capable of doing he did not know how to do, so that he came to ruin at his very beginning.

The senate and the people committed the greatest errors in creating the decemvirate, for although it was said above in the discourse treating the dictator that self-appointed magistrates and not those created by the people are harmful to liberty, the people must, nevertheless, in establishing magistrates, appoint these in such a way that they will hesitate before acting wickedly. Whereas the Romans should have put a safeguard in place in order to keep them good, they removed it, establishing the decemvirate as the sole magistracy in Rome and annulling all the others, as we stated above, because of the senate's excessive desire to eliminate the tribunes and the plebeians' to abolish the consuls; this excessive desire blinded them in such a way that they both contributed to this disorder. As King Ferdinand* used to say, men often act like certain minor birds of prey who have such a strong desire to pursue their prey, being prompted by nature to do so, that they do not hear another larger bird flying above them who is about to kill them. Through this discourse it is possible, therefore, as I proposed in the beginning, to recognize the error the Roman people committed in wishing to save their liberty and the errors Appius committed in wishing to establish a tyranny.

CHAPTER 4I

To Jump from Humility to Arrogance and from Mercy to Cruelty Without the Appropriate Measures Is an Imprudent and Unprofitable Affair

Among the other ill-advised methods Appius used to maintain his tyranny, that of jumping too soon from one state of mind to another was of no little importance. His shrewdness in deceiving the plebeians by pretending to be a man of the people was well used; well used also were the methods that he used in having the decemvirs reappointed; also well used was his audacity in appointing himself against the wishes of the nobility. His shrewdness was well used to appoint associates of his liking; but it was not at all well used, once he had accomplished all of this, following what I said above, in that sudden change of nature from being a friend of the plebeians to being their enemy, from being humane to being arrogant, from being easygoing to being difficult, and to do all of this in such a brief period of time and without any excuse whatsoever so that everyone had to recognize the deceptiveness of his intentions. Thus, anyone who has appeared to be good for a time and intends for his own advantage to become evil must do so through the appropriate measures and in such a manner that he allows himself to be governed by circumstances, so that before your new nature deprives you of old favours, it will have provided you with so many new ones that your authority will not be diminished; otherwise, finding yourself exposed and without friends, you will come to ruin.

CHAPTER 42

How Easily Men May Be Corrupted

It should also be noted, in this matter of the decemvirate, how easily men may be corrupted and how they may transform themselves and give themselves a completely different nature, no matter how good and well educated they may be: consider how the young men whom Appius had chosen to surround him began to be friends of tyranny for the little bit of profit it provided them; or how Quintus Fabius, one of the second group of decemvirs, while an excellent individual, was blinded by a bit of ambition and persuaded by the wickedness of Appius to change his good habits into the worst and became like Appius. Once this is carefully studied, it will make all lawgivers in republics or kingdoms more quick to restrain human appetites and to deprive people of all hope of being able to do evil with impunity.

CHAPTER 43

Those Who Fight for Their Own Glory Are Good and Faithful Soldiers

It should also be considered, concerning the argument above, what a difference there is between a happy army that fights for its own glory and one that is poorly organized and fights for the ambition of others. Roman armies were always accustomed to being victorious under the consuls, while under the decemvirs they always lost. From this example one can understand, in part, some of the reasons for the uselessness of mercenary troops, who have no other reason to stand firmly behind you than the bit of salary you give them. This is not, nor can it be, a sufficient cause to make them faithful to you, nor to make them such good friends that they will want to die for you. In those armies lacking any affection toward the man for whom they are fighting that would make them his strong supporters, there can never be enough of that exceptional skill to withstand a rather unskilful enemy, and because this affection and this spirit of rivalry can arise only from your own subjects, it is necessary, in order to hold on to a government and to maintain a republic or a kingdom, to arm oneself with one's own subjects: this is evident in the actions of all those who have gained great advantages with their armies. The Roman armies under the decemvirs were possessed of the same ability, but because there was no longer the same disposition among them, they did not produce their usual results. But as soon as the magistracy of the decemvirs was eliminated and the Romans began to soldier as free men, the same courageous spirit returned among them and, as a consequence, their undertakings produced the same happy results, in accord with their ancient practice.

CHAPTER 44

A Crowd Is Ineffective Without a Leader; and How One Should Not Make Threats First and Then Request Authority

The Roman plebeians equipped with arms withdrew to the Mons Sacer because of the incident involving Virginia. The senate sent its ambassadors to ask on what authority they had abandoned their commanders and withdrawn to the Mons, and so greatly respected was the authority of the senate that, since the plebeians did not have a leader among them, no one dared to reply. Livy says that they did not lack a response but rather they lacked a person to give it. This demonstrates precisely the ineffectiveness of a crowd without a leader. Virginius was aware of this disorder, and on his command twenty military tribunes were created to act as leaders in responding to and dealing with the senate. When they asked that Valerius and Horatius be sent to them so that they could explain their wishes to them, they did not want to go there unless the decemvirs first relinquished their magistracy, and once they arrived at the Mons Sacer, where the plebeians were located, they were told that the plebeians wanted the appointment of the tribunes of the plebeians, the right of appeal to the people from every magistrate, and the handing over of all the decemvirs to them, for they wanted to burn them alive.

Valerius and Horatius praised their first demands and criticized the last one as impious, saying: 'you are tumbling head-long into that very vice you profess so bitterly to hate.'* And they advised them to avoid saying anything about the decemvirs and to wait until they regained their own authority and power; then, they would not lack the means to obtain satisfaction. In this, one clearly recognizes how much stupidity and how little prudence there is in asking for something and later declaring: 'I want to do such and such evil deed with this', for one must not reveal one's intentions, but instead should attempt to obtain what one wants by any means possible. For it is enough to ask somebody for his weapons without saying, 'I want to kill you with them', because when you have his weapons in hand, you can then satisfy your desire.

CHAPTER 45

It Is a Bad Example Not to Observe a Law that Has Been Passed, Especially on the Part of Its Author; and It Is Extremely Harmful to the Ruler of a City to Open New Wounds Every Day

When the agreement had been made to return Rome to its ancient form of government, Virginius summoned Appius to appear before the people to argue his case. He appeared, accompanied by many noblemen, and Virginius ordered him to be imprisoned. Appius then began to cry out and appeal to the people; Virginius stated that he was not worthy of having that same right of appeal that he himself had destroyed or to have as his defender the people he had harmed. Appius replied that they should not violate the right of appeal which they had so eagerly established. He was, however, imprisoned, and before the day of his trial he killed himself. Although the wicked life of Appius deserves the highest punishment, it was nevertheless very heedless of civic affairs to violate the laws, especially one they had just passed. I do not believe there is any worse example in a republic than to make a law and then not to observe it, and even more so when it is not observed by the person who made it.

After 1494* Florence reorganized its government with the assistance of Brother Girolamo Savonarola, whose writings demonstrate the learning, prudence, and the excellence of his mind, and among other provisions he had enacted to protect the citizens was a law allowing an appeal to the people from the sentences imposed in crimes against the state by the Eight and the Signoria (a law he had long argued for and obtained with the greatest difficulty); it happened that shortly after its approval, five citizens* were condemned to death by the Signoria on behalf of the state, and when these men wanted to make their appeal they were not allowed to do so, and the law was not observed. This diminished the friar's reputation more than any other incident, for if the right of appeal was useful, it should have been observed, and if it was not useful, he should not have caused it to be passed successfully. This incident was remarked upon all the more because in so many of the sermons that the friar delivered after this law had been broken, he never either condemned those who had broken it or excused them—like a man who was unwilling to condemn something that he wanted, as if it were something that turned out to suit his purposes, but who was likewise unable to excuse it. This incident, revealing the friar's ambitious and partisan nature, deprived him of his reputation and brought him much blame.

A government also does damage when on a daily basis it renews the resentment of your citizens through fresh injuries done to one person or another, as occurred in Rome after the decemvirate, for all the decemvirs and other citizens at various times had been accused and condemned, so that a dreadful fear arose among all of the nobility, who thought such condemnations would never end until the entire nobility had been destroyed. This would have generated a great deal of trouble within the city if the tribune Marcus Duellius had not done something about it; he issued an edict* that for one year it would be unlawful for anyone to cite or to accuse any Roman citizen, and this reassured the entire nobility. This demonstrates how harmful it is to a republic or a prince to keep the minds of the citizens anxious and fearful with the threat of continuous offences and punishments. Without a doubt, no one could hold to a more pernicious course, because men who begin to suspect they are about to suffer some evil protect themselves in every possible way from such dangers and become more daring and less cautious in attempting something new. Thus, it is necessary either never to injure anyone or else to inflict the injuries all at once and later on to reassure men and to give them reason to calm down and to quiet their minds.

CHAPTER 46

Men Rise from One Ambition to Another; and First They Seek to Avoid Injury, Then They Injure Others

When the Roman people had recovered their liberty and returned to their original condition, and it was all the greater to the extent that they had passed many new laws confirming the city's strength, it seemed likely that Rome would once again become more tranquil. Nevertheless, experience reveals the contrary, for every day there arose new disturbances and new disagreements. Since Livy very prudently explains the reason why this came about, it seems nothing if not pertinent to refer to his precise words,* where he states that either the people or the nobility was always puffed up with pride when the other one was humbled, and when the people were calm within their proper bounds, the young noblemen began to abuse them and the tribunes could do little to prevent it, for they, too, were under attack. The nobility, on the other hand, even while they felt their young men were too bold, preferred, nevertheless, that if the mean was to be exceeded, they should exceed it and not the plebeians. And so the desire to defend liberty caused each group to prevail to the degree that it oppressed the other. Moreover, the sequence of such events is that while men seek to avoid fear, they begin to make others feel it, and the harm that they drive away from themselves is inflicted upon another, as if it were necessary either to harm or to be harmed. In this can be seen one of the ways, among others, in which republics disintegrate, how men rise from one ambition to another, and the truth of the remark Sallust puts into Caesar's mouth: 'that all examples of evil doing arise from good beginnings.'* As was mentioned above, the first thing ambitious citizens who live in a republic seek is the ability not to be harmed, not only private citizens but even magistrates: in order to accomplish this, they seek out friendships; they acquire these friends by apparently honest means, either by offering them financial assistance or by defending them from the powerful; and because this seems virtuous, they easily fool everyone, and for this there is no remedy, to the point that by persevering, the ambitious citizen, without any obstacles, reaches a position where private citizens are afraid of him and magistrates show him respect. When he has risen to this level and there has been no opposition in the beginning to his ascent, he has attained such a rank that to try to confront him would be extremely dangerous, for the reasons that I mentioned above, where I speak of the danger that exists in confronting a problem that has already grown to a considerable degree within a city. In short, the matter comes down to the fact that it is necessary either to eliminate the problem with the risk of immediate ruin, or, allowing the problem to continue unabated, to enter into an obvious state of servitude, unless death or some accident frees you from it, because once matters reach the point described above, when citizens and magistrates are fearful of offending someone so powerful as well as his friends, not much effort is required later on to make them render judgements and harm others according to his will. For this reason, a republic must have among its institutions some means of ensuring that its citizens cannot do evil under the guise of doing good, and that its citizens possess the kind of reputation that benefits and does not harm liberty, as will be discussed by us in the proper place.

CHAPTER 47

Although Men May Deceive Themselves in General Questions, They Do Not Do So in the Particulars

As was discussed above, when the Roman people had grown sick and tired of the title of consul and wanted either to create consuls from among the plebeians or to curtail the consular authority, the nobility, in order to avoid corrupting consular authority with one option or the other, chose a half measure and were content with the idea that four tribunes with consular powers would be created who could be either plebeians or nobles. This satisfied the plebeians, since they thought they had eliminated the consulate and would have their share in this highest jurisdiction. This gave rise to a noteworthy event: arriving at the moment of electing these tribunes and having the power to elect only plebeians, the Roman people elected only nobles to these offices. Concerning this event, Livy writes these words: 'Men fighting for their own liberty and prestige are very different creatures from men who are called upon to use their judgement, unclouded by passion, when the fight is over.'* And in analysing how this might have come about, I believe it came about because men fool themselves greatly in general questions but not so much in the particular. The Roman plebeians generally thought that they deserved the consulate, because they comprised the largest part of the city; they ran greater risks in the wars; and they kept Rome free and powerful with their own might and muscle. Since, as was mentioned, they felt this desire of theirs was reasonable, they wanted to obtain this authority in any way possible. But when it came to judging their own men in particular, they recognized their weakness and decided that none of them individually deserved what all of them as a group thought they deserved. And thus, ashamed of themselves, they turned back to men who deserved the office. Amazed at this deliberation, Livy justifiably says these words: 'Such decency of feeling, such fairness and magnanimity characterized, on that occasion, the whole body of the Roman commons—where would you find it today in one single man?'*

In confirmation of this it is possible to cite another notable example, which came about in Capua after Hannibal had routed the Romans at Cannae. All of Italy was aroused by this defeat, and Capua was still on the point of riot as a result of the hatred that existed between the people and the senate. In those times Pacuvius Calanus was the supreme magistrate, and understanding the risk of riots the city ran, he developed a plan to reconcile the plebeians with the nobility to his own advantage. After this idea came to him, he had the senate assembled and told them of the loathing the people felt toward them and the dangers the noblemen ran of being murdered by the plebeians and having the city handed over to Hannibal at a time when the Romans were hard pressed: he then added that if they wished to allow him to handle this matter, he would do so in such a way that the city's factions would be united, but he wanted to lock the senators inside the palace* and to save them by giving to the people the power to punish them. The senators yielded to his opinion on the matter, and Pacuvius called the people to assembly after having locked the senate inside the palace. He told them that the time had come for them to check the arrogance of the nobility and to avenge the injuries they had received from them, since he had them all locked up in his custody; that because he believed that they did not want their city to be left without a government, it was necessary, if they wanted to murder the old senators, to appoint new ones; and that he had thus placed all the names of the senators in a bag and would begin to draw them in their presence and would put those selected to death one by one after their successors had been found. Once he had drawn one, at the mention of his name a great clamour arose, calling him proud, cruel, and arrogant, and when Pacuvius asked them to name his replacement the entire assembly calmed down. After some time had passed one of the plebeians was nominated, but at the sound of his name some people began to whistle, others to laugh, and still others to speak badly of him in one way or another, and continuing in this fashion, one by one, they judged all those who were nominated unworthy of the senatorial rank. As a result Pacuvius, seizing the opportunity, stated: 'Since you think this city will fare badly without the senate and that you cannot agree on replacements for the old senators, I think it would be best if you come to a reconciliation with them; for the fear which the senators have just experienced will have humbled them in such a way that the humanity you sought elsewhere you will certainly find in them.'* Once they had agreed to this, unity in the public order followed, for the deception which took them in was uncovered as soon as they were forced to come to grips with the particulars. Besides this, peoples are generally deceived when they judge issues and events which are linked to them, but, later, when they understand things in their particulars, they are no longer deceived.

After 1494 when the rulers of the city had been driven out of Florence and there was no organized government in the city, but rather a kind of ambitious licence, and as public affairs were going from bad to worse, many people, seeing the ruin of the city and finding no other reason for it, blamed it on the ambition of powerful individuals who were fostering disorders, so that they might create a government more to their own liking and deprive the people of their liberty; such individuals stood under the loggias and in the squares speaking ill of many other citizens, threatening that if they ever became part of the Signoria they would uncover this conspiracy of theirs and punish them. It often happened that these men rose to the rank of the supreme magistracy, and when such a man reached that position and saw things more closely, he recognized the origins of such disorders, the dangers they involved, and the difficulty of finding remedies for them. And having witnessed how the times rather than men create disorder, he suddenly changed his mind and his way of doing things, because the knowledge of things in their particulars had removed the element of deception he had taken for granted when he had considered them in general terms. Thus, those who first heard him speak when he was a private citizen, and later observed him remaining silent in the highest magistracy, believed that this came about not through a truer understanding of things but because he had been tricked and corrupted by the powerful. Since this happened to many men on many occasions, a saying arose among them which states: 'Such men have one mind in the public square and another in the palace.' Considering, therefore, everything that has been discussed, it is clear that the quickest way to open the people's eyes, given that a general matter may deceive them, is to make them get down to its particulars, as was done by Pacuvius in Capua and by the senate in Rome. I also believe it possible to conclude that a prudent man should never flee from the popular judgement in particular details regarding the distribution of ranks and positions, because only in this matter do the people avoid deceiving themselves, and if they are deceived on some occasions, they are very seldom deceived more often than the few men who have to make such appointments. Nor does it seem superfluous to demonstrate in the following chapter the means the senate employed to deceive the people in making its appointments.

CHAPTER 48

Anyone Wishing to Prevent a Magistracy from Being Given to a Man of Humble Birth or to an Evil Man Should Have It Requested Either by a Man Who Is Too Humbly Born and Evil or by One Who Is Too Noble and Too Good

When the senate feared that tribunes with consular authority would be chosen from among the plebeians, it adopted one of two methods: either it called on the most renowned citizens of Rome or, indeed, it corrupted by the necessary means some humbly born and extremely ignoble plebeians who would ask for the office and be mixed together with the plebeians of better quality who usually asked for the office. The latter method made the plebeians ashamed of giving the office to such men; the former method made them ashamed to refuse it to worthy individuals. All of this demonstrates the truth of the preceding discourse, where it was demonstrated that if the people are deceived in general questions, they are not deceived in the particulars.

CHAPTER 49

If Those Cities Which Had Free Beginnings Like Rome Experience Difficulty in Finding Laws Which Maintain Them, Those Which Were Servile at the Outset Will Find It Almost Impossible to Do So

How difficult it is to foresee all those laws required to keep a republic free at the moment of its establishment is very well demonstrated by the development of the Roman republic, where, notwithstanding the fact that it was organized by many laws, first by Romulus, then by Numa, then by Tullus Hostilius and Servius, and finally by the ten citizens created for such a purpose, new needs were nevertheless always discovered in the course of governing that city, and it was necessary to create new institutions, as occurred when they created the censors,* with one of those measures that helped to keep Rome free during the period of time it lived in liberty. After the censors had become arbiters of Roman morality, they were a powerful reason why it took such a long time to corrupt the Romans. The Romans, however, made one mistake at the outset in the creation of such a magistracy, by creating it for a five-year term, but after a brief time this was corrected by the prudence of Mamercus, the dictator,* who with a new law reduced this office to a term of eighteen months; the censors who were then in office took it so badly that they deprived Mamercus of his place in the senate, an action that both the plebeians and the elders strongly censured. Since history does not show how Mamercus could have defended himself, either the historian was incomplete,* or in this instance Roman institutions were not good, because it is not beneficial for a republic to be organized in such a way that a citizen who promulgates a law suitable to a free way of life can be injured without any recourse.

But returning to the beginning of this discourse, I would say that with respect to the creation of this new magistracy, it is necessary to consider the fact that if those cities that have had a free beginning and have, like Rome, sustained this freedom on their own experience great difficulty in finding good laws to keep them free, it is no surprise that those cities that were servile at the outset experience not just difficulties but find it impossible to create institutions in such a way that they can live in a civil and peaceful fashion. This can be seen in what came about in the city of Florence, which by reason of being subject to Roman rule at its beginning, and having always lived under the government of others, stood for a time abject and heedless of its own condition; afterwards, when the occasion came for a breath of fresh air, it began to create its own institutions; these being mixed with the ancient ones, which were bad, could not be good; and Florence thus went on managing its affairs in this way for 200 years, of which there remain reliable records, without ever having had a government on account of which it could truly be called a republic. The difficulties that Florence experienced have always been experienced by all those cities with similar beginnings. Although free and public elections have many times bestowed ample authority on a few citizens in order to reform Florence, they have, none the less, never organized the city for the common good but always according to the needs of their own faction; this has not brought order but greater disorder to that city.

And to come to some specific examples, I must say that among the things that the founder of a republic has to consider is the task of examining carefully into whose hands he places the power of life and death over his citizens. This institution was well organized in Rome, because it was normally possible to make an appeal to the people, and if an important decision was made, the execution of which was dangerous to delay through such an appeal, the Romans had a refuge in their dictator who acted immediately; they never had recourse to this remedy except out of necessity. But Florence and other cities born in the same fashion, being servile, vested this authority in a foreigner, who fulfilled this office as a prince's envoy. Later, when they became free, they maintained this authority vested in a foreigner, whom they called a captain: this was an extremely pernicious practice since he was easily corrupted by the powerful citizens.* But later, when this institution was modified by changes in the government, the Florentines appointed eight citizens to carry out the duties of this captain; this institution went from bad to worse for reasons that have been set forth on other occasions, because these few men were always the ministers of the few and the most powerful. The city of Venice has protected itself from this problem by selecting ten citizens* who have the power to punish any citizen without the right of appeal, and because these ten might not be sufficient to punish the powerful, even though they possess the authority to do so, they have constituted the Council of Forty.* Moreover, they wanted their Council of the Pregadi,* which is their Grand Council, to have the power of punishment; in this way, if an accuser is not lacking, there is no lack of a judge to keep powerful men in check. Thus, seeing that in Rome, which was organized by its own inhabitants and by many prudent men, there arose every day new reasons for creating new institutions in support of a free way of life, it is, therefore, not surprising that in other cities, which experienced more disorderly beginnings, there arose so many problems that they could never be reorganized aright.

CHAPTER 50
No One Council or Magistrate Should Be Capable of Blocking Legal Actions in Cities

When Titus Quinctius Cincinnatus and Cnaeus Julius Mento were consuls* in Rome, they blocked all the legal actions of that republic by being disunited. Realizing this, the senate supported the creation of a dictator to do what their disagreements prevented them from doing. But the consuls, disagreeing over everything else, were in agreement only in not wishing to create a dictator. Thus, finding no other remedy, the senate solicited the help of the tribunes, who with the authority of the senate forced the consuls to obey. Here it is necessary to note, first of all, the usefulness of the tribunate, which was useful not only in checking the ambition that the powerful displayed against the plebeians, but also the ambition they displayed among themselves; the second thing to be noted is that one should never create an institution that allows the few to make decisions concerning the laws that are normally necessary to maintain the republic. For example, if you give authority to a council to distribute honours and rewards, or to a magistrate to administer an affair, it is necessary either to force them to take action under all circumstances or to organize things so that, if they do not wish to act, someone else can and must do so; otherwise, this institution would be defective and dangerous, as it clearly was in Rome, had the stubbornness of those consuls not been opposed by the authority of the tribunes.

In the Venetian republic the Grand Council distributes honours and rewards. On occasion it has happened that the majority, either through contempt or some false belief, have failed to appoint successors for the magistrates of the city and for those who administer the city's foreign dominions. This caused great disorder, because all at once both the subject territories and the city itself were without their legitimate judges; nor could anything be done about it if the majority of the council was either dissatisfied or deceived. This difficulty would have brought that city to a bad end had prudent citizens not made some provision for it; once they found the proper occasion, they passed a law which stipulated that all magistrates who served or had served inside the city or abroad could never vacate their offices until new appointments were made and their successors named. And so that council was deprived of the possibility of blocking with great danger the legal actions of the republic.

CHAPTER 51

A Republic or a Prince Should Seem to Do Out of Generosity What Must Be Done Out of Necessity

Prudent men always and in their every action make a merit of doing things even if necessity forces them to act in this way in any case. This kind of prudence was well used by the Roman senate when it decided to give public funds to the men who were fulfilling their military service, even though they were accustomed to serving at their own expense. But realizing that it could not wage war in this fashion for very long, and that for this reason it could neither lay siege to cities nor lead troops far from home, and judging that it was necessary to be able to do both of these things, the senate decided that the previously mentioned stipends would be given; but they did this in such a way that they seemed to do as a favour what necessity forced them to do. And this gift was so welcome to the plebeians that Rome was turned upside down with joy, since this seemed to be a great benefit which they never hoped to have and which they never would have sought on their own. Although the tribunes did their best to annul this act of benevolence, pointing out that it increased rather than eased the plebeians' burdens (since it was necessary to impose a tax to pay for this expense), the tribunes were, nevertheless, unable to do anything to prevent the plebeians from accepting the proposal. The senate only increased their pleasure by the manner in which they assessed the taxes, for they imposed the heaviest and the highest taxes upon the nobility, and these were the first to be paid.

CHAPTER 52

There Is No More Secure and Less Divisive Means of Restraining the Insolence of a Man Who Rises to Power in a Republic Than to Be the First to Occupy the Paths Through Which He May Come into Such Power

We have seen in the discourse above and we have read about how much credit the nobility acquired with the plebeians through its efforts to benefit them, both by the salary they instituted and by the method of imposing the taxes. If the nobility had maintained this institution it would have eliminated every disturbance in that city, and they would have stripped the tribunes of the credit that they enjoyed among the plebeians and, as a consequence, of their authority. Truly there is, in a republic, especially those that are corrupt, no better method, nor one that is less divisive and more simple, of opposing the ambition of any citizen than to be the first to occupy the paths through which he appears to be moving towards the rank he intends to reach. Had this method been used against Cosimo de' Medici, it would have been a much better policy for his adversaries than driving him out of Florence, because had those citizens who were competing with him adopted his method of favouring the people, they would have managed, without strife and without violence, to remove from his hands weapons that served him best.*

Piero Soderini made himself a reputation in the city of Florence with this method alone, that of favouring the people, who considered him devoted to the city's liberty. Truly, it would have been much simpler, easier, more honest, less dangerous, and less damaging to the republic for the citizens who were envious of his greatness to be the first to occupy the paths through which he was making himself great, instead of wanting to oppose him so that at his downfall all the rest of the republic came to ruin.* If they had removed from his hands the weapons with which he was making himself powerful (something they could have easily accomplished), they would have been able to oppose him without suspicion and without regard for anyone in all the councils and all public deliberations. Someone may reply that if the citizens who hated Piero committed an error by not being the first to occupy the paths through which he was winning his reputation with the people, Piero also came to commit the same error in not being the first to occupy those paths through which his adversaries caused him fear. Piero deserves to be excused for this, both because it was difficult for him to do so, and because such a strategy would not have been honest for him, inasmuch as the means through which they did him injury consisted in supporting the Medici, with whose support they fought him and finally destroyed him. Piero could not, therefore, have honestly taken that side, lending it his good name, without destroying that liberty of which he had been appointed guardian; Piero could not, then, offer favours to the Medici secretly and all at once, and these were extremely dangerous for him, because as soon as he had been discovered to be a friend of the Medici, he would have become suspected and hated by the people, and his enemies would have found it even easier to attack him than they had previously. Men must, therefore, consider the defects and the dangers of every decision and avoid adopting the one that is more dangerous than useful, notwithstanding the fact that they might find it to be in accord with their own thinking. By doing otherwise in this case, what happened to Cicero might happen to them; wishing to take away support from Mark Antony, he increased it. Since Mark Antony had been judged to be an enemy of the senate and had assembled that great army in large measure made up of soldiers who had pursued Caesar's cause, Cicero, in order to deprive him of these troops, urged the senate to enhance Octavian's reputation and to send him against Mark Antony with the consuls Hirtius and Pansa,* claiming that as soon as the soldiers following Mark Antony heard the name of Octavian, Caesar's nephew who had adopted Caesar's name, they would abandon him and join Octavian, and thus, once Mark Antony had been stripped of support, it would be easy to overcome him. The affair turned out completely to the contrary, because Mark Antony won the support of Octavian who, abandoning Cicero and the senate, joined forces with him. This affair caused the complete destruction of the aristocratic party. It was easy to speculate that the senate should never have believed the arguments that convinced Cicero, and should have always taken into account the name which with so much glory had extinguished its enemies and acquired for itself the principality of Rome; nor should the senate ever have expected to gain from Caesar's heirs or supporters anything that was compatible with the name of liberty.

CHAPTER 53

The People, Deceived by a False Kind of Good, Often Desire Their Own Ruin, and How Great Hopes and Bold Promises Easily Move Them

Once the city of Veii had been defeated, the Roman people came to be of the opinion that it would be a useful thing for the city of Rome if half the Romans went to live in Veii, concluding that since the city was rich in territory, full of buildings, and near to Rome, it was possible to enrich half of their own citizens due to the proximity of the site without causing any political disorders. This proposal seemed to the senate and to the wisest Romans to be so useless and so damaging that they openly said they would rather suffer death than consent to such a decision. Thus, when the matter came up for debate, the plebeians were so incensed against the senate that they would have come to the point of taking up arms and shedding blood if the senate had not used as a shield some old and esteemed citizens, their reverence for whom restrained the plebeians from pursuing their insolence any further. Here, two things should be noted. The first is that very often the people, deceived by a false image of good, desire their own ruin, and unless someone they trust can make them capable of distinguishing the good from the bad, this will bring endless danger and damage to republics. When fate decrees that the people will have faith in no one, as sometimes occurs, after they have been deceived in the past either by events or by men, this inevitably leads to ruin. In this regard Dante declares in his discourse that makes up *On Monarchy* that the people frequently cry out: 'Long live' their death and 'Death' to their life.* From such scepticism arises the fact that in republics the proper decisions are sometimes not made, as was said above about the Venetians who, when attacked by so many enemies, could not take the decision to win the support of some by restoring to them what they had taken away from others (for this is what caused the war and created the conspiracy of princes against them) before their downfall.*

Thus, turning to consider when it is easy and when it is difficult to persuade a people, this distinction can be made: either what you have to persuade them of represents at first sight either a gain or a loss, or the proposal truly seems either courageous or cowardly. When profit is seen in matters put before the people, even though there may be a loss concealed beneath them, or when something seems courageous, even though the ruination of the republic may be concealed beneath it, it will always be easy to persuade the crowd to follow, and thus, it will always be difficult to persuade them to accept those decisions that appear to involve either cowardice or loss, even though salvation and profit may be concealed beneath them. What I have declared can be confirmed by countless Roman and foreign examples, both modern and ancient. From this attitude arose the unfavourable opinion in Rome that surrounded

Fabius Maximus, who could not persuade the Roman people that it was useful for the republic to proceed slowly with the war and to endure the assaults of Hannibal without actually engaging in battle, because they judged this choice to be cowardly and did not see the usefulness it contained, nor did Fabius have sufficient arguments to prove it to them. Most people are so blinded by bold opinions that, although the Roman people had made the error of authorizing Fabius' master of the horse to engage in battle, even though Fabius was unwilling to do so, and this authority would have led to the destruction of the Roman camp had Fabius' prudence not provided a remedy, this experience was not sufficient; indeed, the Roman people later made Varro consul, for no other merit than because, throughout all the squares and the public places of Rome, he had promised to rout Hannibal whenever he was given the authority to do so. This gave rise to the battle and the defeat of Cannae, and, very nearly, to the fall of Rome.*

I want to set forth yet another Roman example on this subject. Hannibal had been in Italy for eight or ten years, and he had covered the entire province with the dead bodies of Romans, when Marcus Centennius Paenula, a man of extremely low rank (in spite of the fact that he had held some position in the militia), came to the senate and offered to bring them Hannibal in a very short time either dead or captured, if they would grant him the authority to raise a volunteer army in whatever place he wished within Italy. To the senate this request seemed reckless; nevertheless, thinking that if they refused, and the people later came to learn of his request, it would give rise to some disturbance, jealousy, or ill will against the senatorial order, they granted it, preferring to expose all those who might follow him to danger rather than to cause new feelings of indignation to arise among the people, knowing how such proposals were likely to be accepted and how difficult it would be to dissuade them from it. This man, therefore, went with a disorderly and disorganized mob to find Hannibal, and he had barely arrived for the encounter when he and all those who followed him were routed and killed.*

In the Greek city of Athens, Nicias,* a most serious and prudent man, persuaded the people that it was not a good idea to go and attack Sicily, so that when the Greeks took that decision against the wishes of their wise men, the complete destruction of Athens was the result. When Scipio was made consul and wanted the province of Africa, promising the complete destruction of Carthage, and the senate did not agree with the plan given the unfavourable opinion of Fabius Maximus, Scipio threatened to bring the matter before the people, since he knew very well how much such proposals please the people.*

One could also provide examples for this purpose from our own city: for instance, when Messer Ercole Bentivogli, commander of the Florentine troops, together with Antonio Giacomini, after having defeated Bartolommeo d'Alviano at San Vincenti, went into the field at Pisa; this undertaking was decided upon by the people based on the bold promises of Messer Ercole, even though many wise citizens were opposed to it. None the less, they had no way to prevent it, carried away by that general will founded upon the bold promises of the commander.*

I must say, therefore, that there is no easier way to ruin a republic where the people have power than to involve them in bold enterprises, because wherever the people have any importance whatsoever, such proposals will always be accepted, and anyone of a contrary opinion will have no way to prevent this. But if this gives rise to the city's ruin, it even more frequently gives rise to the ruin of particular citizens who are put in charge of such undertakings, because once the people have taken victory for granted, when defeat arrives, neither fortune nor the incompetence of the commander is blamed but, rather, his wickedness and ignorance, and the people usually either kill or imprison or banish him, as happened to countless Carthaginian and Athenian generals. Nor did any of their previous victories prove useful, since the present defeat cancelled them all, as happened to our own Antonio Giacomini who, after failing to take Pisa as the people had assumed and as he had promised them he would, fell into such disgrace among them that, notwithstanding his countless good deeds of the past, he remained alive more due to the humanity of those who had authority over him than to any other argument that might have defended him among the people.*

CHAPTER 54

How Much Authority a Serious Man Possesses in Restraining a Multitude

The second thing to note in relation to the content of the preceding chapter is that there is nothing so apt to restrain an excited mob as their respect for some serious man of authority who confronts them; nor without reason does Virgil declare: 'If it so happens they look round and see | Some dedicated public man, a veteran | Whose record gives him weight, they quiet down, | Willing to stop and listen.'* For that reason, whoever is placed in charge of an army or happens to be in a city when a disturbance occurs ought to present himself before the crowd with the greatest grace and dignity possible, placing around himself the insignia of the rank he holds to inspire still more respect. A few years ago Florence was divided into two factions, the *Frateschi* and the *Arrabbiati** (as they called themselves), and after they came to blows, the *Frateschi* were defeated, among whom was Pagolantonio Soderini, in those days a well-respected citizen. During those disturbances an armed crowd went to his home to sack it, while his brother, Messer Francesco, then bishop of Volterra and today a cardinal, happened to be in the house; as soon as he heard the noise and saw the crowd, Francesco* dressed himself in his most illustrious garments, covering them with his white bishop's rochet, and confronting the armed citizens, he stopped them with his presence and his words, something that was noted and praised throughout the city for many days afterwards.

I conclude, therefore, that there is no more effective or necessary remedy for restraining a multitude than the presence of a single man who appears in person and is revered. It is also evident, if we return to the previously cited text, with what stubbornness the Roman plebeians accepted that decision to go to Veii* because they thought it a useful one and did not recognize the danger that it concealed, and how, after giving rise to numerous disturbances, it would have led to strife had the senate, through men who were serious and highly respected, not curbed their frenzy.

CHAPTER 55

How Easily Affairs Are Conducted in a City
Where the Populace Is Not Corrupted; and That
Where Equality Exists, a Principality Cannot Be
Created, and Where No Equality Exists, a
Republic Cannot Be Created

Although what is to be feared and hoped for from corrupted
cities has been amply discussed above, nevertheless it does not
seem beyond my purpose to consider a decision of the senate
concerning the vow made by Camillus to give Apollo the tenth
part of the spoils taken from the Veientes. These spoils had
already passed into the hands of the Roman plebeians and since
there was no means of accounting for them, the senate issued an
edict ordering everyone to return to the public treasury the
tenth part of what he had seized. Although this decision was not
carried out, since, to the plebeians' satisfaction, the senate later
adopted another means and other ways to please Apollo, it is,
nevertheless, evident from such a decision how much that senate
relied upon the goodness of the plebeians and how it judged that
no one would fail to return exactly what the edict commanded
them to return. On the other hand, it is evident that the plebeians
did not think of cheating on the edict in any way by returning
less than they should, but thought, instead, of freeing themselves from the edict by openly demonstrating their indignation
over it. This example, along with many others that have been
cited above, shows how much goodness and religion were in
that people and how much good was to be expected from it.

And truly, where this goodness does not exist, nothing good
can be hoped for, just as nothing can be hoped for in those
provinces which in our own times are seen to be corrupt, as is the
case in Italy above all others. Even France and Spain share to
some degree in this corruption, and if in these provinces as many
disorders cannot be seen as arise every day in Italy, this derives
not so much from the goodness of their peoples, which in large
measure has disappeared, as from their having a king who keeps
them united, not only through his own exceptional skill but

also through the institutions of those kingdoms, which are not damaged beyond hope. It is quite evident that in the province of Germany this goodness and religion are still strong among the people; this causes many republics there to flourish in liberty and to obey their laws in such a fashion that no one outside or within these republics dares to occupy them. And to show it is true that a good portion of that ancient goodness still prevails in these republics, I wish to give an example similar to the one cited above about the senate and the Roman plebeians. When these republics need to spend some amount of money for the public welfare, the magistracies or councils that have the authority to do so assess all the inhabitants of the city at 1 or 2 per cent of their income. Once they have made this decision, according to the regulations of the city, each citizen comes before the tax-collectors, and after he has taken an oath to pay the proper sum, he throws into a strong-box designated for this purpose what, according to the dictates of his conscience, he thinks he must pay; of this payment there is no other witness except the person who pays. Hence, it is possible to surmise how much goodness and religion still exist in these men. It must be assumed that each citizen pays the right sum, because if this sum were not paid, the tax would not produce the amount they estimated on the basis of what they usually collected in the past; if someone did not pay the fraud would be recognized, and with this recognition, some means other than this would be employed. Such goodness is all the more to be admired in these times since it is so rare; indeed, it is clear that this practice has survived only in that province. This arises from two causes: the first is that they have no extensive contacts with their neighbours, for their neighbours have not gone to visit them, nor have they themselves visited anyone else, because they are content with these goods—to live on the foods, and to dress themselves with the wools the country produces; in this way, the reason for any contact and the beginnings of any kind of corruption have been eliminated, since they have not been able to take up the habits of either the French, the Spanish, or the Italians, nations which taken together constitute the corruption of the world. The other reason is that these republics, where an uncorrupted body politic has been maintained, do not tolerate any of their citizens acting or living like noblemen: on the contrary, they maintain among themselves a clear equality; they are the mortal enemies of those lords and noblemen who live in that province, and if by chance some of them fall into their hands, they are killed as the source of corruption and the cause of every conflict.

To explain more clearly what this title of nobleman means, I will say that men are called noble who, in a state of idleness, live luxuriously off the revenue from their properties without paying any attention whatsoever either to the cultivation of the land or to any other exertion necessary to make a living. Such men as these are pernicious in every republic and in every province, but the most pernicious are those who, besides the aforementioned fortunes, also have castles at their command and subjects who obey them. Of these two kinds of men the kingdom of Naples, the papal states, Romagna, and Lombardy are full. Hence, it happens that in these provinces no republic or any body politic has ever arisen, for men of this kind are completely hostile to any form of civil life. And to try to introduce a republic into provinces organized in a similar way would not be possible, but to try to reorganize them, if there were anyone capable of serving as arbiter in such matters, would mean finding no other solution than to establish a kingdom there. The reason is this: that where there exists so much corrupt material that the laws are insufficient to restrain it, it is necessary to institute there, together with these laws, an even greater force, that is, a royal hand that with absolute and excessive power may impose a restraint on the excessive ambition and corruption of the mighty. This explanation can be verified through the example of Tuscany, where it may be observed how three republics, Florence, Siena, and Lucca, have existed over a long period of time within a small expanse of territory, and although the other cities of that province are in a way subservient to them, it is evident that with their courage or with their institutions, they maintain or would like to maintain their liberty. This is brought about by the fact that there are no lords with castles and very few or no noblemen in this province, but there exists such a state of equality that a prudent man with a knowledge of ancient civilizations could easily introduce a free form of government there. But Tuscany's misfortune has been so great that until recently, it has

not come upon any man who has been capable or knowledgeable enough to accomplish this.

It is possible, therefore, to draw a conclusion from this discourse: that anyone wishing to establish a republic where there
are many noblemen cannot do so unless he first does away with
them all; and that anyone wishing to establish a kingdom or a
principality where there is great equality cannot ever do so
unless he removes from that state of equality a large number of
men with ambitious and restless spirits and makes them noblemen in fact, and not in name only, giving them castles and possessions and favouring them with goods and with men, so that
when he is placed in their midst he may maintain his power
through their support, while through his presence they further
their ambition, and the others are forced to bear the yoke that
force and force alone can make them endure. Since a proportion
is established in this way between those who force and those
who are forced, each man will remain fixed in his own rank. And
since forming a republic out of a province well suited to being a
kingdom, and a kingdom out of one well suited to be a republic,
is a matter for a man who is rare in intelligence and authority,
there have been many who have wished to do so but few who
have known how to carry it out. For the grandeur of the task
frightens men in part and in part hinders them and causes them
to fail in the very first stages. I believe that this opinion of
mine—that where noblemen exist it is impossible to organize a
republic—will seem contrary to the experience of the Venetian
republic, in which no one may hold any rank whatsoever unless
he is a nobleman. To this objection, one can reply that such an
example does not constitute any contradiction, because the
noblemen of that republic are noblemen more in name than in
fact, for they obtain no large revenues from their possessions,
since their great wealth is founded upon commerce and move-
able property. Moreover, none of them possesses a castle or has
any jurisdiction over other men, but for them the title of nobleman is a title of dignity and respect without being based upon
any of those qualities required in other cities for bestowing the
title of nobleman. Just as other republics have divisions under
different names, so Venice is divided into noblemen and commoners, and the Venetians allow only the former to hold (or to

be able to hold) all the offices, while the others are completely excluded. This does not create disorder in that city for the reasons stated on another occasion. The founder of a republic should, therefore, organize it where there exists or has existed great equality, and on the contrary, whoever institutes a principality should do so where there exists great inequality; otherwise, he will do something lacking in proportion and of brief duration.

CHAPTER 56

Before Important Events Happen in a City or a Province, Signs that Foretell Them or Men Who Predict Them Appear

How this comes about I do not know, but both ancient and modern examples demonstrate that no serious event ever occurs in a city or a province that has not been predicted either by fortune-tellers, revelations, extraordinary events, or by other celestial signs. And so as not to stray far from home to prove this, everyone knows that Brother Girolamo Savonarola had foretold before it happened the coming of King Charles VIII of France into Italy,* and that, besides this, throughout all of Tuscany people were said to have seen and heard soldiers fighting against each other in the sky above Arezzo. Everyone knows, besides this, that before the death of Lorenzo de' Medici the elder,* the highest part of the Duomo was struck by a celestial thunderbolt, with very great damage to that edifice. Everybody knows as well that a short time before Piero Soderini, who had been made *gonfaloniere* for life by the Florentine people, was driven out of the city and stripped of his rank, the palace itself was struck by lightning.* More examples of this could be cited, which I shall pass over to avoid tedium. I shall only recount what Livy says about the situation before the Gauls invaded Rome: namely, that a certain plebeian named Marcus Caedicius reported to the senate that, while he was passing through Via Nuova at midnight, he had overheard a superhuman voice warning him to tell the magistrates that the Gauls were coming

to Rome.* The cause of such occurrences, I think, must be discussed and interpreted by men who have the knowledge of
things natural and supernatural, which we ourselves lack. It may
be, however, as some philosophers maintain, that the air is filled
with intelligences, who by means of natural abilities foresee
future events and, having compassion for men, warn them with
similar signs so that they can prepare their defences. Whatever
the case may be, however, it is evidently true, for after such
events, extraordinary and unusual things always happen in
every province.

CHAPTER 57

United the People Are Courageous, but
Divided They Are Weak

After their native city had been destroyed following the invasion of the Gauls, many Romans went to live in Veii against the
statutes and orders of the senate: to remedy this disorderly
behaviour, the senate, through its public edicts, enjoined everyone to return to live in Rome within a certain time period and
under certain penalties. At first these edicts were ridiculed by
those against whom they were passed; later, when the time to
obey them drew near, everyone obeyed. Livy offers these
remarks: 'their united defiance changed to individual obedience,
everyone having fears for himself.'* And truly, nothing can
demonstrate the nature of a crowd any better, in this regard,
than what is shown in this text. A crowd of people is audacious
in speaking out on many occasions against the decisions of their
ruler; then, when they see the penalty in sight, they do not trust
each other and race to obey. Thus, it is quite evident that you
should not give much consideration to what the people say concerning their good or bad inclinations as long as you are organized in such a way as to be able to maintain the people's
goodwill, if they are well disposed, or, if they are ill disposed, to
make provisions so that they cannot harm you. This refers to
those unfavourable inclinations that peoples possess, which
arise from no other cause than either having lost their liberty or

their prince whom they loved and who is still alive: inasmuch as unfavourable inclinations arising from these causes are formidable above all else, strong remedies are required to check them; other unfavourable inclinations of the people are easily remedied when they have no leaders to whom they may turn. Whereas, on the one hand, there is nothing more formidable than an uncontrolled crowd of people without a leader, still, on the other, there is nothing that is weaker, because despite the fact that the crowd may be armed, it will be easy to subdue it provided you have a place where you can take refuge from its first assault, because when their animosity cools down a bit and they all see that they must return home, they begin to have doubts about themselves and think about saving themselves, either by escaping or by coming to terms. Hence, a crowd of people excited in this fashion that wishes to avoid these dangers must immediately select from its own ranks a leader who will guide it, keep it united, and think about its defence, as Roman plebeians did when they left Rome after the death of Virginia, choosing twenty tribunes from their own ranks to save themselves.* If this is not done, then what Livy says in the passage cited above always happens: that all together the people are bold, but when each one then begins to think of the danger he faces, he becomes cowardly and weak.

CHAPTER 58

The Multitude Is Wiser and More Constant Than a Prince

Nothing is more unreliable or inconstant than a crowd of people: so affirms our Livy, like all the other historians. It often occurs that in recounting the deeds of men we see the crowd has condemned someone to death and has later lamented this fact and deeply regretted it, as we see the Roman people did with Manlius Capitolinus, whom they first condemned to death and then deeply regretted it. And these are the words of the author: 'Before long the people remembered only his good qualities, now that there was no danger from him, and regretted their loss.'* Elsewhere, when Livy is recounting the events that arose in Syracuse after the death of Hieronymus, grandson of Hiero, he declares: 'indeed, that is the nature of crowds: the mob is either a humble slave or a cruel master.'* I do not know if, wishing to defend an argument which, as I have said, all writers attack, I may not be assuming a task that is difficult and full of so many problems that it will be necessary for me either to abandon it, earning shame, or to pursue it, earning blame. But however that may be, I do not think, nor shall I ever think, that it is a mistake to defend any opinion through arguments without using either authority or force.

I must say, therefore, that the defect for which writers blame the crowd can be attributed to all men individually and most of all to princes, for each person who is not regulated by the laws will commit the very same errors as an uncontrolled crowd of people. And this can be easily understood, for there exist and have existed many princes, and the good and wise ones have been few in number: I am speaking of princes who have been able to break the constraints that can correct them, among whom may not be numbered those kings who arose in Egypt when, in the most distant antiquity, that province was governed by laws, nor those kings who arose in Sparta, nor those who in our own days arise in France, a kingdom which is regulated more by laws than any other kingdom in our times about which we have information. These kings that arise under such constitutions are not to be placed among that number whose individual natures we must consider in order to see if they resemble the multitude. Such a comparison must be made with a multitude likewise regulated by laws, just as they are, and that same goodness we find in these kings will be seen in that crowd, and we shall see that it neither rules arrogantly nor humbly obeys, just like the Roman people, who never humbly served nor arrogantly ruled, while the republic endured uncorrupted; indeed, with their institutions and magistrates, they held to their ranks honourably. When it became necessary to rise up against a powerful individual, they did so, as can be seen in the cases of Manlius, the decemvirs, and others whom they sought to suppress; and when it was necessary to obey the dictators and the consuls for the public welfare, they did so. If the Roman people regretted the death of Manlius Capitolanus, it is not surprising, for they regretted the loss of his exceptional abilities, which were such that their memory alone aroused everyone's compassion, and they would have had the power to produce the same effect in a prince, because all writers believe the rule that exceptional ability is to be praised and to be admired even in one's enemies. Moreover, if Manlius had been resurrected amidst so much regret, the people of Rome would have pronounced upon him the same judgement as they had before, after they dragged him out of prison and a short time later condemned him to death; notwithstanding this fact, we can see princes reputed to be wise who have put to death some person and then deeply regretted it, as Alexander did in the case of Cleitus and his other friends, and as Herod did with Mariamne.* But what our historian says about the nature of the crowd, he does not apply to a multitude regulated by laws, as was the Roman people, but to an uncontrolled multitude, like the one in Syracuse, which made the same errors that angry and undisciplined men such as Alexander the Great and Herod committed in the cases mentioned. Still, the nature of the multitude is no more to be blamed than that of princes, for all err in equal measure when they err without fear of punishment. Besides those I have mentioned, there are many examples of this both among Roman emperors and among other tyrants and princes, where we can see as much inconstancy and as many changes in character as were ever found in any crowd.

I conclude, therefore, contrary to common opinion that says that peoples (when they hold power) are variable, changeable, and ungrateful, affirming that in them there exist no other sins than exist in particular princes. If anyone were to blame peoples and princes alike, he might be telling the truth; but he would be deceiving himself by excluding princes, for a people that exercises power and is well organized will be stable, prudent, and grateful no differently from a prince, or better than a prince, and will even be considered wise; and, on the other hand, a prince freed from the restraint of the laws will be even more ungrateful, variable, and imprudent than a people. The variation in their conduct arises not from a different nature (for this in all men is the same, and if there is a surplus of good, it resides in the people), but from having more or less respect for the laws under which one or the other lives. Anyone who considers the Roman people will see that for 400 years they were enemies of the very title of king and lovers of the glory and the welfare of their native city, and he will see many examples displayed by them in Rome that bear witness to both of these qualities. If anyone were to remind me of the ingratitude that the multitude displayed against Scipio, I would respond with the same argument I made above when this subject was discussed at length, where it was demonstrated that peoples are less ungrateful than princes.* But with respect to prudence and stability, I would say that a people is more prudent, more stable, and of better judgement than a prince. It is not without reason that the voice of a people is compared with that of God, for it is obvious that popular opinion is wondrously effective in its predictions, to the extent that it seems to be able to foresee its own good and evil fortune through some occult power. As for making judgements, when the people hear two opposing speakers of equal skill taking different sides, it is only on the rarest occasions that it does not select the best opinion and that it is not capable of understanding the truth it hears. If in matters of courage or of seeming utility, as was mentioned above, the people errs, a prince will also often err because of his own passions, which are more numerous than those of a people. It is also evident that in the selection of magistrates the people make far better choices than a prince, for one can never persuade the people that it is good to elect to public office an infamous man with corrupted habits, something that a prince can be persuaded to do easily and in a thousand ways. It can be seen how a people may begin to loathe something and will remain of this opinion for many centuries, something that is not true of a prince. In both of these two matters I think the Roman people bears sufficient witness, for in so many hundreds of years and in so many elections of consuls and tribunes, they did not make four choices which they were forced to regret. And, as I have mentioned, the Roman people so hated the very title of king that no merit on the part of any citizen who aspired to that title could enable him to avoid the just penalties. Besides this, it is evident that cities where the people hold power quickly make enormous conquests and much greater ones than cities which have always been under the rule of a prince, as Rome did after she drove out the kings, and Athens after she freed herself of Pisistratus. This can arise from nothing other than the fact that governments by peoples are better than governments by princes. Nor would I wish that all of what our historian says on this matter in the previously cited passage or in any other be used to counter this view of mine, because if we are to discuss all the disorders under peoples and all those under princes, all the glories under peoples and all those under princes, we shall see that in goodness and in glory, the people are by far superior. And if princes are superior to the people in enacting laws, forming civil societies, establishing statues and new institutions, the people are so much superior in maintaining the things established that, without any doubt, they add to the glory of those who established them.

Finally, to conclude this argument, let me say that just as the states of princes have long endured, the states of republics have long endured, and both have needed to be regulated by laws, because a prince who is able to do what he wishes is mad, and a people that can do what it wishes is not wise. If, therefore, we are discussing a prince legally bound by the laws and a people enchained by them, more ability can be observed in the people than in the prince; if we are discussing both of them in an unregulated state, fewer errors will be observed in the people than in the prince, and these will be less serious and will have greater remedies. But a good man can speak to an intractable and unruly people and can easily lead them back down the right path; nobody can speak to an evil prince, nor is there any other remedy for him than the sword. From this, one can speculate about the importance of their respective maladies: that is, if words are enough to cure the malady of the people, and that of the prince requires a sword, there will never be anyone who will not judge that where there is greater need for a cure, there exist greater flaws. When a people is thoroughly unrestrained, neither its foolish actions nor the evil at hand need be feared, but rather the evil that may arise from them, since a tyrant may arise amid so much confusion. But with evil princes the opposite happens: the present evil is to be feared and the future holds hope, since men persuade themselves that the prince's wicked life can cause a state of liberty to arise. Thus, you see the difference between the two, which is the difference between things that are and things that are to be. The cruelties of the multitude are directed against those whom they fear will take possession of the public property; those of a prince are directed against anyone he fears will take possession of his own property. But this sentiment against the people arises because everyone speaks badly about the people without fear and in complete freedom even while the people rule; everyone always speaks badly about princes with a thousand fears and a thousand reservations. Nor does it seem beside the point to me, since this subject leads me to it, to discuss in the following chapter the kinds of confederations that are most reliable, those created with a republic or those created with a prince.

CHAPTER 59

Which Confederation or Other Kind of League Is Most Reliable, That Created With a Republic or That Created With a Prince

Because it happens every day that one prince and another, or one republic and another forge a league and a friendship with each other, and, likewise confederations and agreements are also formed between a republic and a prince, it seems proper to me to examine whose word is more reliable and should be given greater consideration, that of a republic or that of a prince. After examining everything, I believe that in many cases they are similar, and that in some cases there is some difference. I believe furthermore that agreements made by force will never be observed either by a prince or by a republic; I believe that when the fear of losing the state arises, both kinds of government will break faith with you and will treat you with ingratitude in order to avoid losing it. Demetrius, the man who was called conqueror of cities, had bestowed countless benefits upon the Athenians: then it happened that after he had been defeated by his enemies and sought refuge in Athens, as in a friendly city obligated to him, he was not received by that city; this grieved him even more than if he had suffered the loss of his troops and his entire army.* Defeated by Caesar in Thessaly, Pompey took refuge in Egypt with Ptolemy, whom in the past he had put back on the throne, and he was killed by him.* Such things are seen to have the same causes; none the less, more humanity was displayed and less injury inflicted by the republic than by the prince. Wherever fear exists, however, we shall in fact discover the same kind of loyalty. And if it is discovered that either a republic or a prince runs a risk in keeping faith with you, this can also arise from similar causes. As for the prince, it can very well happen that he may be the friend of some other powerful prince who lacks the opportunity to defend him at that moment, but he can still hope that with the passage of time his ally will restore him to his principality, or he may certainly believe that, since he has followed him as a supporter, this prince will make no agreements or treaties with his enemies. Of this type were those princes of the kingdom of Naples who supported the French factions, and among republics of this type were Saguntum in Spain,* which awaited its destruction because it took the side of Rome, and Florence, which in 1512 supported the French factions. When everything has been taken into account, I believe that in these cases, where danger is imminent, somewhat more stability will be found in republics than in princes. Yet, although republics may possess the same courage and inclinations as a prince, the fact that they move more slowly will always cause them to find it more difficult to come to a decision than a prince, and, as a result, they will always find it more difficult to break their word than he will. Confederations are broken to gain some advantage. In this respect, republics are far more likely to abide by agreements than princes. And, it is possible to cite examples where the smallest advantage has caused a prince to break his word, but where even an enormous advantage has not caused a republic to break its word: for example, the policy Themistocles proposed to the Athenians, to whom in a speech he claimed to have some advice that would be highly beneficial to their city but that he could not say what it was in order to avoid revealing it, since to do so would deny them the opportunity of discovering it. As a result, the people of Athens elected Aristides to whom he might communicate the proposal, so that they could later decide according to Aristides' opinion in the matter; Themistocles demonstrated to Aristides that the fleet of all the Greeks, while it was still bound by their word of honour, was in a position where it could easily be captured or destroyed, which would make the Athenians sole arbiters of that province. When Aristides reported to the people that the proposal of Themistocles was most advantageous but extremely dishonest, the people completely rejected it for that reason.* Philip of Macedonia and other princes would not have acted in this fashion, for they sought and gained more advantage by breaking their word than by any other method. With respect to breaking pacts on account of some failure to comply with them, this is a normal occurrence about which I shall speak, but I shall speak about those treaties which are broken for extraordinary reasons, and in these cases, from what we have seen, I believe that the people commit less serious errors than the prince, and that for this reason, it is possible to place more trust in the people than in the prince.

CHAPTER 60
How the Consulate and Every Other Magistracy in Rome Were Bestowed Without Respect to Age

It is evident from the unfolding of history that after the consulate came to the plebeians, the Roman republic granted this office to its citizens without respect to age or family; indeed, respect for age never existed in Rome, but the city always sought to discover exceptional ability, whether it was to be found in the young or the old. The example of Valerius Corvinus, who was made consul at the age of 23, bears witness to this fact; and when speaking to his soldiers, this Valerius declared that the consulate was 'the reward of ability, not of birth'.* Whether this opinion was a well-considered one or not should be thoroughly discussed. As for birth, it was disregarded out of necessity, and, as we have remarked on another occasion,* the same necessity experienced by Rome will be felt in every city that wishes to produce the same results Rome did, because men cannot be burdened by hardships without a reward, nor can they be deprived of the hope of obtaining such a reward without danger. And it soon seemed appropriate, therefore, that the plebeians should have the hope of obtaining the consulate, and that they should nourish this hope for a time without its being fulfilled; later, hope alone was no longer enough, and it was necessary to make it a reality. For the city that does not make use of its plebeians in some glorious enterprise can treat them as it wishes, as has been argued elsewhere,* but the city that wishes to do what Rome did does not have to make this kind of distinction. Given that this is the case, the distinction based on time has nothing to be said for it, and on the contrary must be disregarded, and when the multitude elects a young man to a position which needs the prudence of an older man, some illustrious action on his part should be the cause for elevating him to that rank. When a young man has such exceptional ability that he makes himself known through some illustrious deed, it would be a most damaging thing if the city were not able to avail itself of his talent, and if it had to wait until age has affected that strength of mind and readiness of his early years of which at that age his native city could have availed itself, as Rome availed itself of Valerius Corvinus, of Scipio, of Pompey, and of many others who triumphed while still very young.

BOOK II

PREFACE

Men always praise ancient times and condemn the present, but not always with good reason, and they are such partisans of the past that they celebrate not only those eras they have come to know through the records that historians have left behind but also those that they, having grown old, remember having seen in their younger days. When their opinion is mistaken, as it is most of the time, I am persuaded that there are several reasons leading them to make this error. The first reason is, I believe, that we do not know the complete truth about ancient affairs, and that most frequently those matters that would bring disgrace on those times are hidden, while other matters that would bestow them with glory are recounted most fully and magnificently. Most historians follow the fortune of the conquerors, and in order to render their victories more glorious not only amplify what they have most skilfully achieved but also magnify the actions of their enemies in such a fashion that anyone born afterward in either of the two provinces, that of the victor or that of the vanquished, has reason to marvel at those men and those times and is compelled to the highest degree to admire and to love them. Besides this, since men hate things either out of fear or out of envy, two very powerful explanations for hatred of things in the past are eliminated, for they cannot harm you nor can they give you cause for envy. But the contrary occurs with those matters which you handle or observe, no part of which is hidden from you, because you know them in great detail, and recognizing in them along with the good, numerous other details which are not so pleasing, you are constrained to judge them as being much inferior to ancient affairs even though, in reality, present affairs may be much more deserving of glory and fame; I am not discussing matters pertaining to the arts, which shine with so much brilliance in themselves that the times can neither take much away from them nor bestow much more glory upon them than they intrinsically deserve, but I am speaking rather of those matters pertaining to the lives and customs of men, for which we do not see such clear evidence.

I repeat, therefore, that this general practice of praise and condemnation described above exists, but it is not true that those who engage in it are always in error. It is sometimes necessary for people to make judgements, since human affairs are always in motion and are either on the rise or in decline. It is possible for a city or a province to possess a body politic well organized by some excellent man, and, for a time, by virtue of the skill of such a founder, always to progress toward the better. Anyone, therefore, who is born in such a state and praises ancient times more than modern ones is deceiving himself, and his deception is brought about by those matters that have been discussed above. But those who are born later on in that same city or province after the time of its decline toward the worst has arrived do not, then, deceive themselves. As I reflect upon how these affairs proceed, I conclude that the world has always been in the same state, and that although there has always been as much good as evil in it, this evil and this good vary from province to province; this can be seen from what we know of ancient kingdoms that differed from one another according to the variations in their customs, while the world remained as it always had been. There is only this one difference, that the world first lodged its exceptional ability in Assyria, then moved to Media, and later passed into Persia, and from there it entered Italy and Rome.* If, after the Roman empire, no other empire has followed it that has endured, nor a single place in which the world has gathered together all its exceptional ability, it can be seen nevertheless that this ability has been distributed among many nations where men live ably, such as the kingdom of the Franks, the kingdom of the Turks—that of the Sultan—and, today, the peoples of Germany, and before them that Saracen sect that achieved so many great things and occupied so much of the world that it destroyed the Roman empire of the east.* In all these provinces, therefore, after the Romans came to ruin, as well as in all these sects, this exceptional ability has existed and still exists in those where such ability is still sought after and justly praised. Anyone who is born in these provinces and praises past times more than present ones may be deceiving himself, but whoever is born in Italy or Greece and has not become either an Ultramontane in Italy or a Turk in Greece has reason to condemn his times and to praise others, because in those of the past many things existed that made them marvellous, while in present times nothing whatsoever redeems them from utter misery, infamy, and disgrace, in these places where there is no regard for religion, laws, or the profession of arms but only stains of the worst kind of filth. And these vices are all the more detestable as they are found among those who sit on tribunals, command others, and want to be revered.

But returning to our argument, let me say that if human judgement is corrupted in judging whether the present is better than the ancient past, which, because of its antiquity, men cannot know as perfectly as their own times, it should not be corrupted in those who are older as they judge the periods of their youth and their old age, since they have known and observed both equally. This would be true if men throughout all the periods of their lives retained the same opinions and the same appetites. But since these vary, while the times do not, the same opinions and appetites cannot appear in men, since they have other desires, other pleasures, and other concerns in their old age than those they had in their youth. When men grow older, they lose strength but gain in judgement and prudence, and, of necessity, the things that seemed bearable and good in their youth later come to be unbearable and bad as they grow older, and although they ought to place the blame for this on their own judgement, they blame the times instead. Besides all this, human appetites are insatiable,* for while we are endowed by nature with the power and will to desire everything, and by fortune with the ability to obtain little of it, the result is a continuous discontent in the minds of men and a dissatisfaction with the things they possess; this causes them to condemn present times, to praise the past, and to long for the future, even though they do so without any reasonable motive. I do not know, therefore, whether I deserve to be considered among those who deceive themselves if, in these discourses of mine, I praise too lavishly the times of the ancient Romans and condemn our own. Certainly, if the exceptional ability that prevailed then and the vice that prevails today were not clearer than the sun, I would speak more cautiously for fear of falling into the same deception for which I criticize others. But since the matter is so obvious that everyone can see it, I shall boldly proclaim in an open way what I understand of ancient times and of our own, so that the minds of the young men who will read these writings of mine can avoid the errors of the present and be prepared to imitate the past whenever fortune provides them with the proper occasion. Thus, it is the duty of a good man to teach others the good you yourself were unable to accomplish due to the malignity of the times or to fortune, so that among the many people capable of such actions, some of those more favoured by heaven may accomplish it. And since I have discussed the decisions the Romans took in matters pertaining to their internal affairs in the discourses of the preceding book, in this one we shall speak of those decisions the Roman people made pertaining to the expansion of their empire.*

CHAPTER I

What Was the Main Reason for the Empire the Romans Acquired, Ability or Fortune?*

Many have held the opinion, among them Plutarch, a most authoritative writer,* that the Roman people, in acquiring their empire, were favoured more by fortune than by exceptional ability. Among the other reasons he sets forth, Plutarch declares that the Roman people by their own admission attributed all their victories to fortune, since they built more temples to the goddess of fortune than to any other deity. It seems that Livy adheres to the same opinion, because he rarely has any Roman deliver a speech in which he speaks of ability without mentioning fortune. This is an argument I do not want to accept, nor do I believe that it can be supported, because, if no republic has ever made gains equal to those of Rome, this arises from the fact that no republic was ever organized so that it could acquire territory as Rome did. The exceptional ability of its armies enabled Rome to acquire its empire, and its mode of conduct and its own way of existence, discovered by its first lawgiver, allowed it to hold on to its conquests, as will be recounted in more detail in the discourses to follow. These writers declare that it was due to fortune and not the exceptional ability of the Roman people that they never became involved in two great wars at the same time; for they did not go to war against the Latins until they not only defeated the Samnites but actually waged war in their defence; nor did they ever fight the Etruscans until they had first subjugated the Latins and had completely weakened the Samnites by frequent routs: if two of these powers had joined together when they were fresh and whole, it is no doubt possible to speculate that the downfall of the Roman republic would have ensued. But, however these things came about, the Romans never happened to wage two crucial wars at the same time: on the contrary, it seems that the beginning of one war always saw the end of another, or the ending of one war gave rise to another. This can easily be seen from the order of the wars they waged, because, if we set aside the wars they waged before Rome was sacked by the Gauls, we see that while they fought with the Aequi and the Volscians, so long as these two peoples were powerful no others ever engaged them in warfare. After they had been subdued the war against the Samnites broke out, and although the Latin peoples rebelled against the Romans before this war was over, when this rebellion took place the Samnites had nevertheless already formed an alliance with Rome, and they assisted the Romans with their armies to curb the insolence of the Latins. When the Latins were subdued, the war with the Samnites broke out again. Once the Samnites were broken by the many defeats they suffered, the war against the Etruscans began. When this one was concluded, the Samnites once again rose up when Pyrrhus passed into Italy. After Pyrrhus was repulsed and driven back into Greece, the Romans started the first war against the Carthaginians, which scarcely ended before all the Gauls on both sides of the Alps conspired together against the Romans until, between Popolonia and Pisa, where the tower of St Vincent stands today, they were overcome in a great slaughter. When this war was over, for the space of twenty years the Romans experienced wars of little consequence, because they did not fight with anyone except the Ligurians and the Gauls who remained in Lombardy. And they continued in this fashion until the second Carthaginian war broke out, which kept Italy occupied for sixteen years. When this war ended with the greatest glory, the Macedonian war broke out; when this was over, the war with Antiochus and Asia followed. After that victory there remained in all the world neither prince nor republic that, individually or altogether, could oppose Roman forces.

But before this last victory, anyone who will give careful thought to the order of these wars and the manner in which they were conducted will discover in them good fortune mixed with exceptional skill and the greatest prudence. Thus, anyone examining the cause of such good fortune would find it quite easily, because it is certainly true that when a prince or a people achieves such a reputation that every other prince or people nearby is afraid to mount an attack alone and remains in a state of fear, it will always happen that none of them will ever attack unless driven by necessity, so that such a powerful prince or people will have, as it were, the choice of waging war upon whichever of its neighbours it chooses, while holding the others at bay with its diligence. Such neighbours will easily be kept at bay, partly because they respect this power and partly because they are deceived by the means used to lull them to sleep. Other, more distant powers which have no dealings with them will consider these matters too remote to concern them; they will continue in this error until the fire reaches them, and when this occurs they will have no means of extinguishing it, unless they employ their own forces, and their own forces will be insufficient, since this one will have become extremely powerful. I should like to pass over how the Samnites stood by and watched while the Roman people conquered the Volscians and the Aequi, and in order not to be too long-winded, I shall mention only the Carthaginians, who were a great power and enjoyed great esteem when the Romans were fighting with the Samnites and the Etruscans, because they already held all of Africa, Sardinia, and Sicily, and they had partially conquered Spain. Their power, along with their great distance from the confines of the Roman people, caused them never to think about attacking

Rome or of assisting the Samnites and the Etruscans; on the contrary, they acted as people are apt to act when things progress more or less in their favour, forging links with the Romans and seeking their friendship. Nor did they ever become aware of the error they had made until the Romans, having conquered all the peoples between them and the Carthaginians, began to fight them for control of Sicily and Spain. The same thing happened to the Gauls that happened to the Carthaginians, and also to King Philip of Macedonia and to Antiochus: each one of them believed that while the Roman people were occupied with another power, this other power would conquer the Romans and that they would have time to defend themselves against them through either peace or war. In this sense, I believe that the good fortune the Romans enjoyed in this regard would be enjoyed by all those rulers who would conduct themselves as did the Romans and who possessed the same special ability as they did.

It would be pertinent to demonstrate the means adopted by the Roman people in entering the territories of others if we had not discussed them at length in our treatise on principalities,* where this matter is discussed at length. I shall say only this, to be brief: the Romans always sought to have some friend in new territories to serve as a ladder to climb up or a gate through which to enter or as a means to hold on to them; this is evident from the way they entered Samnium with the assistance of the Capuans,* Etruria with that of the Camertines,* Sicily with that of the Mamertines,* Spain with that of the Saguntines,* Africa with that of Masinissa,* Greece with that of the Aetolians,* Asia with that of Eumenes and other Asian princes,* and Gaul with that of the Massilienses and the Aedui.* And so the Romans never lacked such support to facilitate their undertakings, or to acquire and to hold such provinces. Thus, the peoples who observe their practice will discover that they have less need of fortune than those who are not good observers. So that everyone can better understand how much more effective their exceptional skill was than their fortune in acquiring their empire, we shall discuss in the following chapter the character of those peoples with whom the Romans had to fight, and the stubbornness with which they defended their liberty.

CHAPTER 2

What Kinds of Peoples the Romans Had to Fight, and How Stubbornly These Peoples Defended Their Liberty

Nothing made it more difficult for the Romans to overcome the surrounding peoples and parts of the more distant provinces than the love many peoples in those times had for liberty, which they defended so stubbornly that they would never have been subjugated except by extraordinary ability. The dangers to which they exposed themselves to preserve or to regain their liberty, and the revenge they took against those who had deprived them of it are known through many examples. The lessons of history also teach us the injuries those peoples and their cities suffered because of their servitude. Whereas in our own times only a single province can be said to contain within it free cities, in ancient times many entirely free peoples lived throughout the provinces.* It is evident that in those times which we are presently discussing, throughout Italy, from the Alps that now divide Tuscany from Lombardy down to the toe of Italy, all the peoples were free, as were the Etruscans, the Romans, the Samnites, and many other peoples who lived in the rest of Italy. Nor has it ever been argued that there was any king other than those who reigned in Rome and Porsenna, king of the Etruscans, the extinction of whose lineage is not explained by history. But it is quite evident that in those times when the Romans went to lay siege to Veii, Etruria was free, and it took such pleasure in its liberty and so hated the very name of prince that when the Veientes created a king in Veii for their defence and asked the Etruscans for assistance against the Romans, the Etruscans, after much consultation, decided not to give help to the Veientes as long as they lived under a king, judging that it was not good policy to defend the native city of those who had already made it subject to someone else. It is easy to understand how this affection for a free way of life arose in those peoples, because experience demonstrates that cities have never enlarged their dominion or increased their wealth unless they have lived in liberty. It is truly a marvellous thing to consider what greatness Athens achieved in the space of one hundred years after the city freed itself from the tyranny of Pisistratus.* But it is even more wondrous to consider how much greatness Rome achieved after it freed itself of its kings. The reason is easy to understand, because it is not the private good but the common good that makes cities great. And without any doubt, this common good is pursued only in a republic, because everything that meets its needs is carried out, and however much harm might be done to this or that private individual, there are so many who benefit from this common good that they are able to promote it, despite the inclination of the few who are oppressed by it. The opposite occurs when there is a prince, for in most cases whatever works to his benefit harms the city, while whatever works to the city's benefit harms him. As a result, as soon as a tyranny arises to replace a free government, the least amount of harm that may occur in such cities is that they no longer move forward or grow either in power or wealth; in most cases—actually, in all of them—it happens that such cities go into decline. And if fate might act in such a way that a tyrant of exceptional ability were to arise, whose boldness and skill at arms might increase his dominion, this would result in no benefit to the republic but, rather, to him alone, because he cannot honour any of the citizens over whom he exerts his tyranny, no matter how brave or good they might be, since he will not wish to be suspicious of them. Nor can he subjugate or make the cities he conquers tributaries to the city in which he acts as tyrant, since making the city powerful does not work to his benefit, but rather it works to his benefit to keep the state disunited and to have each city and province acknowledge him alone. In such a way, only he profits from his acquisitions and not his native city. And anyone who wishes to confirm this opinion with countless other arguments should read Xenophon's treatise entitled *On Tyranny*.* It is not surprising, therefore, that ancient peoples persecuted their tyrants with such hatred and loved a free way of life, and that the very name of liberty was so revered by them. This was the case when Hieronymus, the grandson of Hiero of Syracuse, was assassinated in Syracuse, for when the news of his death reached his army, which was not far from Syracuse, the troops first began to run riot and to take up arms against his killers, but when they heard that in Syracuse the word 'liberty' was being proclaimed, they calmed down completely, captivated by that name, and putting aside their anger against the tyrannicides, they began considering how a free way of life might be organized in that city. It is also no wonder that such peoples carried out extraordinary acts of revenge against those who had deprived them of liberty. There have been numerous examples of this, but I shall refer only to one of them, which occurred in Corcyra, a Greek city, during the Peloponnesian War; Greece was at that time divided into two factions, one of which followed the Athenians and the other the Spartans, and as a result, in many cities that were divided between the two factions, one faction sought Sparta's friendship, and the other that of Athens; and it happened that in Corcyra the nobles prevailed and took away the people's freedom, but the popular party, with Athenian assistance, regrouped their forces, and after they had laid hands on all the nobility they locked them inside a prison large enough to hold them all; from which they then took them out, eight or ten at a time, under the guise of sending them into exile in different places, and put them to death in many cruel ways. When those who remained realized what was taking place, they decided, in so far as it was possible, to avoid such an ignominious death, and arming themselves as best they could, they fought with those who tried to enter, defending the entrance to the prison, so that when the people heard the noise, coming together, they exposed the upper part of the building and suffocated the prisoners under the debris.* Many other similar horrible and noteworthy events subsequently took place in that province, and this clearly demonstrates how the liberty that has been taken from you is avenged with greater ferocity than the liberty that someone tried to take away from you.*

In considering, therefore, why all the peoples of ancient times were greater lovers of liberty than those of our own day, I believe this arises from the same cause that today makes men less strong, which I believe lies in the difference between our education and that of antiquity, based upon the difference between our religion and that of antiquity. For, while our religion has shown us truth and the true path, it also makes us place a lower value on worldly honour, whereas the pagans,* who greatly

valued honour and considered it the highest good, were more
ferocious in their actions. This can be seen in many of their customs, beginning with the magnificence of their sacrifices as
compared to the modesty of our own, in which there is some
pomp that is more delicate than magnificent but no bold or ferocious action. In their rites neither pomp nor magnificence was
lacking in the ceremonies, but there was, in addition, the act of
sacrifice full of blood and cruelty, and the slaughter of a great
number of animals, a spectacle which inspired awe and rendered
the men who witnessed it equally awesome. Besides this, ancient
religion beatified only men fully possessed of worldly glory,
such as the leaders of armies and the rulers of republics. Our religion has more often glorified humble and contemplative men
rather than active ones. Moreover, our religion has defined the
supreme good as humility, abjection, and contempt of worldly
things; ancient religion located it in greatness of mind, strength
of body, and in all the other things apt to make men the
strongest. And if our religion requires that you have inner
strength, it wants you to have the capacity to endure suffering
more than to undertake brave deeds. This way of living seems,
therefore, to have made the world weak and to have given it over
to be plundered by wicked men, who are easily able to dominate
it, since in order to go to paradise, most men think more about
enduring their pains than about avenging them. Although it
appears that the world has become soft and heaven has been disarmed, without a doubt this arises more from the cowardice of
men who have interpreted our religion according to an ideal of
freedom from earthly toil and not according to one of exceptional ability. For if they would consider how our religion permits us to exalt and defend our native land, they would see that
it also wants us to love and honour it and to prepare ourselves in
such a way that we can defend it. It is, therefore, that other type
of education and these false interpretations that explain why we
no longer find as many republics in the world as existed in
ancient times, nor, as a consequence, as much love of liberty
among the peoples as there was then. Yet, I also believe the
reason for this to be that the Roman empire with its arms and its
grandeur destroyed all the republics and all the self-governing
states. Although this empire later disintegrated, the cities have

still not been able to regroup themselves again nor to reorganize themselves into a body politic except for a very few places within that empire. Still, be that as it may, in even the very remotest parts of the globe the Romans encountered alliances among republics that were extremely well armed and obstinate in the defence of their liberty. This demonstrates that the Roman people would never have been able to overcome such republics without rare and extraordinary ability.

To give an example of a member of such a confederation, I want that of the Samnites to suffice: it seems a marvellous thing, and Livy admits it, that the Samnites were so powerful and their armed strength so effective that they were able to resist the Romans until the time of the consul Papirius Cursor, son of the first Papirius (which was a space of forty-six years), following many defeats, the destruction of their lands, and many massacres within their own territory; especially if one sees that this land, where there were so many cities and men, is today almost uninhabited, since at that time it was so well organized and had so much strength that it would have been invincible had it not been assaulted by Roman skill.* It is easy to discern the origins of such order and such disorder, because it all comes from living at one time in a free society and then in one that is servile. As I said above, all countries and provinces living in liberty have gained enormous advantages from it, because wherever there is a larger population, marriages are easier and more desirable on the part of men; since each man willingly procreates those children he believes he can support without fearing that their patrimony will be taken away from them and knowing not only that they will be born free and not as slaves, but that they may, through their own exceptional ability, become leaders in the city. Wealth will be seen to increase more rapidly there, both that which derives from agriculture and that from crafts and trade, because each man more willingly increases those things and seeks to acquire those goods that he believes, once acquired, he can enjoy. Thus, it comes about that men competing with each other think about both private and public benefits, and both increase at a miraculous rate.

The opposite of all these things follows in those countries that live in servitude; the further away they move from their accustomed good, the harsher is their servitude. And of all the harshest forms of servitude, the most harsh is that which subjugates you to a republic: first, because it is the most long-lasting and offers less hope of escaping from it; secondly, because the goal of a republic is to enervate and weaken all other bodies in order to strengthen its own. This is not done by a prince who subjugates you, as long as this prince is not some barbarian ruler or a destroyer of lands and a devastator of all human civilization, like the oriental rulers. But, if such a prince possesses humane and ordinary methods, in most instances he will love his subject cities equally and leave to them all their crafts and almost all their ancient institutions. As a result, although they are unable to grow as if they were free, they will not come to ruin as if they were enslaved, and here I mean the kind of servitude which develops in cities subject to a foreigner, since I spoke earlier about those cities subjugated to one of their own citizens. Anyone, therefore, who considers everything that has been said will not be amazed at the power the Samnites possessed when they were free and at their weakness when they subsequently fell into servitude, and Livy testifies to this fact in more than one passage, and especially in discussing the war with Hannibal, where he shows that when the Samnites were oppressed by a legion of men stationed in Nola, they sent ambassadors to Hannibal to beg him to come to their rescue; in their speech, these ambassadors stated that they had fought with the Romans with their own troops and their own commanders for a hundred years, and on many occasions they had withstood two consular armies and two consuls, but now they had come to such a sorry state that they could hardly defend themselves from a small Roman legion in Nola.

CHAPTER 3

Rome Became a Great City by Destroying the Surrounding Cities and by Freely Receiving Foreigners into Its Ranks

'A result of the fall of Alba was an increase in the size of Rome.'*
Those who design a city to create a great empire must strive

with great diligence to fill it full of inhabitants, because without this abundance of men it will never succeed in becoming a great city. This may be done in two ways: either through love or through force. It is done through love by keeping the pathways open and safe for foreigners who wish to come there to live, so that everyone may live there willingly; it is done through force, after nearby cities are destroyed, by sending their inhabitants to live in your city. This method was so strictly observed by Rome that in the era of its sixth king,* 80,000 men capable of bearing arms lived in Rome, for the Romans wished to act like good farmers who, in order to make a plant grow and produce mature fruit, prune off the first branches it puts out, so that the sap* remaining in the root of the plant will cause it to grow greener and bear more fruit with the passage of time. That this means of enlarging a city and creating an empire is both good and necessary may be demonstrated by the examples of Sparta and Athens, two extremely well-armed republics organized by the best laws, which none the less never brought them to match the grandeur of the Roman empire; and Rome seemed far more disorderly and much less well organized than these republics. No other reason can be cited for this than the one presented above: Rome, having enlarged its population through those two methods, was already capable of putting 80,000 armed men in the field, while Sparta and Athens never surpassed a total of 20,000 each. This situation arose not because Rome had a more advantageous location than these two cities, but only because of a different mode of conduct. Lycurgus, the founder of the Spartan republic, believing that nothing was more likely to corrupt his laws than the admixture of new inhabitants, did everything to prevent outsiders from having any contact with Sparta, and besides preventing intermarriage and the exchange of civilities or other types of social intercourse that bring people together, he ordered that in his republic people should use only leather money* so that nobody might be tempted to come there to carry on commerce or to practise any other kind of craft or trade, with the result that the city was never able to enlarge its population. Since all our actions imitate nature, it is not possible nor natural for a slender trunk to support heavy branches. Thus, a small republic cannot occupy cities or kingdoms that are stronger or larger than it is; and if, nevertheless, it does occupy them, such a republic will experience the same fate as the tree whose branches are larger than its trunk, which, sustaining its branches with difficulty, will be bent by every little breeze that blows. This situation is seen to have come about in Sparta after it had occupied all the cities of Greece, for no sooner did Thebes rebel than all the other cities rebelled as well, and the trunk remained alone without any branches. The same thing could not happen to Rome, since its trunk was so large that it could easily support any branch. Thus this mode of conducting affairs, together with the others that will be described below, made Rome great and extremely powerful. Livy demonstrates this in a few words when he says: 'A result of the fall of Alba was an increase in the size of Rome.'*

CHAPTER 4
Republics Have Employed Three Methods of Expansion

Anyone who has studied the ancient histories discovers that republics have employed three methods of expansion. One is that which the ancient Etruscans employed, which consisted of a confederation of many republics in which none surpassed the others in either authority or rank; and as they acquired territory, they made the other cities their companions just as the Swiss have done in our own times, and as in ancient times the Achaeans and the Aetolians did in Greece. Since the Romans waged many wars with the Etruscans, I shall present a detailed account of them in order better to demonstrate the merits of this first method.

In Italy before the advent of the Roman empire, the Etruscans were extremely powerful on both land and sea, and although no detailed historical account of their affairs exists, there nevertheless still remain some brief record and some trace of their greatness. It is known that they sent a colony, which they called Adria, to the sea-coast above them, which was so noble that it gave its name to the sea that the Latins still call the Adriatic. It is also known that their forces were obeyed from the shore of the Tiber to the foot of the Alps that now circle the largest section of Italy, notwithstanding the fact that 200 years before the Romans grew so greatly in strength, the Etruscans lost their dominion over that territory which is now called Lombardy, the province which was occupied by the Gauls. Driven either by necessity or attracted by the sweetness of the fruits, and especially of the wine, the Gauls entered Italy under their duke Bellovesus. After defeating and driving away the inhabitants of that province, they settled in that place where they built many cities; they called the province Gaul after the name they then bore, and they retained this land until they were conquered by the Romans. Thus, the Etruscans lived in equality and proceeded to enlarge their territory employing the first method that was mentioned above: there were twelve cities, among which were Chiusi, Veii, Arezzo, Fiesole, Volterra, and other such cities, which governed their empire through a confederation. Nor were they able to pass beyond Italy in making conquests, and the greater part of Italy remained intact for reasons that will be explained below.

The second method is to make alliances for yourself, but not to the extent that you do not retain the position of command, the seat of the empire, and the credit for its achievements: the method that was employed by the Romans. The third method is quickly to obtain subjects rather than allies for yourself, as did the Spartans and Athenians. Of these three methods, this last one is entirely useless, as can be seen in the cases of the two republics mentioned above, which came to ruin for no other reason than because they had acquired territory that they were unable to hold. Thus, assuming the burden of ruling a city with violence, especially those accustomed to living in liberty, is a difficult and trying undertaking, and if you are not armed and well equipped, you can neither command nor rule them. In order to be organized like this, it is necessary to have allies who will assist you and increase the population of your city. Since these two cities did neither the one nor the other, their mode of conduct was useless; since Rome, which is an example of the second method, did both the one and the other, it rose to the heights of power. And since it was the only city to live in this manner, it was also the only one to become so powerful; for after it had made many allies for itself throughout all of Italy who lived, in many respects, under laws similar to its own, and on the other hand, as was previously mentioned, since Rome always retained the seat of empire and the position of command, its allies, without realizing it, came to subjugate themselves through their own labours and with their own blood. Thus, the Romans began to march outside of Italy with their armies, where they reduced kingdoms to provinces, and subjugated peoples who, accustomed to living under kings, did not care about becoming subjects and who, having Roman governors and being conquered by armies with the Roman name, recognized no superior other than Rome itself; so that Rome's allies inside Italy all at once found themselves surrounded by Roman subjects and overcome by an enormous city as Rome then was. When they recognized the deception under which they had been living, they were not in time to find a remedy, because Rome had assumed so much authority with its foreign provinces and had created so much strength within its own walls, being in possession of an enormous and extremely well-armed city. Even though Rome's allies formed an alliance against that city in order to avenge themselves for their injuries, they lost the war in a short time, making their conditions worse, since from being allies they, too, were reduced to subjects. This mode of conduct, as has been said, has been employed only by the Romans; nor can a republic wishing to expand its territory employ any other method, because experience has shown us none other more certain or more true.

The previously mentioned method employed by the leagues, under which the Etruscans, the Achaeans, and the Aetolians lived and under which the Swiss live today, is the next best after that of the Romans, because although it is impossible to expand very much with it, two benefits derive from it: first, you do not easily bring wars down on your own back; secondly, you can easily keep all that you take. The reason for not being able to expand is because such a republic is disjointed and has several seats of power, which makes it difficult for them to consult and reach decisions. It also makes them less anxious to acquire power, because, with so many communities participating in the dominion, they do not place as high a value on such acquisitions as a single republic, which can hope to enjoy them all by itself. Besides this, leagues govern themselves through councils and are necessarily slower in deliberation than those who live within the same circle of walls. It is also evident from experience that a similar mode of conduct has a fixed limit, which no example proves capable of being exceeded; and this is to arrive at a confederation of twelve to fourteen communities and then to cease trying to expand any further, since when they reach the level where they feel able to defend themselves from everyone else, they seek no greater dominion, both because necessity does not force them to acquire more power and because they do not recognize any utility in such acquisitions, for the reasons stated above.

Thus, they would have to do one of two things: either they must continue to make allies for themselves (and their great number would create confusion), or they must create subjects for themselves (and since they see the difficulty and not the advantage in this course of action, they do not value it). Consequently, whenever they reach such a number that they seem to be living in security, they turn to two other policies: first, they receive taxes and take protectorates, and through these means obtain money from every direction, which they can easily distribute among themselves; secondly, they fight for others and take money for doing this from the prince who hires them on for his undertakings, as we see the Swiss doing today, and as we read that the previously mentioned confederations once did. Livy bears witness to this, where he declares that Philip, king of Macedonia, who came to confer with Titus Quinctius Flaminius, discussed an agreement in the presence of a praetor of the Aetolians, and when the praetor began arguing with Philip, the king rebuked him for avarice and infidelity, declaring that the Aetolians were not ashamed to fight with one man and later to send their men off into the service of his enemy, so that the banners of Aetolia were often seen flying in two opposing camps. It is evident, therefore, that this mode of conduct on the part of leagues has always been similar and has always produced similar effects. It is also clear that this method of acquiring subjects has always been weak and has always produced little gain, and that when these confederations go beyond their limits, they soon come to ruin. Furthermore, if this method of acquiring subjects is ineffective in armed republics, it is totally ineffective in republics that are unarmed, as the republics of Italy have been in our own times.

It is evident, therefore, that the only effective method is the one followed by the Romans, which is even more admirable in so far as no example of it existed before that of Rome, and after Rome's fall, no one has been capable of imitating it. As for leagues, only the Swiss and the Swabian League imitate them. And, as will be discussed in the conclusion to this book, so many of the institutions set up by Rome, as relevant to domestic affairs as to foreign affairs, are not only not imitated in our present times but are not even taken into account, since some people judge them as being untrue, others as impossible, and still others as inappropriate or useless, so that remaining in this state of ignorance, we are prey to anyone who wants to invade this province. Even though imitation of the Romans may seem difficult, imitation of the ancient Etruscans should not seem so difficult, especially to the Tuscans of the present, for if the Etruscans were unable to establish an empire similar to that of Rome for the reasons we outlined, they were still able to acquire in Italy that power that their mode of conduct accorded them. This power was secure for a long period of time, accompanied by the highest glory in empire and arms and the greatest renown for their customs and religion. Their power and glory were first diminished by the Gauls and later destroyed by the Romans: they were so completely destroyed that there is hardly any record of them at the present, even though 2,000 years ago the power of the Etruscans was immense. This has caused me to reflect upon how things fall into oblivion, as will be discussed in the following chapter.

CHAPTER 5

How the Changes in Religious Sects and Languages, Along With Such Occurrences as Floods and Plagues, Erase the Memory of Things

To those philosophers who have claimed that the world has existed eternally, I believe one could reply that if it really were this old, it would be reasonable to assume that there is some record of it dating back more than 5,000 years, were it not for the fact that we see how records of past times are destroyed for many different reasons, some of which originate with men themselves, and others with heaven. Those originating with men are changes in religious sects and in languages. Thus, whenever a new sect springs up—that is, a new religion—its first inclination is to extinguish the old religion in order to enhance its reputation, and whenever it happens that the founders of the new sect speak a different language, they can easily destroy it. This matter can be understood by considering the methods the Christian sect employed against that of the pagans; they obliterated all of its institutions, all of its religious ceremonies, and suppressed the memory of its ancient theology. It is true that they did not succeed in destroying the entire record of the deeds accomplished by the illustrious men of that time; this occurred because they maintained the Latin language, which they were forced to do, because they had to write down their new law in this language. Thus, had they been capable of writing in a new language, considering the other persecutions they committed, there would have remained no record whatsoever of past events. And anyone who reads of the methods employed by St Gregory and by other leaders of the Christian religion will witness with what stubbornness they pursued every record from ancient times, burning the works of poets and historians, destroying images, and ruining everything else that retained any sign of antiquity. Thus, had they added a new language to this persecution, everything would have been forgotten in a very short period of time. It is credible to suppose, moreover, that what the Christian sect wanted to do to the pagans, the pagans did to the religion that preceded their own. And, because these sects change two or three times in five or six thousand years, the recollection of things done long before is lost, and even if some traces remain, they are considered to be mythical and nobody believes them, as occurred in the case of the history by Diodorus Siculus,* which provides an account of between forty and fifty thousand years but is nevertheless considered untrustworthy, as I believe it to be.

As for the causes that originate in heaven, those are the ones which destroy the human race and reduce the inhabitants in one region to a bare few, and this occurs either because of pestilence, famine, or flood, and the most important cause is this last one, both because it is the most universal and also because those who save themselves are all mountaineers and crude people who, having no knowledge of anything from antiquity, cannot bequeath it to posterity. If among them someone is saved who has some knowledge of it, he conceals it and modifies it to his own purposes in order to enhance his reputation, so that nothing is left for the survivors but what he has wished to set down in writing and nothing else. And that such floods, pestilences, and famines occur, I believe there can be no doubt, because all the histories are full of them, both because this effect of things falling into oblivion is an obvious one, and also because it seems reasonable that this should be the case. Thus, just as in a simple body, when too much superfluous material accumulates, nature herself moves it on many occasions and effects a purgation which restores it to health, so this also occurs in the mixed body of the human race, for when all the provinces are full of inhabitants (so that people are unable to live there, nor are they able to go elsewhere, since every other place is occupied and filled), and when human cunning and wickedness have increased as much as they can, the world of necessity must purge itself in one of three ways, so that men, having been reduced in number and vanquished, will live more comfortably and become better. Thus, as was said above, Etruria was once powerful, full of religion and ability; it possessed its own customs and native language, all of which were destroyed by Roman power, so that as was said, only the memory of its name remains.

CHAPTER 6
How the Romans Proceeded in Waging War

Having discussed how the Romans proceeded in increasing their territory, we shall now discuss how they proceeded in waging war; and in each one of their actions, it will be seen with what prudence they deviated from the universal methods of others in order to clear their path to supreme greatness. The intention of those who make war by choice or out of ambition is to acquire territory and to maintain it, and to proceed in such a way that it enriches but does not impoverish their native city and the countryside. It is necessary, therefore, both in acquiring territory and in maintaining it, to try not to spend, but rather to undertake everything in a way that benefits the public treasury. Anyone who desires to do all these things must follow the Roman style and method: this was first of all to make wars short and massive, as the French say, because by fielding enormous armies, the Romans brought to a very swift conclusion all the wars that they waged against the Latins, the Samnites, and the Etruscans. If we take note of all those wars they fought from the beginnings of Rome until the siege of Veii, we shall see that all of them were expedited, some in six days, others in ten, and still others in twenty days. Thus, this was their custom: as soon as war was declared, they marched forth against the enemy with their armies and immediately waged a decisive battle. When they were victorious, the enemy, in order to avoid the total destruction of their territory, came to terms, and the Romans condemned them to give up part of their lands; they allotted these lands as private property or consigned them to a colony, which, placed at their frontiers, came to serve as a guard-post at the Roman borders to the profit of the colonists, who owned these lands, as well as to Rome's public treasury, which maintained these guard-posts without expense. Nor could this method be any more secure or stronger or more profitable: while the enemy did not march into the field, this guard-post was sufficient; if the enemy came out in force to attack the colony, then the Romans came out in force themselves and did battle with them; and once they had done this and won the day, they imposed upon the enemy even more onerous conditions and then returned home. In this way, step by step, they came to gain a reputation over that of their enemy and internal strength.

They adhered to this method until they altered their method of proceeding in war; this happened after the siege of Veii when, in order to wage war over a longer period of time, they decided to pay the soldiers, whom they did not pay earlier, since the brevity of the wars made it unnecessary. Even though the Romans paid them and by virtue of such payments were able to wage longer wars, and, by waging them further away, had to remain in the field, they none the less never varied from their first method of ending them quickly, based on the place and time, nor did they ever vary from their system of sending out colonies. With regard to keeping wars brief, besides their normal practice, the ambition of the consuls also held them to this first method: since they were elected for a single year, for six months of which they were confined at home, they wanted to end wars in order to enjoy a triumph. In the matter of sending out colonies, the profit and the great convenience held them to it. They did somewhat alter their way of distributing the booty, in which they were not as liberal as they once had been, both because it did not seem so necessary, since the soldiers had a salary, and also because they planned, once the booty was much greater, to fatten the public treasury, so that they would not be forced to pay for their undertakings with taxes levied on the city. In a short time this system made their treasury extremely rich. These two methods, therefore, both that of distributing the spoils and that of sending out colonies, made Rome grow rich from warfare, whereas other princes and less wise republics were impoverished from it. And things were finally reduced to a state in which a consul was unable to enjoy a triumph if he did not carry in his triumphant procession a great deal of gold and silver and every other sort of booty into the treasury. Thus the Romans, with the provisions described above and with their practice of ending wars quickly, by being skilful in wearing down their enemies with long delays, and through routs, raids, and treaties made to their advantage, became ever richer and more powerful.

CHAPTER 7

How Much Land the Romans Gave to Their Colonists

I believe it is difficult to discover the truth about the amount of land the Romans distributed to each colonist, since I think they gave more or less according to the places where they sent their colonies. It can be assumed that in every way and in every place the distribution was moderate, first, in order to send more men, since they were deputized to guard that countryside, and then, since these men lived in poverty at home, it was not reasonable for the Romans to want their men to grow too rich outside the city. And Livy describes how once they had taken Veii, the Romans sent a colony there and distributed to each soldier 3 *jugera* and 7 *unciae* of land (which is the equivalent, in our system, of . . .),* because, in addition to what was discussed above, they also judged highly tillable land, rather than a sizeable piece of land, to be sufficient. And it is certainly necessary for each colony to have public pastures where each colonist can pasture his livestock and woodlands where they can cut wood for their fires; without such things, a colony cannot establish itself.

CHAPTER 8

The Reason Why Peoples Leave Their Homelands and Overrun the Lands of Others

Since we have discussed above the method of proceeding in war used by the Romans and how the Etruscans were attacked by the Gauls, I feel it is not unrelated to the subject to explain that there are two causes for war. One type is waged because of the ambition of princes or republics that seek to extend their empire, such as the wars waged by Alexander the Great, those waged by the Romans, and those waged every day by one power against another. These kinds of wars are dangerous but they do not drive the inhabitants completely out of a province, because the victor is satisfied with the obedience of the people, and in most cases he allows them to live under their own laws and always in their own homes and with their own property. The other cause for war is when an entire people with all its families leaves a place, driven either by famine or by war, and goes to seek out a new location and a new province, not to rule over it as those above do but, rather, to possess it, even the private property, and to drive out or murder its ancient inhabitants. This kind of war is extremely cruel and frightful. It is about this type of war that

Sallust speaks at the end of his history of Jugurtha, when he declares that once Jugurtha was defeated, the movement of the Gauls who were coming into Italy began to be felt; he then states that with all other peoples, the Romans fought only about who was to be in command, while with the Gauls they always fought for their safety.* Accordingly, for a prince or a republic that attacks a province, it is sufficient to destroy only those who are in command, but populations such as these need to destroy everyone since they wish to live off the resources that supported others. The Romans waged three of these extremely dangerous wars. The first occurred during the occupation of Rome, when the city was captured by those Gauls who had taken Lombardy from the Etruscans, as was mentioned above, and made it their territory; Livy sets forth two reasons for this invasion: first, as was mentioned above, the Gauls were attracted by the sweetness of the fruits and wines of Italy, which were lacking in France; secondly, the kingdom of Gaul was so overpopulated with men that it could no longer support them, and the rulers of those places decided that it was necessary for part of them to seek new land. Once they had made this decision, they elected as captains of the people who had to leave Bellovesus and Sicovesus, two kings of the Gauls; Bellovesus came into Italy and Sicovesus went on to Spain. It was Bellovesus' passage into Italy that brought about the occupation of Lombardy and, as a result, the first war that the Gauls waged against Rome.* Then came the war that the Gauls waged after the First Carthaginian War, when between Piombino and Pisa the Romans killed more than 200,000 Gauls.* The third war occurred when the Teutones and the Cimbri came into Italy: having defeated several Roman armies, they were destroyed by Marius. The Romans, therefore, won these three extremely dangerous wars. Nor was only minor ability required to win them, because it can be seen later on that once Roman ability grew faint and their arms lost their ancient valour, their empire was destroyed by similar peoples, such as the Goths, the Vandals, and other like tribes who occupied the entire Western empire.

Peoples such as these leave their own lands, as was mentioned above, driven out by necessity, and this necessity arises either from famine or from a war and the oppression they have experienced in their own country, which has compelled them to seek new homelands. Such peoples come in great numbers, and then they violently enter the lands of others, murder the inhabitants, take possession of their property, create a new kingdom, and change the very name of the province, just as Moses did and as those other peoples did when they occupied the Roman empire. Accordingly, these new names, which exist in Italy and in other provinces, arise from nothing other than the fact that they have been named in this way by the new occupants: just so Lombardy used to be called Cisalpine Gaul; France used to be called Transalpine Gaul and now is named after the Franks, the name of the peoples who occupied it; Slavonia was called Illyria; Hungary Pannonia; England Britannia; and so many other provinces changed their names that it would be tedious to recount them. Moses also called that part of Syria he had occupied Judaea. Since I declared above that on some occasions such peoples are driven out of their own territory by war and are therefore compelled to seek new lands, I should like to cite the example of the Maurusians, peoples who lived in Syria in ancient times. Upon hearing that the Jewish peoples had arrived and deciding that they were unable to resist them, they thought it preferable to save themselves and to abandon their own country rather than to perish while trying to save it, and after gathering up their families they left for Africa, where they established their territory, driving out the inhabitants that they found in those places. Thus, these peoples, who could not defend their own land, were able to occupy that of another people; and Procopius, who wrote a history of the war that Belisarius waged against the Vandals, who had occupied Africa, refers to the fact that he had read inscriptions written upon certain columns in the places where these Maurusians lived which said: 'We Maurusians who fled before Joshua the Robber, son of Nava'—which reveals the reason for their departure from Syria.* Such peoples as these are, therefore, extremely formidable, since they are driven by extreme necessity, and if they do not encounter good armies, they will never be stopped.

But when peoples who are compelled to abandon their homeland are not numerous, they are not as dangerous as those we have discussed, because they cannot employ such violence and are obliged to occupy some location with cunning and, once it has been occupied, to maintain themselves there by means of allies and confederations. This can be seen from what Aeneas, Dido, the Massilienses, and other similar peoples did, all of whom with the consent of their neighbours were able to remain in the places to which they had come.*

The most numerous peoples leave the lands of Scythia, and almost all of them have left these cold and impoverished places from which, due to the large number of inhabitants and land of a quality that cannot support them, they are forced to migrate, having much to drive them away and nothing to hold them back. If none of these peoples have poured into another country during the last 500 years, this has come about for several reasons. The first is the enormous evacuation that this territory experienced during the decline of the Roman empire, when more than thirty different peoples left. The second is that Germany and Hungary, places from which these people still used to leave, have now reclaimed their lands in such a way that people can live there with ease, and are, therefore, not forced to move elsewhere. Moreover, their men are extremely bellicose and serve as a bastion to keep the Scythians, whose country borders theirs, from presuming to conquer them or to pass through them. Enormous movements of the Tartars have often occurred, which the Hungarians and the peoples of Poland have stopped, and they often boast that if it had not been for their swords, Italy and the church would on numerous occasions have felt the weight of the Tartar armies. But I wish this to suffice concerning the previously mentioned peoples.

CHAPTER 9

The Causes that Commonly Provoke Wars Among the Powerful

The cause of the war that broke out between the Romans and the Samnites, who had long been allies, is a common one that arises among all powerful states. This cause either comes about by chance or is brought about by someone who wants to start a war. The war between the Romans and the Samnites arose by chance, for the intention of the Samnites in waging war against the Sidicini and then the Campanians was not to extend it to the Romans. But after the Campanians were conquered, contrary to the expectation of both the Romans and the Samnites, they ran to Rome for help, and after the Campanians had placed themselves under Roman protection, the Romans were forced to defend them as if defending themselves, and to engage in a war they felt they could not honourably avoid. Thus, it seemed reasonable to the Romans not to defend their friends the Campanians against their friends the Samnites, but it seemed shameful not to defend them as subjects or as people under their protection, since they thought that if they did not take up their defence, it would place an obstacle in the path of all those who might wish to place themselves under Roman power. Thus, valuing empire and glory over tranquillity, as its goal, Rome could not refuse this undertaking. This same cause gave rise to the First Punic War against the Carthaginians, when the Romans took up the defence of the people of Messina in Sicily; this was also by chance. But later the Second Punic War did not break out by chance, because Hannibal, the Carthaginian general, attacked the Saguntines, the allies of the Romans in Spain, not in order to harm the Saguntines but, instead, by provoking the Roman armies, to have the opportunity to do battle with them and to pass over into Italy. This method of starting new wars has always been customary among the powerful who hold in respect their word of honour and other such agreements. Thus, if I wish to wage war with a prince and between us there are firm pacts which have been observed over a lengthy period of time, I will attack one of his friends with another justification or another excuse, rather than attacking him, knowing full well that if I attack his friend he will either resent it, and I shall fulfill my intention of waging war upon him, or by not resenting it, he will reveal his weakness or lack of faith by not defending someone under his protection. And either of these two things is sufficient to lessen his prestige and to make my plans easier to carry out. With respect to starting wars, the submission of the Campanians must therefore be noted as was mentioned above; moreover, one should also note the remedy a city has when it cannot defend

itself and wishes to defend itself in any way possible from anyone who attacks it. That remedy is to give yourself voluntarily to
anyone whom you wish to defend you, as the inhabitants of
Capua* did with the Romans or the Florentines did with King
Robert of Naples, who, although he did not want to protect
them as allies, later defended them as subjects against the forces
of Castruccio of Lucca who was attacking them.*

CHAPTER 10

Wealth Is Not, Contrary to Popular Opinion, the Sinew of Warfare

Because anyone can begin a war but cannot bring it to a conclusion whenever he pleases, a prince must take the measure of his
forces before he undertakes an enterprise and govern himself
accordingly. But he must possess enough prudence not to
deceive himself about his strength; and he will always deceive
himself when he measures it either by money, by location, or by
the goodwill of men while, on the other hand, lacking troops of
his own. All of these things certainly increase your power, but
they do not give it to you, and, by themselves, they are worth
nothing and serve no good purpose without faithful troops.
Great wealth is insufficient without them, and the strength of
the country is of no use to you, nor can the faith and goodwill of
men endure, because they cannot remain faithful to you if you
cannot protect them. Every mountain, every lake, every inacces-
sible position becomes a plain, where strong defenders are lacking. Money, moreover, not only will not defend you but will
cause you to be plundered all the sooner. Nor could any idea be
more false than the popular opinion of wealth as the sinew of
warfare. This maxim was enunciated by Quintus Curtius concerning the war between Antipater of Macedonia and the king of
Sparta, where he recounts how the king of Sparta was forced to
fight and was defeated for lack of money, and how, if he had
postponed the battle for a few days, the news of Alexander's
death would have reached Greece and he would have remained
the victor without fighting.* But lacking money and fearing that

his army would for this reason abandon him, he was compelled to try his luck in battle, causing Quintus Curtius to affirm that wealth is the sinew of warfare. This maxim is cited every day, especially by princes, who follow it without being sufficiently prudent. Basing their actions upon this maxim, they believe that it is sufficient to have a great deal of money to defend themselves, and they do not consider the fact that if money were sufficient to produce victory, then Darius would have defeated Alexander, the Greeks would have defeated the Romans, and in our own times, Duke Charles would have defeated the Swiss and, just a few days ago, the pope and the Florentines together would have had no difficulty in defeating Francesco Maria, the nephew of Pope Julius II, in the war over Urbino.* But all those mentioned above were defeated by those who believed that good soldiers, not money, are the sinew of warfare. Among the other things Croesus, king of the Lydians, showed to Solon, the Athenian, was an immense treasure; when Solon was asked what he thought of the king's power, Solon replied that he did not consider him more powerful for it, because war is waged with steel and not with gold; and somebody possessing more steel could come along and take his treasure away from him. Besides this, after the death of Alexander the Great, when a multitude of Gauls passed into Greece and then into Asia and sent envoys to the king of Macedonia to negotiate a certain agreement, that king, in order to demonstrate his power and to frighten them, showed them a great deal of gold and silver. As a result the Gauls, who had almost decided on a peace agreement, broke it, because they had been seized by such a strong desire to take that gold away from the king, and, in this way the king was dispossessed of the very thing he had accumulated for his own defence. A few years ago the Venetians lost their entire state even though their treasury was full of money, since it could not be used in their defence.*

I must declare, therefore, that good soldiers are the sinew of war and not gold, because gold is an insufficient means of finding good soldiers, but good soldiers are a more than sufficient means of finding gold. If the Romans had insisted on waging war with money rather than steel, all the treasure in the world would not have sufficed, considering the greatness of their undertakings and the difficulties they encountered in accomplishing them. But by waging their wars with steel, they never lacked for gold, because those who feared them brought it to them even inside their encampments. And if that Spartan king* through a lack of money had to tempt the fortunes of war, what happened to him because of money has often happened for other reasons, because it is obvious that when an army lacks provisions and must either die of hunger or fight a battle, it always chooses to fight, since this is the most honourable course and the one in which fortune may favour you in some way. It has also happened many times that when a leader sees assistance coming to an opposing army, he finds it advisable to engage that army in battle and to test the fortunes of war, rather than waiting until the enemy army grows larger and then be forced to fight in any case with a thousand disadvantages. It has also been observed (as happened to Hasdrubal* when he was attacked in the Marches by Claudius Nero together with the other Roman consul) that when a leader is obliged either to retreat or to fight, he will always elect to fight, believing that even though it is extremely doubtful, this decision might lead him to victory, while the opposite decision would force him into defeat in any case. There are many necessities, therefore, that force a leader, contrary to his intentions, to make the decision to fight, among which may well be, on some occasions, the lack of money; but money should not, for this reason, be judged the sinew of warfare any more than the other things that lead men into such difficulties. Again I must repeat that good soldiers are the sinew of warfare, not gold.

Money is certainly necessary as a secondary consideration, but it is a need that good soldiers overcome by themselves, because it is impossible for good soldiers to lack money, just as it is impossible for wealth alone to create good soldiers. Every history in a thousand places demonstrates that what we are saying is true, notwithstanding the fact that Pericles advised the Athenians to make war upon the entire Peloponnesus, arguing that they could win that war with their industry and the power of their wealth. Even though in that war the Athenians sometimes experienced good fortune, they ultimately lost the war, for the fitness and good soldiers of Sparta were worth more than the

industry and the wealth of Athens. But Livy is a better witness
to the truth of this statement than anyone else, when he discusses whether Alexander the Great would have conquered the
Romans if he had invaded Italy, and demonstrates that three
things are required in war: many soldiers and good ones, prudent leaders, and good fortune; upon considering whether the
Romans or Alexander would have prevailed in these matters,
Livy then reaches his conclusion without ever mentioning
money.* When the Capuans were asked by the Sidicini to take
up arms with them against the Samnites, they must have mea-
sured their power in terms of wealth rather than the quality of
their soldiers, because having decided to assist the Sidicini, they
were forced, after two defeats, to become tributaries of the
Romans if they wished to save themselves.*

CHAPTER 11

It Is Not a Prudent Policy to Form a Relationship With a Prince Who Has More Prestige Than Power

In his wish to demonstrate the error of the Sidicini in trusting the
assistance of the Campanians and the error of the Campanians in
believing that they could defend the Sidicini, Livy could not
have employed more lively words than by saying: 'The Campanians had brought a reputation rather than actual strength to
protect their allies.'* In this regard, it should be noted that
alliances concluded with princes who possess neither the ability
to assist you because of their distance from you, nor the power
to do so on account of their poor organization, or for some other
cause, offer more fame than real assistance to those who entrust
themselves to them; this happened in our times to the Florentines when, in 1479, the pope and the king of Naples attacked
them, because, as allies of the king of France, they derived from
that relationship 'a reputation rather than actual strength';* this
would happen as well to any prince who, having placed his trust
in Maximilian the emperor,* would engage in some enterprise,
for this is one of those relationships that would offer to the one
who makes it 'a reputation rather than actual strength', just as

Livy says in this passage the alliance with the Capuans offered to the Sidicini.*

The Capuans, therefore, erred in this matter by assuming that they possessed greater forces than they had. Thus, the small measure of prudence possessed by men is such that, not knowing how or not being able to defend themselves, they sometimes wish to engage in the enterprise of defending others; the Tarentines once did this by sending ambassadors to the Roman consul, while the Roman armies were marching against the Samnites, to inform him that they desired peace between those two peoples and that they were disposed to wage war upon the party that rejected peace, so that the consul, amused by this proposal, sounded the battle-cry and ordered his army to confront the enemy in the presence of the said ambassadors, demonstrating to the Tarentines with his actions and not with words the reply they deserved. After having discussed in the present chapter the poor decisions that princes make in the defence of others, I should like in the following chapter to speak of the decisions they make in their own defence.

CHAPTER 12

Whether It Is Preferable, Fearing an Assault, to Start a War or to Await Its Outbreak

I have overheard men very experienced in warfare debate this question on occasion: if there are two princes of almost equal power and the bolder one has declared war on the other, what would be the best choice for the second prince: to wait for the enemy within his borders or to seek him out in his homeland and attack him? I have heard arguments on both sides. Those who argue in favour of attacking others cite the advice that Croesus gave to Cyrus when, after his arrival at the borders of the Massagetans to make war on them, their queen Tomyris sent him a message saying that he might wish to choose one of two alternatives: either enter her kingdom, where she would await him, or wait for her to come to attack him. When the question came to be debated, Croesus, against the opinion of others, said to go and to seek her out, claiming that if he defeated her at a distance from her kingdom he would be unable to seize the kingdom from her, because she would have the time to regroup, but that if he conquered her within her own borders he could follow her as she fled, and, by not giving her time to regroup, seize the state from her. They also cite the advice that Hannibal gave to Antiochus when that king developed a plan to wage war upon the Romans, in which he demonstrated that the Romans could not be conquered except inside Italy, because an invader could make use of their arms, wealth, and allies, but that anyone who fought the Romans outside of Italy and left Italy free would leave them a source that would never fail to supply them with forces wherever necessary; and Hannibal concluded that Rome could be more quickly taken from the Romans than the empire, and Italy before the other provinces. They also cite the example of Agathocles,* who, being unable to sustain the war at home, attacked the Carthaginians, who were again waging war against him, and forced them to sue for peace, as well as that of Scipio, who, in order to stop the war in Italy attacked Africa.

Those who hold a contrary opinion declare that whoever wishes harm to befall an enemy should draw him away from home. They cite the Athenians, who remained superior as long as they waged a convenient war in their own backyard, but upon finding themselves at a distance from home, they went with their armies to Sicily and lost their liberty.* They cite the poetic fables that show how Antaeus, king of Libya, under attack by Hercules the Egyptian, was invincible as long as he remained within the confines of his kingdom, but when he went beyond them, because of Hercules' ingenuity, he lost his state and his life. This gave rise to the fable that while Antaeus stood on the ground, he regained his strength from his mother who was the earth, and when Hercules realized this, he lifted him up and moved him away from the earth.* They also cite modern opinions. Everyone knows that Ferdinand, king of Naples, was considered to be a very wise prince in his own times, and two years before his death, when he heard a rumour about how Charles VIII, the king of France, wanted to come to attack him, he fell ill after having made a great many preparations, and as he was dying, among the other pieces of advice he left Alfonso, his son, was that he should wait for the enemy inside the kingdom and that for no reason in the world should he take his forces outside his state, but rather await Charles inside his domain with his entire army. This advice was not followed by Alfonso, but, upon sending an army into the Romagna, Alfonso lost it without fighting, along with his state.*

Besides the ones already mentioned, the arguments brought forward by each side are these: anyone who attacks does so with more courage than anyone who awaits an attack, which makes the attacker's army more confident; attacking also takes away many of the enemy's advantages by depriving him of his ability to avail himself of his possessions, since he cannot avail himself of subjects who are being plundered; and with the enemy in his home territory, a ruler is obliged not to overtax his subjects or to overburden them, so that the invader can eventually dry up the source that, as Hannibal declared, makes it possible for the defender to sustain the war. Besides this, the attacker's soldiers, by virtue of being in another country, are more obliged to fight, and this necessity produces exceptional skill, as we have stated many times. On the other hand, it is said that when you await the enemy you wait with a considerable advantage, since without any hardship of your own you can cause him great hardships in securing provisions and everything else an army requires; you can more efficiently impede his plans through your greater knowledge, and you can confront him with greater forces and easily keep them united, even though you cannot move them all away from home; you can easily reorganize if you are defeated, because most of your army will save itself by virtue of having refuges nearby and reinforcements that need not come over a long distance, so that you eventually risk all your forces but not your entire fortune, whereas going off to a distant place, you risk your entire fortune but not all of your forces. And there have been some who, in order to weaken the enemy more efficiently, have allowed them to enter for a few day's march into their own territory and to seize a number of towns, so that by leaving garrisons in them all, they have weakened their army, and it is then easier to fight them.

But in order to say now what I understand of this matter, I believe that one must make this distinction: either I possess my own armed country, like the Romans in the past or the Swiss in the present; or I possess an unarmed country, like the Carthaginians in the past or the king of France and the Italians in the present. In the latter case, an enemy must be kept far from your home territory because your strength resides in your wealth and not in your army, so that whenever access to your wealth is cut off, you are finished, and nothing will block access to your wealth more than a war in your home territory. As examples, we have the Carthaginians who, while their homeland was free, could wage war against the Romans with their income, but when it was attacked, could not resist Agathocles. The Florentines had no remedy whatsoever against Castruccio, lord of Lucca, because he waged war on them in their own home territory, to the point that, in order to defend themselves, they had to give themselves over to King Robert of Naples. But once Castruccio was dead, these same Florentines had the courage to attack the duke of Milan in his home territory and to hope to take his kingdom away from him, so much of that exceptional ability did they demonstrate in distant wars and so much weakness in those nearby.* But when kingdoms are armed, as Rome was armed and as the Swiss are now armed, it is much more difficult to conquer them the nearer you come to them, because these bodies can unite more forces to resist an onslaught than to attack someone else. Nor does the authority of Hannibal convince me in this instance, because passion and profit made him give the advice he gave to Antiochus. If the Romans had suffered in France in the same space of time the three defeats Hannibal inflicted on them in Italy, they would undoubtedly have been crushed, because they would not have been able to avail themselves of the remainder of their armies, as they did in Italy; in reorganizing themselves, they would not have been able to enjoy the advantages they enjoyed, nor could they have resisted the enemy with the forces that they employed. There are no instances of the Romans attacking a province without sending armies that exceeded the number of 50,000 men, but to defend their home territory, after the First Punic War, they assembled against the Gauls 1,800,000 armed men.* Nor could they have defeated them in Lombardy as they defeated them in Etruria, because against such a large number of enemies they could not have moved so many forces over such a distance, nor could they have fought them with such ease. The Cimbri routed a Roman army in Germany, nor had the Romans any remedy there. But when the Cimbri reached Italy and the Romans were able to bring together all their forces, they destroyed the Cimbri.* The Swiss are easily conquered outside their home territory, where they cannot send more than 30,000 or 40,000 men, but to conquer them at home, where they can put together 100,000 men is extremely difficult. Once again I conclude, therefore, that the prince whose people are armed and organized for warfare should always wait at home for a violent and dangerous war and should not go out on the attack. But the prince who has unarmed subjects and a country unused to war should always go as far away from home as possible. In this way, both the one and the other, each according to his own circumstances, will defend himself more effectively.

CHAPTER 13

That One Moves from Humble to Great Fortune More Often Through Fraud Than Through Force

I consider it to be very true that it rarely or never happens that men of humble fortune rise to high positions without the use of force and fraud, although others obtain this rank either as a gift or by inheritance. Nor do I believe that force ever suffices by itself, whereas it is often the case that fraud alone will suffice, as anyone who reads the life of Philip of Macedonia or that of Agathocles the Sicilian and of many other similar men will clearly see, for from the most humble, or at least a very humble fortune, they attained either kingdoms or very great empires. Xenophon demonstrates the necessity for deception in his *Life of Cyrus*, considering that the first expedition Cyrus carried out against the king of Armenia was full of fraud and that Cyrus occupied his kingdom by means of deceit, not force. No other conclusion can be drawn from his action except that a leader who wishes to undertake great enterprises must learn how to deceive. Xenophon also says that Cyrus deceived his maternal uncle, Cyaxares, king of the Medes, in several ways, and he demonstrates that without such deception, Cyrus could never have attained the greatness he achieved. Nor do I believe that anyone who has been placed in humble circumstances has ever attained supreme authority purely by means of open force and sincerity, but this has certainly been the case for those who have employed fraud alone, as Giovan Galeazzo did when he seized the state and the supreme authority in Lombardy from his uncle, Messer Bernarbò.*

What princes are obliged to do at the beginning of their expansion republics must do as well, until they have become powerful and force alone proves sufficient, and because Rome, in every instance, employed either by chance or by choice all the methods necessary to achieve greatness, it did not fail to employ this one either. Nor could the city have chosen a more useful deception at the beginning than to select the method (the one we discussed above) of making allies for itself, for under this name the Romans made them their slaves, as were the Latins and the other peoples surrounding them. Accordingly, Rome first used its own armies to subdue the peoples nearby and to acquire the reputation of a powerful state; then, once the city had subdued them, it achieved such growth that it could defeat any one of them; and the Latins never realized that they had become completely enslaved until they saw the Samnites twice defeated and forced to come to terms.* With this victory the Romans acquired great renown among far-away rulers, who in this way heard of the Roman name but not of their armies, and so they generated envy and suspicion in those who saw and felt the force of their arms, among whom were the Latins. This envy and this fear were so powerful that not only the Latins but also the colonies they possessed in Latium, along with the Campanians, who had shortly before been defended by the Romans, conspired against the Roman people. The Latins started this war in the way that we noted above, the way in which most wars are started, not by attacking the Romans but by defending the Sidicini against the Samnites, who were making war on the Sidicini with the permission of the Romans. Livy demonstrates that the Latins started the war once they recognized this deception, when he puts the following words in the mouth of Annius

Setinus, the Latin praetor, who spoke in their council: 'For if we are able to endure slavery even now when we have the pretence of a fair treaty, etc.'* It is evident, therefore, that in their early expansions even the Romans did not fail to employ fraud, which must always be used by those who from small beginnings wish to ascend to sublime heights, and which is much less deserving of condemnation the more it is concealed, as it was in the case of the Romans.

CHAPTER 14

Men Often Deceive Themselves, in the Belief that They Will Conquer Pride With Humility

It is evident on many occasions that humility not only does no good but may cause harm, especially when it is used with arrogant men who, either out of envy or for some other reason, have conceived a hatred for you. Our historian bears witness to this in discussing the cause for the war between the Romans and the Latins. When the Samnites complained to the Romans that the Latins had attacked them, the Romans did not insist on prohibiting the Latins from waging war, not wishing to provoke them; not only did their decision not provoke them but it made them grow even more spirited against the Romans, and they soon revealed themselves as enemies. Testimony of this is provided in the words used by the previously mentioned Latin praetor Annius, who declared in the same council: 'You have tried their patience by refusing them troops; who doubts that they were furious when we broke the tradition of 200 years? Yet they swallowed their resentment... They have heard how... we are preparing armies against the Samnites, their allies under treaty; but they have not bestirred themselves to leave the City. Where does this excess of restraint on their part spring from if not from an awareness of our strength in comparison with their own?'* Thus, we clearly see by means of this text how much the patience of the Romans increased the arrogance of the Latins. A prince must never, therefore, allow his dignity to be diminished and must never give up anything willingly, if he wishes to give it up honourably, except when he can or believes he can keep it, because it is almost always better, when the matter has come to the point that you cannot give up a possession in the manner just described, to allow it to be taken from you by force rather than by the fear of force. Thus, if you allow it to be taken through fear, you do so to avoid a war, and in most instances you will not avoid it, because the person to whom you have conceded this possession through obvious cowardice will not stand still but will want to deprive you of other possessions, and, esteeming you less, he will be incited to act against you, and among those who support you, you will find your defenders lukewarm, since they will feel that you are either weak or cowardly. But if you prepare your forces immediately, once you have discovered the enemy's designs, even if they are inferior to his, he will begin to esteem you; other princes nearby will esteem you even more, and when you have taken up arms they will wish to assist you, whereas if you give up, they will never come to your assistance. This applies when you have a single enemy, but when you have more than one, even though war has already broken out, it is a prudent policy to give up some of the things you possess to one of them to win him back and to divide him from his other allies.

CHAPTER 15

Weak States Are Always Ambiguous in Their Decisions; and Slow Decisions Are Always Harmful

In this same matter and in these same beginnings of war between the Latins and the Romans, we can observe how in every assembly it is well to come to the specifics of what must be decided and to avoid being ambiguous and uncertain about the case. This can be clearly seen in the assembly the Latins called when they were thinking about severing relations with the Romans, for once the Romans had anticipated the evil humour that had affected the Latin peoples, in order to assess the matter and to see whether, without resorting to arms, they could regain the support of those peoples, the Romans let it be known that they should send eight citizens to Rome, because they needed to consult with them. Having understood this and being aware that they had done many things against the will of the Romans, the Latins held a council to determine who should go to Rome and to give them instructions about what they should say. While in the council during this debate, their praetor Annius spoke these words: 'I still think that how we should act will affect the main issue more than what we should say. It will be easy to find words to fit our actions once we have set our plans in order'.* These words are without any doubt completely true, and they should be valued by every prince and by every republic, because in the midst of doubt and uncertainty about what others wish to do, it is impossible to match words with deeds, but once a decision has been taken and what is to be done has been determined, it is an easy matter to find the right words. I have all the more willingly stressed this point, inasmuch as I have on many occasions known such ambiguity to have harmed public actions, to the damage and the disgrace of our republic. And it will always happen that in doubtful cases and where courage is required for making decisions, such ambiguity will exist when it is weak men who deliberate and make such decisions. Nor are slow and tardy decisions any less harmful than the ambiguous ones, especially those which must be decided in favour of some ally, since slowness helps no one and is harmful to oneself. Decisions of this kind derive either from weakness of mind or weakness in your forces, or from some malignant disposition on the part of those who have to deliberate, who, moved by their own selfish passion to destroy the state or to fulfil some other desire, do not allow any decision to be reached but impede and block it. Good citizens, even when they see popular sentiment turning toward a pernicious choice, never impede the deliberations, and especially in matters where there is little time.

After the death of Hieronymus, the tyrant of Syracuse, while there was a great war raging between the Carthaginians and the Romans, the citizens of Syracuse argued about whether they should pursue the friendship of Rome or of Carthage. So great was the fervour of the parties that the question remained unsettled and no decision was ever reached, until Apollonides, one of the foremost Syracusan citizens, demonstrated in an oration full of prudence that no one was to be blamed for holding the opinion that they should ally themselves with Rome, just as no one was to be blamed for wishing to take the Carthaginian side; that it was well to detest such uncertainty and tardiness in choosing a policy, since he saw in such uncertainty the ruin of the republic; and that once a decision was taken, no matter what it might be, it was possible to hope for some good to result from it.* Nor could Livy demonstrate any better than in this section the damage that remaining undecided brings along with it. He demonstrates it again in this case of the Latins, since once they had asked the Lavinians for assistance against the Romans, the Lavinians delayed so long in deliberating the question that they had scarcely gone through the city gates with their men to bring the Latins help when news arrived that the Latins had been routed. At this point, their praetor Milionius declared: 'This short march will cost us dearly with the Roman people.'* Thus, if the Lavinians had decided at first either to aid or not to aid the Latins, they would not have provoked the Romans by not aiding them; by aiding them and by sending aid in time, they could have made the Latins victorious with the addition of their forces, but by deferring the decision, they would have come to lose in any case, as happened to them. If the Florentines had noted this passage, they would not have had so much damage or trouble inflicted upon them by the French as they had during the expedition of King Louis XII of France into Italy against Ludovico, duke of Milan,* since in making preparations for this expedition, the king sought out an alliance with the Florentines, and the ambassadors at the king's court agreed with him that they would remain neutral and that when the king entered Italy, he would have to maintain their state and receive them under his protection; and he gave the city the space of one month to ratify this agreement. The ratification was postponed by those who, out of a lack of prudence, took the side of Ludovico until finally, when the king was already certain of victory and the Florentines wanted to ratify the agreement, the ratification was not accepted, since the king recognized that the Florentines had allied themselves with him out of necessity and not of their own will. This cost the city of Florence a great deal of money and left it on the verge of losing control of the government, as later happened for a similar reason.* Thus, this decision deserves condemnation, because it was of no use to Duke Ludovico, who, if he had won, would have shown many more signs of hostility against the Florentines than did the king. Although the harm which arises in republics on account of this weakness has been discussed above in another chapter,* none the less, having another occasion to discuss it because of a new circumstance, I have decided to discuss it again, since it is, in my opinion, a most important matter of which republics similar to our own ought to take note.

CHAPTER 16

How Far the Soldiers of Our Times Have Strayed from Ancient Institutions

The most important battle the Roman people ever fought in any war with any nation was the one they fought with the Latin peoples during the consulate of Torquatus and Decius. Every argument confirms that, just as the Latins became slaves by having lost the battle, so the Romans would have become slaves had they not won it. Livy is of this opinion, for he writes that the two armies were equal in every way—organization, exceptional ability, stubbornness, and number; the only difference between them was that the leaders of the Roman army were more able than those of the Latin army. Furthermore, it is evident that in the handling of this battle, two incidents occurred that were never before observed and rarely repeated afterwards: that is, in order to keep their soldiers firm in their convictions, obedient to the consuls' orders, and resolute in battle, one consul killed himself and the other killed his son.* The parity that Livy declares to have existed between these two armies came about because, having fought together for a long time, they were alike in speech, organization, and arms, for in organizing the battle they held to the same methods, and the formations and the leaders of these formations bore the same names. Given that they were equal in forces and equal in ability, it was therefore necessary for something extraordinary to arise that would make the spirit of one army more determined than the other; as has been said on other occasions, victory depends upon such obstinacy, because while it abides in the hearts of those who are fighting, armies never turn their backs in retreat. And so that such obstinacy would abide longer in the hearts of the Romans than in the Latins, it was partly fate and partly the exceptional ability of the consuls that brought Torquatus to kill his son and Decius to kill himself.

In the course of demonstrating this equality of forces, Livy reveals in its entirety the organization maintained by the Romans in their armies and their battles. Since he explains it in great detail I shall not repeat it all, but I shall examine only what I deem notable and what, having been neglected by all the military leaders of these times, has created disorder in armies and battles. Let me say, therefore, that from the passage in Livy we can discern that the Roman army had three principal divisions, which in Tuscan could be called *schiere* [formations]: they named the first *hastati*, the second *principes*, the third *triarii*, and each of these formations had its own cavalry.* In drawing up the order of battle, the Romans placed the *hastati* in front; in the second place directly behind them they positioned the *principes*; and in the third place in a similar line they put the *triarii*. They positioned the cavalry of these three ranks to the right and to the left of the three lines; the formations of these cavalry, from their form and placement, were called *alae* [wings] because they looked like two wings on that body. They organized the first group, the *hastati*, which was in front, in a locked formation so that it could attack or resist the enemy. The second formation of the *principes* was not the first to offer combat but rather had the task of supporting the first formation when it was beaten or attacked, and it was not tightly ordered but rather kept its ranks open so that it could receive the first formation within its ranks without becoming disorganized, whenever the first formation was forced to retreat by the enemy's onslaught. The third formation of *triarii* kept its ranks even more open than the second in order to receive, whenever necessary, the first two formations, of the *hastati* and the *principes*. Arranged in this manner, then, these formations gave battle, and if the *hastati* were forced back or conquered, they retreated into the openings in the ranks of the *principes*, and, all united together, they created one body out of the two formations and re-entered the battle. If these two formations were repulsed and driven back, they all retreated into the openings in the ranks of the *triarii*, and all three formations having become a single body renewed the struggle; if they were overcome at this point, because they could no longer reorganize, they would lose the battle. And since whenever this last formation of *triarii* was employed, the army was in grave danger, this proverb arose: 'to have reached the *triarii*', which in Tuscan usage would mean: 'we have played our last card.'*

Military leaders of our times, who have abandoned all the other institutions and who fail to observe any part of ancient discipline have likewise abandoned this one, which is of no little importance, for anyone who organizes himself so that he can regroup three times in a battle will lose only if fortune is hostile to him three times, and he must encounter a skill that is capable of conquering him three times. But anyone who is organized to stand up only against the first assault, like all Christian armies today, can easily lose, because any disorder, any mediocre skill can snatch the victory away from him. The thing that makes our armies incapable of regrouping three times is that they have lost the method of taking one formation into another. This has arisen because at present, battles are organized with one of these two defects: either the formations are placed shoulder to shoulder one after the other, and create a battle line that is wide across but thin toward the rear, which makes it weaker, because there is no depth from front to rear; or when instead, in order to make it stronger, they shorten the formations in the Roman manner, and if the first line is broken, since there is no arrangement for receiving them into the second line, they become entangled and break themselves up. For, if the formation in front is pushed back, it collides with the second, and if the second wants to advance, it is impeded by the first, so that with the first formation colliding with the second and the second with the third, so much chaos arises that often only a very small incident can destroy an army. The Spanish and French armies at the battle of Ravenna (where Monsieur de Foix, leader of the French troops, was killed), a battle considered in our times to be very well fought, organized themselves in one of the ways described above: that is, both armies advanced with all their troops lined up shoulder to shoulder, so that neither could have more than a single front line, and they were much stronger in breadth than in depth.* This always happens to them wherever they have a large battlefield, as they had at Ravenna. For, knowing the disorder they produce in retreating, they avoid it when they can by placing their soldiers in a single file, and creating a broad front, as we have said, but, when the countryside restricts them, they remain in the poorly organized position described above without thinking of any remedy. With this same poor organization they ride through hostile territory, either plundering or carrying on any other tactic of warfare. At Santo Regolo in the Pisan territory and elsewhere, wherever the Florentines were defeated by the Pisans during the war between Florence and Pisa after the Pisan rebellion when Charles, king of France, passed through Italy, such ruin arose from nothing other than friendly cavalry: being situated in the front line and driven back by the enemy, it ran through the Florentine infantry and broke it up, so that all the rest of the soldiers turned back. And Messer Ciriaco dal Borgo, the old leader of the Florentine infantry, has affirmed in my presence many times that he was never defeated except by friendly cavalry. The Swiss, who are the masters of modern warfare, above all else take care when they fight with the French to put themselves on one side so that friendly cavalry, if driven back, will not run into them. Although these matters seem easy to understand and extremely easy to put into practice, nevertheless, not even one of our contemporary commanders can be found who imitates ancient institutions and reforms the modern ones. Although they may still have three parts in their army, one called the vanguard, one the main force, and one the rearguard, these divisions serve no other purpose than to keep them under control in camp, but in using them, as we have said above, it is rare that they do not make all these forces subject to the same destiny.

And because many, to excuse their ignorance in these matters, allege that the violence of artillery does not permit many of these ancient institutions to be employed in these times, I want to debate this subject in the following chapter, and I want to examine the question of whether artillery prevents us from employing ancient skill.

CHAPTER 17

How Much Value Should Armies in the Present Day
Place on Artillery; and If the Generally Held
Opinion About Artillery Is True

Besides the matters discussed above, having considered how
many battles in the field (in our times called *giornate*,* a French
word, and *fatti d'arme** by the Italians) were fought by the
Romans at different times, I have decided to consider the common opinion of many who wish to argue that if artillery had
existed in those days, the Romans would not have been able to
seize provinces and make peoples their tributaries as easily as
they did, nor would they have in any way achieved such great
acquisitions. They also declare that with firearms men cannot
demonstrate or make use of their exceptional ability as they
were able to do in ancient times. They add a third point: it is now
more difficult to engage in battle than it was then, and it is
impossible to retain the battle formations of those times, with
the result that, in time, war will be fought only with artillery. In
the belief that it is not outside my topic to debate whether such
opinions are true and how much artillery has increased or
diminished the strength of armies, and whether artillery has
eliminated or provided opportunities for good military leaders
to act skilfully, I shall begin to discuss the first of these opinions:
that the ancient Roman armies would not have made the acquisitions they made had artillery been in existence.

On this subject, in responding, I must say that one makes war
either to defend oneself or to go on the attack; we must first,
therefore, examine the question of which of these two aspects of
war artillery benefits or harms the most. Although there are
arguments on both sides of the issue, I nevertheless believe that
without comparison, artillery causes more damage to the
defence than to the offence. My reason for saying this is that
anyone who is on the defence is either inside a city or in the field
within a fortified camp. If he is inside a city, either this city is
small, as the majority of fortresses are, or it is large: in the first
case, anyone on the defence is completely lost, because the
impetus of the artillery is such that there is no wall so thick that

it will not collapse in a few days, and if the person inside does not possess good wide spaces to which he may retreat, furnished with trenches and fortifications, he is lost, nor can he resist the impetus of the enemy who will later try to enter through the breach in the wall, nor can the artillery that he possesses be of any use to him in this, because it is a maxim that wherever a large body of men can go with force, artillery cannot stop them. Thus, the fury of the Ultramontanes during the defence of cities is not withstood, but Italian assaults are withstood, because they are conducted not with a large body of men but in little groups during the battles, which the Italians call, quite appropriately, skirmishes. Soldiers who go forth with such poor organization and such a lack of ardour to attack the breach in a wall where they face artillery march to an obvious death, for against such men artillery is effective, but when a large number of soldiers is grouped together so tightly that one pushes the other forward, and they march toward a breach, if they are not held off by trenches or embankments they will enter at every point and artillery will not stop them; and if any of them die, the casualties will not be sufficiently high to prevent a victory. The truth of this can be seen in the many expeditions that the Ultramontanes have made into Italy and particularly the one against Brescia, for after that city had rebelled against the French and while its fortress still held out for the French king, the Venetians, in order to withstand the onslaught that might come against the city from the fortress, lined the entire street that descended from the fortress into the city with artillery and placed artillery in front and on the flanks and in every other suitable spot. Monsieur de Foix paid no attention whatsoever to this artillery; on the contrary, with his squadron dismounted, he passed through the middle of the artillery pieces and occupied the city, nor have we heard that he incurred any damage worthy of note. Thus, the defender of a small city, as we have said, who finds his walls levelled to the ground, lacks space with embankments and trenches to which he can retreat, and has no choice but to rely upon artillery, will quickly lose.

If you are defending a large city and you have the opportunity to retreat, artillery is, nevertheless, beyond any comparison more useful to those who are outside than to those who are inside. First of all, in order for artillery to harm those outside you must raise yourself above ground level, for if you are standing on a level plane, every small embankment or barrier the enemy creates makes him safe and you cannot harm him. Thus, since you must raise your artillery and put it upon the walkway atop the walls or in some manner or another raise yourself up from the ground, you expose yourself to two difficulties: the first is that you cannot bring up artillery that is of the size and power that can be used by those outside, since it is difficult to manage large objects in small spaces; the other difficulty is that when you actually can bring up the artillery, you cannot build effective and secure embankments to protect it in the same way as can those outside, since they are standing on solid ground and enjoy all the conveniences and the space they might wish: it is, as a result, impossible for anyone who is defending a city to keep his artillery in high places when those outside have many good and powerful artillery pieces, and if it must be positioned in low places it becomes largely useless, as was said. Thus, the defence of a city is reduced to defending it with hand-to-hand combat, as was done in ancient times, and with light artillery; even if some benefit may be derived from this light artillery, a disadvantage results that counterbalances the advantage of artillery, since on this account the walls of cities have been lowered and almost buried in the trenches, so that when it comes to hand-to-hand combat, either because the walls have been demolished or because the trenches are filled, whoever is inside has many more disadvantages than he might have had in ancient times. Hence, as was mentioned above, these weapons are of much more use to anyone besieging a city than to the besieged.

As for the third issue, that of encamping inside a stockade in order not to give battle unless it is to your benefit or advantage, I must say that in this case you ordinarily have no greater means to avoid fighting than the ancients had, and sometimes, on account of your artillery, you have a greater disadvantage. Accordingly, if the enemy comes upon you and has a slight advantage in his position, as can easily happen, when he is on higher ground than you are, or if at the time of his arrival you have not yet built your embankments or shielded yourself well with them, he will dislodge you immediately and you will have no remedy whatsoever and be forced to leave your fortresses and enter into battle. This happened to the Spanish at the battle of Ravenna; they were dug in between the Ronco river and an embankment, and because they did not make it as high as was necessary, while the French had a slight advantage in their position, they were forced by the artillery to leave their fortresses and to enter the fray. But given that, as is usually the case, you have chosen a place for your camp that is higher than the others opposed to it and that its embankments are good and secure, the enemy would not dare to attack you, considering the site and your other preparations; in this case the same methods will be used that were employed in ancient times when an army was in a position that could not be attacked; the enemy's methods are to overrun the countryside, plunder or seize cities friendly to you, and prevent you from receiving provisions. They will do this until you are forced by some necessity to leave your camp and to come into combat, in which case the artillery, as will be said below, accomplishes very little. Considering, therefore, the kinds of wars the Romans fought, and seeing that they fought almost all their wars to attack others rather than to defend themselves, it will be clear, if the things said above are true, that they would have had a greater advantage and would have made their gains more rapidly if artillery had existed in those times.

As for the second issue, that because of artillery men cannot demonstrate their exceptional ability as they were able to do in ancient times, I must say that it is true that where men have to appear in scattered groups, they run more risks than in ancient times when they had to scale a city wall or engage in similar assaults, in which men were not gathered close together but had to appear by themselves one after another. It is also true that commanders and leaders of armies are more exposed to the peril of death than before, since they can be reached by artillery in any spot, nor does it avail them to be in the rear squadrons surrounded by extremely powerful men.

It is clear, nevertheless, that both of these two dangers rarely do serious damage, because well-fortified city walls cannot be scaled, nor does one proceed to attack them with feeble assaults, but if they are to be taken it comes down to a siege, as it did in ancient times. Even in those cities taken by assault, the dangers are not much greater than in ancient times, because even in those days the defenders of cities did not lack for weapons to hurl, and even if they were not as violent, in so far as killing men is concerned, they produced the same effect. As for the deaths of commanders and *condottieri*, there are fewer examples of this during the last twenty-four years of warfare in recent times in Italy than in ten year's time among the ancients, since after Count Ludovico della Mirandola, who died at Ferrara when the Venetians attacked that state a few years ago, and after the duke of Nemours, who died outside of Cirignola, no such leader has been killed by artillery, because Monsieur de Foix died at Ravenna from sword wounds and not from cannon shot.* Hence, if men as individuals do not demonstrate their exceptional skill, this arises not from the presence of artillery but from inferior institutions and the weakness of their armies which, lacking this exceptional skill as a whole, are unable to show it in any way.

As for the third of their declarations, that it is not possible to fight hand to hand and that war will be conducted entirely with artillery, I can say that this idea is completely false, and it will always be held false by those who wish to make use of their armies according to the standard of ancient excellence, because anyone who wishes to create a good army must, with feigned or genuine battles, accustom his soldiers to approach the enemy, to engage in a sword fight, and to seize him by the throat, and he must rely primarily upon infantry rather than upon cavalry for reasons that will be explained below. When we rely upon infantry and upon the methods previously discussed, artillery becomes completely useless, because infantry, in approaching the enemy, can with more facility avoid cannon shots than soldiers in ancient times could avoid the onslaught of elephants, chariots armed with scythes, and other unexpected opposition that the Roman infantry encountered and against which they always found a remedy. They would have found one more easily against artillery, since the time during which artillery can do you harm is far shorter than the one during which elephants and chariots can hurt you. Thus, the latter throw you into disarray in the midst of a battle, whereas artillery impedes you only before the battle is joined, and such an obstacle is easily avoided by the infantry, either by marching under the natural cover of the terrain or by lying on the ground when these weapons are fired. Experience shows that even this is not necessary, especially to defend oneself from heavy artillery pieces which cannot be balanced in any way, so that if their aim is high they do not hit you, or if their aim is low they do not reach you. After armies have engaged in hand-to-hand combat, it is clearer than the light of the sun that neither heavy nor light artillery can hurt you, because if the artillerymen are in front of you, they become your prisoners; if they are behind you, they damage their friends more than you; if the guns are on your flanks, they cannot hurt you in such a way that you cannot proceed to attack them, and the result will be the effect that we have discussed. This cannot be disputed, because we have seen the example of the Swiss, who at Novara in 1513 without artillery and without cavalry went to meet the French army equipped with artillery inside their fortified positions, and they defeated this army without any hindrance whatsoever from the artillery. The reason for this, besides those mentioned above, is that artillery needs to be protected if it is to work properly, either by a wall or by trenches or by embankments, and if one of these protections is missing, it is captured or becomes useless, in the same way as when it has to be protected by men, which occurs in battles and other actions in the field. On the flank, artillery cannot be used except in the way that the ancients employed the weapons they hurled, which they placed outside their squadrons, so that they could fight outside the lines of battle, and every time that they were charged by cavalry or were pushed back by other kinds of troops, the artillerymen found refuge behind the ranks of the legions. Anyone who relies upon artillery in any other way does not understand the matter very well and relies upon something that can easily deceive him, and if the Turk has won victories with artillery against Sophy and the Sultan,* this has arisen not from some special excellence in artillery itself, but from the terror that its unusual noise spread through their cavalry.

I conclude, therefore, coming to the end of this discourse, that artillery is useful in an army where ancient excellence has been firmly implanted, but without it, artillery is quite useless against an excellent army.

CHAPTER 18

Why One Should Hold the Infantry in Higher Regard Than the Cavalry, Based on the Authority of the Romans and the Example of the Ancient Militia

It can be clearly demonstrated through many arguments and examples that the Romans in all their military actions valued foot-soldiers more than those on horses and based all the battle plans for their forces on them; this can be seen in numerous examples, including the occasion when the Romans were fighting the Latins near Lake Regillus,* where with the Roman army already faltering, the Romans ordered the men on horseback to dismount in order to give assistance, and in this way, having renewed the battle, they achieved victory. In this case, it is obvious that the Romans had more confidence in having their troops on foot than in keeping them mounted on horseback. They employed this same expedient in many other battles, and they always found it to be an excellent remedy to their dangers.

We should not counter this with the judgement of Hannibal, who, upon seeing that the consuls had made their cavalrymen dismount from their horses during the battle of Cannae, declared, mocking such a decision: 'Quam mallem vinctos mihi traderent equites!'—that is to say: 'I would have preferred that they hand them over to me in chains.'* Although this judgement came from the mouth of a most excellent man, none the less, if one must believe in authority, it is necessary to give more credence to the Roman republic and to the many excellent military leaders that it possessed than to the single example of Hannibal. Furthermore, without citing any authorities, there are obvious reasons for this: a foot-soldier can go in many places where a horse cannot follow; it is possible to teach a foot-soldier to stay in formation and, whenever he falls out of line, to return to it; it is difficult to make horses stay in formation, and it is impossible, whenever they fall out of line, to reorder them. Besides this, some horses, just like some men, have little courage and others have a great deal of it, and it often occurs that a courageous horse is ridden by a cowardly man and a cowardly horse by a courageous man; and whatever the form this disparity may take, disadvantage and disorder arise from it. Infantry in formation can easily break the cavalry and can be broken by them only with difficulty. This opinion is corroborated not only by many ancient and modern examples but also by the authority of those who make rules for civic affairs, where they show that wars first began to be waged with cavalry, because the institution of the infantry did not yet exist; but as these foot-soldiers were organized, it was immediately recognized that foot-soldiers were more useful than cavalrymen. It is not for this reason true, however, that cavalry is unnecessary in armies to do reconnaissance, to raid and plunder the countryside, to pursue the enemy when they are in flight, or to provide some opposition for the enemy's cavalry; but the foundation and the sinew of the army, and the type of troops that should be valued most, must be the infantry.

Among the sins of Italian princes, who have made Italy the slave of foreigners, there is none more serious than to have paid little attention to the institution of the infantry and to have turned all of their attention to the militia on horseback. This disorder has arisen because of the wickedness of commanders and the ignorance of those who have ruled states. Some twenty-five years ago,* once the Italian militia had been given over to the command of men without states who were like soldiers of fortune, these commanders immediately thought about how to maintain their own prestige, since they were armed and the princes unarmed. Since they could not continuously pay a large number of foot-soldiers, and did not have subjects they could make use of, and since a small number of men would not bring them any reputation, they turned to keeping cavalry, because two or three hundred horsemen who were paid by a *condottiere* would maintain his prestige, and the payment was not such that it could not be met by men who ruled a state. So that this would more easily come to pass and bring them more prestige, they took all of the esteem and reputation away from the infantry and bestowed it upon their cavalry, and they so enlarged on this confused policy that in the greatest army there was only a minimal number of infantry. This practice, along with many defects mixed in with it, made the Italian militia so weak that this province has been easily trampled upon by all the Ultramontanes.

This error of holding the cavalry in higher esteem than the infantry can be shown even more clearly in another Roman example. The Romans were encamped at Sora, and when a squadron of cavalry went forth from the city to attack their camp, the Roman master of horse went to meet them with his own cavalry; once they charged each other, fate decreed that in the first encounter both commanders would die, and although the rest of the men were left without their commanders and the battle nevertheless went on, the Romans dismounted in order more easily to overcome the enemy, and they compelled the enemy cavalry to do the same, if they wished to defend themselves; and with this tactic the Romans carried off the victory. There could be no better example to demonstrate how much more ability there is in infantry than in cavalry, because if in other actions the consuls made their cavalry dismount, it was to give assistance to the infantry who were suffering and needed help; in this instance, however, the cavalry dismounted, not to assist the infantry nor to combat the enemies on foot, but while fighting on horseback against cavalry, they concluded that if they could not overcome the enemy on horseback, they could, by dismounting, conquer them more easily. I should like to conclude, therefore, that a well-organized infantry can be overcome only with the greatest difficulty, except by another infantry. The Romans Crassus and Mark Antony marched for many days through the dominion of the Parthians with very few cavalry and many infantry, and in opposition to them they had the innumerable cavalry of the Parthians. Crassus was killed with a part of his troops; Mark Antony saved himself through great skill. Nevertheless, in the hardships the Romans experienced, it is evident that the infantry prevailed over the cavalry, because while being in a large country with few mountains and even fewer rivers, far away from the sea and from any assistance, Mark Antony nevertheless saved himself, in the judgement of the Parthians themselves, through the greatest skill; nor did all the Parthian cavalry ever dare to test the formations of his army. If Crassus died there, anyone who reads about his actions with attention will see that he was deceived rather than overwhelmed by force; never in all his troubles did the Parthians ever dare to charge him directly; on the contrary, remaining on his flanks at all times, they cut off his supplies, and by making promises which they did not observe, they brought him to a state of utter distress.

I should think I need to take more trouble to argue the case that the ability of infantry is so much greater than that of cavalry, if there were not so many modern examples that provide the most abundant testimony. As we mentioned earlier, we have seen 9,000 Swiss soldiers at Novara march to confront 10,000 cavalry and as many infantry and overcome them; the cavalry could not harm them, and since the infantry were largely men from Gascony and very poorly organized, the Swiss considered them of little consequence. Then we have seen 26,000 Swiss troops north of Milan* march to attack Francis, king of France, who had with him 20,000 cavalry and 40,000 foot-soldiers along with 100 artillery pieces, and if the Swiss did not carry the day as they did at Novara, they fought valiantly for two days, and then, when they were defeated, half of them escaped. Marcus Regulus Attilius was so bold as to attack not only cavalry with his infantry but elephants as well, and if his plan did not succeed, it was not because the skill of his infantry was such that he could not rely upon them well enough to believe he could overcome that difficulty. I repeat, therefore, that to overcome well-organized infantry, it is necessary to oppose them with infantry even better organized than they are; otherwise one marches to certain defeat. In the times of Filippo Visconti, duke of Milan, around 16,000 Swiss troops descended into Lombardy, whereupon that duke, who, at that time, had Carmignuola as his general, sent him with about 1,000 cavalry and a few foot-soldiers to confront the Swiss. Not knowing their battle formation, Carmignuola attacked the Swiss with his cavalry, presuming he would immediately be able to defeat them. But when he found them invincible, he retreated after losing many of his men, and since he was a most capable man and knew how to design new policies according to new circumstances, Carmignuola reinforced his army and went to meet the Swiss; and when he approached, he made all his men-at-arms dismount, and after placing them at the head of his infantry, he went to assault the Swiss. The Swiss had no remedy for this, because Carmignuola's men-at-arms were on foot and well armed and could easily enter the Swiss formations without suffering any harm, and once they had entered them, they could easily harm them, with the result that of this entire number, only those who were spared by Carmignuola's humanity remained alive.*

I believe that many recognize the difference in ability between these two different kinds of military institutions, but so great is the wretchedness of these times that neither ancient examples nor modern ones, nor even the confession of error, suffices to make modern princes reconsider and understand that in order to give prestige to the militia of a province or of a state, it is necessary to restore these institutions, to observe them closely, to give them prestige, to give them life, so that they may bring him strength and prestige.* But since they deviate from these methods, they also deviate from the other methods discussed above. Hence, it happens that acquisitions bring harm rather than greatness to a state, as will be discussed below.

CHAPTER 19

Conquests Made by Republics Which Are Not Well Organized, and Which Do Not Proceed According to Roman Standards of Excellence, Bring About Their Ruin Rather Than Their Glorification

These opinions contrary to the truth and founded upon the bad examples that our corrupted times have introduced prevent men from thinking about deviating from their usual methods. Could one have persuaded an Italian of thirty years ago that 10,000 infantrymen could attack 10,000 cavalry and as many infantry on level ground and not only fight them but defeat them, as we have seen in the example of Novara that we have so frequently cited? Even though histories are full of such examples, men nevertheless refuse to believe in them; or if they had believed in them, they would have said that in those times men were better armed and that a squadron of armed men on horseback would rather charge a rock than a body of infantrymen; and thus, with such false excuses, they have corrupted their judgement. Nor would they have considered how Lucullus,* with just a few foot-soldiers, defeated 150,000 of Tigranes' cavalry, and that among those cavalrymen was a type of cavalry very much like our own men-at-arms on horseback. Thus, just as this fallacy has been revealed by the example of the Ultramontane soldiers (and for that reason, we see that everything the histories tell us about the infantry is true), so they ought to believe that all the other ancient institutions are true and useful.

If this were believed, republics and princes would err a great deal less and they would be stronger to oppose any attack made against them; they would not place their trust in flight, and those who had a civil society in their hands would know better how to direct it, either by expanding it or by maintaining it. They would believe that increasing the number of inhabitants in their city, making allies and not subjects, sending colonies to watch over acquired territories, making capital out of the spoils of war, subduing the enemy with raids and battles rather than sieges, keeping the public treasury wealthy and private citizens poor, and sustaining military training with the highest degree of diligence would be the true path to making a republic great and to acquiring power. If this method of growth is not acceptable to them, they should remember that acquisitions by any other means are the ruin of republics, and they should rein in every ambition, regulating the city carefully from within through laws and customs and prohibiting expansion, thinking only of defending themselves and keeping their defences well organized, as do the republics of Germany, which by following these methods live free and have lived free for some time. Nevertheless, as I said earlier when I discussed the difference between establishing institutions for expansion and establishing institutions for stability, it is impossible for a republic to succeed in standing still while enjoying its liberty within its narrow borders, because if the republic does not trouble others, others will trouble it, and from being troubled arises the will and the necessity for expansion, and when you have no enemy outside you will find one at home, as it seems occurs necessarily in all the great cities. If the republics of Germany can live in that manner and have endured for a long while, this arises from certain conditions that exist in that country which do not exist elsewhere and without which they could not hold on to such a way of life.

That part of Germany of which I am speaking was subjected to the Roman empire as were France and Spain, but when the imperial power later began to decline and the title of that power was transferred to that province, the most powerful of these cities, according to the cowardice or the needs of the emperors, began to free themselves, redeeming themselves from the empire by reserving for it a small annual tribute, so that little by little all those cities that were direct dependants of the emperor and were subject to no other prince redeemed themselves. At the same time that these cities were redeeming themselves, it happened that certain communities subject to the duke of Austria rebelled against him, among them being Fribourg and the Swiss and other similar communities; they prospered in the beginning and little by little they managed to expand so much that not only did they not return to the yoke of Austria, but caused all their neighbours to fear them, and these are the people who are called the Swiss.*

This province is, therefore, divided among the Swiss, into republics (which they call free cities), princes, and the emperor. And the reason that among so many diverse kinds of government wars do not arise or, if they do arise, do not last for long, is that symbol of the emperor, who, while having no forces, nevertheless has so much prestige among them that he acts as their conciliator and, interposing himself with his authority as a mediator, quickly puts a stop to any disagreements. The greatest and longest wars that have occurred there are those between the Swiss and the duke of Austria, and although the emperor and the duke of Austria have been one and the same thing for many years, he has nevertheless been unable to overcome the daring of the Swiss, with whom no agreement is ever possible without force. Nor has the rest of Germany given the emperor much help, both because these communities do not wish to attack any-one who wishes to live free like themselves, and also because some of those princes cannot, since they are poor, while others will not, since they are jealous of his power. These communities can, therefore, live content with their small dominion, since they have no reason, with respect to imperial authority, to desire to become larger; they can live united within their city walls, since they possess a nearby enemy who would seize any opportunity to attack them whenever they find themselves at odds. Thus, if that province were set up differently, it would be necessary for them to seek to expand and to destroy their own tranquillity.

But since such conditions cannot be found elsewhere, it is not possible to choose this way of life, and it is necessary either to expand by means of leagues or to expand as the Romans did. Anyone who acts otherwise seeks not his life but his death and ruin, since in a thousand ways and for many reasons, conquests are damaging. Thus, it is quite possible to acquire dominion but not strength at the same time, and anyone who acquires dominion but not strength along with it of necessity comes to ruin. Anyone who is impoverished by wars cannot acquire strength, even if he is victorious, since he puts more into the affair than he derives from his acquisitions: just as the Venetians and the Florentines did, who were much weaker when Venice held Lombardy and Florence controlled Tuscany than they were when one was content with the sea and the other with six miles of surrounding territory. In fact, all this is born from wishing to expand without knowing how to select the method of doing so; and these cities deserve even more criticism inasmuch as they have less excuse, since they saw the method employed by the Romans and could have followed their example, while the Romans, without any example to follow, through their own prudence knew on their own how to find the right method.

Besides this, conquests sometimes cause no little damage to a well-organized republic, when a city or a province full of luxuries is acquired, where it is possible to take on some of those habits through one's own experience with them; this happened first to Rome, in the acquisition of Capua, and then to Hannibal. And if Capua had been farther away from Rome, so that the remedy for the soldiers' error was not so close at hand, or if Rome had been corrupt to some degree, without a doubt this acquisition would have been the ruin of the Roman republic. Livy bears witness to the truth of this with these words: 'Capua was even then a most unhealthy spot for military discipline, seducing the minds of the soldiers by all the pleasures it could provide, so that they forgot their homeland.'* And truly, such cities or provinces have their revenge against the conqueror without battles or shedding of blood, because by filling him with their own bad habits, they make him vulnerable to being conquered by anyone who attacks him. And Juvenal could not have said it better when, in considering this matter in his *Satires*, he declares that as a result of acquiring foreign territories, foreign customs entered Roman hearts, and in place of frugality and other excellent qualities, 'gluttony and luxury took over, avenging the conquered world'.* If expansion risked being harmful to the Romans during the times when they were conducting themselves with so much prudence and skill, what will happen, then, to anyone who proceeds in a way which deviates so far from their methods and who, besides the other mistakes they make, which I have discussed in some detail above, also chooses soldiers who are either mercenaries or auxiliaries? As a result of this, they often suffer the kinds of damage that will be noted in the following chapter.

CHAPTER 20

What Kind of Danger a Prince or a Republic Employing Auxiliary or Mercenary Soldiers Incurs

If I had not discussed in detail in another work of mine* the question of how useless mercenary or auxiliary troops are and how useful one's own soldiers are, I would extend my discussion in this chapter farther than I have already done, but since I have spoken of this question at length elsewhere, I shall at this point be brief. It has not seemed appropriate to pass over it entirely, since I have found so many examples of relevance to the topic of auxiliary troops in Livy; auxiliary soldiers are those, led and paid by you, that a prince or a republic may send to assist you. With respect to Livy's text, let me say that having defeated two Samnite armies in two different places with their own troops, which they had sent to assist the Capuans and thus to free the Capuans from the war the Samnites were waging against them, and wishing to move back toward Rome, the Romans left two legions behind in the city of Capua to defend it, so that the Capuans, deprived of protection, would not once again become prey to the Samnites. These legions, wasting away in idleness, began to take such pleasure in it that, having forgotten their native city and their reverence for the senate, they pondered the possibility of taking up arms and making themselves rulers of the city that they had defended with their own valour, feeling that the inhabitants were not worthy of possessing property they did not know how to defend. This matter, when discovered, was dealt with and corrected by the Romans, as will be amply demonstrated when we deal with conspiracies.* Let me say again, therefore, that of all the kinds of soldiers, auxiliary troops are the most harmful, for the prince or the republic that adopts their assistance possesses no authority whatsoever over them, but the one who sends them alone possesses such authority. Thus, auxiliary soldiers are those who are sent to you by a prince, as I have said, under his captains, under his banners, and paid by him, as was the army the Romans sent to Capua. These kinds of soldiers, once they have gained victory, in most cases prey upon the one who has hired them as well as the one against whom they are hired, and they do this either because of the wickedness of the prince who sends them or because of their own ambition. Although it was not the intention of the Romans to break the agreement and the conventions they had established with the Capuans, nevertheless, the ease with which they could take the city was so obvious to those soldiers that they were able to persuade themselves to think about taking it from the Capuans. It is possible to cite many examples of this, but I should like this one along with one other to suffice, that of the people of Rhegium, whose lives and land were seized by a legion that the Romans had placed there as a garrison.* A prince or a republic must, therefore, first choose any other policy but that of bringing auxiliary troops into their state for their own defence when it is necessary to rely upon them completely, because every pact, every convention with the enemy, no matter how long it lasts, will be less burdensome than this policy. And if we read about past events and discuss those of the present, we shall discover that for each one who has benefited from this policy, countless numbers have been deceived, and a prince or an ambitious republic cannot have a better opportunity to occupy a city or a province than to be invited to send its armies to their defence. Thus, anyone who is so ambitious that he calls in such assistance not only to defend himself but also to attack others, seeks to acquire what he cannot hold and what can easily be taken away from him by the same one who acquired it for him. But the ambition of man is so great that, in order to satisfy a desire of the moment, he does not think about the evil that can result from it in a very short time. Nor do ancient examples move him any more in this matter than in the others we have discussed, because if men were moved by such examples, they would see that the more generosity they demonstrate toward their neighbours and the less inclined they are to occupy their territory, the more likely such neighbours will be to throw themselves into their laps, as will be discussed below through the example of the Capuans.

CHAPTER 21

The First Praetor the Romans Sent Anywhere Was Sent to Capua, Four Hundred Years After They Had Begun to Wage War

How different the Romans' mode of conduct in making conquests was from those who in the present day increase their territory has been amply discussed above, as well as how they allowed the cities they did not destroy to live under their own laws, even those which had surrendered to them not as allies but as subjects; in such cities they left no sign of Roman power but rather obliged them to observe certain terms, and if these were observed, they maintained those cites in their own condition and dignity. It is known that these methods were observed until the Romans went outside of Italy and began to turn kingdoms and states into their own provinces.

A clear example of this is the fact that the first praetor they sent to any location was sent to Capua, and they sent him not out of any ambition of theirs but rather because it was something sought by the Capuans, who, upon experiencing internal conflict, thought it necessary to have within the city a Roman citizen who would reorganize and reunite it. Inspired by this example and constrained by the same necessity, the people of Antium then requested a prefect for themselves, and about this incident and this new method of achieving dominance, Livy says: 'and the power not only of Roman arms but of Roman law began to be widely felt.'* It is evident, therefore, how much this method facilitated Roman expansion. Since cities, particularly those which are used to living free or normally govern themselves through their own citizens, are more content living in some tranquillity under a dominion they do not see, even if there is some harshness in it, than under one that they see every day and that seems every day to reproach them with their servitude. Another benefit, then, accrues to the ruling power, for since its own ministers do not have power over the judges and magistrates who render justice in the civil and criminal cases in these cities, no judicial sentence can ever be pronounced to the detriment or disgrace of the ruler, and in this way, such cities come to avoid many causes for false accusation and hatred toward the ruler. To show that this is true, besides the ancient examples that one might cite, there is a fresh example in Italy. As everybody knows, after Genoa had been occupied numerous times by the French, that king always, except in recent times, sent a French governor there to rule in his name. Only now, and not by the king's choice but rather because necessity has required it, has the king left that city to rule itself and to do so with a Genoese governor. Without doubt, anyone who seeks to discover which of these two methods brings more security to the king in his possession of the city and more contentment to the people will without hesitation approve this latter method. Besides this, men are much more likely to throw themselves into your lap the less inclined you seem to take possession of them, and they fear you so much the less, with regard to their freedom, the more humane and kind you are with them. This kindliness and generosity made the Capuans run to ask the Romans for a praetor; yet, if the Romans had shown the least desire to send him there, the Capuans would have instantly grown suspicious and would have distanced themselves from Rome.

But why is it necessary to go to Capua and to Rome for examples when we have those of Florence and Tuscany? Everyone knows how long ago the city of Pistoia placed herself voluntarily under Florentine rule. Everyone also knows how much enmity has existed among Florentines, Pisans, Lucchese, and Sienese, and this difference of feeling has not arisen because the people of Pistoia do not value their liberty just like the others and do not judge themselves equal to the others, but rather because, with them the Florentines have always acted like brothers, while they have acted like enemies with the others. For this reason, the people of Pistoia have willingly come under their control; the others have made and still make every effort not to fall under it. Undoubtedly, if the Florentines, either by way of leagues or assistance, had domesticated and not exasperated their neighbours, at this hour they would no doubt be the lords of Tuscany. I do not, for this reason, think that one should not employ arms and force, but they must be reserved for the last resort, when and where other methods are not sufficient.

CHAPTER 22

How Often the Opinions of Men Are Mistaken
in Their Judgements About Important Matters

How false the opinions of men are on many occasions, those who have been witnesses of their decisions have seen and still see; often when such decisions are not made by excellent men, they are contrary to every truth. Because excellent men in corrupt republics (especially in tranquil times) are considered enemies, both out of envy or other ambitions, the people follow either a man who is judged to be good by common self-deception or someone put forward by men who are more likely to desire special favours than the common good. Later, in adverse times, this deception is revealed, and out of necessity the people turn to those who in tranquil times were almost forgotten, as will be amply discussed in the appropriate place.* Certain situations also arise in which men who have little experience of things are easily deceived, since in such incidents there is much that seems so true that it makes men believe their judgements in these matters are accurate. I have made these remarks because of what Numisius, the praetor, persuaded the Latins to do after they were defeated by the Romans,* and also because of what many people were given to believe a few years ago when Francis I, king of France, came to take possession of Milan, which was defended by the Swiss. On that account, let me say that after Louis XII died* and Francis of Angoulême ascended the throne of France, desiring to restore the duchy of Milan to his kingdom, which a few years before had been occupied by Swiss troops with the encouragement of Pope Julius II, Francis wanted to have allies in Italy who would facilitate the undertaking; and besides the Venetians, whose support Louis had regained, he sounded out the Florentines and Pope Leo X, since he thought the enterprise would be easier once he had regained their support, since the king of Spain had soldiers in Lombardy and the emperor additional forces in Verona. Pope Leo did not yield to the king's wishes but was persuaded by those who gave him counsel (according to what is said) to remain neutral, demonstrating to him that in this plan lay certain victory, since it did not serve the church to have either the king or the Swiss with power inside Italy, and that if he wished to restore Italy's ancient liberty, it was necessary to liberate Italy from servitude to both of them. Because it was not possible to conquer one or the other, either by themselves or both together, the pope needed to have one of them conquer the other, and afterwards the church with its allies could attack the one who then emerged victorious. It was impossible to find a better opportunity than the present one, since both of them were in the field and the pope's forces were organized in such a manner that they could present themselves on the borders of Lombardy near both armies under the pretence of wishing to guard his possessions and remain there until they engaged in battle. Since both armies were strong, it could reasonably be assumed that the battle would be very bloody for both parties and would leave the victor in a weakened condition, so that it would be easy for the pope to attack and defeat him, and thus the pope would become, to his great glory, lord of Lombardy and arbiter of all of Italy. Just how false this opinion was can be seen in the actual unfolding of this incident, because once the Swiss were overcome after a lengthy struggle, the pope's troops and those of Spain did not have the courage to attack the victors but prepared to retreat, and this would not have helped them had it not been for the humanity or the irresoluteness of the king, who did not seek a second victory but for whom it was enough to come to an agreement with the church.*

Certain arguments supporting this opinion seem true from

afar but are altogether extraneous to the truth. For it rarely occurs that the victor loses too many of his troops, because victorious troops perish in the midst of the battle, not in flight; and in the heat of battle when men are face to face, few of them actually fall, mainly because the combat lasts for a brief period of time in most cases; and even if it lasts for a long while and many of the victors perish, their victory enhances their prestige so greatly and creates so much fear that it far outweighs the damage they have suffered through the death of their soldiers. Thus, if an army, in the belief that the victor has been weakened, goes to attack him, it will find itself greatly deceived, unless the army was already such that at any time, either before or after the victory, it was capable of engaging the victor in combat. In this case it could win or lose according to its fortune and its exceptional ability, but the army that had fought earlier and won would still have the advantage over this one. The truth of this can be recognized in the experience of the Latins and the error made on the part of Numisius, the praetor, and by the damage caused to the peoples who believed him. After the Romans had conquered the Latins, he proclaimed throughout all the territory of Latium that the moment was ripe to attack the Romans, who were weakened from the battle they had waged with them; that the Romans had gained nothing more than the name of victory, while all the other damage they had suffered was tantamount to having been defeated; and that any little force which attacked them again would destroy them. As a result, the peoples who believed him created a new army and were quickly defeated, and they suffered the harm that those who hold such an opinion will always suffer.

CHAPTER 23

To What Extent the Romans Avoided a Middle Course of Action in Passing Judgements on Subjects for Some Incident Requiring Such a Verdict

'The situation in Latium was already one where peace and war were equally intolerable.'*

Of all the unhappy situations, the most unhappy is that of a prince or a republic reduced to a state where it can neither accept the peace nor continue the war; and those are reduced to such a state who, by the terms of a peace agreement, are harmed too much and who, on the other hand, are obliged to become prey to those who assist them or to the enemy, in their wish to make war. All of them finish in such dire straits through poor advice and poor planning, through not having taken careful measure of their own forces, as we said above.* Thus, any republic or prince who takes good measure of these matters will only with great difficulty be brought to the end suffered by the Latins, who, when they should not have reached an agreement with the Romans, did so, and when they should not have declared war upon the Romans, did so, and in this way managed to bring about a situation in which both the enmity and the friendship of the Romans were equally damaging to them. The Latins were therefore defeated and totally overwhelmed, first by Manlius Torquatus and later by Camillus,* who, after forcing them to surrender and to place themselves back in the hands of the Romans, and after placing garrisons in all the cities of Latium and taking hostages from them all, returned to Rome and reported to the senate that the entire territory of Latium was in the hands of the Roman people. And because this judgement is notable and worthy of being observed by those rulers who might imitate it when similar situations arise, I should like to cite Livy's own words placed in the mouth of Camillus, which bear witness both to the means employed by the Romans in expansion and to the fact that, in governmental decisions, the Romans always avoided a middle course of action and turned to extreme measures.

In substance, a government is nothing more than the control of subjects in such a way that they cannot and must not harm you; this is achieved either by making yourself completely safe from them, by taking away from them every means of doing you harm, or by bringing them benefits in such a way that it would not be reasonable for them to desire some change in fortune. All this is perfectly clear, first from Camillus' remarks and then from the judgement pronounced on them by the senate. His words were these: 'The immortal gods have put you in control of the situation, so that the decision whether Latium shall exist in future or not is left in your hands; as far as the Latins are concerned, therefore, you have the power to create a permanent peace for yourselves by exercising either cruelty or forgiveness. Do you wish to adopt harsh measures against men who have surrendered or suffered defeat? You may destroy the whole of Latium, and create vast deserts out of the places from where you have often drawn a splendid allied army to make use of in many a major war. Or do you want to follow the example of your ancestors and extend the State of Rome by admitting your defeated enemies as citizens? The material for such increase is there in abundance, with glory to be won of supreme kind. Certainly by far the strongest government is one to which men are happy to be subject. But whatever you decide to do, you must make haste; you are keeping so many peoples in suspense, between hope and fear. You must resolve your own doubts concerning them as soon as possible, and while their minds are benumbed with apprehension, give them either the certainty of punishment or generous treatment.'* The deliberation of the senate following this proposal was in accord with the words of the consul, and city by city, bringing forward all those of some importance, the Romans either rewarded them or destroyed them; to those they rewarded, the Romans granted exemptions, privileges, and citizenship, in every way making them secure; as for the other cities, their lands were destroyed or colonies were sent there or their citizens were sent back to Rome, scattering them so that they could nevermore do harm through arms or intrigue. Nor did the Romans, as I have stated before, ever take a neutral course in these matters of crucial importance.

Rulers should imitate this judgement. The Florentines should have followed this course of action when Arezzo and the entire Valdichiana rebelled in 1502;* had they done so, they would have secured their dominion and made the city of Florence great, and they would have given it the countryside that it lacked for provisions. But they employed that middle course of action which is extremely damaging in passing judgement on men; they banished some of the citizens of Arezzo, and they condemned others to death; they took away their honours and ancient ranks from everyone in the city; and they left the city intact. But if some citizen in the course of their deliberations advised that Arezzo be destroyed, those who seemed to be wiser declared that would bring little honour upon the city, since it would appear that Florence lacked the strength to hold it. These arguments are of the kind that appear to be true but are not, because by this same reasoning one would never execute a traitor or a wicked and seditious man, since to do so would shamefully demonstrate that the ruler lacked the power to restrain a single individual. Those men who hold such opinions fail to see that men taken individually, and a city as a whole, sometimes sin against the state in such a way that in order to make an example to others for one's own security, a ruler has no other remedy than to destroy them. Honour consists in being able and knowing how to punish them, not in being able to hold them amidst a thousand dangers, because a ruler who does not punish a man who errs in such a way that he cannot err again is held to be either ignorant or cowardly.

The necessity of the judgement that the Romans rendered is also confirmed by the sentence they pronounced upon the people of Privernum. In this matter, two things in Livy's text must be noted: first, as was mentioned above, that subjects must be either given benefits or destroyed; secondly, how much generosity of spirit and telling the truth matters when speaking in the presence of wise men. The Roman senate was gathered together to pass judgement upon the people of Privernum, who had rebelled and had then been brought back by force under Roman control. Many citizens were sent by the people of Privernum to ask for the pardon of the senate, and when they were in the senators' presence, one of the senators asked one of them: 'what punishment he thought the Privernates deserved.'* To this the citizen of Privernum replied: 'the punishment deserved by those who think themselves worthy of freedom'. To this the consul replied: 'Suppose we let you off punishment, what sort of a peace may we hope to have with you?' To this the citizen of Privernum responded: 'If you grant us a good one, it will be loyally kept and permanent. If a bad one, it will not last long.' At this point, the wisest part of the senate, even though many others were angered, declared that 'the voice they heard was that of a man, and a man free-born. Was it credible, they asked, that any people, or indeed, individual, would remain longer than was necessary in a situation that was painful? A peace was loyally kept when its terms were voluntarily accepted; loyalty could not be expected from those on whom they wished to impose servitude.' On the basis of these words the senators decided that the people of Privernum should become Roman citizens, and they honoured them with the privileges of citizenship, saying, 'only those who took thought for nothing except freedom are worthy of becoming Romans'. This sincere and generous reply greatly pleased generous spirits, because any other reply would have been deceptive and cowardly. Those who believe otherwise about men, especially about those accustomed to being, or thinking themselves, free, are deceiving themselves; and under this deception, they choose policies that are neither good for themselves nor likely to satisfy others. From this circumstance arise frequent rebellions and the ruin of states. But to return to our topic, let me conclude by saying that, based on this judgement and the one pronounced against the Latins, when one has to judge powerful cities and cities that are accustomed to living in liberty, it is necessary either to destroy them or to give them benefits; otherwise every judgement is made in vain. Above all one must avoid a middle course of action, which is harmful, as it was to the Samnites when they trapped the Romans at the Caudine Forks and did not wish to accept the opinion of the old man who advised them that all the Romans should either be released with honour or killed, but, choosing a middle course of action, they disarmed the Romans and forced them to march under the yoke, allowing them to depart full of shame and indignation. As a result, not long afterwards they learned, at great cost to themselves, that the old man's judgement had been useful and their own decision harmful, as will be discussed at greater length in the proper place.*

CHAPTER 24

Fortresses Are Generally Much More Harmful Than Useful

To the wise men of our times, it will perhaps seem a matter not well considered that the Romans, in their desire to secure themselves from the peoples of Latium and the city of Privernum, did not think of building fortresses, which would have served as a check to keep those peoples faithful, especially given the existence of a saying in Florence, cited by our own wise men,* that Pisa and other cities like it must be held with fortresses. And truly, if the Romans had been made like these Florentines they would have thought about building fortresses, but because they possessed a different kind of ability, a different kind of judgement, and a different kind of power, they did not build them. While Rome lived in freedom and maintained her institutions and her virtuous laws, she never built fortresses in order to hold either cities or provinces, but she did conserve some of those already built. Hence, seeing how the Romans conducted themselves in this matter and how the rulers of our times have acted, I should like to consider whether building fortresses is a good idea and whether they bring harm or advantage to those who construct them.

It should, then, be considered whether fortresses are constructed to defend against one's enemy or against one's subjects. In the first case they are not necessary, in the second they are harmful. And beginning with the reasons why in the second case they are harmful, I would say that where a principality or a republic fears its subjects and the possibility of their rebellion, such a fear must arise first of all from the hatred that its subjects harbour for it, hatred for its evil conduct; this evil conduct arises either from the belief that it can hold its subjects with force, or from the lack of prudence of the one who governs them. One of the things that makes him believe he can then rule them by force is having fortresses nearby, because the bad treatment causing their hatred derives in good measure from the fact that such a ruler or such a republic possesses fortresses, which, when this is true, are far more harmful than useful. For in the first place, as was mentioned, they make you more bold and violent toward your subjects, and then they fail to give you the security within, which you were convinced would exist, since all the forces and all the violence used to hold a people are worth nothing, with two exceptions: either you must always put a good army in the field, as the Romans did, or you disperse, destroy, disorganize, and disunite the people in such a way that they cannot unite to harm you. Thus, if you impoverish them, 'to those despoiled, arms remain';* if you disarm them, 'anger supplies weapons';* if you kill their leaders and continue to injure the others, these leaders will be reborn like heads of the Hydra; if you build fortresses, they will be useless in peacetime, because they make you more inclined to mistreat your subjects, but in times of war they are completely useless, because they are assaulted both by the enemy and by your subjects, nor is it possible to offer resistance to both one and the other. And if fortresses ever were useless, they are especially so in our own times against artillery, the destructive power of which makes small locations, where it is impractical to retreat behind embankments, impossible to defend, as was discussed earlier.

I should like to discuss this matter in greater detail. Either you, prince, desire to hold in check the people of your own city or you, prince or republic, wish to hold in check a city seized through warfare. I now wish to turn to the prince and declare to him that such a fortress cannot be more useless to hold one's citizens in check, for the reasons cited above, because they make you more ready and less hesitant to oppress your subjects, and this oppression makes them so disposed to seek your ruin that it inflames them to the degree that such a fortress, which is the cause of all this, can no longer defend you. Hence, in order to maintain his reputation, a wise and good prince will never build a fortress, to avoid giving his sons either a reason or the temerity to become wicked, and to make them rely not upon their fortresses but upon the goodwill of their people. And if Count Francesco Sforza,* who became duke of Milan, was reputed to be a wise man and none the less constructed a fortress in Milan, let me say that in this respect he was not wise, and the result of such a fortress has demonstrated that it has brought harm rather than security to his heirs.* Because, thinking that by means of this fortress they could live securely and would be able to offend their citizens and their subjects, they spared their subjects no kind of violence, making themselves so despised that they lost their state when the enemy first attacked them; nor did that fortress protect them or prove useful in war, and in peace it did them great harm, because had they not possessed it and, through a lack of prudence, treated their citizens harshly, they would all the sooner have discovered this danger and might well have restrained themselves; and they would have then been able to resist with greater courage the French onslaught with their subjects as friends and without a fortress, rather than with a fortress and all their subjects as enemies. Fortresses are of no use to you whatsoever, because you lose them either through the treachery of those who guard them or the violence of those who attack them, or through starvation. If you wish them to be useful to you and to help you regain a government that you have lost, where only the fortress remains in your hands, you need an army with which you can attack the person who has driven you out, and when you possess this army you will regain the state in one way or another, just as if the fortress did not exist, and you will do it much more easily, since men will be friendlier to you than they were after you treated them badly because of the pride you took in your fortress. Experience has shown that this fortress in Milan has in no way benefited either the Sforza family or the French in adverse times; on the contrary, it has brought much harm and damage to them all, since with the presence of this fortress they have not thought about a more honourable method of holding on to that state.

Guidobaldo, duke of Urbino and the son of Federigo, who was in his day a greatly esteemed military leader, was chased out of his state by Cesare Borgia, the son of Pope Alexander VI; later, after an unforeseen incident, Guidobaldo returned there, and he had all the fortresses in that province destroyed, judging them harmful. Because he was loved by his people, he did not need fortresses to protect himself, and he saw that he could not defend them against the enemy, since they required an army in the field to defend them; thus, he chose to destroy them.* After having driven the Bentivoglio family from Bologna, Pope Julius II constructed a fortress in that city, and then allowed one of his governors to brutalize that people. As a result the Bolognese rebelled, and the pope immediately lost the fortress, and it therefore served no good purpose and did him harm, whereas had he acted differently it would have been useful to him.* Niccolò da Castello, the father of the Vitelli, upon returning to his homeland from which he had been exiled, immediately dismantled two fortresses that Pope Sixtus IV had built there, judging that not a fortress but, rather, the goodwill of his people would have to maintain him in that state.*

But of all the other examples, the freshest and most notable in every regard, and the one most likely to demonstrate the uselessness of constructing fortresses and the usefulness of tearing them down, is what happened in Genoa in recent times. Everyone knows that Genoa rebelled in 1507 against King Louis XII of France, who personally came with all his troops to reconquer the city, and once he had retaken it he built a fortress, which was stronger than all of those we know about up to the present day, because its location and every other detail made it impregnable, situated as it was atop some hills extending toward the sea, called Codefà by the people of Genoa; and with it he dominated the entire port and a large part of the city of Genoa. Then, in 1512 when the French troops were driven out of Italy, Genoa, notwithstanding the fortress, rebelled and the state was seized by that Ottaviano Fregoso, who with great effort, at the end of sixteen months, took the fortress by means of starvation. Everyone thought (and many advised) that he should preserve the fortress as a refuge for any emergency, but being a most prudent man and recognizing that it is not fortresses but, rather, the will of the people that maintains rulers in their position of power, he destroyed it. Thus, without basing his power upon the fortress but upon his own exceptional ability and prudence, he has held and still holds it, and whereas to change the government of Genoa it was once enough to employ a thousand foot soldiers, his adversaries have attacked him with ten thousand and have not been able to do him harm. It is obvious, therefore, from this example that tearing down the fortress has done no harm to Ottaviano and that constructing one did not protect the king, for when the king was able to come into Italy with an army, he was able to recover Genoa without having a fortress, but when he was unable to come into Italy with an army, he could not hold Genoa even while having one there. It was, then, expensive for the king to build it and shameful for him to lose it, while for Ottaviano, reacquiring it was glorious, and destroying it was useful.

But let us come to republics that build fortresses not in their homeland but in lands that they conquer. To demonstrate the fallacy of relying on fortresses, if the example we have cited of France and Genoa is not enough, I believe that of Florence and Pisa will suffice; the Florentines, in this case, built fortresses to hold that city, not realizing that in a city to which the very name of Florence had always been inimical, which had lived in freedom, and which had in that freedom a reason to rebel, it was necessary, if one wished to hold it, to follow the Roman method: either make it your ally or destroy it. The merit of fortresses is shown by what happened upon the arrival of King Charles, to whom they were given up either because of the treachery of those who defended them or fear of greater harm; if the fortresses had not existed there, the Florentines would not have based their capability to hold Pisa upon them, and that king would not have been able in that way to deprive Florence of that city; and the methods by which Florence held Pisa until that time would have perhaps been sufficient to save it, and without doubt they would have given no worse an account of themselves than with the fortresses.

Let me conclude, therefore, that to hold one's own native city, a fortress is harmful, and for holding cities that have been acquired, fortresses are useless. As for me, I want the authority of the Romans to suffice, for in the cities they wished to hold with force, they tore down walls instead of building them. To anyone who would cite contrary to this opinion the example of Tarentum* in ancient times or that of Brescia in the present day, places which were recaptured by means of fortresses after a rebellion of their subjects, I would reply that for the recovery of Tarentum, Fabius Maximus was sent at the beginning of a year with an entire army, which would have been enough to regain the city even if no fortress had existed there; and even though Fabius employed this method, had it not existed, he would have used another means which would have produced the same result. I do not know of what use a fortress is if, in the retaking of a city, you need a consular army and a Fabius Maximus as general in order to do so. That the Romans would have captured the city in one way or another can be seen from the example of Capua,* where there was no fortress and which was recaptured through the army's exceptional skill. But let us turn to Brescia.* Let me say that what happened in that rebellion rarely happens:

that is, the fortress remains in your hands after the city has rebelled, and you have a large army close by like the one the French had, for when Monseigneur de Foix, the king's general, had heard about the loss of Brescia while in Bologna with his troops, without delay he went there directly; and arriving in three days, he retook the city using the fortress. Still, to serve any useful purpose, the fortress needed a Monseigneur de Foix and a French army to come to its assistance within three days. Certainly, this example as compared to the contrary ones does not really suffice, because in the wars of our times, many fortresses have been taken and retaken with the same kind of fortune with which the countryside has been captured and recaptured, not only in Lombardy but also in Romagna, in the kingdom of Naples, and throughout Italy.

But with respect to building fortresses to defend yourselves from foreign enemies, I must say that they are unnecessary for those peoples and kingdoms that have good armies, and for those that do not have good armies they are useless, because good armies without fortresses are sufficient to defend themselves, while fortresses without good armies cannot defend you. This is seen through the experience of those who have been considered excellent in governmental affairs and in other matters as well, such as the Romans and the Spartans: if the Romans did not build fortresses, the Spartans not only abstained from doing so but also did not permit their city to have walls, because they wanted the exceptional ability of the individual man, and no other type of defence, to protect them. Hence, when a Spartan was asked by an Athenian if the walls of Athens seemed beautiful to him, he replied: 'Yes, if there were only women living there.'* That prince who has good armies will sometimes, therefore, find fortresses on the coasts and borders of his state useful in holding back the enemy for a few days until he has put things in order, but they are not essential. Furthermore, when a prince lacks a good army, possessing fortresses in his state or on his borders is either harmful or useless to him: they are harmful, because he can easily lose them, and losing them, they can be used to make war against him, or even if they are so strong that the enemy is unable to occupy them, they are left behind the enemy army and come to be of no use, because good armies, when they meet no strong resistance, enter enemy territory without respect to the cities or fortresses they may leave behind, as we can see in ancient histories and in the actions of Francesco Maria,* who in recent times in order to attack Urbino left behind ten enemy cities without concern.

That prince, therefore, who can create a good army can do so without building fortresses; the prince who lacks a good army must not build them. He must carefully fortify the city in which he lives and keep it supplied and its citizens well disposed, in order to hold back the enemy attack long enough to free himself either through an agreement or through outside help. All other plans are expensive in peacetime and useless in times of war. Thus, anyone who will consider everything I have said will recognize that the Romans, so wise in every other institution, were also prudent in their judgement concerning the Latins and the Privernates; giving no thought to building fortresses in this situation, they ensured their own security with more skilful and wiser methods.

CHAPTER 25

That It Is a Mistaken Policy to Attack a Divided City in Order to Occupy It as a Result of Its Disunity

There was so much disunity within the Roman republic between the plebeians and the nobility that the Veientes, along with the Etruscans, thought that through such disunity they could extinguish the very name of Rome. After they had raised an army and conducted raids upon the Roman countryside, the senate sent against them Gaius Manlius and Marcus Fabius, who led their army near that of the Veientes, but the Veientes did not cease, both with attacks and insults, to harm and to tarnish the reputation of Rome: and so great was their temerity and their insolence that the Romans, once disunited, became united and turning to battle, defeated and conquered them. It is, therefore, evident, as we have written previously,* how greatly men deceive themselves in making certain decisions, and how frequently, thinking they will gain something, they lose it. The

Veientes thought they would attack the Romans while disunited and conquer them, and this attack was the cause of the unity among the Romans and of their own ruin, for the cause of disunity in republics is in most cases idleness and peace; the cause of unity is fear and warfare. Hence, if the Veientes had been wise, the more disunited they perceived Rome to be, the more they would have avoided war with that city and the more they would have sought to overcome it through the arts of peace. The proper method is to seek to gain the confidence of the city that is disunited and, until the people come to the point of fighting, to act as their arbiter, manœuvring between the factions. When fighting breaks out, it is appropriate to give small favours to the weakest faction, so that they continue fighting for a longer time and wear themselves down, and so that larger forces never make them all suspect that you intend to overcome them and become their ruler. When such a policy is well handled, it will almost always result in reaching the goal you have set for yourself. The city of Pistoia, as I stated in another discourse on a different subject,* did not come under the rule of the Florentine republic by any other method than this one; since it was divided and the Florentines favoured first one faction and then another, without being blamed by either side, they brought the city to such a state that, worn out from its tumultuous civic life, it spontaneously threw itself into their arms. The political status of Siena has never changed with favours from the Florentines except when these favours have been weak and of little account, for when they have been generous and bold, they have made the city unified in defence of the government in place. I want to add to the examples cited above yet another example. Filippo Visconti, duke of Milan, often declared war on the Florentines, basing his decision upon their disunity, and he always remained the loser, to the extent that he was accustomed to declare, complaining about his undertakings, that the follies of the Florentines had caused him uselessly to spend 2 million gold florins.

The Veientes and the Etruscans were, therefore, deceived in this opinion, as was mentioned above, and they were finally overcome by the Romans in a battle. Thus, in the future, anyone who thinks he can conquer a people in a similar way or for a similar cause will also be deceived.

CHAPTER 26

Insults and Abuse Generate Hatred Against Those Who Employ Them, Without Profit

I believe that one of the great means of exercising prudence that men can employ is to abstain either from threatening anyone or from injuring them with words, for neither of these actions takes any strength away from the enemy, but the first makes him more cautious and the second increases his hatred toward you and makes him think more actively of harming you. This can be seen in the example of the Veientes, who were discussed in the preceding chapter; they added the injury of words to the damages of war inflicted on the Romans, something every prudent commander must make his soldiers refrain from doing, because these are the things that inflame the enemy and incite him to take revenge, and in no way, as is said, do they hinder him from harming you, to the degree that these are all weapons that are turned against you.

A noteworthy example of this occurred once in Asia, where Cobades, commander of the Persians, having been encamped before the city of Amida for some time, decided to leave, exhausted by the tedium of the siege, and after he had already struck camp, the city's inhabitants came out on the walls and, puffed up with pride, did not hesitate to employ every kind of insult, vituperating, disparaging, and reproaching the cowardice and the worthlessness of their enemy. Enraged by this, Cobades changed his mind, and once he returned to the siege his indignation over the injury was so great that in a few days he had taken the city and sacked it. This same thing happened to the Veientes, for whom, as was mentioned, it was not enough to make war upon the Romans; they also abused them with their words; and going even as far as their stockades to insult them, they irritated the Romans far more with their words than with their weapons, and those soldiers who initially fought against their will forced the consuls to take up the fight, so that like the others mentioned above, the Veientes suffered the penalty of their insolence. Good leaders of armies and good rulers of republics must, therefore, take every opportune measure to ensure that such injuries and reproaches are not used either in their cities or in their armies, either among themselves or against the enemy, because when employed against an enemy, the above-mentioned disadvantages result, and employed among themselves they would produce even worse effects, unless proper remedies were taken in the way prudent men have always taken them. After the Roman legions who were left in Capua conspired against the Capuans, as will be recounted in the appropriate place,* this conspiracy gave birth to a mutiny, and when this was put down by Valerius Corvinus, among the other articles contained in the agreement, very severe penalties were stipulated for anyone who might ever reproach the soldiers for that mutiny. Tiberius Gracchus, who during the war against Hannibal had become commander of a certain number of slaves armed by the Romans because of a shortage of men, decreed, among his very first acts, that capital punishment would be suffered by anyone who reproached any of these soldiers for their former servitude. The Romans considered insulting men and reproaching them for any disgrace on their part to be extremely harmful, as was mentioned above, because nothing inflames their spirits more nor generates greater indignation, whether it is said in earnest or in jest. 'But crude jests, when based on truth, they rankle.'*

CHAPTER 27

Victory Should Be Sufficient for Prudent Princes and Republics, for Most Often When It Does Not Suffice, They Lose

Employing insulting words against the enemy arises, in most instances, from an insolence you gain either from victory or from the false hope of victory; this false hope makes men err not only in their speech but also in their actions. For when this kind of hope enters men's breasts, it makes them go too far and, in most cases, lose the opportunity of possessing a certain good in the hope of acquiring an uncertain but better one. Given that this is a rule that deserves consideration, since men are very often deceived about it to the detriment of their state, I think it is fit to demonstrate it in detail with ancient and modern examples, since it is impossible to provide as clear a demonstration solely with arguments. After he had defeated the Romans at Cannae, Hannibal sent his emissaries to Carthage to announce his victory and to ask for assistance. The senate debated over what was to be done. Hanno, an old and prudent Carthaginian citizen, advised them to employ this victory wisely in making peace with the Romans, since they had won and could obtain it with honourable conditions, something they could not expect to do after a defeat, because the intention of the Carthaginians should be to demonstrate to the Romans that defeating them was enough and that after having achieved their victory, they did not seek to lose it in the hopes of gaining even a greater one. This policy was not adopted, but it was later recognized as a very wise one by the Carthaginian senate, when the opportunity was lost.

After Alexander the Great had already conquered the entire East, the republic of Tyre—in those times a noble and powerful republic, because its city was surrounded by water, like that of the Venetians—recognized Alexander's greatness and sent him emissaries to inform him that they wished to be his good servants and to give him the obedience he required, but that they were not yet prepared to accept either him or his troops inside their city; whereupon, indignant that a city would wish to close their gates to someone to whom the entire world had thrown them open, Alexander rebuffed them and, refusing to accept their conditions, besieged the city. The city was surrounded by water and was well supplied with provisions and other munitions necessary for its defence; after four months, Alexander finally realized that a single city, to its glory, was taking more of his time than many of his other acquisitions had taken, and he decided to try to come to an agreement and to concede to them what they themselves had asked of him. But the citizens of Tyre, puffed up with pride, not only were unwilling to accept such an agreement but they murdered the envoy who came to negotiate it. Indignant at this, Alexander turned to the assault with such force that he took the city and destroyed it and killed and enslaved its people.

In 1512 a Spanish army entered Florentine territory to restore the Medici in Florence and to levy a tribute upon the city; they had been brought there by citizens inside who had led them to hope that as soon as they were inside Florentine territory, the inhabitants would take up arms in their support; and after they entered the plain and no one showed himself, the troops tried to reach an agreement, since they were short of provisions; the people of Florence, puffed up with pride, did not accept it, which resulted in the loss of Prato and the ruin of the Florentine state.*

Rulers who are attacked cannot, therefore, commit a greater error, when the attack is carried out by men of far greater power than their own, than to refuse every agreement, especially when it is offered to them, because there will never be an offer so mean that it will not contain something beneficial to the party who accepts it and will, in some respects, represent a partial victory for him. Thus, it should have been enough for the people of Tyre that Alexander accepted the conditions he had initially refused, and it was victory enough to have constrained such a man to their will with arms in hand. It should also have been enough for the Florentine people, since it was a sufficient victory for them, that the Spanish army yielded to some of their demands and did not satisfy all its own, because the aim of that army was to overturn the Florentine state, to remove it from the alliance with France, and to extract money from it. Once the army had achieved two of its three goals, that is, the last two, and the Florentines had achieved one of theirs, which was the preservation of their government, each party in this affair had some honour and satisfaction. The people should not have cared about the first two goals, since they remained alive, nor should they have been willing, even though they looked toward an even greater and almost certain victory, to leave the outcome in any way at the discretion of fortune, thus going to their last stake, which no prudent man ever risks unless he is forced to do so.

Having left Italy where he had gained glory for sixteen years, recalled by his own Carthaginians to rescue his native city, Hannibal found Hasdrubal* and Syphax defeated, the kingdom of Numidia lost, and Carthage confined within the limits of its city walls, with no other refuge remaining except him and his army. Recognizing that this was his city's last stake, he did not, first of all, want to put his city at risk until he had exhausted every other remedy, and he was unashamed to sue for peace, concluding that if his native city had any remedy, it lay in that and not in war; but when peace was denied to him, he decided not to avoid fighting even if he had to lose, concluding that he might yet be able to win or, losing, to lose gloriously. If Hannibal, who was so able and had his army intact, first sought peace rather than a battle when he saw that if he lost the battle, his native city would become enslaved, what should another man of less ability and experience do? But men commit this error, that is, they do not know how to set limits to their hopes, and when they base their actions on such hopes, without otherwise measuring themselves, they come to ruin.

CHAPTER 28

How Dangerous It Is for a Republic or a Prince
Not to Avenge an Injury Committed Against
the Public or Against a Private Individual

What indignation causes men to do can easily be ascertained by what happened to the Romans when they sent the three Fabii as emissaries to the Gauls, who had come to attack Etruria and Chiusi in particular. For, after the people of Chiusi had sent to Rome for assistance against the Gauls, the Romans sent ambassadors to the Gauls, who, in the name of the Roman people, told them to cease waging war upon the Etruscans. When these emissaries were on the spot and proved themselves more capable of acting than speaking, they placed themselves among the first to fight against them when the Gauls and Etruscans engaged in battle, and after they were recognized by the Gauls, the Gauls turned all the indignation they had felt against the Etruscans against the Romans. This indignation became greater, because, after the Gauls through their ambassadors had lodged a complaint with the Roman senate about this injury and had asked that the previously mentioned Fabii be delivered to them in satisfaction for the damage, not only did the Romans fail to turn the Fabii over to them or punish them in any way, but when elections came around, they were made tribunes with consular authority. Thus, once the Gauls saw them honouring the men who should have been punished, they thought that all this had been done with contempt and to their disgrace, and burning with indignation and wrath, they came to attack Rome and took the city, except for the Capitol. This disaster came upon the Romans solely because of their failure to observe justice, for after their ambassadors had transgressed 'against the law of nations' and should have been punished, they were honoured. Nevertheless, it must be considered how much care every republic and every prince should take not to commit such an injury, not only against a mass of people but also against any single individual, because if a man is greatly offended either by the state or by a private person and is not avenged to his own satisfaction, he will, if he lives in a republic, seek to avenge himself, even if it results in the republic's ruin, and if he lives under a prince and has any inner strength, he will never be appeased until in some way he has avenged himself upon the prince, even if he sees his own harm in it.

To verify this, there is no finer nor truer example than that of Philip of Macedonia, the father of Alexander. He had in his court a handsome young nobleman named Pausanias, with whom Attalus, one of the foremost men in Philip's court, fell in love, and after trying to obtain his consent on numerous occasions, and discovering that Pausanias was contrary to such things, he decided to take with deceit and force what he saw he was unable to obtain in any other way. Having organized a formal banquet to which Pausanias and many other noble barons came, after each guest was full of food and drink, he had Pausanias seized and brought to him with no hope of escape, not only fulfilling his own lust by force but also, to bring him even greater dishonour, allowing many others to violate him in the same way. Pausanius complained more than once about this insult to Philip; after keeping him for some time in the hope of being avenged, Philip not only failed to avenge him but made Attalus governor of a province in Greece; hence Pausanius, seeing his enemy honoured and unpunished, turned all his indignation not against the man who had done him the injury but against Philip who had not avenged him. One solemn morning, at the time of the wedding feast of Philip's daughter whom he had married to Alexander of Epirus, while the king was going to the temple to celebrate the wedding, Pausanius killed him as he stood between the two Alexanders, son-in-law and son. This example is very similar to the one concerning the Romans and it is worthy of note to anyone who governs: he must never esteem a man so lightly that, piling injury upon injury, he believes that the injured man does not think about taking revenge despite all the danger and harm that might befall him.

CHAPTER 29

Fortune Blinds Men's Minds When She Does Not Wish Them to Oppose Her Plans

If we consider carefully how human affairs proceed, we shall see that things frequently arise and incidents occur against which the heavens have not wished any provision to be made. And if what I am discussing happened in Rome (where there existed so much ability, so much religion, and such order), it is no surprise that it may happen even more often in a city or a province lacking in such elements. Since this instance is of considerable note in illustrating the power of heaven over human affairs, Livy explains it at length and in the most effective language, stating that since heaven for some reason wished the Romans to recognize its power, it first caused the Fabii who went as emissaries to the Gauls to make a mistake and through their actions to incite the Gauls to wage war on Rome. Then it ordained that nothing should be done in Rome worthy of the Roman people to stop this war, by having first arranged for Camillus, who might have been by himself the sole remedy for such a great ill, to have been sent in exile to Ardea. Then, when the Gauls marched toward Rome, those who had often created a dictator to deal with the assault of the Volscians and other neighbouring enemies did not do so when the Gauls came. Also, in drafting soldiers, they did so in an unsound way and without any special care, and they were so slow in taking up arms that they barely managed to engage the Gauls on the River Allia, ten miles from Rome.

There the tribunes set up their camp without their usual care, neglecting first to inspect the place and to surround it with a moat and a stockade, employing no precautions human or divine. In drawing up the order of battle, they made the ranks thin and weak, so that neither the soldiers nor the commanders accomplished any deed worthy of Roman discipline. Then they fought without shedding any blood, for they fled before they were attacked, and the majority went to Veii, while the rest retreated to Rome where, without even returning to their homes, they went to the Capitol, so that, without thinking about Rome's defence, the senate did not even shut Rome's gates, and part of it fled while part went with the others to the Capitol. Still, in the defence of the Capitol the senate employed methods that were not chaotic; they did not make it over-crowded with useless people; they stocked within it all the grain possible in order to survive a siege; and the majority of the use-less crowd of old people, women, and children fled to sur-rounding cities, while the rest remained inside Rome at the mercy of the Gauls. Thus, anyone who reads about the things accomplished by that people so many years before and then reads about these later times could not believe in any manner that this was the same people. Once Livy has described all the previously mentioned disorders, he concludes with these words: 'Destiny blinds men's eyes, when she is determined that her gathering might shall meet no check!'* This conclusion could not be more true; hence men who normally live under great adversity or in great prosperity deserve less praise or blame. For in most cases it is clear that they have been led to a disastrous or a grandiose action by an unusual situation that the heavens have created, granting them the opportunity or depriv-ing them of the capability of acting with great valour.

Fortune does this well: when she wants to accomplish great deeds, she selects a man with such spirit and such exceptional ability that he recognizes those occasions that she offers him. Thus, in like manner, when she wishes to bring about great calamities, she places men in charge who will contribute to that disaster. If there is anyone who might be able to oppose her, she either kills him or deprives him of all the means to achieve some good. We recognize very well from this passage that in order to make Rome more powerful and to bring the city to the level of greatness it achieved, fortune judged it necessary to strike it down (as we shall discuss at length in the beginning of the following book), although she did not wish to destroy the city completely. This can be seen in the fact that she had Camillus sent into exile but not killed; she had the city of Rome taken but not the Capitol; she ordained that the Romans would not think of any good way to protect Rome, but then did not overlook any good measure to protect the Capitol. To ensure that Rome might be taken, she caused most of the soldiers who were routed at the River Allia to go to Veii, and in this way she blocked every method of defending the city. And in organizing all this, she prepared everything for the regaining of the city, having taken an entire Roman army to Veii and Camillus to Ardea, so that it would be possible to create a large vanguard with a commander unsullied by the disgrace of defeat and with his reputation intact to reclaim his native city.

In confirmation of the matters discussed, some modern examples might be cited, but I shall omit them, judging them unnecessary, since this should be sufficient to satisfy anyone. Again, I want to affirm it as being very true, according to what can be seen in all the histories, that men can side with fortune but not oppose her; they can weave her warp but they cannot tear it apart. They must never give up, for without knowing her goals as she moves along paths both crossed and unknown, men always have to hope, and with hope, they should never give up, no matter what the situation or the difficulty in which they find themselves.

CHAPTER 30
Truly Powerful Republics and Princes Do Not Buy Friendships With Money But, Rather, With Their Exceptional Skill and the Reputation of Their Forces

The Romans were besieged in the Capitol, and although they were expecting help from Veii and Camillus, driven by hunger, they came to an agreement with the Gauls to ransom themselves for a certain quantity of gold, and while the gold was being weighed out according to this pact, Camillus arrived with his army; fortune brought this about, says the historian, so that the Romans would not 'owe their lives to a cash payment'.* This is worth noting not only in this case but also in the series of actions taken by the republic, where it can be seen that the Romans never acquired territory with money, never made peace with money, but always did so with their exceptional skill at arms, something I do not believe ever to have occurred in any other republic. Among the other signs through which the power of a strong state is recognized is the manner in which it lives with its neighbours. When it governs itself in such a way that its neighbours are its tributaries in order to keep it friendly, this is a sure sign that such a state is powerful, but when these neighbours, even while inferior to it, take money from it, then this is a significant sign of its weakness.

Read all the Roman histories, and you will see that the Massilienses, the Aedui, the Rhodians, Hiero of Syracuse, kings Eumenes and Masinissa, who all lived near the confines of the Roman empire, competed with payments and tributes to Rome's needs to gain her friendship, seeking nothing else from her but to be defended. The opposite is seen in weak states. Beginning with our state of Florence, in times past when her reputation was greatest there was not a single lord in Romagna who did not receive some payment from her, and besides, she gave money to the Perugians, the inhabitants of Città di Castello, and to all her other neighbours. If this city had been armed and bold, everything would have gone in the opposite direction, for many cities would have given money to her in order to have her protection, and would have sought not to sell their own friendship but to purchase hers. Nor did the Florentines live alone in this cowardice, but also the Venetians and the king of France, who, with such a great kingdom, lives as a tributary of the Swiss and the king of England. All this arises from the fact that this king disarmed his peoples and from the fact that he and the others mentioned above have preferred to enjoy the immediate benefit of being able to plunder their people and to avoid imaginary and unreal danger, rather than to accomplish things that would make them secure and their states happy in perpetuity. This disorder, even when it creates some tranquillity, is necessarily the cause, with the passage of time, of damage and irremediable ruin. It would take far too long to recount how many times the Florentines, the Venetians, and that kingdom of France have bought themselves out of a war and how often they have exposed themselves to a disgrace to which the Romans were on the point of exposing themselves only a single time. It would take too long to recount how many cities the Florentines and the Venetians have bought off; disorder was later seen in them, and it was evident that those things acquired with gold cannot be defended with steel. The Romans observed this proud conduct and this way of life as long as they lived in liberty, but later, when they came under the rule of emperors and the emperors began to be evil and to love the shade more than the sun, the Romans also began to buy themselves off from the Parthians, then from the Germans, and then from other nearby peoples, and this was the beginning of the ruin of so great an empire.

Similar disadvantages arise, then, from having disarmed your peoples; from this arises another, even greater disadvantage, for the nearer the enemy comes to you, the weaker he will find you. Anyone who lives in the ways outlined above treats the subjects inside his dominion badly and those who live on its borders well, in order to have men strongly disposed to keeping the enemy at a distance. As a consequence, in order to keep the enemy further off he makes payments to those rulers and peoples living near his borders. Hence, states of this kind put up very little resistance on their borders, but when the enemy passes nearby they have no remedy whatsoever, and they do not realize that their mode of conduct is contrary to every good institution. Accordingly, the heart and the vital organs of a body, and not its extremities, have to be kept armed, since without the latter the body is alive, but if the former are harmed it dies; and these states keep the heart disarmed while arming the hands and feet.

What this disorder has brought about in Florence has been seen and can still be seen every day, because whenever an army crosses the borders and comes near to its heart, it has no other remedy left. A few years ago* the same thing was true of the

Venetians, and if their city were not surrounded by water, it would have seen its end. This experience is not so commonly seen in France, which is such a large kingdom that it has few enemies that are superior to it in number; none the less, when the English attacked that kingdom in 1513* the entire country trembled, and the king himself and everyone else thought that a single defeat could take the kingdom and the state from him. Exactly the opposite happened to the Romans, for the nearer the enemy came to Rome, the more powerful he found that city in resisting him. This is evident in Hannibal's invasion of Italy, because after three defeats and so many dead commanders and soldiers, the Romans were not only able to hold out against the enemy but to win the war. This arose from the fact that they had armed their heart well and paid less attention to the extremities. Thus, the foundation of their state was the people of Rome, the Latin nation, the other allied cities in Italy, and their colonies, from which they drew so many soldiers that with them they were able to fight and to hold on to the entire world. The truth of this is obvious in the question that Hanno, the Carthaginian, asked the emissaries of Hannibal after the defeat of Cannae, for after they had glorified Hannibal's deeds, they were asked by Hanno if anyone from the Roman people had come to sue for peace and if any among the Latin nations or the colonies had rebelled against the Romans, and when they replied in the negative to both these questions, Hanno declared: 'This war is still as undecided as it was before.'*

Both this discourse and what we have said elsewhere many times before show how greatly the mode of conduct in republics of the present differs from that in republics of ancient times. Thus, we see miraculous losses and miraculous gains every day, because when men possess little of that exceptional ability, fortune shows her power all the more; and because fortune is changeable, republics and states often change, and they will continue to change until someone rises up who is so devoted to antiquity that he will regulate fortune in such a way that she will have no cause to demonstrate, with every revolution of the sun, how powerful she can be.

CHAPTER 31

How Dangerous It Is to Believe Exiles

It does not seem beside the point to discuss somewhere in these discourses how dangerous a thing it is to believe those who have been driven from their native land, since those who rule states must deal with such matters everyday, and since this idea can be demonstrated with a memorable example cited by Livy in his histories, even though it was outside the scope of his topic. When Alexander the Great passed through Asia with his army, his brother-in-law and uncle Alexander of Epirus came into Italy with his troops, summoned by the exiled Lucanians, who gave him hope that with their help he could occupy that entire country. Whereupon, based upon their word and in that hope, he entered Italy and was killed by them once their fellow-citizens promised them they could return home if they murdered him.* One must consider, therefore, how vain are both the word and promises of those who find themselves deprived of their homeland. Accordingly, with respect to their word, it must be assumed that any time they can return to their native land by any other means than with your assistance, they will abandon you and draw near to others, notwithstanding whatever promises they have made to you. As for their vain promises and hopes, their desire to return home is so intense that they naturally believe many things which are false, and to them they add many things with guile, so that between the things they believe and the things they say they believe to fill you with hope, they fill you up with so much hope that if you rely upon it, you either incur expenses or undertake an enterprise in which you are ruined.

I want the previously mentioned example of Alexander to suffice, along with that of Themistocles of Athens, who, after being declared a rebel and fleeing to Darius in Asia, promised him so much, if he would attack Greece, that Darius undertook the invasion. Unable to keep these promises later on, Themistocles poisoned himself, either out of shame or for fear of retribution.* And if this error was committed by Themistocles, a man of great excellence, it must be assumed that those men of lesser ability who allow themselves to be pulled along by their desire and their passion make even more mistakes. A prince must, therefore, go slowly in undertaking actions based upon the report of an exile, because most often he will end up suffering either shame or very serious harm. And also, since taking cities by stealth or through intelligence from others on the inside rarely succeeds, it does not seem beside the point to discuss this subject in the following chapter, adding to this discussion material about the many methods by which the Romans acquired them.

CHAPTER 32

In How Many Ways the Romans Took Towns

Since all Romans were dedicated to war, they always waged it with every advantage, both with respect to expenses and with respect to every other thing. This gave rise to the fact that they avoided taking towns by siege, because they thought that this method involved far more expense and inconvenience than the benefit they could derive from the acquisition. For this reason, they believed that it was better and more useful to subjugate cities by any other means than by laying siege to them, with the result that in so many wars and over so many years, there are extremely few examples of sieges that they carried out. The methods with which they took cities were, therefore, either by assault or surrender. Assault was either by force and open violence or by force mixed with fraud. Open violence was either when they conducted an attack without battering the walls, which they called 'putting a crown around the city',* because they surrounded the city with the entire army and attacked it from all sides (and they were often successful in taking a city in a single assault, even though it was very large, as when Scipio took New Carthage in Spain);* or when this attack was not enough and they turned to breaking the walls down with battering-rams and other machines of war, to digging a tunnel through which they entered the city (the way in which they captured the city of Veii), to constructing wooden towers so that they were level with those who defended the city walls, or to putting up earthen embankments supported by the outside walls in order to reach the height of the walls above them. In the first instance, that of being attacked from all sides, the men defending the city against such assaults were subject to more immediate danger and had more uncertain remedies, because they required numerous defenders in all positions, but their troops were not so numerous that they could provide men for all positions or for replacements, or if they could, they did not all possess the same courage to resist, and if the battle were to shift in one direction, they would all be lost. On that account, as I have said, this method often met with happy success. But when it did not succeed at first, the Romans did not often make another attempt, for it was a method that was very dangerous to the army, since by stretching itself over so much space, it remained totally vulnerable to any sortie that those inside the walls might have made, and it also disorganized the troops and left them fatigued; still, on a single occasion and as a surprise measure, the Romans might use this method. With respect to destroying the city walls, those inside would oppose this method with the same kind of fortifications as are used today. To resist against tunnels they would dig a counter-tunnel, and they would, in this way, oppose the enemy both with arms and other devices, among which was this one: they would fill large containers with feathers in which they lit a fire, and once they were aflame they placed them in the tunnel so that, with the smoke and the smell, they blocked the entrance against the enemy. If they were attacked with towers, they made every attempt to destroy them with fire. With respect to the earthen embankments, they would break up the wall which supported the embankment at its base, pulling into the city the earth that those outside the walls were piling up, so that as earth was put outside and taken away inside, the embankment did not grow.

These methods of capturing cities could not be employed over a long period of time, and it was necessary either to strike camp or to seek through other means to win the war (as Scipio did when, after invading Africa and having attacked Utica without succeeding in taking it, he struck camp and sought to destroy the Carthaginian armies); or to resort to a siege, as the Romans did at Veii, Capua, Carthage, and Jerusalem and other similar cities that they took by means of a siege. With respect to taking cities by clandestine violence, this occurs as it did at Paleopolis, which the Romans occupied by agreement with those inside the city. This kind of attack has been attempted many times, by the Romans and by others, and it has met with success on few occasions; the reason is that every small obstacle breaks up the plan, and obstacles arise easily, because the conspiracy is discovered before the plot is carried out, and it may be discovered without much difficulty, both because of the infidelity of the people with whom you are conspiring and because of the difficulty of putting the plan into action, since you have to come to an agreement with your enemies and with people with whom it is not permissible to speak except under some pretext. But if the conspiracy is not discovered during the planning, a thousand problems then arise in putting it into action, because either you arrive before the appointed time or you arrive afterwards, which spoils everything, or if an accidental noise is raised, as with the geese on the Capitol, or if normal routine is broken, the slightest error and the smallest mistake ruin the whole enterprise. To this must be added the shadows of the night, which cause even more fear in those who participate in such dangerous affairs. And since the majority of men who undertake such enterprises are inexperienced in the lay of the land or in the places where they are led, they are confused, they grow fearful, and they become unsettled at the least unforeseen incident, and every deceptive appearance is sufficient to make them take flight. Nor has anybody ever been more fortunate in these fraudulent and nighttime expeditions than Aratus of Sicyon,* who, as valiant as he was in these, was something of a coward in open operations in daylight; it is necessary to conclude that this was because he had some special hidden talent rather than because such undertakings are naturally more successful. Of these methods, therefore, many are tried, few are actually tested, and very few succeed.

With respect to taking cities by surrender, either they give themselves up voluntarily or they are taken by force. The will to give up voluntarily arises either from some external necessity that constrains them to take refuge under your protection, as did Capua with the Romans, or from a desire to be well governed, being attracted by the good government that such a prince maintains in those who have voluntarily placed themselves in his arms, as the Rhodians, the Massilienses, and other similar cities did when they gave themselves up to the Roman people. With respect to forced surrender, either such force originates in a lengthy siege, as was stated above, or it comes from continual oppression through raids, pillaging, and other bad treatment, which cities may wish to avoid by surrendering. Of all these methods mentioned, the Romans employed this last one more than any other, and they spent more than 450 years wearing down their neighbours with routs and raids and increasing their reputation among them by means of treaties, as we have discussed on many other occasions. They always relied upon this particular method, even though they tried all of them, but in other methods they found elements that were either dangerous or useless. In a siege, there are the length of time and the cost; in an attack, doubt and danger; in conspiracies, uncertainty. They saw that they could acquire a kingdom in a single day by defeating an army, and that they wasted many years in taking a stubborn city by siege.

CHAPTER 33

How the Romans Gave the Commanders of Their Armies Full Discretionary Powers

I reckon that, while reading Livy's history and wishing to derive some profit from it, it is necessary to consider all the methods of proceeding employed by the people and the Roman senate. Among other matters worthy of consideration is an examination of the kind of authority with which they sent out their consuls, dictators, and other military commanders. It is evident that such authority was extremely great, and that the senate reserved nothing for itself except the authority to start new wars and to confirm peace treaties, while leaving everything else to the will and power of the consul. For this reason, once the people and the senate had decided to wage a war, for example against the Latins, they left all the rest to the will of the consul, who could fight a battle or avoid it and besiege one city or another, just as he saw fit. These policies can be confirmed through many examples, and especially through what happened during an expedition against the Etruscans. Because after Fabius the consul had defeated them near Sutrium and then planned to pass through the Ciminian forest with his army to go into Etruria, not only did he fail to consult the senate, but he gave it no information whatsoever about his plans, even though he was about to wage a war in an unknown territory, which was risky and dangerous. The decisions taken in regard to this policy by the senate also testify to this; the senate, upon learning of the victory that Fabius had won, fearing that he would decide to march through that forest into Etruria, and deeming it unwise to attempt such a war and to run such a risk, sent two legates to make him understand that he was not to march into Etruria; the legates arrived after Fabius had already done so and won his victory, so that instead of preventing the war, they returned as emissaries to announce his conquest and the glory he had earned. Anyone who considers this approach well will see that it was very prudently employed, for if the senate had wished for a consul to proceed in war little by little according to what tasks they entrusted to him, they would have made him less diligent and slower, because he would have felt that the glory of the victory was not entirely his, but that the senate had shared in it through the advice by which he had been guided. Besides this, the senate would have been obliged to give advice on a matter about which it could not have known anything, since notwithstanding the fact that the senate was filled with men highly experienced in warfare, nevertheless, not being on the spot and not knowing the countless details that must be known in order to give good advice, they would have committed countless errors in giving it. For this reason, they wanted the consul to act on his own and for the glory to be entirely his own, his love of which they judged to be the best check and rule of thumb to make him do his best. This is a policy I most willingly note because I see that the republics of the present day, such as the Venetian and Florentine republics, understand the question differently, and if their military leaders, quartermasters, and agents have to set up a single artillery piece, they want to know about it and give advice on it. This method deserves the same praise as the others, all of which taken together have led them into the situation in which they find themselves at present.*

BOOK III

CHAPTER I

In Order for a Religion or a Republic to Have a Long Life, It Is Often Necessary to Bring It Back to Its Beginnings

It is very true that all the things of this world have a limited existence, but those which go through the entire cycle of life ordained for them by heaven are generally those which do not allow their bodies to fall into disorder but maintain them in an orderly way, so that either nothing changes, or if it changes, it is to their welfare, not to their detriment. Since I am speaking of mixed bodies, such as republics and religions, let me say that changes which bring such bodies back to their beginnings are healthy. The ones that have the best organization and the longest lives are, however, those that can renew themselves often through their own institutions, or that come to such a renewal through some circumstance outside these institutions. And it is clearer than light itself that if they do not renew themselves, these bodies will not endure.

The method of renewing them is, as was stated, to bring them back to their beginnings, because the beginnings of religions, republics, and kingdoms must always contain in themselves some goodness through which they may regain their early prestige and their early expansion. And because in the course of time that goodness is corrupted, if something does not come about to bring it back to its proper limits, it will, of necessity, kill that body. Those doctors of medicine declare, speaking of human bodies: 'Every day the body absorbs something that requires a cure from time to time.'* This process of bringing something back to its beginnings, when referring to republics, is produced either by some extrinsic accident or by some intrinsic prudence. As for the first means, it is evident how necessary it was for Rome to have been taken by the Gauls in order for it to be reborn, and in being reborn, to take on new life and new vigour and to take up once again the observance of religion and of justice, which were beginning to become corrupt. This is very clearly understood through Livy's history, where he demonstrates that in calling out their army against the Gauls and in creating tribunes with consular authority, the Romans failed to observe any religious ceremony. Likewise, they not only failed to punish the three Fabii who had fought against the Gauls 'in opposition to the law of nations',* but they made them tribunes. It is easy to speculate that they began to take less account of the good regulations instituted by Romulus and other prudent rulers than was reasonable and necessary to maintain a free way of life. This blow from the outside occurred, therefore, so that all the institutions of that city might be reclaimed, and so that the Roman people would see not only that it was necessary to maintain religion and justice, but also to hold good citizens in high esteem and to place a higher value on their exceptional abilities than on those conveniences they felt were lacking because of their actions. It is evident that this is exactly what happened, because as soon as Rome was retaken, the Romans renewed all the institutions of their ancient religion, punished the Fabii who had fought 'in opposition to the law of nations', and then honoured the exceptional ability and goodness of Camillus to such a degree that the senate and the others set aside their envy and placed back in his hands the entire burden of that republic. It is therefore necessary, as was said before, for men who live together under some kind of order to be required to reflect upon themselves, either by these extrinsic accidents or by the intrinsic ones. With respect to the latter, they must arise either from some law, which obliges the men who belong to that body to re-examine their affairs with some frequency, or, indeed, from one good man who is born among them and who, by his exemplary deeds and his exceptional works, produces the same effect as the regulation.

Such good, therefore, arises in republics either through the exceptional ability of a single man or through the special excellence of a single regulation. With respect to the latter, the institutions that brought the Roman Republic back to its beginnings were the tribunes of the plebeians, the censors, and all the other

Discourses on Livy

laws that were passed against the ambition and the insolence of men. These regulations must be given life by the exceptional ability of a single citizen, who courageously strives to enforce them against the power of all those who fail to observe them. Among the ways in which these laws were applied before Rome was taken by the Gauls, the most notable examples were the deaths of the sons of Brutus, the deaths of the decemvirs,* and the death of Melius the grain-dealer; after Rome was taken, these examples included the death of Manlius Capitolinus, the death of the son of Manlius Torquatus, the attempt by Papirius Cursor to execute Fabius, his master of cavalry, and the charges against the Scipios. Because these events were unusual and worthy of note, each time one of them occurred they made men move back toward their proper limits, and when such events became more rare, they also began to give more space to men to become corrupt and to conduct themselves in a far more dangerous and disorderly manner. Thus, not more than ten years should pass between one of these applications of the law and another, because after such a period of time has passed, men begin to change their habits and break the laws, and if nothing arises to remind them of the punishment and to renew the fear in their hearts, the number of delinquents will soon become so large that they can no longer be punished without danger. Those who governed the Florentine state from 1434 until 1494 used to say in this regard that it was necessary to take the state back every five years or it was otherwise difficult to preserve it, and what they called 'taking the state back' meant striking the same terror and fear into the hearts of men that they had instilled upon first taking power, when they struck down those who had, according to that way of life, governed badly. But when the memory of such a beating fades away, men grow bolder in making new attempts and in speaking evil, and it is therefore necessary to make provision against this by bringing the state back to its beginnings.

This return to the beginnings in republics also arises from the simple talents of a single man, without depending upon a law which drives you on to its execution; such men are nevertheless of such reputation and exemplary behaviour that good men wish to imitate them and evil men are ashamed to lead a life contrary to theirs. Those men in Rome who produced particularly good results were Horatius Cocles, Scaevola, Fabricius, the two Decii, Regulus Atilius, and some others, all of whom with their uncommon and worthy examples created in Rome almost the same effect that was created by the laws and institutions.* If the enforcement of the laws noted above, along with these particular exemplary actions, had occurred at least every ten years in that city, it would have necessarily followed that Rome would never have become corrupted, but as they became both few and far between, corruption began to increase. For this reason, after Marcus Regulus no similar exemplary actions were seen in Rome, and although the two Catos* rose up in Rome, there was too great a space of time between him and them, and then between the two of them, and they remained so isolated that they could not, with their good examples, accomplish any good work; this is especially true of the last Cato who, finding the city for the most part corrupt, could not, with his own example, make the citizens better. And this should suffice as far as republics are concerned.

But as for religions, it is also evident that these revivals are necessary through the example of our own religion which, had it not been brought back to its beginnings by Saints Francis and Dominic, would have died out completely; for these men, with their poverty and the example of Christ's life, restored religion to the minds of men where it had been extinguished; and their new institutions were powerful enough to prevent the dishonesty of the priests and leaders of this religion from ruining it; and by continuing to live in poverty and enjoying such trust among the people in the confessional and in their preaching, they made them understand that it was evil to speak ill of the evil, that it was good to live in obedience to them, and that if these priests committed errors, they should be left to the punishment of God. Thus, the clergy do the worst they can, because they do not fear that punishment they do not see and in which they do not believe. Thus, this revival has maintained and still maintains this religion.*

Kingdoms also need to renew themselves and to bring their laws back to their beginnings. What good effects this practice achieves can be seen in the kingdom of France, which lives under laws and institutions to a greater degree than any other kingdom. The parliaments maintain these laws and institutions, especially the one in Paris, which renews them every time it takes an action against a prince of that kingdom and condemns the king in its judgements. Until now it has maintained itself as the obstinate opponent of the nobility, but any time it allows them to go unpunished and allows such offences to increase, then without a doubt these offences will either have to be corrected with great disorder or that kingdom will fall apart.

To conclude, therefore, nothing is more necessary in a community, whether it be a religion, kingdom, or republic, than to restore it to the reputation it enjoyed at its beginnings and to strive to ensure that either good institutions or good men achieve this effect and that it does not have to be brought about by some external force, for although an external force may sometimes be the best remedy, as it was in Rome, it is so dangerous that it is in no way to be desired. In order to demonstrate to everyone the extent to which the actions of individual men made Rome great and produced many good results in that city, I shall proceed to a narration and discussion of them; this third book and last part of the commentary on these first ten books of Livy will conclude within the boundaries of this topic. Although the actions of the kings were great and noteworthy, nevertheless since history treats them at length I shall leave them out and mention them only when they did something pertaining to their own private interests; and we shall begin with Brutus, father of Roman liberty.*

CHAPTER 2

How Very Wise It Is to Pretend to Be Mad at the Proper Moment

No one was ever as prudent as Junius Brutus, nor was anyone ever held in such high regard for any of his remarkable actions as he was for feigning stupidity. Although Livy expresses no more than one reason that led him to such pretence, which was to be able to live more securely and to maintain his patrimony, nevertheless, considering his method of conduct, it can also be believed that he feigned this in order to be less closely observed and to have greater ease in overthrowing the king and in liberating his native land, whenever he was given the opportunity. The fact that he was contemplating this can be seen first in his interpretation of the oracle of Apollo, when he pretended to fall down in order to kiss the ground, judging that if he did so he would have the gods in favour of his plans, and then when standing over the dead Lucretia in the presence of her father, husband, and other relatives, he was the first to pull the dagger out of her wound and to make the bystanders swear that they would never in the future tolerate any king ruling in Rome.*

From his example, all those who are dissatisfied with a ruler have something to learn; they must first measure and weigh their own forces, and if they are so powerful that they can reveal themselves as his enemy and wage war openly upon him, they must select this path, as less dangerous and more honourable. But if their condition is such that their forces are insufficient to wage open war on him, they must seek with great diligence to make themselves his friend, and to this end they must enter upon all those paths they deem necessary, following his wishes and taking pleasure in all those things in which they see he takes delight. This intimacy will, in the first place, allow you to live in safety and, without the risk of danger, to enjoy the ruler's good fortune along with him; it also provides you with every opportunity to carry out your plans. It is true that some will declare you ought not to live so close to rulers that their downfall will harm you as well, nor so far away that when they come crashing down, you would not have time to climb up on their ruins; this middle course would be the most reliable if it could be followed, but since I believe that it is impossible, it is necessary to reduce one's choices to the two methods described above, that is, either to keep your distance or to remain close to them. Anyone who does otherwise and is a man known for his merit will live in continuous danger. Nor it is enough to declare: 'I pay no attention to such things, I seek neither honours nor profit, I wish to live quietly and without trouble', for these excuses are heard and not accepted; nor can men who possess standing choose to do nothing, even if they truly choose to do so and are without any ambition whatsoever, because no one believes them, so that even if they wish to be left alone, others will not leave them alone. It is necessary, therefore, to play the fool like Brutus, and in playing the fool, it is enough to give praise, to speak, to see, and to do things contrary to your character in order to please the ruler. And since we have spoken about this man's prudence in regaining the liberty of Rome, now we shall speak of his severity in maintaining it.

CHAPTER 3

How Necessary It Is to Kill the Sons of Brutus in Order to Maintain a Newly Acquired Liberty

No less necessary than useful was Brutus' severity in maintaining in Rome the liberty that he had acquired there, which is an example quite rare in all of recorded history: to see a father sit as judge and not only condemn his sons to death but to be present at their execution. Those who read ancient histories will always recognize that after the transformation of the state either from a republic into a tyranny or from a tyranny into a republic, a memorable action must be taken against the enemies of present circumstances. Anyone who creates a tyranny without killing Brutus, and anyone who creates a free government and does not kill the sons of Brutus, will not sustain himself for long. Since this subject has been discussed at length above,* I shall refer to what was said at that time; I shall add only one example to the argument which, in our own times and in our own native city, has been worthy of note. This is the example of Piero Soderini, who thought that he might overcome with his patience and goodness the desire of Brutus' sons to return under a new government, and who deceived himself in this matter.* Although Soderini was a prudent man who recognized the necessity of doing this, and even though chance and the ambition of those who stood against him gave him the opportunity to defeat them, none the less, he never made up his mind to do so, because, besides believing that he could dissolve evil humours with his patience and kindness, and, with rewards for some of them, end part of their hostility toward him, he thought (and many times assured his friends of this) that in order to confront his opposition boldly and to strike down his adversaries, he would need to seize extraordinary authority and, by means of the laws, destroy equality among the citizens. Such a thing, even though he had not employed it later on in a tyrannical fashion, would have so terrified all the citizens that after it they would never have again agreed, after his death, to elect another standard-bearer for life, an institution he believed it would be good to strengthen and to maintain. His fear for this was wise and good; none the less, one must never allow an evil to continue on for the sake of a good, when that good can easily be destroyed by that evil. Since his undertakings and his intentions would be judged by their results, he should have believed that when fortune and life were in his company, he could have convinced anyone that what he had done was for the well-being of his native city and not because of his own ambition; and he could have settled things in such a way that his successor could not have done for a wicked reason what he had done for a good one. But he was deceived in the first opinion, failing to realize that wickedness is not subdued by time nor appeased by any gift. Thus, for not knowing how to be like Brutus, he lost, along with his native city, both the government and his reputation. And just as it is difficult to save a free state, so it is difficult to save a kingdom, as we shall show in the following chapter.

CHAPTER 4

A Prince Cannot Live in Safety in a Principality While Those Whom He Deprived of It Are Still Alive

The death of Tarquinius Priscus, caused by the sons of Ancus, and the death of Servius Tullius, caused by Tarquinius Superbus, show how difficult and dangerous it is to deprive a man of a kingdom and to allow him to live, even though the new man may seek to win him over with some reward.* It is evident that Tarquinius Priscus was deceived into believing that he possessed that kingdom lawfully, since it had been given to him by the people and confirmed by the senate, nor did he believe that the indignation of the sons of Ancus was so strong that they would not be satisfied with what had satisfied all of Rome; and Servius Tullius was deceived in believing that he could win over the sons of Tarquinius with new rewards. Accordingly, with respect to the first example, every prince should be warned that he will never live in security in his principality as long as those whom he deprived of it are alive. With respect to the second example, every powerful man should be reminded that old injuries are never cancelled by new benefits, and this is even less likely when the new benefit is less important than the old injury. Undoubtedly, Servius Tullius was imprudent to believe that the sons of Tarquinius would be willing to remain the sons-in-law of one over whom they thought they should be king. This thirst to rule is so great that not only does it enter the hearts of those who have the right to rule but also the hearts of those who have no such right, as it did in the case of the wife of the young Tarquinius, the daughter of Servius, who, moved by this rage, against all paternal piety roused her husband against her father to take from him both his life and his kingdom, so much more did she value being a queen than the daughter of a king. If, therefore, Tarquinius Priscus and Servius Tullius lost their kingdom by not knowing how to secure themselves against those from whom they had usurped it, Tarquinius Superbus lost his for not observing the practices of the ancient kings, as will be demonstrated in the following chapter.

CHAPTER 5

What Causes a King to Lose a Kingdom of the Hereditary Kind

After Tarquinius Superbus had killed Servius Tullius, who left no heirs, he came to possess his kingdom in security, since he did not have to fear those things that had harmed his predecessors. Although his method of occupying the kingdom had been extraordinary and detestable, nevertheless, if he had observed the ancient practices of the other kings, he would have been tolerated, and would not have stirred up the senate and plebeians against him to take away the state from him. He was not, therefore, driven out because his son Sextus raped Lucretia, but because he had broken the laws of the kingdom and governed it tyrannically, after taking from the senate every kind of authority and transferring it to himself; and the affairs that had been carried on in public places with the approval of the Roman senate came to be carried on in his palace, bringing blame and envy upon him, in such a way that in a brief time he stripped Rome of all the liberty she had maintained under the other kings. Nor did it suffice him to make the Fathers his enemies, for he aroused the people against him as well, exhausting them with hard labour of a kind completely different from that in which his predecessors had employed them. Thus, when Rome was full of his cruel and proud acts, he had already disposed the hearts and minds of all the Romans to rebellion whenever the occasion arose. If the incident involving Lucretia had not occurred, then as soon as another such incident had come about it would have produced the same result, because if Tarquinius had lived like the other kings and his son Sextus had committed that crime, Brutus and Collatinus would have appealed to Tarquinius for vengeance against Sextus and not to the Roman people. Princes should know, therefore, that they begin to lose the state the moment they begin to break the laws and those ways and customs that are ancient and under which men have lived for a long period of time. If, after being deprived of the state, they ever become so prudent that they recognize how easily principalities are held by those who receive wise counsel, their loss will become even more painful and they will condemn themselves to a greater penalty than any to which others might condemn them, because it is much easier to be loved by good men than by wicked ones and to obey the laws rather than to take control of them. If they want to understand the method they must employ in accomplishing this, they need endure no other labour than to select as their mirror the lives of good rulers, such as Timoleon of Corinth, Aratus of Sicyon, and others like them, in whose lives they would discover so much security and satisfaction on the part of the ruler and the ruled alike that they would have a desire to imitate them, being able easily to do so for the reasons given.

When men are governed well, they do not seek, nor do they desire, any other liberty: this was true of the peoples governed by the two men named above, whom they compelled to be princes as long as they lived, even though they tried on many occasions to return to private life.

And because in this and the two preceding chapters we have discussed the humours stirred up against rulers and the conspiracies carried out by the sons of Brutus against their native city as well as those against Tarquinius Priscus and Servius Tullius, it does not seem to me to be beyond our subject to discuss them in detail in the following chapter, since they are matters worthy of being noted both by rulers and by private citizens.

CHAPTER 6

On Conspiracies*

I did not think I should omit an analysis of conspiracies, since they represent a grave danger both for princes and for private citizens. It is evident that many more princes have lost their lives and their states through conspiracies than through open warfare, because being able to wage open war against a prince is within the reach of very few, while the possibility of conspiring against him is open to everyone. On the other hand, private citizens cannot enter into a more dangerous or more foolhardy enterprise that this one, because it is difficult and extremely dangerous at every one of its stages, which results in the fact that many conspiracies are attempted but very few reach their desired goal. Thus, so that princes may learn to guard themselves from these dangers and private citizens may enter into them more cautiously (or rather, so that private citizens may learn to live content under whatever dominion has been imposed on them by fate), I shall speak of conspiracies in great detail, not omitting any noteworthy case of relevance to either sort of person. Truly golden is that maxim of Tacitus, which declares that men must honour past affairs and endure present ones, and that they should desire good princes, but regardless of what they are like, should tolerate them.* And truly, anyone who does otherwise most often ruins himself and his native land.

In approaching the subject, we must, therefore, consider first the issue of against whom conspiracies are formed, and we shall find that they are formed either against one's native city or against a prince; I want to begin by discussing these two kinds, because those that are formed to give a city over to the enemies who are besieging it, or those that are formed for some reason similar to this, have already been discussed at sufficient length above.* Hence, we shall treat in this first part conspiracies against a prince, and we shall first examine the reasons for these conspiracies, which are numerous. But one of these reasons is much more important than all the others, and that is being hated by the people, because when a prince has aroused such universal hatred, it is reasonable to assume that there are private individuals who have been harmed by him and who desire to take revenge. Their desire is increased by the universally hostile disposition which they see aroused against him. A prince, therefore, must avoid this public condemnation (and how he must act in order to avoid it is something I do not wish to discuss here, since I have dealt with this matter elsewhere),* for by guarding himself against this, simple individual offences will bring him less hostility. The first reason for this is that he will rarely encounter men who will judge one injury to be so important that they will place themselves in great danger to avenge it; the second is that, even when men have the courage and power to do so, they are held back by the universal goodwill they see the prince inspires.

Injuries must either be against property, lifeblood, or honour. To threaten someone's lifeblood is more dangerous than to execute him; or rather, making threats is extremely dangerous, while ordering executions involves no danger whatsoever, because a dead man cannot think about a vendetta, while those who remain alive most often leave the thinking to the dead. But anyone who is threatened and forced by necessity either to act or to suffer will become a very dangerous man to the prince, as we shall discuss in detail in the proper place. Besides this kind of necessity, injuries to property and honour are the two things that offend men more than any other kind of attack, and the prince must protect himself against them, because he can never strip a man of so much that he will not have a knife left with which to take his revenge; nor can he ever dishonour a man so much that he does not retain a heart and mind stubbornly intent on revenge. Of the honours that may be taken away from men, those relating to women are most important; after that comes an outrage committed against one's person. This kind of disgrace armed Pausanias against Philip of Macedonia and has armed many others against many other princes; in our own day, Giulio Bellanti did not set out to conspire against Pandolfo, the tyrant of Siena, for any other reason than that Pandolfo had given Giulio one of his daughters as his wife and then had taken her away, as we shall discuss in the proper place. The chief motive that caused the Pazzi family to conspire against the Medici was the question of the inheritance of Giovanni Bonromei, which was taken from them at the Medici's orders.

There is another motive, and it is very important, that drives men to conspire against a prince; this is the desire to free one's native city from the one who seized it. This motive moved Brutus and Cassius against Caesar; it also moved many others against Phalaris, Dionysius, and those who seized their native cities. Nor can any tyrant protect himself against this humour except by abandoning his tyranny, and since there is no one who will do such a thing, there are few tyrants who do not end badly; whence arises that verse from Juvenal: 'Few are the kings who descend without wounds or murder to Pluto. Few tyrants die a dry death.'*

The dangers incurred in conspiracies, as I stated above, are great, and they are incurred at every stage, because in such cases, one runs a risk in planning them, in executing them, and even after they have been executed. Those who form conspiracies are either single individuals or they are many. A single individual cannot be said to form a conspiracy but, rather, this represents the firm determination aroused in a single man to kill the prince. Of the three kinds of dangers incurred in conspiracies, this single individual avoids the first, for prior to the execution he runs no risk whatsoever, since others do not share his secret, nor is there any danger that news of his plan will reach the prince's ear. Resolve of this kind can arise in any man of whatever rank, great, small, noble, ignoble, familiar, or not familiar to the prince, because everyone has the power to give vent to his own feelings. Pausanias, who has been mentioned before, killed Philip of Macedonia while he was going to the temple surrounded by a thousand armed men and standing between his son and his son-in-law. But he was a noble and known to the prince. A poor and abject Spaniard stabbed King Ferdinand of Spain in the neck with a dagger; the blow was not a mortal one, but this shows that the man had the courage and the opportunity to do it. A dervish, a Turkish priest, struck at Bajazet (father of the present Turk) with a scimitar; he did not wound him but he still possessed the courage and the opportunity to do so.* Many men with such dispositions can, I believe, be found who would like to undertake such a thing, because there is no penalty or any danger in wishing to do it, but few people do so, and of those who do, very few or none avoid being killed on the spot, but no one can be found who wants to go to certain death. Hence, let us set aside the discussion of these individual actions and come to conspiracies with a number of people involved.

I must say that all conspiracies are found in the histories to have been organized by great men or by those closest to the prince, because others, unless they are completely mad, cannot conspire, since weak men and those not close to the prince are entirely lacking in all those hopes and all those opportunities required for carrying out a conspiracy. In the first place, weak men cannot find supporters who will keep faith with them, because the latter cannot yield to the will of the weak with any of those hopes that make men expose themselves to great dangers; so that as the number of conspirators is widened to two or three people, they find a traitor among them and come to ruin. But even when they are fortunate enough to avoid such an accuser, they are surrounded by such difficulties in the execution of the conspiracy by lacking easy access to the prince that it is impossible for them not to come to ruin in the process, because if great men and those who have easy access are overwhelmed by the difficulties discussed below, it follows that in weak men these difficulties will endlessly increase. Thus, since men are not completely mad in matters concerning their lives and property, when conspirators see that they are weak they become cautious, and when they grow tired of a ruler they turn to cursing him, and they wait for those who have greater merits than their own to avenge them. And if by chance anyone of this rank were to attempt such a thing, one should praise their intentions but not their prudence.

It is evident, therefore, that those who have organized conspiracies have all been great men or close to the prince, and that many of these organized conspiracies were motivated as much by too many favours as by too many injuries; this was the case with Perennius against Commodus, Plautianus against Severus, and Sejanus against Tiberius.* All these men were accustomed to so much wealth, honour, and rank by their emperors that they felt nothing was lacking in the perfection of their power except the empire itself, and not wishing to lack even that, they set about conspiring against the prince. Their conspiracies all met the end that their ingratitude deserved, even though in more recent times some similar efforts have met with success, such as the conspiracy of Jacopo di Appiano against Messer Piero Gambacorti, ruler of Pisa; Jacopo, raised, nourished, and given prestige by Messer Piero, then took away his state.* The conspiracy of Coppola in our own times against King Ferdinand of Aragon was one of this type: Coppola, who had achieved such greatness that he thought he lacked nothing but a kingdom, lost his life for trying to acquire that as well.* Truly, if any conspiracy organized against princes by great men ought to have succeeded, it should have been this one, which was executed, one might say, by another king, and by a man who had such great opportunity to fulfil his desire. But the lust for power which blinds conspirators blinds them even more in executing their plans, for if they knew how to accomplish such an evil deed with prudence, it would be impossible for them not to succeed. A prince who wishes to protect himself from conspiracies should, therefore, fear those for whom he has done too many favours more than those upon whom he has inflicted too many injuries; because the latter lack opportunities, while the former have them in abundance, and their desires are similar, since the desire for power is just as great or even greater than the desire for revenge. Consequently, princes should give only as much authority to their friends as will leave some distance between their authority and that of the principality, with something to be desired in the middle; otherwise, it would be most unusual if they did not come to the same end as the princes mentioned above. But let us return to our argument.

Let me say that, since those who organize conspiracies must be great men with easy access to the prince, the results of their undertakings remain to be discussed and the reasons for their success or failure remain to be examined. As I said above, there are three dangerous moments in conspiracies: before, during, and after the fact. Few conspiracies can be found with an advantageous outcome, because it is almost impossible to pass through these three moments safely. To begin with a discussion of the preliminary dangers, which are the most important ones, let me say that it is necessary to be very prudent and very lucky to avoid being discovered in carrying out a conspiracy. Conspiracies are discovered either through information or indications. Information arises from encountering a lack of loyalty or prudence among the men with whom you discuss the conspiracy. This lack of loyalty is easily encountered, for you cannot discuss the conspiracy except with your most trusted friends, who will face death out of their love for you, or with men who are discontented with the prince. It is possible to find one or two trusted friends, but when you try to extend this number to many, it is impossible to find them; even then the goodwill they bear you must be great, so that the danger and the fear of punishment will not seem greater. Furthermore, men in most instances deceive themselves in the matter of the love they judge that someone bears for them; nor can you ever be sure of this love unless you test it, and testing it in this type of action is extremely dangerous. Although you may have put it to the test in some other dangerous enterprise, in which these men have proven faithful, you cannot measure this kind of loyalty by that, since this by far surpasses any other kind of danger. If you measure loyalty by the discontentment a man feels for the prince, you can easily deceive yourself in this matter, because as soon as you have revealed your intention to this malcontent, you give him the means to become contented, and his hatred must be great or your own authority must be extremely great to maintain his loyalty.

As a result, many conspiracies are discovered and broken up

in their beginning stages, and when one has been kept secret for
a long time among many men, it is considered a miraculous
achievement, as was the conspiracy of Piso against Nero, and in
our own times that of the Pazzi against Lorenzo and Giuliano
de' Medici, which was known to more than fifty men and discovered only at the moment it was to be carried out.* With
respect to being discovered through lack of prudence, this
comes about when a conspirator speaks carelessly in such a way
that a servant or a third party overhears you; which happened
to the sons of Brutus, who were overheard by a servant who
denounced them as they were planning the affair with the emissaries of Tarquinius, or when you carelessly reveal your plans to
a woman or a young boy you love or some similarly careless
individual, like Dymnus, one of the conspirators with Philotus
against Alexander the Great, who revealed the conspiracy to
Nicomachus, a young boy he loved, who immediately reported
it to Cebalinus his brother, and Cebalinus to the king.* With
respect to being discovered through indications, there is the
example of the plot Piso organized against Nero in which
Scaevinus, one of the conspirators, the day before he was to
assassinate Nero, made out his will, ordered Milichus, his freed-
man, to sharpen one of his old, rusty daggers, freed all his slaves
and gave them money, and ordered bandages to be made to bind
up wounds; when Milichus became aware of the plot through
these indications, he denounced Scaevinus to Nero. Scaevinus
was seized and with him, another conspirator, Natalis, the two
of whom had been seen the day before speaking to each other at
length and in secret, and when their accounts of this discussion
did not agree, they were forced to confess the truth, so that the
conspiracy was discovered, resulting in the ruin of all the
conspirators.*

Concerning the causes for the discovery of conspiracies, it is
impossible to protect oneself from malice, imprudence, or
thoughtlessness so that the plot will not be discovered whenever
those aware of it exceed the number of three or four. When more
than one of the conspirators is caught, it is impossible to make
their stories agree, because two men cannot agree on all the
details of their explanations. When only one of the conspirators
is taken, if he is a strong man he can, with courage and fortitude,

keep silent about the others, but the other conspirators must possess no less courage than he to stand firm and not reveal themselves by taking flight, because if courage is lacking on even one side, either in the man who is arrested or in the one who is free, the conspiracy will be discovered. The example brought forward by Livy from the conspiracy organized against Hieronymus, king of Syracuse, is an unusual one. In this case, when Theodorus, one of the conspirators, was arrested, he concealed with exceptional strength the names of all the conspirators, and he denounced the friends of the king, and for their part, the conspirators trusted so completely in Theodorus' exceptional courage that none of them left Syracuse or showed any sign of fear.* In the planning of a conspiracy, then, all these dangers must be passed through, even before reaching the point of executing the plan, and in order to avoid these dangers the following remedies exist. The first and the most reliable, or rather, to put it better, the only remedy is not to give the conspirators time to denounce you but to communicate the details of the matter to them when you want to execute it and not before. Those who have done so have clearly avoided the dangers that exist in the preparation of the conspiracy and, in most cases, the other dangers as well; indeed, all such conspiracies have come to a successful conclusion, and any prudent man would take the opportunity to conduct himself in such a manner. I want two examples of this to suffice.

Unable to tolerate the tyranny of Aristotimus, tyrant of Epirus, Nelematus gathered in his home many of his relatives and friends, and after he had urged them to liberate their native city, some of them asked him for time to think about it and to make plans; whereupon, Nelematus had his servants lock up the house, and he declared to those who had made such a request: 'Either you will swear to go now to put this plan into effect, or I shall deliver you all as prisoners to Aristotimus'. Stirred by these words, they all swore to do so and they went, without any delay, and successfully executed Nelematus' plan.* After one of the Magi through deception seized the kingdom of the Persians, and Ortanes and one of the noblemen of the kingdom learned of this deceit and exposed it, he conferred with six other princes of that state, declaring that he intended to liberate the kingdom from the tyranny of this Magus, and when one of them requested more time, Darius, one of the six princes summoned by Ortanes, arose and declared: 'Either we shall all go now to execute this plan or I shall go to accuse you all.'* Thus, all in agreement, they arose and, without giving anyone time to change his mind, they successfully executed their plans.* Also similar to these two examples is the method the Aetolians used to kill Nabis, the Spartan tyrant; they sent their fellow citizen Alexamenes with thirty cavalrymen and 200 foot-soldiers to Nabis under the pretence of sending him aid, and they communicated the secret only to Alexamenes, while upon the others they imposed the duty of obeying Alexamenes in anything and everything under penalty of exile. Alexamenes went to Sparta, and he never informed anyone of his mission until he wanted to accomplish it, with the result that he succeeded in killing Nabis.* Through these methods, therefore, these men avoided those dangers that are incurred in planning conspiracies, and anyone who imitates them will always avoid such risks.

In order to demonstrate that anyone may do as they did, I want to offer the example of Piso referred to above. Piso was a very distinguished and renowned man, an intimate friend of Nero, who confided in him a great deal. Nero often went to eat with Piso in his gardens; Piso, then, was able to make friends with men of courage and determination whose characters were suited to execute such a plan (which is extremely easy for a great man); and when Nero was in Piso's gardens, the latter could have communicated the matter to them and, with the appropriate words, encouraged them to do what they would not have time to refuse to do, and what could not fail to succeed.* And so, if we examine all the other conspiracies, we shall discover few of them that could not have been carried out in the same way, but men usually have so little understanding of the ways of the world that they often commit extremely serious errors, and they commit much greater ones in those affairs which are most extraordinary, as are these conspiracies.

A conspiracy should never be revealed, therefore, unless it is necessary, and only at the moment of its execution, and if you wish to inform someone of it anyway, inform only a single person with whom you have had long experience or who is motivated for the same reasons as you are. To find one individual such as this is much easier than to find several of them, and for this reason there is less danger; then, even if you are deceived by a single person, there still remains the remedy of defending yourself, which does not exist when many conspirators are involved; I have heard it said by some prudent man that you can speak of anything with one man, because the 'yes' of one man is worth as much as the 'no' of another, if you do not allow yourself to write anything out in your own hand; and every man should guard himself against writing as if avoiding a reef, for nothing can more easily convict you than the writing of your own hand. When Plautianus wanted to kill the Emperor Severus and his son Antoninus, he informed the tribune Saturninus; Saturninus wished to denounce Plautianus rather than to follow him, but fearing that when he came to make his accusation he would be no more credible than Plautianus, Saturninus asked him for an order written in his own hand to confirm the commission; blinded by ambition, Plautianus did so, which resulted in his being accused by the tribune and convicted; and without that written order and certain other evidence, Plautianus would have emerged the victor, so resolutely did he deny the charges. It is possible, therefore, to find some remedy against the accusation of a single person, when you cannot be convicted by something in writing or some other evidence; against this one must protect oneself. In Piso's conspiracy a woman named Epicharis, who had been Nero's mistress in the past, thought it would be useful to have among the conspirators a captain of some of the triremes Nero kept as his guard and informed him about the conspiracy but not the names of the conspirators. As a result, when that captain betrayed her and denounced her to Nero, Epicharis was so resolute in denying the accusation that Nero, who remained confused, did not condemn her. In revealing the conspiracy to a single person, there are, therefore, two dangers: one is that he may denounce you with proof; the other is that he may denounce you once he is convicted and forced to do so by torture, after being arrested on some suspicion or for some sign of guilt he has shown. But for both of these two dangers, there are some remedies, since it is possible to deny the first kind of accusation, citing the hatred that the accuser has for you, as well as to deny the second by citing the force employed in forcing the accuser to tell lies about you. It is prudent, therefore, not to inform anybody about the matter, but to follow the examples cited above, or even, if you must inform someone about it, not to tell more than one person, for in this instance, even if some danger exists, there is much less than when many people are informed about it.

Related to this method is the one used when necessity forces you to do to the prince what you see the prince would like to do to you, an emergency so great that it does not allow you time even to think about protecting yourself. This kind of necessity almost always brings the conspiracy to its desired conclusion, and two examples suffice to demonstrate this. The Emperor Commodus counted Laetus and Eclectus, the leaders of the Praetorian guards, among his best friends and closest companions; Marcia was among the first of his concubines or mistresses; and because he was often reproached by them for the ways in which he disgraced himself and his imperial office, Commodus decided to have them killed, and on a list he wrote the names of Marcia, Laetus, and Eclectus, and some others whom he wanted to have killed on the following evening, and he put this list under the bolster on his bed. And when he had gone to wash himself, a young boy who was one of his favourites, playing around the bedroom and on the bed, came upon the list, and leaving the room with it in his hand, he ran into Marcia, who took it from him, and after she had read it and seen its contents, she immediately sent for Laetus and Eclectus, and recognizing the danger they were in, all three decided to take preventive action, and without delaying, on the following night they killed Commodus.*

Antoninus Caracalla, the emperor, was with his armies in Mesopotamia, and he had as his prefect Macrinus, a man who was more a civilian than a soldier. As it happens that princes who are not good always fear that others work against them in a manner they feel they deserve, Antoninus wrote to his friend Maternianus in Rome, asking him to find out from the astrologers if there was anyone who aspired to the imperial power and to inform him of it. As a result, Maternianus wrote him that Macrinus was the man who aspired to such power, and when the letter reached the hands of Macrinus before the emperor, and he recognized the necessity of either killing the emperor before a new letter arrived from Rome, or of dying himself, he commissioned Martial, a trusted centurion, whose brother had been put to death only a few days before by Antoninus, to kill him, a task Martial carried out successfully.* It is evident, therefore, that the kind of emergency that allows no time creates almost the same effect as the method I mentioned above as being employed by Nelematus of Epirus. It is also evident that what I declared almost at the beginning of this discourse is true: that is, that making threats does more damage to princes and is the cause of more effective conspiracies than injuries; a prince should guard against making such threats, because it is necessary to treat men with kindness or to secure oneself against them, and never to reduce them to the condition where they believe they must either die or kill someone else.

With respect to the dangers incurred during the execution of a conspiracy, they arise either from changing the plan; or from a lack of courage on the part of the man who carries it out; or from an error that the executor commits out of a lack of prudence; or from failing to execute the conspiracy perfectly, with part of those who were supposed to be killed remaining alive. I must say, therefore, that nothing disrupts or impedes all human actions as much as being forced in an instant, without having any time, to change a plan and to alter it from what had been planned earlier. If such change causes disorder in anything, it does so in matters of war and in matters similar to those of which we are speaking, because in such actions, there is nothing so necessary for men to do as to summon up their courage to perform the role assigned to them. And if men have focused their minds for many days upon one method and one plan and this suddenly changes, it is impossible for this not to upset everyone and ruin everything, so that it is much better to execute a thing according to the established plan, even if some drawback is discovered in it, than it is to encounter a thousand obstacles by wanting to cancel it. This occurs whenever there is no time to make new plans, for when time is available, a man can manage affairs in his own way.

The conspiracy of the Pazzi against Lorenzo and Giuliano de' Medici is well known. The established plan was that the

Medici would serve the cardinal of San Giorgio* the midday meal and that they were to be killed at that repast; it had been decided who would kill them, who would seize the palace, and who would race through the city and call the people to liberty. It happened that while the Pazzi, the Medici, and the cardinal were hearing a solemn rite in the cathedral of Florence, it became known that Giuliano would not eat with them that morning; this caused the conspirators to gather together, and what they were to have done in the Medicis' home they now decided to do in the church. This upset the entire plan, because Giovambattista da Montesecco did not wish to take part in the murder, declaring that he did not want to do it in a church, so that they had to entrust every action to new agents, who did not have sufficient time to summon up their courage, and they committed such errors that they were beaten down while carrying out their plan.*

The courage of anyone who executes the plan fails either out of respect for the victim or out of his own cowardice. The majesty and reverence inspired by the presence of a prince is so great that it is a simple matter for this either to weaken or frighten a conspirator. When Marius was captured by the people of Minturnae, a slave was sent to murder him; terrified by the presence of such a man and by the memory of his name, he became afraid and lost the strength to kill him.* If such power resides in a man bound and imprisoned and overcome by bad luck, it is even easier to maintain that this power is so much greater in a prince who is free, with the majestic aspect of his ornaments, his pomp and ceremony, and his royal court! As a result, such pomp may frighten you or soften you, when it is accompanied by some pleasant greeting. A few men were conspiring against Sitalces, king of Thrace;* they had fixed the day the plot would be carried out; they gathered together at the appointed place where the prince was located; none of them made a move to harm him; they eventually left without having attempted anything, without knowing what had stopped them; and they blamed each other. They lapsed into this error several times until the conspiracy was discovered and they suffered the penalty for the crime they could have but would not commit. Two of his brothers conspired against Alfonso, duke of Ferrara, and they employed as their go-between Giannes, a priest and the duke's cantor,* who at their request brought the duke into their presence on more than one occasion, so that they would have the freedom to murder him. Nevertheless, neither of them ever had the courage to do it, so that when they were discovered, they suffered the penalty for their wickedness and their lack of prudence. This negligence could not have arisen from anything other than the fact that either the duke's presence must have frightened them or some act of humanity on his part must have humiliated them.

In such plans a drawback or error arises either through a lack of prudence or through a lack of courage, since both of these two things can obsess you and make you say and do something you should not say or do, carried away by the confusion in your mind. The fact that men are obsessed and confused by these things cannot be better demonstrated than in Livy's description of how Alexamenes the Aetolian wanted to assassinate Nabis the Spartan, of whom we have spoken above, because when the time for executing the plan arrived, and he had revealed to his men what was to be done, Livy says this: 'He for his part summoned up his courage—for his mind was confused by the contemplation of the great task that faced him.'* Thus, it is impossible for anyone, even a man who is steady of mind and accustomed to killing men and to using the sword, not to be confused. Still, men of experience in such matters must be selected, and no others should be trusted, even if they are considered to be extremely courageous, because where courage is required in great undertakings, if it has not been tested by experience, there is no one who can promise a certain outcome. This confusion can, therefore, either make you drop the weapon from your hand or make you say things that produce the same effect. Lucilla, the sister of Commodus, ordered Quintianus to kill him. He waited for Commodus at the entrance to the amphitheatre, and drawing near to him with a drawn dagger, he cried: 'The senate sends you this!' His words caused him to be seized before he had brought his arm down to strike Commodus. Messer Antonio da Volterra, assigned (as we said above) to kill Lorenzo de' Medici, shouted 'Ah, traitor!' while drawing close to him. His voice was Lorenzo's salvation and the downfall of that conspiracy.

A conspiracy can fail to be executed perfectly when it is directed against one leader for the reasons already provided, but it can also easily fail to be executed perfectly when the conspiracy is directed against two leaders; in truth, this kind of conspiracy is so difficult that it is almost impossible for it to succeed. To undertake a similar enterprise at the same time in different places is almost impossible, because it cannot be carried out at different times if the first is not to spoil the second. Thus, if a conspiracy against one prince is an uncertain, dangerous, and imprudent affair, conspiring against two rulers is completely vain and foolhardy. If it were not for the respect in which I hold this historian, I would never believe possible what Herodian says of Plautianus, when he commissioned the centurion Saturninus alone to assassinate Severus and Antoninus, who lived in different places, because the plan is so far removed from what is reasonable that no one but this authority could ever make me believe it.* Certain young Athenians organized a conspiracy against Diocles and Hippias, tyrants of Athens; they killed Diocles but Hippias remained alive and avenged him.* Chion and Leonidas, citizens of Heraclea and disciples of Plato, conspired against the tyrants Clearchus and Satirus; they killed Clearchus but Satirus, who remained alive, avenged him.* The Pazzi conspirators, cited by us numerous times, did not succeed in killing anyone but Giuliano. Hence, everyone should avoid conspiracies such as these aimed at more than one leader, because they do not benefit the conspirators, the city, or anyone else; on the contrary, survivors who remain become even more insufferable and harsher, as Florence, Athens, and Heraclea all know, which I mentioned earlier.

It is true that the conspiracy Pelopidas organized to liberate Thebes, his native city, met with all these difficulties, but it had, nevertheless, a successful conclusion. Pelopidas conspired not only against two tyrants but against ten of them; not only was he not their confidant and without easy access to them, but he was a rebel in exile; he was, none the less, able to enter Thebes, assassinate the tyrants, and liberate his native city. Furthermore, he accomplished this with the assistance of a certain Charon, an advisor to the tyrants, from whom he gained easy access to carry out his plan. Nevertheless, no one should use him as an example, because this was an impossible undertaking that succeeded miraculously, and it was so viewed by historians at the time, who celebrate it as a rare and almost unparalleled event.*

The execution of a plan can be interrupted by a false supposition or by an unforeseen event that occurs on the spot. The morning that Brutus and the other conspirators wanted to kill Caesar, it happened that Caesar spoke at length to Gnaeus Popilius Laenas, one of the conspirators, and seeing this long conversation, the others feared that this Popilius had revealed the conspiracy to Caesar and were about to try to kill him right there without waiting for him to go to the senate; they would have done so if the conversation had not ended, and if, having seen that Caesar made no unusual movement, they had not been reassured. These are the kinds of false assumptions to be considered and kept carefully in mind, especially in so far as it is easy to make them, because anyone with a guilty conscience can easily believe that people are speaking of him; you can hear a word that is spoken for another reason that troubles your mind and makes you believe that it is spoken about your own case; and it can cause you either to flee and to expose the conspiracy by yourself, or to make a muddle of its execution by taking action sooner than you planned. This comes about more easily when many people are aware of the conspiracy.

With respect to accidents, since they are unexpected, they can only be illustrated through examples which will make men cautious. Giulio Bellanti from Siena, whom we have mentioned above, because of the indignation he felt against Pandolfo, who had taken away the daughter he had previously given Bellanti as a wife, decided to kill him and had selected a certain time. Almost every day Pandolfo went to visit one of his sick relatives, and on his way he passed by Giulio's home. Thus, once Giulio noticed this, he arranged to have his fellow conspirators in the house in order to kill Pandolfo as he walked by, and after he had placed them, armed, inside the entrance he kept one man at the window, so that as Pandolfo passed by the man would make a sign when he was near the entrance. It happened that, as Pandolfo was approaching and after the man had made the sign, Pandolfo ran into a friend who stopped him, while some of those who were with him went on ahead, and once they heard the noise made by the weapons and saw them, they discovered the ambush, so that Pandolfo was saved and Giulio and his companions were forced to flee from Siena.* This accidental meeting prevented any action and brought Giulio's enterprise to ruin. There is no remedy against such accidents, which are rare. Still, it is necessary to examine all those that may arise and to provide a remedy against them.

Presently there remains only for us to discuss the dangers that are incurred after the execution of a plan, and these involve primarily one, and that is, when someone remains alive to avenge the dead prince. Those who remain, then, to undertake such a vendetta may be his brothers, his sons, or other followers of his who expect to inherit the principality (and they may remain alive either because of your negligence or for the reasons given above): this happened to Giovanni Andrea da Lampognano who, along with his other co-conspirators, murdered the duke of Milan, but since one of his sons and two of his brothers remained alive, they in time avenged the dead man.* And truly, in these cases the conspirators are to be excused because they had no other remedy, but when someone remains alive because of their lack of prudence or negligence, then they do not deserve to be excused. Some conspirators from Forlì killed their lord Count Girolamo and took his wife and small children hostage, and since they felt they could not live in security unless they took possession of the fortress, and since the castellan would not surrender it to them, Madonna Caterina (this was the countess's name) promised the conspirators that if they were to allow her to enter the fortress, she would turn it over to them, and they could keep her children with them as hostages. With this promise they allowed her to enter the fortress, and once inside, she reproached them from the walls for the death of her husband and threatened them with all kinds of vendettas. To show that she was not concerned for her children, she showed them her genitals, declaring that she still had the means to create more of them. Thus, the conspirators, not knowing what choice to make and only too late realizing their error, suffered perpetual exile as the punishment for their lack of prudence. But of all the dangers that can be incurred after the execution of such a plan, there is matter came to the attention of those in Rome, they commissioned Rutulus, the new consul, to take care of the matter; ar[...] to lull the conspirators to sleep, Rutulus spread the news th[...] the senate had confirmed the assignments of the Capu[...] legions. Believing this and thinking that they had time to car[...] out their plan, those soldiers did not try to accelerate it, ar[...] they stood firm until they began to see that the consul was se[...] arating them one from the other; this action aroused their su[...] picion, causing them to reveal themselves and to put their pl[...] into operation.* A better example of the two sides of the iss[...] could not be found, because it shows how slowly men act [...] matters in which they believe they have time, and how swif[...] they act when necessity drives them. Nor can a prince o[...] republic that wishes in an advantageous way to delay expos[...] a conspiracy adopt a better expedient than cleverly offering [...] conspirators an opportunity in the near future, so that wh[...] they wait for that opportunity or think they have ample tin[...] that prince or republic has time to punish them. Anyone w[...] has acted differently has hastened his own ruin, as the duke [...] Athens and Guglielmo de' Pazzi both did. Once the duke h[...] become tyrant of Florence and had learned that there wa[...] conspiracy against him, without examining the problem [...] more detail, he had one of the conspirators taken; this act[...] immediately caused the others to take up their arms and to ta[...] the state away from him.* Guglielmo, [the Florentine] co[...] missioner in the Valdichiana in 1501, learned of a conspiracy [...] Arezzo in favour of the Vitelli family to seize that city from [...] Florentines; he immediately went to that city and, witho[...] thinking about the strength of the conspirators or his own, a[...] without preparing some kind of military force for himself, [...] had one of the conspirators arrested upon the advice of [...] bishop, his son, after which the others immediately took [...] arms and took the city from the Florentines; and Guglielr[...] went from being a commissioner to being a prisoner.* B[...] when conspiracies are weak, they should and must be su[...] pressed without fail.

Nor are two methods which are almost the opposite of ea[...] other to be imitated in any way: the first one was employed [...] the previously mentioned duke of Athens, who, in order [...]

none more certain or more to be feared than when the people are the friend of the prince that you have murdered, because conspirators have no remedy against this danger and can never secure themselves against it. As an example, there is Caesar, who had the people on his side and was avenged by them, and for this reason, after the conspirators were chased out of Rome they were all killed at various times and places.*

Conspiracies planned against one's native city are less dangerous for those who plan them than conspiracies planned against princes, because in organizing them, there are fewer dangers in the former than in the latter; in carrying them out, the dangers are the same; and after they have been executed, there is no danger of any kind. In organizing them there are not many dangers, for a citizen can make preparations to acquire power without revealing his mind or his plan to anyone; if these preparations are not interrupted, he can successfully carry out his undertaking; and if his preparations are interrupted by some law, he can bide his time and employ other measures. It is to be understood that this occurs in a republic where some corruption already exists, because in an uncorrupted republic where no evil principle has taken root, such thoughts cannot occur in the minds of its citizens. Citizens can therefore aspire to take over the principality, in many ways and by many means, without suffering the danger of being crushed, both because republics are slower to act than a prince, less suspicious, and, as a result, less cautious, and also because they pay their most important citizens more respect, with the result that such men are more daring and courageous in acting against them. Everyone has read about the conspiracy of Catiline described by Sallust and knows how, after the conspiracy was discovered, Catiline not only remained in Rome but came to the senate and said insulting things both to the senate and to the consul, so great was the respect that city paid to its citizens. After he left Rome and was already with his armies, Lentulus and those others would not have been arrested if letters had not existed in their own handwriting which clearly implicated them.* Hanno, a very distinguished citizen of Carthage who aspired to tyranny, had made plans during the wedding of one of his daughters to poison the entire senate and then to make himself prince. When it became known, the senate made no other provision against it than a law which placed limits on the expenses of banquets and weddings,* such was the respect they had for this man's merits.

It is certainly true that in carrying out a conspiracy against one's native city, there are more difficulties and greater dangers, because your own forces are rarely sufficient in conspiring against so many, and everyone is not the commander of an army as was Caesar or Agathocles or Cleomenes and other men like them, who have, in a single stroke and with their own forces, seized control of their native cities. Men such as these find the path very easy and very safe, but others, who do not have these additional forces, must do things either with deception and guile or with foreign troops. In regard to deception and guile, after Pisistratus the Athenian had defeated the inhabitants of Megara and had, for this reason, gained the favour of the people, he went out one morning, wounded, declaring that the nobility had injured him out of envy, and demanded that he be allowed to have armed men with him for his protection. With this authority, he easily rose to such greatness that he became tyrant of Athens.* Pandolfo Petrucci returned with other exiles to Siena and was given the guardianship of the public square with a command, an office others refused as a menial task; none the less, his armed men with the passage of time earned him such prestige that in a short while he became the ruler of the city.* Many others have employed different schemes and methods and have, in the course of time and without danger, achieved their goal. Those who have conspired to seize power in their native city with their own forces or with foreign armies have achieved different results, according to fortune. Catiline, who was previously cited, was ruined in this fashion. Hanno, who was mentioned above, armed his partisans, many thousands of people, and when poison failed, both he and they were killed. Some of the foremost citizens of Thebes called a Spartan army in to help them set themselves up as tyrants, and they established a tyranny in that city.* Thus, when all the conspiracies people have mounted against their native land have been examined, you will find none, or very few, that have been suppressed in the process of being organized, but all have either succeeded or come to ruin while being carried out. After they are executed, no

dangers are incurred other than those inherent in the nature of the principality itself, because when someone has become a tyrant, he faces the natural and ordinary dangers which tyrannicide brings upon him, against which he has no other remedies than those discussed above.

This is as much as I need to write about conspiracies, and if I have analysed those that are accomplished not with poison but with the sword, this arises from the fact that they all have a similar organization. It is certainly true that those carried out with poison are more dangerous by virtue of being more uncertain: not everyone has the opportunity to use it, and it becomes necessary to confer with those who do, and this necessity of conferring with others places you in danger. Then, for a number of reasons a drink of poison may not be fatal, as happened to those who killed Commodus, for after he had thrown up the poison they had administered to him, they were forced to strangle him if they wished for him to die.

Princes, therefore, have no greater enemy than a conspiracy, because if a conspiracy is organized against them, it either kills them or disgraces them; if it succeeds, they die, and if it is discovered and they kill the conspirators, people always believe that the conspiracy was an invention of the prince to give vent to his avarice and cruelty against the lives and property of those whom he has killed. Yet, I do not wish to fail to warn that prince or republic against whom a conspiracy has been planned to be cautious, so that when a conspiracy is revealed to them, before they make an effort to avenge themselves, they will seek to understand very well its characteristics, and they will take careful measure of the conditions of the conspirators as well as their own, and when they find that the conspiracy is widespread and powerful, they will never reveal it until they have prepared themselves with forces sufficient to suppress it; acting otherwise, they would discover only their own ruin. For this reason, they must make every effort to pretend to dissimulate, since once the conspirators find themselves exposed, driven by necessity they will act without scruples. For example, when the Romans left two legions of soldiers behind to guard Capua against the Samnites, as we said elsewhere,* the leaders of these legions conspired together to oppress the Capuans; once this

demonstrate his belief that he enjoyed the goodwill of the Florentine citizens, put to death a man who revealed a conspiracy to him; the other was employed by Dion of Syracuse who, to test the intentions of a man against whom he harboured suspicion, allowed Callippus, whom he trusted, to pretend to organize a conspiracy against him. And both of these men ended badly: for the former discouraged informers and encouraged those who wished to plot against him, while the latter provided an easy avenue to his own death, or, on the contrary, actually led the conspiracy against himself, because events were to prove that Callippus, who was able to conspire against Dion with impunity, did it so well that he deprived Dion of his state and his life.*

CHAPTER 7

Why Changes from Liberty to Servitude and from Servitude to Liberty Are Sometimes Without Bloodshed and Sometimes Full of It

Some will perhaps ask themselves why, in the many changes from free government to tyranny and the opposite, some occur with bloodshed and others without it; because, as we learn from the histories, during similar changes a great many men on some occasions, have been killed, while on others no one has been injured: this happened in the transition that Rome underwent from the kings to the consuls, where no one was exiled except the Tarquins, without harm to anyone else. This depends on the following circumstance: that is, the state that is changing is either born in violence or it is not, and since when it is born in violence, it is, of necessity, born amid injuries to many people, it is then necessary that in their downfall, the injured wish to seek revenge, and that from this desire for revenge arises bloodshed and the death of men. But when such a state is created by the common consensus of an entire people who have made it great, that people has no reason later on, when the state collapses, to attack anyone but the leader. The state of Rome after the exile of the Tarquins was of this type, as was, too, the government of the

Medici, since when they came to ruin in 1494, no one was injured except them. Thus, such transitions do not turn out to be very dangerous, but those that are brought about by men who have to seek revenge are extremely dangerous and have been of the kind that, if nothing else, terrify those who read about them. But since the histories are full of such examples, I want to leave them out.

CHAPTER 8

Anyone Wishing to Alter a Republic Must Consider Its Basic Material

It has been discussed above how a wicked citizen cannot do evil in a republic that is not corrupted, and that conclusion is strengthened, beyond the reasons that were then set forth, with the examples of Spurius Cassius* and Manlius Capitolinus.* Being an ambitious man, this Spurius wanted to seize extraordinary authority in Rome and to gain the support of the plebeians by doing them many favours (such as dividing among them the lands the Romans had taken from the Hernici), and his ambition was exposed by the city fathers, who brought it so clearly under suspicion that, when Spurius spoke to the people and offered to give them the money that had been obtained from the grain imported by the state from Sicily, they absolutely refused, in the belief that Spurius was trying to give them the price of their liberty. But if that people had been corrupt, they would not have refused such a price, and they would have opened up the path to tyranny that they closed off to him. A much more important example of this is Manlius Capitolinus, for his case shows how great strength of mind and body and how many good works done for the benefit of one's own city can be later cancelled out by an evil passion to rule; it is evident that this desire arose in Manlius because of the envy he felt at the honours bestowed upon Camillus, and his mind became so blinded that, failing to consider the city's way of life, or to examine its basic material, which was not yet receptive to a wicked form of government, he began to create disturbances in

Rome against the senate and against the laws of the city. This event reveals the perfection of that city and the goodness of its social fabric, for in his case, no one from the nobility, even though they were extremely fierce supporters of one another, did anything to assist him; none of his relatives did anything on his behalf: for other accused men they usually appeared in mourning, dressed in black and full of sorrow in order to seek compassion for the accused, but with Manlius not one of them was seen. The tribunes of the plebeians, who always used to encourage matters that seemed likely to result in the people's benefit and who pushed them forward all the more when they were directed against the nobility, in this case united with the nobles to suppress a common plague. The people of Rome, extremely eager for their own gain and lovers of policies that opposed the nobility, did Manlius many favours, but nevertheless, when the tribunes summoned him and submitted his case to the judgement of the people, that people, transformed from defender to judge, without any hesitation condemned him to death. For this reason, I do not believe that there is an example in Livy's history more apt to demonstrate the goodness of all the institutions of that republic than this one, seeing that no one in that city made a move to defend a citizen full of exceptional abilities, who had publicly and privately done many praiseworthy deeds. For, love of their native city was stronger than anything else in all of the people, and they gave more consideration to the present dangers for which he was responsible than to his past merits, to the extent that with his death, they set themselves free. And Livy declares: 'Such was the end of a man who would have been memorable had he not been born in a free state.'*

In relation to this, two things are to be considered: the first is that different methods of seeking glory have to be used in a corrupted city than in one still living according to the rule of law; and the second (which is almost the same as the first) is that, in their conduct and even more in their great actions, men ought to consider the times and adapt to them.

Those who, through bad choices or by natural inclination, are out of tune with the times live unhappy lives in most cases and their actions have a bad outcome; the opposite happens to those who are in harmony with the times. And without any doubt, based upon the previously cited words of the historian, it can be concluded that if Manlius had been born in the times of Marius or of Sulla, when the social fabric was already corrupted, and upon which he would have been able to imprint the form of his ambition, he would have enjoyed the same results and successes as Marius and Sulla and the others who after them aspired to tyrannical power. Likewise, had Sulla and Marius lived in the times of Manlius, they would have been crushed during their first undertakings. A man, with his methods and his wicked actions, can easily begin to corrupt the people of a city, but it is impossible for him in one lifetime to corrupt the city to such an extent that he can derive any benefit from it; and even if it were possible for him to do so, given the length of time, it would be impossible due to the way in which men conduct themselves, since they are impatient and cannot long hold off their desires. Eventually, they deceive themselves in their affairs and especially in those that they desire above all else, so that either for a lack of patience or through deceiving themselves, they will undertake an enterprise at odds with the times and will end up very badly. It is necessary, then, in order to seize authority in a republic and imprint an evil form upon it, to find that the social fabric has broken down over time, and that little by little and from generation to generation, it has been thrown into disorder; this will come about by necessity, as was discussed above,* when it is not often renewed by good examples or by new laws to bring it back to its beginnings. Thus, Manlius would have been a rare and memorable man had he been born in a corrupt city. Citizens who carry out some undertaking in republics either in favour of liberty or of tyranny should, then, consider the basic material of their society and should judge by that the difficulty of their undertakings, because it is as difficult and as dangerous to try to liberate a people that wishes to live in slavery as it is to try to enslave a people that wishes to live in freedom. And because it was said above that men in their activities must consider the condition of the times and proceed accordingly, we shall speak at length about this in the following chapter.

CHAPTER 9

That It Is Necessary for Those Who Wish Always to Enjoy Good Fortune to Change With the Times

I have considered on many occasions* that the cause of the bad and good fortune of men lies in how well their mode of conduct fits the times. Because it is evident that in their works some men proceed with impetuosity, others with care and caution; and because either of these methods may exceed the proper limits, being unable to follow the true path, one may err in employing either one. But an individual comes to make fewer mistakes and to enjoy a favourable fortune, as I have said, when his methods fit the times, and he always proceeds as nature compels him. Everyone knows how carefully and cautiously Fabius Maximus advanced with his army, far removed from any impetuous act and Roman daring, and good fortune caused his method to fit well with the times.* Thus, when Hannibal had invaded Italy as a young man and, with fresh fortune, had already defeated the Roman people twice, and when that republic was almost completely stripped of its good militia and terrified, Rome could not have enjoyed a better fortune than having a general who, with his deliberateness and caution, held the enemy at bay. Nor could Fabius have encountered times any more suitable to his methods than those from which he emerged in glory. It is evident that Fabius did this by nature rather than by choice, because when Scipio wished to move into Africa with his armies to conclude the war, Fabius strongly opposed him, being unable to detach himself from his methods and his habits. Thus, had it been up to Fabius, Hannibal would still be in Italy, for Fabius was a man who did not see that the times had changed and that it was necessary to change the methods of warfare. And if Fabius had been king of Rome, he could easily have lost the war, because he would never have known how to vary his conduct in accord with the variation of the times. But he was born in a republic, where there are different citizens and different humours, and just as Rome once had Fabius, who was the best leader in those times requiring a prolonged war, so it later had Scipio in times requiring a victory.

Thus, it happens that a republic has a longer life and much greater fortune than a principality, because it can more easily adapt itself to the diversity of circumstances than can a prince, through the diversity of the citizens who inhabit it. Accordingly, a man who is used to conducting himself in one way never changes, as we have said, and of necessity, when the times change and are at variance with his methods, he comes to ruin.

Piero Soderini, already cited several times, proceeded in all his affairs with humanity and patience. When the times were in conformity with his mode of conduct, he and his native city prospered, but when later times arrived in which he had to break with his patience and humility, he did not know how to do so, so that, along with his native city, he came to ruin. Pope Julius II conducted himself during the entire period of his pontificate with impetuosity and fury, and because the times fitted him perfectly, all his undertakings were successful. But if other times had arrived requiring different qualities, he would of necessity have come to ruin, because he would never have changed either his methods or his system of managing his affairs. And there are two causes for our inability to change: the first is that we cannot oppose our natural inclinations; the other is that, when a man with one mode of conduct has been very prosperous, it is impossible to persuade him that he can do as well by proceeding in a different manner; it happens in this way that fortune varies for a single man, because she brings about the changes in the times while he fails to modify his methods. The downfall of cities also arises from their failure to modify the institutions of their republics over time, as we discussed at length above. But they move more slowly, finding it more difficult to change, because to do so brings times that shake the entire republic, and for this to happen, it is not enough for one man alone to change his mode of conduct.

And since we have mentioned Fabius Maximus who kept Hannibal at bay, it seems fitting to discuss in the following chapter whether the commander who insists on fighting a battle with the enemy under any circumstances can be prevented by someone who refuses to do so.

CHAPTER 10

That a Commander Cannot Avoid a Battle When His Opponent Insists on Fighting Under Any Circumstances

'But the dictator was very reluctant to risk his fortune before it was absolutely necessary against an enemy who was becoming weaker with every day he had to linger in an unfriendly country.'*

When an error persists into which all men or the majority of them fall, I cannot believe that it is a bad idea to criticize it repeatedly. Hence, even though I have demonstrated above how unlike our actions in great affairs are from those of ancient times, it does not, none the less, seem superfluous at present to repeat this. If in anything we deviate from ancient practices, we deviate especially in military engagements, where at present none of those things so highly esteemed by the ancients are practised. This difficult situation has arisen because republics and princes have imposed such duties upon others, and to avoid danger they have kept at a distance from this kind of exercise, and if we do occasionally witness a king of our times go to war in person, we do not believe, nevertheless, that his actions will give rise to other methods that deserve higher praise. Hence, if kings engage in such an exercise at all, they do so with great pomp and not for any other laudable purpose. Yet these kings make fewer mistakes than republics do, especially those in Italy, in that they sometimes review their armies in person and keep for themselves the title of commander; by placing their trust in others, republics do not, in any way, understand the matters pertaining to war, but on the other hand, they insist on making such decisions in order to appear to be acting like a prince, and in these decisions they commit a thousand errors.

Although I have spoken about some of these errors elsewhere, I wish at present to avoid remaining silent about a very important one. When these lazy princes or weak republics send forth one of their commanders, the wisest order they think they can give him is not to engage in battle for any reason but rather, above all else, to avoid any encounter; and in the belief that they are imitating the prudence of Fabius Maximus who, by deferring combat, saved their state for the Romans, they fail to understand that most of the time this order is worthless or harmful. Hence, it is necessary to draw this conclusion: a commander who wishes to remain in the field cannot avoid battle if the enemy insists on fighting under any circumstances. This kind of command is tantamount to saying: 'Fight the battle when the enemy wants, not when you want to.' For, if you want to remain in the field without engaging in battle, there is no other remedy more secure than to put at least fifty miles between you and the enemy and then to keep good spies, so that as he approaches you, you have time to fall back. There is another choice, that is, to shut yourself within a city; and both of these choices are extremely damaging. With the first, you abandon your countryside to the enemy, and a capable prince will prefer to tempt fortune in battle rather than to prolong the war with so much damage to his subjects. With the second choice, your loss is obvious, because by withdrawing with your army into a city, you necessarily come under siege, and very soon suffer hunger and eventually surrender. Thus, avoiding battle in these two ways is extremely damaging. The method that Fabius Maximus employed, remaining in strongholds, is good when you have such an able army that the enemy lacks the courage to come and to confront you on your own terms. No one can say that Fabius fled from the fight but, rather, that he wanted to engage the enemy on his own terms, because if Hannibal had marched to find him, Fabius would have waited for him and engaged him in battle, but Hannibal never dared fight Fabius on the latter's terms. As a result, engaging in battle was avoided as much by Hannibal as by Fabius, but if one of them had decided to fight no matter what the circumstances, the other would have had only one of three remedies: the two mentioned above, or to run away.

That what I say is true can be clearly seen in a thousand examples, especially in the war that the Romans waged against Philip of Macedonia, the father of Perseus,* because when he was attacked by the Romans he decided not to go into battle, and in order to avoid it, he decided first to do as Fabius Maximus had done in Italy, and he camped with his army on the summit of a mountain, where he marshalled his forces, thinking that the

Romans would not dare go to find him. But going there and fighting him, they drove him off the mountain-top, and being unable to resist, he fled with the greater part of his forces. What saved him from being totally destroyed was the rugged nature of the countryside, which prevented the Romans from following him. Not wishing to engage in battle, and being encamped near the Romans, he was forced to flee, and after he learned from this experience that it was not enough to remain on the mountain-tops if he wished to avoid fighting, and since he did not wish to shut himself up inside his cities, he decided to choose the other method, that of remaining many miles away from the Roman camp. Hence, if the Romans were in one province, he went into another, and likewise, when the Romans moved out, he always moved in. Yet seeing at the end how, by prolonging the war in this way, his conditions were growing worse and his subjects were being oppressed first by him and then by the enemy, he decided to tempt the fortunes of war, and so he engaged the Romans in a proper battle. It is useful, therefore, to avoid combat when armies enjoy conditions similar to those of the army of Fabius or that of Gneus Sulpicius,* that is, to have an army so good that the enemy does not dare confront you inside your fortresses, and to have an enemy in your territory who has not gained much ground, so that he suffers from a lack of food. In this instance, the decision was useful for the reasons given by Livy: 'But the dictator was very reluctant to risk his fortune before it was absolutely necessary against an enemy who was becoming weaker with every day he had to linger in an unfriendly country.'* But in every other situation you cannot avoid battle, except with dishonour and danger to yourself, because to flee, as Philip did, is like being defeated, and with more shame, in so far as you have given less proof of your exceptional ability. And if Philip managed to save himself, another man would not have done so, unless he had been assisted by the countryside as Philip was.

No one would ever say that Hannibal was not a master of warfare, and in his confrontation with Scipio in Africa, if he had seen an advantage in prolonging the war he would have done so, and perhaps, being a good commander with a good army, he could have done so, as Fabius did in Italy, but since he did not, we must believe that some important motive prompted him. Thus, a prince who has put together an army and sees that, for lack of money or friends, he cannot keep such an army together for long is completely mad if he does not tempt fortune before that army falls apart, because by waiting he will certainly lose, and by trying he may win. Another thing to be considered carefully here is that even if one is going to lose, one must wish to acquire glory, and there is more glory in being defeated by force than by some other difficulty that has caused you to lose. Thus, Hannibal must have been constrained by this necessity. And on the other hand, had Hannibal delayed the battle and Scipio lacked the courage to go and confront him in his strongholds, Scipio would not have suffered, because he had already defeated Syphax and taken so many cities in Africa that he could remain safely and in comfort, as in Italy. This is not what happened to Hannibal when he was facing the opposition of Fabius, nor to those Gauls when they were facing that of Sulpicius.

It is even less possible for a commander to avoid engaging in battle when he and his army are attacking another country, because if he wants to march into an enemy's country, he must go into battle when the enemy meets up with him, and if he besieges a city, he is even more obliged to go into battle; this happened in our times to Duke Charles of Burgundy who was besieging Morat, a Swiss city, when he was attacked by the Swiss and routed, and to the French army, which was besieging Novara, when it was likewise routed by the Swiss.*

CHAPTER II

That Anyone Who Has to Fight Many Enemies, Although He Is Inferior in Numbers, May Yet Win the Victory If He Can Withstand the First Onslaught

In the city of Rome, the power of the tribunes of the plebeians was great, and it was necessary (as we have said many times), because otherwise it would not have been possible to place a check on the ambition of the nobility, which would have corrupted that republic much earlier than actually occurred.

Nevertheless, because everything holds within it some hidden evil that can give rise to new circumstances, as we have said on other occasions, it is necessary to provide against such evils with new institutions. Once tribunal authority became insolent and frightening to the nobility and to all of Rome, some difficulty would therefore have arisen that would have been harmful to Roman liberty, if Appius Claudius had not demonstrated the method by which they could defend themselves against the ambition of the tribunes; his method was to find among the tribunes someone who was either fearful or corruptible or who loved the common good so much that they could persuade him to oppose the will of those who wanted to bring forward some resolution against the will of the senate. This remedy was a great moderating force against such authority, and it was useful to Rome for many years. This example moves me to observe that, whenever many powerful men are united against another powerful man, even though all of them together are much more powerful than he is, one must, nevertheless, always expect more from that one man alone who is less bold than from those many men, no matter how bold they are. For leaving aside all those things in which a single person can prevail over many people, which are countless, this will always occur: the single person, with a bit of effort, can disunite the many and weaken the body that was so bold. I do not wish to cite any ancient examples of this, though there would be many of them, but I wish modern ones from our own times to suffice.

In 1483 all of Italy conspired against the Venetians, and since they were completely defeated and could no longer remain with their army in the field, they bought off Lord Ludovico who ruled Milan, and through these efforts they made an agreement in which not only did they take back the lands they lost, but occupied part of the state of Ferrara as well. In this way, those who lost the war stood in a better position after the peace.* A few years ago everyone conspired against France; nevertheless, before the end of the war Spain broke with her allies and made a truce with France, so that these allies were constrained shortly thereafter to come to terms themselves.* Thus, one should undoubtedly always make the judgement that whenever a war is started by many against one, that single individual will remain in

a better position when he possesses sufficient ability to withstand the first onslaught and can temporize to await the proper
moment. Whenever this is not the case, he will encounter a thousand dangers, as happened in 1508 to the Venetians, who, had
they been able to temporize with the French army, and to find
the time to win over some of those who were allied against them,
would have avoided their downfall; but being without able
armies so that they could temporize with the enemy, and for this
reason lacking the time to separate any of them from the alliance,
they came to ruin. Subsequently, we saw that the pope, once he
regained his possessions, became their friend, and the king of
Spain did the same, and had they been able, both of these two
rulers would very willingly have saved the state of Lombardy
for them against the king of France, in order to keep him from
becoming too powerful in Italy. The Venetians, therefore, could
have given up part in order to save the rest; if they had done so in
time to make it look as if they were not forced to do so, especially before the events of war, this would have been an
extremely wise plan; but as a result of the events of this war, their
policy was contemptible and perhaps less than profitable. But
before the war broke out few of the citizens in Venice could see
the danger, very few could see a remedy, and nobody advised it.
But to return to the beginning of this discourse, let me conclude
by saying that, just as the Roman senate had a remedy for the
health of their native city against the ambition of the tribunes by
virtue of being many, in like manner any prince who is attacked
by many will have a remedy whenever he knows how, with prudence, to employ measures apt to disunite them.

CHAPTER 12

Why a Prudent Commander Must Impose on His Troops the Absolute Necessity to Fight, While Taking It Away from Those of the Enemy

On other occasions we have discussed how useful necessity is in
human actions and the glory to which it has brought them; and
how some moral philosophers have written that the hands and

the tongues of men, two most noble instruments that ennoble mankind, would not have functioned perfectly nor brought human endeavours to that height that they have attained had they not been driven on by necessity. Since the ancient commanders of armies understood the power of such necessity, as well as the extent to which it made the spirits of their soldiers stubborn in combat, they made every effort to ensure that it would constrain their soldiers, and on the other hand, they took great pains to free their enemies from such constraint. For this reason, they often opened to the enemy a path that they could have closed to him, while to their own troops they closed a path they could have left open. The commander who, therefore, desires a city to defend itself stubbornly or an army in the field to fight stubbornly, must, above everything else, strive to place such necessity in the hearts of those who are to fight. Hence, a prudent commander who has to march out to seize a city must measure the ease or difficulty in the seizing of it by recognizing and considering what necessity will force the inhabitants of that city to defend themselves, and whenever he discovers that a great necessity forces them to defend it, he will judge the city difficult to capture; otherwise, he will judge it easy. Thus, it happens that after a rebellion cities are more difficult to capture than they are during the first conquest, because in the beginning, lacking a reason to fear punishment since they have not given offence, they surrender easily, but later, having rebelled, they feel they have given offence, and fearing punishment for this reason, they become difficult to defeat. This stubbornness is also produced by the natural hatreds that neighbouring princes or republics harbour for each other; this arises from the ambition to rule and the jealousy of their states, especially if they are republics, as occurred in Tuscany, where conflict and competition have made and always will make the capture of one city by another difficult. Consequently, anyone who gives careful consideration to the neighbours of the city of Florence and the neighbours of the city of Venice will not be amazed, as many are, that Florence has spent more on its wars and acquired less than Venice. This results from the fact that the Venetians have not had nearby cities so stubborn in their own defence as Florence has had, since all the cities near Venice are accustomed to living under a prince and not in liberty, and those cities used to living in servitude think nothing of changing their master frequently, indeed, many times they desire to do so. Thus, although Venice had more powerful neighbours than Florence, finding nearby cities less obstinate, it was able to overcome them more quickly than Florence, which was surrounded by nothing but free cities.

To return, then, to the beginning of this discourse, when a commander attacks a city he must employ every means available to eliminate such necessity on the part of its defenders and, as a consequence, such stubbornness, promising pardons if the defenders are afraid of punishment, and if they are fearful of losing their liberty, demonstrating how he will act not against the common good but only against a few ambitious citizens in the city; this approach has on many occasions facilitated such undertakings and the seizures of cities. Although such ruses are easily recognized, especially by prudent men, they have, nevertheless, often deceived people who, eager for immediate peace, close their eyes to any other trap concealed beneath such generous promises. In this way countless cities have become enslaved, as happened to Florence in recent times; and as happened to Crassus and his army. Although he recognized the vain promises of the Parthians, which were made to deprive his soldiers of the necessity they felt to defend themselves, he was still unable to keep them obstinate, since they were blinded by the offers of peace which had been made to them by their enemies, as can be seen in greater detail by reading the life of this commander.*

Let me say, therefore, that when the Samnites, breaking the terms of the agreement because of the ambition of a few, raided and plundered the lands of their allies and then sent ambassadors to Rome to sue for peace, offering to restore the property plundered and to imprison those who had caused the rioting and plundering, they were rebuffed by the Romans. Upon returning to Samnium without any hope of an agreement, Claudius Pontius, then commander of the Samnite army, in a noteworthy oration demonstrated that the Romans wanted war at all costs, and although the Samnites, for their part, wanted peace, necessity forced them to turn to war, and these were his words: 'War is just, Samnites, when it is necessary, and arms are righteous for those whose only hope remains in arms';* on this necessity he and his soldiers founded their hopes for victory.

In order to avoid returning to this subject later, it seems advisable to cite those examples from Roman history that are most worthy of being noted. Gaius Manlius* and his army faced the opposition of the Veientes; when part of the army of Veii had invaded Manlius' fortifications, he went swiftly with a company of men to the assistance of these troops; and so that the Veientes could not escape, Manlius occupied all the exits of the camp. For this reason, when the Veientes realized they were trapped they began to fight with such ferocity that they killed Manlius and would have overwhelmed all the rest of the Romans if the prudence of a tribune had not opened to them a path for escape. Here it is evident that when necessity forced the Veientes to fight, they fought most fiercely, but when they saw the path of escape open, they gave more thought to escaping than to fighting.

With their armies, the Volscians and the Aequi had invaded Roman territory. The consuls were sent to oppose them. As the battle wore on, the army of the Volscians, whose commander was Vettius Messius, suddenly found itself trapped between its stockades, occupied by the Romans, and the other Roman army and realizing that they had either to die or to cut their way through with their swords, Vettius spoke these words to his troops: 'There is no wall of earth or stone to stop you—but armed men like yourselves; in courage you are as good as they— in the ultimate and most powerful weapon of all—desperation—you have the advantage!'* Livy calls this necessity the 'ultimate and most powerful weapon of all'. Camillus, the most prudent of all Roman commanders, was already inside the city of Veii with his army when, in order to facilitate its capture and to deprive his enemies of the ultimate necessity of defending themselves, he gave the command, in such a way that the Veientes heard that no one would be harmed who was without a weapon, so that the Veientes threw their arms to the ground, and the city was taken almost without bloodshed. This method was later employed by many commanders.*

CHAPTER 13

Where Should One Place More Trust, in a Good Commander With a Weak Army, or in a Good Army With a Weak Commander?

After Coriolanus had gone into exile away from Rome, he went to the Volscians, from where, after having raised an army to take revenge against his fellow citizens, he marched on Rome, from which he then departed, owing more to his mother's piety than to the strength of the Romans.* Concerning this matter, Livy says it reveals that the Roman republic grew more through the exceptional ability of its commanders than of its soldiers, considering that the Volscians had in the past been defeated and only later had won when Coriolanus was their commander. Although Livy holds this opinion, it is nevertheless evident in many passages in his history that the exceptional ability of soldiers without a commander accomplished miraculous feats, and that they were more organized and ferocious after the death of their consuls than before they were killed. This happened to the army the Romans had in Spain under the Scipios; after the two commanders were killed, the army, through its exceptional ability, was not only able to save itself but to vanquish the enemy and to save that province for the republic.* Thus, all things considered, many examples can be found where only the exceptional skill of the troops will win the day, and many others where only the exceptional skill of the commanders will produce the same effect, so that it can be determined that the former has need of the latter and the latter of the former.

It is well to consider, first, what is most to be feared, either a good army badly commanded or a good commander accompanied by a bad army. Following the opinion of Caesar on this matter, either choice can be deemed of little use. Thus, when Caesar marched into Spain against Afranius and Petraeus, who had an excellent army, he declared that he had little esteem for them, 'since he went against an army without a leader', pointing out the weakness of the commanders. On the contrary, when he marched into Thessaly against Pompey, he stated: 'I go against a leader without an army.'*

It is possible to consider something else: is it easier for a good commander to create a good army or for a good army to create a good commander? On this topic, I would say that this question seems settled, because it is much easier for many good men to find or to instruct one man so that he may become good than it is for one to do so with many. When Lucullus was sent against Mithridates, he was completely inexperienced in war; nevertheless, this good army which contained many outstanding leaders very quickly turned him into a good commander.* For lack of men, the Romans armed many slaves, and for training gave them to Sempronius Gracchus, who in a brief time created an excellent army.* As we have said elsewhere,* Pelopidas and Epaminondas, having negotiated to free Thebes, their native city, from enslavement by the Spartans, in very little time created out of Theban peasants excellent soldiers, who were able not only to withstand the Spartan militia but to conquer it. Hence, the matter is even, because one good thing can find another. None the less, a good army without a good leader usually becomes insolent and dangerous, like the army of Macedonia after the death of Alexander, and the Roman soldiers who were veterans of the civil wars. For this reason, I believe more confidence can be placed in a commander who has the time to teach his men and the opportunity to arm them than in an insolent army with a leader created by the army on the spur of the moment. On that account, double glory and praise are due to those commanders who have not only had to vanquish the enemy but, before they came to blows with them, were forced to teach their army and to make it good; because in such men a double ability is demonstrated, and this is so rare that if such a labour were assigned to most men, they would be respected and esteemed much less than they are.

CHAPTER 14

What Effects Are Produced by the Strange Contrivances that Appear and the Strange Sounds that Are Heard in the Midst of a Battle

The importance in conflicts and battles of a strange event that arises by means of something unexpectedly seen or heard is demonstrated in many passages, and especially in an example that occurred in the battle the Romans waged against the Volscians: Quinctius, seeing one of the wings of his army giving way, began to shout loudly that they should stand firm, since the other wing of the army was winning: encouraging his men and frightening the enemy with these words, he was victorious.* If such cries produce a strong effect in a well-organized army, in an unruly and badly organized army they produce an even stronger one, because the entire group is swayed by like winds. I want to cite a noteworthy example of this which occurred in our own times. A few years ago, the city of Perugia was divided into two factions, the Oddi and the Baglioni families. The latter were in power; the former were in exile. With the assistance of their friends, the Oddi family raised an army and assembled it in one of their towns near Perugia, and with help of their allies they entered Perugia one night, and without being discovered, they came to take the main square. Since that city had chains at all its street-corners to keep the streets blocked, the Oddi troops put at their head a man holding an iron mace to break the locks on the chains, so that the horses could pass through; only the chain that blocked the street into the main square remained to be broken when the call to arms was raised, but since the man who was breaking the chains was hampered by the crowd coming up behind him, so that he was unable to raise his arms properly to break the chain, in order to be able to move he cried: 'Move back!'; his cry, passing from rank to rank, became 'Retreat!', so that the last ranks began to flee first, then one by one the others, with such haste that they broke up their own ranks; and thus the plan of the Oddi family came to nothing because of such an insignificant event.*

There still remains to be considered the fact that good battle formations in an army are necessary in order to be able to fight in an orderly fashion, so that every little incident does not throw you into confusion. For this reason, if for no other, the popular multitude is useless in war because every noise, every cry, every uproar upsets them and causes them to flee. Still, every good commander among his other dispositions must appoint those who are to take his spoken commands and pass them to others, and he must accustom his troops to pay attention to these men alone and his captains to say nothing but what he has commissioned them to say, because if this practice is not well observed, it has frequently been seen to have created serious disorders.

With respect to seeing strange sights, every commander should strive to make something appear while his armies are engaged in hand-to-hand combat that gives his soldiers courage and takes it away from the enemy, because among the incidents that give you the victory, this is most efficacious. As evidence of this it is possible to cite the case of Caius Sulpicius,* the Roman dictator, who while engaging the Gauls in battle armed all his support troops and others in the field lacking their own arms, and after he had mounted them on mules and other pack-animals with arms and banners to make them appear to be cavalry, he placed them under his banners behind a hill and ordered that, on a given signal, when the battle was at its fiercest pitch, they should appear and show themselves to the enemy. This stratagem organized and executed in this way terrorized the Gauls to such an extent that they lost the battle. A good commander must, however, do two things: the first is to see if he can frighten the enemy with some of these strange inventions; the second is to be prepared, so that if they are used against him he will detect them and make them of no avail against him. This is what the king of India did to Semiramis who, upon noticing that the king had a large number of elephants, constructed a number of them with buffalo and cow hides placed over camels and sent them forward, in order to frighten him and to demonstrate to him that she too had many of them, but since the king recognized her trick, he made her plan not only useless but even harmful.* Mamercus, the dictator, was waging war upon the people of Fidenae, who, in order to frighten the Roman army, planned that at the height of the battle a number of soldiers would march out of Fidenae with torches on their lances, so that the Romans, distracted by the novelty of the thing, would break ranks.* On this subject, it should be noted that when such inventions contain more truth than fiction, they can then certainly be staged for men, because they are so bold that their weakness cannot quickly be discovered, but when they are more fictitious than true, it is best either not to stage them or, if you must do so, to keep them at a distance so that they cannot be so quickly discovered, as Caius Sulpicius did with his muleteers. Thus, when such deceptions are weak, drawing near to them will quickly expose them, and this will do you harm instead of good, as the elephants did to Semiramis and the torches to the people of Fidenae. Although these torches disturbed the army slightly at the beginning, none the less, when the dictator arrived, he began to shout out to his men that they should be ashamed to flee from smoke like bees and that they should turn around and face the enemy, declaring: 'Destroy Fidenae with her own flames, since generous kindness could not make her your friend!'* This contrivance proved useless to the people of Fidenae, and they were left the losers in that battle.

CHAPTER 15

That One Man and Not Many Should Be Placed in Command of an Army, and How More Than One Commander Is Harmful

After the people of Fidenae rebelled and massacred the colony the Romans had sent to that city, the Romans created four tribunes with consular power to respond to this attack; one of them was left to guard Rome, and three others were sent against the people of Fidenae and the Veientes; and since these men were divided among themselves and disunited, they derived dishonour from the campaign but not harm, because they brought dishonour upon themselves, while the fact that they were not harmed was due to the exceptional ability of their soldiers. Upon seeing such disorder, the Romans had recourse to the creation of the dictator, so that a single man would reorganize what three others had disorganized. Hence, it is possible to recognize the uselessness of having many commanders in a single army or in a city that has to be defended, and Livy cannot say it any more clearly than with these words: 'Three tribunes with consular power were appointed ... where they gave signal proof of the inefficacy of a divided command. Unable ever to agree with his colleagues, each man persisted in following his own judgement, to the obvious advantage of the enemy.'* Although this example is sufficient to demonstrate the disorder that more than one commander can create in a war, I should like to cite a few others, both modern and ancient, for a fuller explanation of the matter.

In 1500, after the king of France, Louis XII, recaptured Milan, he sent his troops to Pisa to restore that city to the Florentines; Giovambattista Ridolfi and Luca di Antonio degli Albizi were sent to that city as commissioners. Since Giovambattista was a man of some renown and was older, Luca left the task of managing everything completely to him; and if he did not display his ambition by opposing Giovambattista, he displayed it by keeping his silence and by disregarding and showing his contempt for everything, so that he failed to assist actions in the field either through deeds or counsel, as if he had been a man of no importance. But then completely the opposite was observed when Giovambattista, through a certain turn of events, had to return to Florence; now alone, Luca showed how much his spirit, hard work, and counsel were worth, all of which had been lost while he had a companion.* In confirmation of this, I want to cite once again the words of Livy, who tells us that when Quinctius and Agrippa, his colleague, were sent by the Romans against the Aequi, Agrippa wanted the entire administration of the war to be in Quinctius' control, and Livy declares: 'It is most salutary that in tne administration of great undertakings, the supreme command should be in the hands of a single man.'* This is exactly the opposite of what our republics and principalities do today, when, in order to administrate them better, they send into places more than one commissioner and more than one leader; this creates an immeasurable confusion. If the reasons for the ruin of the Italian and French armies in our times were to be sought, this would be the principal explanation. It is truly possible to conclude that it is better to send one man of average prudence on an expedition alone than two extremely capable men with the same authority together.

CHAPTER 16

True Ability Is Sought in Difficult Times, and in Easy Ones, Men With Wealth or From Good Families, Rather Than Men of Ability, Find More Favour

It always was and always will be the case that great and uncommon men are neglected in times of peace, because the envy brought upon them by the reputation their exceptional ability has earned them causes numerous citizens to desire not only to be their equals but their superiors. A good passage regarding this is found in the Greek historian Thucydides, who shows that after the Athenian republic remained the victor over its enemies in the Peloponnesian War, having checked the pride of the Spartans and subjugated all the rest of Greece, Athens gained so much prestige that it planned to invade Sicily. This enterprise came under debate in Athens; Alcibiades and some other citizens advised that the invasion be made, like men who, thinking very little of the public good, thought only of their own honour, planning to become leaders in such an enterprise. But Nicias, who was the first among the distinguished citizens of Athens, advised against it, and the strongest reason he brought forth when addressing the people to persuade them to trust him, was this: that is, in advising them not to wage this war, he was advising them in a matter which was not in his own interest, for with Athens at peace, he knew that there were countless citizens who would want to surpass him, but with Athens at war, he knew that no citizen would be superior or even equal to him.*

It is evident, therefore, that a certain disorder exists in republics, which is that of holding worthy men in little esteem in peaceful times. This causes such men to feel indignant in two ways: the first is that they see themselves deprived of their proper rank; the other is that they see as their companions and superiors men who are unworthy and of lesser competence than they. This disorder in republics has caused many to collapse, because those citizens who see themselves slighted for no reason and understand that this is caused by the safe and easy times, contrive to stir things up, instigating new wars to the detriment of the republic. In thinking about what remedies might exist for this, I have come upon two of them: the first is to maintain the citizens in poverty, so that, lacking in exceptional ability, they cannot corrupt themselves or others with riches; the second is to be prepared for war, as the Romans were in their early days, so that it can always be waged and distinguished citizens will always be needed. Since that city always maintained armies outside the city, there was always a place for men of exceptional ability, nor was it possible to take away a rank or position from a man who had earned it and give it to another who did not deserve it, because even if this was done on some occasions by error or as a test, it immediately brought about such disorder and danger that the city quickly returned to the true path. But other republics which are not organized like Rome and who wage war only when necessity forces them to do so cannot defend themselves from such difficulties; on the contrary, they are always coming up against such difficulties, and disorder always arises from them when the neglected and able citizen is vengeful and enjoys some reputation or following in the city. At one time the city of Rome protected itself against this, but after Rome had conquered Carthage and Antiochus (as we have said elsewhere),* this city too, no longer fearing wars, believed it could entrust its armies to anyone it wished, without giving as much consideration to exceptional ability as to other qualities that find favour with the people. For this reason, Paulus Aemilius was many times refused the consulship, nor was he made consul before the Macedonian War broke out, but since this was judged a dangerous war, the consensus of the entire city entrusted the office to him.*

After 1494 in our own city of Florence, following many wars in which Florentine citizens had all made a very bad showing, the city by chance encountered a man who demonstrated how one had to command an army: this was Antonio Giacomini. While dangerous wars were to be waged, the ambition of other citizens died out, and in the election for commissioner and the leader of the army Antonio had no other competitor, but when it came to waging a war where there was no doubt of the outcome and much honour and rank involved, Antonio discovered so many competitors there that when three commissioners were elected to besiege Pisa, he was left out entirely. Although it was not immediately evident that failing to send Antonio caused harm to the public, it was, none the less, easy to speculate about this, because the Pisans no longer had anything to defend themselves with or to live on, and if Antonio had been in command he would have pressed them so hard that they would have surrendered unconditionally to the Florentines. But since they were besieged by military leaders who understood neither how to besiege them nor how to weaken them with force, they held out for so long that the city of Florence bought them off, when it could have taken them by force. Antonio's indignation must necessarily have been great, and he must have been very patient and good not to desire to take revenge for this, either through the downfall of the city, if he could bring it about, or through the injury of some individual citizen. A republic must guard itself against this, as will be discussed in the following chapter.

CHAPTER 17

That You Should Not Offend a Man and Then Appoint Him to an Important Governmental Post

A republic must carefully consider whether or not to place anyone in any important administrative post who has been offended in some noteworthy way by others. Claudius Nero, who left the army with which he was opposing Hannibal, and with part of it went off to the Marches to look for the other consul in order to engage Hasdrubal in battle before he joined up with Hannibal, had found himself on a previous occasion confronting Hasdrubal in Spain. Having closed in on him with his army in a location that forced Hasdrubal either to fight to his own disadvantage or to die of starvation, Claudius Nero was so cleverly held off by Hasdrubal with certain arrangements for a treaty that the latter slipped through his hands and deprived Claudius Nero of the opportunity to defeat him. Once this was learned in Rome, it earned the condemnation of both the senate and the people, and he was criticized in an offensive way throughout the city, much to his dishonour and disdain. But later, when he was made consul and was sent to oppose Hannibal, he chose the above-mentioned policy, which was extremely dangerous, so much so that all of Rome remained doubtful and anxious until news of the rout of Hasdrubal arrived. Later, when Claudius was asked why he had taken such a dangerous decision, in which without dire necessity he had almost gambled Roman liberty away, he replied that he had done it because he knew that if he succeeded, he would regain the glory that he had lost in Spain, and that if he failed and this decision of his had the opposite outcome, he realized that he would avenge himself upon the city and those citizens who had so ungratefully and shamelessly insulted him.* When the passions of such offences can be so powerful in a Roman citizen and at a time when Rome was still not corrupt, one must imagine how powerful they would be in a citizen of another city that was not like Rome in those days. Since no certain remedy can be offered for such disorders which arise in republics, it follows that it is impossible to organize an everlasting republic, because its downfall can come about in a thousand unforeseen ways.

CHAPTER 18

Nothing Is More Worthy of a Commander Than to Anticipate the Decisions of the Enemy

Epaminondas the Theban used to say that nothing was more necessary and more useful to a commander than having some knowledge of the deliberations and decisions of the enemy. Since such knowledge is difficult to obtain, the commander deserves even more praise when he does so by speculation. It is not as difficult to understand the enemy's plans as it is sometimes difficult to understand his actions, and not so much the actions carried out by him some distance away but, rather, those which are present and nearby. Accordingly, it has happened many times that when a battle has lasted into the night, the victor believes he has lost and the vanquished thinks he has won. This kind of error has brought about decisions contrary to the well-being of the person who made them; this occurred to Brutus and Cassius, who by virtue of such an error lost the war, because after Brutus had won on his wing, Cassius believed that he had lost and that the entire army was routed; and in despair over this misjudgement of the situation, he killed himself.* In our own times, in the battle that Francis, king of France, fought in Lombardy at Santa Cecilia with the Swiss, the part of the Swiss army that remained intact thought they had won when night fell, unaware that their fellow-soldiers had been routed and killed; this error made them fail to save themselves, since to their great disadvantage they waited to fight again the next morning; this mistake also caused the army of the pope and Spain to commit another error, and because of it they were on the verge of ruin, for after false news of the Swiss victory, they crossed the Po River, and if they had proceeded too far forward they would have remained prisoners of the French who were victorious.*

This same mistake happened in Roman camps and in those of the Aequi;* Sempronius the consul had marched with his army to face the enemy, and once he had initiated the battle, the two armies struggled until evening with changing fortunes on both sides. When night came, since both armies were half destroyed, neither one returned to its camp; on the contrary, each army withdrew into the nearby hills, where it thought it would be more secure; and the Roman army divided itself into two parts: one went with the consul, and the other went with a certain centurion named Tempanius, through whose skill the Roman army that day had not been entirely destroyed. When morning came, the Roman consul, without learning anything further about the enemy, drew back towards Rome; the army of the Aequi did likewise, because each side thought the enemy had won, and each, therefore, withdrew, caring very little about leaving behind their camps as spoils of war. It happened that while Tempanius, who was with the rest of the Roman army, was also retreating, he learned from some wounded Aequi that their commanders had departed and had abandoned their camps. Hence, upon hearing this news, Tempanius marched into the Roman camps and saved them, then sacked the camps of the Aequi, and returned to Rome victorious. This victory, it is evident, was only a matter of who among them was first to understand the disarray of the enemy. Here, it must be noted that it can often happen that two armies which are confronting one another are in the same disarray and suffering from the same necessities, and that the one which remains the victor is the first to understand the necessities of the other.

I want to give a domestic and modern example of this. In 1498, when the Florentines had a huge army in Pisan territory and were besieging the city, which the Venetians had taken under their protection, the Venetians saw no other means of saving Pisa and decided to create a diversion in the war by attacking the dominion of Florence from another side, and after they had created a powerful army they entered the Val di Lamona, occupied the town of Marradi, and besieged the stronghold of Castiglione, which stood on a hill above. When the Florentines heard this, they decided to send help to Marradi without diminishing the forces they had in Pisan territory, and after they had raised new infantry and organized new cavalry, they sent them in that direction under the command of Jacopo IV d'Appiano, lord of Piombino, and Count Rinuccio da Marciano. When these troops were then led to the top of the hill overlooking Marradi, the enemy lifted the siege around Castiglione and withdrew into the town, and since both of these two armies had opposed each other for some days, both were very short of provisions and every other necessary thing. Lacking the courage to attack each other or any knowledge of the problems each was suffering, they both decided on the same evening to strike camp the following morning and to draw back in retreat, the Venetians toward Bersighella and Faenza and the Florentines toward Casaglia and the Mugello. When morning came and each of the camps began to send their baggage ahead, by chance a woman left the village of Marradi and went toward the Florentine camp, feeling safe because of her old age and her poverty, wishing to see certain of her relatives who were in that camp; when she told the commanders of the Florentine forces that the Venetian army had departed, this news raised their courage, and changing their decision, as if they had dislodged the enemy, they marched against them and wrote to Florence that they had driven the Venetians back and won the war.* This victory arose from nothing but having understood, before the enemy, that they were marching away; had this news reached the other side first, it would have produced the same effect against our troops.

CHAPTER 19

Whether Deference or Punishment Is More Necessary to Restrain a Multitude

The Roman republic was stirred up by the enmities between the nobles and the plebeians; none the less, when war was upon them they sent out Quinctius and Appius Claudius with their armies.* Appius, who was cruel and harsh as a commander, was so rarely obeyed by his troops that, on the brink of defeat, he fled from his own battlefield. Quinctius, who was kind and gracious of spirit, had obedient soldiers and carried off the victory. Thus, it appears that it is better, in governing a multitude, to be more humane than arrogant, more merciful than cruel. Nevertheless, Tacitus, with whom many other writers agree, in one of his maxims reaches exactly the contrary conclusion when he says: 'In governing a multitude, punishment is more valuable than indulgence.'* In considering how both of these opinions can be reconciled, I will say: either you have to control men who are usually your companions, or men who are always your subjects. When they are your companions, it is impossible wholly to use punishment or that severity Tacitus describes, and because the Roman plebeians shared equal power in Rome with the nobility, a single man who became ruler for a limited time could not handle them with cruelty and harsh treatment. Often it is clear that Roman commanders who made themselves loved by their armies and who treated them with deference achieved better results than those who made themselves extraordinarily feared, unless, of course, they were endowed with enormous ability as was Manlius Torquatus. But anyone who commands subjects, such as those Tacitus discusses, must lean more towards punishment than deference, so that they will not become insolent and ride roughshod over you because of your excessive kindness. But even this kind of punishment must be moderate in a way that avoids hatred, because making oneself hated never turns out well for any ruler. The way to avoid hatred is to leave the property of one's subjects alone, because unless it conceals his desire for plunder, no ruler is eager to spill blood, except when driven to it by necessity, and such necessity comes about only on rare occasions; but when such eagerness is mixed with a desire for plunder, this necessity always appears, and the reasons and the desire to shed blood are never lacking, as was discussed at length in another treatise on this subject.* Quinctius, therefore, deserved more praise than Appius, and the maxim of Tacitus, within its limits and not in the ways it was observed by Appius, deserves to be approved.

Since we have spoken of punishment and deference, it does not seem superfluous to me to demonstrate how an example of human kindness could accomplish more with the inhabitants of Falerii than arms.*

CHAPTER 20

One Example of Humanity Towards the Inhabitants of Falerii Achieved More Than Any Use of Roman Power

When Camillus had drawn his army around the city of Falerii and had besieged it, a schoolmaster of the most noble children of that city, thinking he could ingratiate himself with Camillus and the Roman people, left the city with these children under the pretence of taking some exercise, and brought them all to the Roman camp before Camillus, and having presented them to him, he declared that through these children, the city would place itself in his hands. This gift was not only refused by Camillus, but after he had stripped the schoolmaster and bound his hands behind him and had placed a switch in the hands of each of these schoolchildren, he had them accompany the schoolmaster back to the city while giving him a good beating. When the citizens learned of this incident, they were so pleased by the humanity and integrity of Camillus that, without wishing to defend themselves further, they decided to give him the city. Thus, with this perfect example, it must be considered how much more can be accomplished on occasion in the hearts of men by a single humane act full of charity than an act which is ferocious and violent, and how on many occasions in those provinces or cities where weapons, instruments of war, and every other human power have been unable to open a breach, one example of humanity and mercy, of chastity or of generosity, has done so. Many other examples of this are found in the histories besides this one. It is evident that Roman arms could not drive Pyrrhus from Italy, but the generosity of Fabricius* drove him away when Fabricius showed Pyrrhus the offer that one of his confidants had made to the Romans to poison him. It is also evident that Scipio Africanus did not gain as much renown in Spain from the destruction of New Carthage as he earned from that example of chastity by which he restored the young and beautiful wife untouched to her husband; the fame of this act won him the friendship of all of Spain.* It is also evident how strongly people desire this quality in great men, and how it is praised by writers and by both those who describe the lives of princes and those who prescribe how princes ought to live. Among these, Xenophon takes great pains to demonstrate how many honours, victories, and distinctions Cyrus attained by being kind and humane and by giving no indication in his actions of pride, cruelty, lust, or any of the other vices that sully the lives of men. None the less, given that Hannibal won great fame and great victories with contrary methods, it seems to me that in the following chapter we should discuss how this comes about.

CHAPTER 21

How It Came About that Hannibal, With a Different Mode of Conduct from that of Scipio, Achieved the Same Results in Italy that Scipio Achieved in Spain

I think some will be amazed to see that certain commanders, notwithstanding the fact that they have led completely different lives, have nevertheless achieved results similar to those of men who have lived in the way described above; thus, it seems that the reason for their victories does not derive from the previously mentioned causes, but rather, it seems that these methods do not bring you any more power or fortune, since it is possible to acquire glory and renown through contrary methods. Hence, in order not to avoid discussing the men mentioned above and to clarify more precisely what I tried to say, let me say that when Scipio invaded Spain it is evident that his humanity and mercy immediately made that province his friend and made him adored and admired by the people. On the other hand, it is evident that when Hannibal invaded Italy and with completely opposite methods—that is, with cruelty, violence, pillage, and every kind of treachery—he achieved the same result that Scipio had achieved in Spain, because all the cities of Italy revolted in Hannibal's favour and all the peoples followed him.

In thinking about what might have caused this to happen, several reasons are evident. The first is that men are desirous of new things to such an extent that those who are faring well wish for change as much as those who are faring badly, because, as was mentioned on another occasion*—and it is the truth—men become bored with the good and grieve for the bad. This desire, then, opens the gates to anyone in a province who makes himself the leader of some reform; if he is a foreigner, everyone pursues him, and if he is a fellow-citizen, they crowd around him, increasing his strength and granting him their favour to such an extent that, in whatever way he proceeds, he succeeds in making great progress in those places. Besides this, men are driven by two principal impulses, either by love or by fear, so that anyone who makes himself loved can command them just as easily as anyone who makes himself feared; on the contrary, anyone who makes himself feared is in most cases more readily followed and obeyed than anyone who makes himself loved.*

It matters very little, therefore, which of these two paths a commander takes as long as he is an extremely able man and this exceptional ability makes him esteemed among men, because when his ability is great, as it was in Hannibal and in Scipio, it cancels all those errors that he commits in order to make himself either loved or feared too much. Thus, from both of these two methods great difficulties can arise that are apt to cause the downfall of a prince: the man who has too great a desire to be loved becomes despicable every time he strays from the true path; the other man, who has too great a desire to be feared, becomes odious each time he exceeds the mean. Keeping to the middle course is not possible precisely because our nature does not allow us to do so, but it is necessary to mitigate those things that are in excess with enormous ability, as did Hannibal and Scipio. None the less, it is evident that just as both one and the other were damaged by their different ways of life, so both of them were glorified as well.*

The glorification of both men has already been mentioned. With respect to Scipio, the harm he experienced was that his troops in Spain mutinied along with some of his allies, a matter that arose from nothing else but the fact that he was not feared; for men are so restless that once the smallest door is open to their ambition, they immediately forget all the love they bore for their prince because of his humanity, as did his previously mentioned soldiers and allies, to the extent that, to remedy this problem, Scipio was obliged to employ some of those cruel measures he had avoided. With respect to Hannibal, there is no particular example of his cruelty and deceitfulness harming him, but one can certainly presume that Naples and many other cities which remained faithful to the Roman people did so out of fear of his cruelty. It was certainly evident that his merciless way of life made him more odious to the Roman people than any other enemy that republic ever had, to the extent that when Pyrrhus was with his army in Italy the Romans denounced the man who wished to poison him, but they never pardoned Hannibal, even when he was disarmed and in exile, until they brought about his death. Thus, these disadvantages arose for Hannibal because he was considered merciless, faithless, and cruel; but his behaviour resulted, on the other hand, in a great advantage for him, one admired by all the historians: that is, in his army, although composed of various kinds of men, no dissension ever arose either among the men or against Hannibal himself. This could not derive from anything other than the terror inspired by his own person, which was so great that, mixed with the reputation his exceptional ability gave him, it kept his troops subdued and united. I will conclude, therefore, that the method of conduct a commander employs is of little importance, provided that he harbours within himself a very great ability that conditions either one of these different ways of life, because as was mentioned, in both methods exists a defect and a danger when it is not corrected by extraordinary ability. If Hannibal and Scipio, one with laudable deeds, the other with detestable ones, accomplished the same result, I would prefer not to omit here a discussion of two Roman citizens who, with different methods but both praiseworthy ones, attained the same glory.

CHAPTER 22

How the Hardness of Manlius Torquatus and the Humaneness of Valerius Corvinus Acquired for Each Man the Same Glory

Living in Rome at the same time were two excellent commanders, Manlius Torquatus and Valerius Corvinus, who were equal in ability, in triumphs, and in glory; each of them, in so far as the enemy was concerned, had acquired this glory with equal skill, but in matters concerning their armies and the treatment of soldiers they proceeded very differently. Thus, Manlius commanded his men with every kind of severity, without giving his troops any respite from their toil or pains; Valerius, on the other hand, controlled them by using every humane method and expedient, tempered by an intimate friendliness. For it can be seen that, in order to have the obedience of his troops, one man put his son to death while the other never harmed anyone. Nevertheless, with very different conduct, each man achieved the same result against the enemy and to the benefit of the republic and himself, because no soldier either ever deserted from a battle or rebelled against them or was in any way disobedient to their wishes, even though the commands of Manlius were so harsh that all the other commands that exceeded the normal method were called 'Manlian commands'.* Here we must consider, first, how it came about that Manlius was constrained to conduct himself so rigorously; next, why Valerius was able to proceed so humanely; again, why different methods produced the same result; and finally, which of them is best and most useful to imitate. If one carefully examines Manlius' nature, from the time Livy first mentions him one will discover him to be extremely strong, devoted to his father and his native city, and extremely respectful of his superiors. These qualities can be recognized in the killing of the Gaul, in the defence of his father against the tribune, and in what he said when he went to the consul before he went off to do battle with the Gaul: 'Without an order from you, sir . . . I would never fight out of my rank, even if I were certain of victory.'* Thus, once a man like this comes to the rank of command, he wants to find all men similar to himself, and his great inner strength makes him give strong orders, and that same inner strength expects his commands to be carried out when they are given. It is a rule most true that when harsh orders are given, it is necessary to act harshly to ensure that they are executed; otherwise you will find yourself deceived. Here, it must be noted that in order to be obeyed, it is necessary to know how to command, and they know how to command who match their own qualities with those of the men who have to obey, and if they see a balance, they then give orders, but if they see an imbalance, they refrain from giving orders.

A prudent man* once declared that in order to hold a republic with violence, a balance has to exist between the one who exerts the force and those against whom the force is exerted. Whenever this balance exists, it can be assumed that such violence will endure, but when the person subjected to violence is more powerful than the person who employs it, we cannot doubt that one day this violence will cease.

But in returning to our discourse, let me say that to command strong measures requires a strong man, and the man who possesses such strength and orders such measures cannot later on with gentleness cause his orders to be obeyed. But anyone who does not possess such inner strength must guard against the use of extraordinary commands, and, in ordinary situations, employ his humanity, because ordinary punishments are not blamed upon the leader but, rather, upon the laws and institutional arrangements. Thus, it should be assumed that Manlius was constrained to proceed so inflexibly by the extraordinary circumstances of the commands toward which his nature inclined him; such orders are useful in a republic, because they bring the institutions of the republic back toward their beginnings and ancient excellence. If a republic were so fortunate, as we have stated above, that it could often have a man who, with his exemplary action, could renew its laws and who would not only prevent it from racing toward ruin but would pull it back, that republic would be everlasting. Manlius was just one of those men who with the harshness of his commands maintained military discipline in Rome, constrained first by his nature and then by the desire he had to ensure that what his natural inclination made him command would be accomplished. On the other hand, Valerius was able to conduct himself in a humane fashion, like a man for whom it was sufficient to observe the usual practices followed in the Roman armies. These customary practices, because they were good, were sufficient to do him honour; it was not difficult to follow them, and it did not force Valerius to punish the transgressors, both because there were none in that time and because, had there been any, as was mentioned, the men would have blamed their punishment on the institutions and not on the cruelty of their prince. In this way, Valerius was able to show that he was the source of every humane act, which enabled him to acquire the gratitude of his soldiers and their contentment. Hence, it happened that while both commanders enjoyed the same obedience, they were able, operating differently, to achieve the same result. Those who might wish to imitate them can fall into the vices of contempt and hatred that I mentioned above in the discussion of Hannibal and Scipio, two qualities that can be avoided only with enormous skill and not otherwise.

It now remains to consider which of these modes of conduct is most praiseworthy. This is, I think, open to dispute, because historians praise both methods. Nevertheless, those who write about how a prince should govern are more sympathetic to Valerius than to Manlius, and the remarks of Xenophon, whom I cited earlier, in offering numerous examples of Cyrus' humanity, correspond closely to what Livy says about Valerius Corvinus. When he was made consul against the Samnites and the day arrived in which he had to fight, he spoke to his troops with that humanity by which he governed himself, and after this speech, Livy writes these words: 'There was nowhere a commander on more friendly terms with his men. Valerius cheerfully shared all their duties with the humblest of his soldiers; in military sports too, when trials of speed and strength took place among men of the same age, he was pleasant and courteous, accepting victory and defeat with the same expression on his face, and spurning no one who offered himself as a match for him. His practical kindliness fitted every situation, his speech showed as much concern for the other man's freedom as for his own dignity, and he conducted himself in office in the same manner as when he was a candidate; nothing wins greater popularity than this.'* Likewise, Livy speaks honourably of Manlius, demonstrating that his severity in the death of his son made the army so obedient to the consul that it was the cause of the victory the Roman people won over the Latins; and Livy goes so far in praising him that, after this victory, having described the entire order of that battle and shown all the dangers that the Roman people incurred in it as well as the difficulties involved in winning, he comes to this conclusion: that is, only the exceptional skill of Manlius delivered that victory to the Romans. In comparing the strength of both armies, he affirms that the other side would have won if Manlius had been their consul.

Considering, then, everything that the historians have said about these two methods, it would be difficult to choose between them. Nevertheless, in order not to leave this question undecided, I must say that as a citizen who lives under the laws of a republic, I believe Manlius' conduct is more laudable and less dangerous; because this method is in complete support of the public good and is not in any way directed at private ambition; because no one can acquire supporters through this method, showing himself always to be harsh and to love the common good alone; and because anyone who uses this method will not acquire special friends, or what, as was mentioned above, we call supporters. Thus, such a mode of conduct cannot be more useful nor more desirable in a republic, since it is not lacking in public benefits and contains no suspicion of private power. But in Valerius' mode of conduct, the contrary occurs, because even if it produces the same effects in so far as the public good is concerned, many doubts none the less arise from it because of the particular goodwill that such a person acquires with the troops, which might produce bad effects against liberty in a lengthy period of command. If such evil effects did not arise with Publicola,* it was because the minds and spirits of the Romans were not yet corrupted and he was not continuously in government over a long period of time.

But if we have to consider a prince, as Xenophon did, we would side completely with Valerius and abandon Manlius, because a prince must seek in his soldiers and subjects both obedience and love. Respecting institutions and being considered a man of exceptional ability bring him obedience; kindness, humanity, mercy, and the other qualities that were typical of Valerius and which, according to Xenophon, were typical of Cyrus, bring him love.* For being a prince particularly well loved who counts the army among his supporters is in conformity with all the other duties of his position, but being a citizen who counts the army among his supporters is not in conformity at all with the other requirements which oblige him to live under the laws and to obey the magistrates.

Among the ancient records of the Venetian republic, one can read that when the Venetian galleys returned to Venice, a certain dispute arose between those aboard the galleys and the people, which led to disturbances and fighting, nor could the matter be laid to rest through the power of government officials, through respect for citizens, or through their fear of the magistrates, but when suddenly before those sailors a gentleman appeared,* who had been their captain the year before, out of love for him they departed and abandoned the struggle. Their obedience generated such suspicion in the senate that a short time afterwards the Venetians protected themselves against him either by prison or by execution. I must conclude, therefore, that the conduct of Valerius is useful in a prince and harmful in a citizen, not only to his native city but to himself as well: to his native city, because such methods prepare the path to tyranny; to himself, because in suspecting his mode of conduct, the city is forced to protect itself against his methods to his detriment. And so I affirm, on the contrary, that the conduct of Manlius is damaging in a prince but useful in a citizen, especially to his native country, and yet it rarely does injury, unless the hatred your severity brings you is increased by the suspicion your other abilities bring upon you as a result of your great reputation, as will be shown below in the case of Camillus.

CHAPTER 23

Why Camillus Was Driven Out of Rome

We have concluded above that in conducting himself like Valerius, a man harms his native city and himself; in conducting himself like Manlius, a man benefits his native city and sometimes harms himself. This is well demonstrated by the example of Camillus, who in his conduct resembled Manlius rather than Valerius. Hence Livy, when speaking of Camillus, says that 'the soldiers hated but admired his exceptional ability'.*

What caused him to be considered marvellous was his solicitude, prudence, greatness of heart, and the good organization that he displayed in using and commanding armies; what made him hated was that he was more severe in punishing his men than generous in rewarding them. Livy cites these reasons for this hatred: first, that the money which was derived from selling the property of the Veientes was added to the public treasury and was not divided among the soldiers along with the spoils of war; next, that in his triumph he had his triumphal chariot drawn by four white horses, which caused people to say that because of his pride he was trying to rival the sun; third, that he made a vow to give to Apollo the tenth part of the spoils from the Veientes, which, in trying to fulfil this vow, he had to take from the hands of soldiers who had already seized it. Here, it is easy to note clearly those things which make a prince hated by his people, the most important of which is to deprive them of some benefit. This is a matter of great importance, because when you are deprived of things which in themselves possess some benefit, you will never forget it; every little necessity causes you to remember it, and because necessities arise every day, you remember them every day. The other thing is to appear puffed up with pride, which could not be any more odious to a people, especially if they are free. And although such pride and pomp cause them no inconvenience, none the less, they hate anyone who displays them; a prince must guard against this as he would against a reef, because to bring hatred on himself without any benefit is a completely reckless and imprudent policy.

CHAPTER 24

The Prolongation of Military Commands Enslaved Rome

If the conduct of the Roman republic is considered carefully, it will be evident that two things were the cause of that republic's dissolution: one was the struggles that arose over the agrarian laws; the other was the prolongation of military commands; if these two things had been well understood from the beginning, and the proper remedies for them taken, a free way of life would have lasted longer and, perhaps, have been more peaceful. Although the prolongation of military command apparently never caused any disturbances in Rome, nevertheless, it is, in fact, evident how much harm it did to the city when the citizens seized that authority in making such decisions. If the other citizens for whom this appointment was extended had been wise and good, as was Lucius Quinctius,* the city would not have experienced this difficulty. His goodness provides an example worthy of note. After an agreement between the plebeians and the senate had been reached, and the plebeians had extended the command of the tribunes, judging them strong enough to resist the ambition of the nobles, the senate, in competition with the plebeians and in order not to appear weaker than they, decided to prolong the consulate of Lucius Quinctius. But he completely refused to accept this decision, stating that bad examples should be eliminated and not multiplied with even worse examples, and he insisted that new consuls be appointed. His goodness and prudence, had they been possessed by all Roman citizens, would not have allowed the introduction of that practice of prolonging magistracies, and from these prolongations the Romans would not have come to those of military commands: with the passage of time, this practice ruined that republic. The first for whom a military command was extended was Publilius Philo,* who was in the field at the city of Palaeopolis and when he came to the end of his consulate, the senate, feeling that he had victory in his grasp, did not send his successor but made him proconsul; thus, he was the first proconsul. Although this action was carried out by the senate in the public interest, in time it enslaved Rome, because the more the Romans went abroad with their armies, the more it seemed to them that such an extension was necessary and the more they made use of it. This produced two disadvantages: first, that fewer men were experienced in military command, and because of this, reputation became restricted to a few; second, that when a citizen was commander of an army for a lengthy period of time, he gained its support and made it his supporter, because that army in time forgot the senate and recognized him as its leader. For this reason, Sulla and Marius were able to find soldiers who, contrary to the public good, would follow them, and for this reason, Caesar was able to seize his native city. If the Romans had never prolonged the magistracies and military commands, they would not have so quickly come into such great power, and if their conquests had come later, they would also have fallen more slowly into servitude.

CHAPTER 25

On the Poverty of Cincinnatus and Many Roman Citizens

We have explained elsewhere* that the most useful thing instituted in a free society is a way to keep the citizens poor. Although it is not apparent which institution had this effect in Rome, especially since the agrarian law encountered so much opposition, experience none the less reveals that 400 years after Rome had been founded, there existed great poverty in the city; nor can it be believed that any other institution was more important in producing this effect than the understanding that poverty did not close the path to any rank or honour whatsoever, and that exceptional ability was sought after wherever it made its home. This way of living made wealth less desirable. This is clearly evident, because when Minucius the consul along with his army was under siege by the Aequi, Rome was so fearful that this army would be lost that they had recourse to the creation of a dictator, the last remedy in critical situations. They appointed Lucius Quinctius Cincinnatus, who was at that time on his small farm, which he worked with his own hands. The event is celebrated by Livy with these golden words when he says: 'Now I would solicit the particular attention of those numerous people who imagine that money is everything in this world, and that rank and ability are inseparable from wealth.'* Cincinnatus was ploughing his little farm, which was no longer than four *jugers*, when the senate's legates arrived from Rome to notify him of his election to the dictatorship and to show him the danger in which the Roman republic found itself. Donning his toga, he came to Rome, and after assembling an army, he marched off to free Minucius; and having routed and plundered the enemy and freed Minucius, he did not wish for the besieged army to share the spoils, speaking these words to them: 'I do not want you to share in spoils taken from those who almost despoiled you'; and he deprived Minucius of the consulate and made him a legate, saying to him: 'You will remain in this rank until you learn to know how to be consul.'* He had made Lucius Tarquitius his master of horse, who was so poor he fought as a foot-soldier.

It is notable, so it is said, that in Rome honour was paid to poverty, and that, for a good and valiant man like Cincinnatus, four *jugers* of land were enough to feed him; this same poverty is also seen in the times of Marcus Regulus: when he was in Africa with the armies, he asked the senate for leave to return to take care of his farm which was being ruined by his workers.* Here, two things of great note can be seen: one, poverty, and how they were content with it; and the other, how winning honour from war was enough for those citizens, and how they left all profit to the public. Clearly, if Regulus had thought about making himself rich from the war, he would scarcely have troubled himself over the fact that his fields were being ruined. The second thing to consider is the generosity of spirit of those citizens, whose grandeur of heart rose above that of any prince when they were placed in command of an army; they did not overestimate kings or republics, nor did anything dismay or frighten them, and upon having later returned to being private citizens, they became frugal, humble, guardians of their own small pieces of land, obedient to the magistrates, and respectful to their superiors, so that it appears impossible for one and the same mind to undergo such a transformation. This poverty endured until the times of Paulus Emilius, which were practically the last happy times in that republic, where a citizen whose triumph enriched Rome nevertheless remained poor himself. And poverty was still so highly esteemed that, in honouring anyone who had conducted himself well in the war, Paulus gave to his son-in-law a silver cup, which was the first piece of silver in his home. It would be possible to demonstrate with a long discussion how much better are the fruits of poverty than of wealth and that poverty has honoured citizens, provinces, sects, while wealth has destroyed them, if this subject had not on many occasions been celebrated by other writers.

CHAPTER 26

How a State Is Ruined Because of Women

Riots arose in the city of Ardea between the patricians and plebeians over a marriage; a rich woman of this city, who was to be married, was asked for by both a plebeian and a nobleman, and since she had no father, her guardians wished to join her to the plebeian, while her mother preferred the nobleman.* This gave rise to such an uproar that they came to the point of taking up arms; all the nobility took up arms on behalf of the nobleman and all the plebeians on behalf of the plebeians. Then, having been defeated, the plebeians left Ardea and sent to the Volscians for assistance, while the nobles sent to Rome. The Volscians were first, and upon their arrival they encamped around Ardea. The Romans came next and hemmed in the Volscians between the city and themselves, so that they compelled them, overwhelmed with hunger, to surrender themselves to the Romans' discretion. After the Romans marched into Ardea and executed the leaders of the uprising, they settled the affairs of that city.

There are many things in this text to note. First, it is evident that women have been the cause of many downfalls, have done great damage to those who govern a city, and have caused many divisions; as we have seen in this history of ours, the abuse committed against Lucretia took the state from the Tarquins, and the one committed against Virginia deprived the Ten of their authority. Among the principal causes Aristotle gives for the downfall of tyrants is the one of having injured others through women by raping them, violating them, or breaking up marriages, as we discussed at great length in the chapter we wrote about conspiracies. Let me say, therefore, that absolute rulers and the governors of republics must not take this matter lightly; rather, they must consider the disorders that through such an unforeseen event can arise and remedy them in time, so that the remedy does not bring with it damage and disgrace to their state or their republic; this happened to the inhabitants of Ardea, who allowed this rivalry among their citizens to grow and came to experience divisions among themselves, and when they wished to reunite, they had to send for outside assistance, which is a principal starting-point for imminent servitude. But let us come to another issue of note, the method of reuniting cities, about which we shall speak in the following chapter.

CHAPTER 27

How to Unify a Divided City, and Why the Opinion that It Is Necessary to Keep Cities Divided in Order to Hold Them Is Not True

By the example of the Roman consuls who reconciled the inhabitants of Ardea, the method of how to reunite a divided city may be noted; this method consists of nothing else, nor can the wound be healed in any other way, but executing the leaders of the disturbances. For it is necessary to choose one of three methods: either execute them, as the Romans did; or remove them from the city; or force them to make peace among themselves under the obligation of causing no more harm. Of these three methods, the last is the most damaging, the least certain, and the most useless, because where much blood has been spilled or other similar injuries have been inflicted, it is impossible for a peace made by force to endure, with the parties meeting face to face every day; it is difficult for them to abstain from offending each other, with new occasions for complaints arising among them every day through their close association.

On this subject, no better example can be given than the city of Pistoia. That city was divided fifteen years ago* (as it still is) into the Panciatichi and the Cancellieri factions, but at that time Pistoia was up in arms, while today it has laid them down. After many disputes between them, the factions came to bloodshed, to the destruction of one another's houses, to plundering each other's property, and to every other sort of hostility. The Florentines, who had to reconcile them, always employed this third method there, and greater disorders and greater embarrassments always arose from it until, exhausted, they came to the second method, that of removing the leaders of the factions, some of whom were sent to prison while others were confined in various places, so that the accord reached could endure, and it has up to the present day. But without any doubt, the first method would have been more secure. But, since such punishments have in them something of the great and generous, a weak republic will not know how to carry them out and is so reluctant to use such methods that it barely manages to make use of the second remedy. As I said at the beginning,* these are the kinds of errors that princes of our times commit when they have to make decisions on important matters; thus, they should want to hear how those who in ancient times had to make decisions in similar cases took action. But the weakness of men in the present, caused by their poor education and their slight knowledge of affairs, makes them consider ancient punishments as partly inhumane and partly impossible. And they hold certain modern opinions far removed from the truth, such as the one the wise men of our city used to repeat some time ago— that it was necessary to hold Pistoia with factions and Pisa with fortresses; they did not realize that both of these two methods are useless.

I want to omit fortresses, because we spoke of them at length above,* and I want to discuss the disadvantage that derives from keeping the cities you possess divided.* In the first place, it is impossible for you to keep both factions your friends, whether you who are governing them are a prince or a republic, because nature causes men to choose sides in any matter with two sides, where one side may please them more than the other. Thus, by having one part of that city discontented, you lose the city in the first war that arises, because it is impossible to guard a city with enemies both inside and outside. If a republic governs it, there is no finer method of making your citizens wicked and causing divisions in your own city than to control a city that is divided, because each faction seeks to win favours and each creates friends through various corrupt means. Thus, two extremely great disadvantages arise from this: one is that you never make them your friends, for the reason that you cannot govern them well, since you must often vary the government, now with one humor, now with another; the other is that such concern with factions of necessity divides your republic. Biondo, speaking of the Florentines and the Pistoians, bears witness to this when he says: 'while the Florentines tried to reunite Pistoia, they divided themselves.'* It is easy, however, to consider the harm that arises from such a division.

In 1502, when Florence lost Arezzo and the entire Valditevere and the Valdichiana, which had been occupied by the Vitelli family and Duke Valentino, a certain Monsieur de Lant* came on the scene, sent by the king of France to restore all those lost cities to the Florentines, and when de Lant found in every castle men who, in paying him honour, declared that they were in the Marzocco faction,* he harshly criticized this division, stating that if in France one of the king's subjects declared he was in the king's faction, he would be punished, because such a statement signified nothing other than that people who were the king's enemies lived in that city; and that this king wanted all the cities to be friendly to him, united, and without factions. But all these methods and opinions contrary to the truth arise from the weakness of those who are rulers; with the realization that they cannot hold states with force and with exceptional skill, they turn to similar schemes, which are occasionally useful in quiet times, but when adversities and hard times arrive, they display their fallacious nature.

CHAPTER 28

That One Must Pay Attention to the Deeds of Citizens, Because a Worthy Act Often Conceals the Beginnings of Tyranny

When the city of Rome was afflicted with hunger and public provisions were insufficient to stop it, a certain Spurius Melius, being very rich, in the manner of those times, took it in mind to create a private supply of grain and to feed the plebeians with it at his own expense. For this reason, he had such a company of people in his favour that the senate, thinking about the difficulty that might arise from his generosity, created a dictator on his account and had him put to death* to suppress the problem before it gained more strength.

Here it is to be noted that on many occasions actions which seem worthy and cannot reasonably be condemned may become cruel and extremely dangerous for a republic, if they are not punished in time. In order to discuss this matter in more detail, I will say that a republic without citizens who have a good reputation cannot stand, nor can it conduct itself well in any way. On the other hand, the reputation of citizens is the cause of tyranny in republics. In order to regulate such a thing, it is necessary to be organized in such a way that citizens will enjoy the kind of reputation that does good and not harm to the city and to its liberty. It is necessary, therefore, to examine the methods by which reputation is obtained, of which there are, in effect, two: either public or private. Public methods are those by which a person, giving good advice and taking even better actions on behalf of the common good, acquires reputation. The path to this type of honour must be opened up to citizens, and rewards must be set up both for their advice and for their deeds, so that they will be honoured and satisfied. When such reputations, earned in these ways, are transparent and simple, they will never be dangerous, but when they are obtained by private means, which is the other method cited above, they are extremely dangerous and entirely harmful. Private means involve doing favours for this or that other private citizen, by loaning him money, marrying off his daughters, defending him from officials and magistrates, and doing him other similar personal favours, which make men partisans and give the man who is so favoured the courage to corrupt the public and to weaken the laws. Consequently, a well-organized republic must open the way, as was said, to anyone who seeks favours through public means and close it to anyone who seeks them through private means. As is evident, this is what Rome did; for to reward anyone who worked productively for the public good, the city instituted triumphs and all the other honours that it bestowed upon its citizens, and as a punishment for anyone who, under various pretexts and through private means, sought to become great, it instituted accusations, and if these were insufficient, when the people were blinded by a false appearance of good, it instituted the dictator, who with his kingly authority made anyone who had exceeded the proper bounds return within them, as Rome did in punishing Spurius Melius. One such case which goes unpunished is sufficient to ruin a republic, because it is difficult with such an example to return to the true path later on.

CHAPTER 29

That the Faults of Peoples Begin With Their Princes

Princes should not complain of any sin committed by the people they have under their control, because such sins of necessity arise either from his negligence or from his being tainted by similar errors. Anyone who will examine the peoples who in our times have been considered abounding in robberies and similar faults will see that all of them begin with those who govern them and who are of a similar nature. The Romagna, before Pope Alexander VI destroyed the lords who were once in control there, was an example of every kind of wicked living, because in that region the slightest causes brought about murders and the greatest robberies. This situation arose from the wickedness of those princes and not from the wicked nature of men, as they claimed. Since those princes were impoverished but wanted to live as if they were rich, they had to turn to frequent robberies, employing a variety of means. Among the other dishonest methods they adopted, they passed laws and prohibited certain actions; later, they were the first to provide opportunities for breaking the laws, nor did they ever punish those who broke them, except when they saw that many others had become involved in the same violation, and then they turned to punishment, not out of any zeal for the enacted law but rather out of their greed to collect the fine. Hence, many difficulties arose, and above all else, the peoples grew poor and were not corrected, and those who were impoverished managed to avenge themselves on those who were less powerful than they. Hence, all those evils recounted above emerged, the cause of which was the prince.

Livy shows that this is true when he relates how the Roman legates, while carrying the gift of the spoils taken from the Veientes to Apollo, were captured by the pirates of Lipari in Sicily and brought to that city, and how once Timasitheus their prince understood what kind of gift this was, where it was going, and who was sending it, he conducted himself, although born in Lipari, like a Roman, and showed his people how impious it was to seize such a gift, so that, with the consensus of the entire population, he let the legates go with all their possessions. These are the words of the historian: 'Timasitheus instilled religious fear into the crowd, which always resembles its leader.'* Lorenzo de' Medici, in confirmation of this maxim, declares:

> What the ruler does, many do afterward,
> For the eyes of all are fixed on their lord.*

CHAPTER 30

That a Citizen in His Own Republic Who Wishes to Employ His Authority for Some Good Work Must First Extinguish Envy; and How to Organize the Defence of a City When the Enemy Is Coming

When the Roman senate had learned that all of Etruria had conducted a new levy of soldiers to do harm to Rome and that the Latins and the Hernici, who had in the past been friends of the

Roman people, had sided with the Volscians, perpetual enemies of Rome, the senate decided that this war would be dangerous. Since Camillus was tribune with consular power, he was of the opinion that they could do without creating a dictator if the other tribunes, his colleagues, were willing to concede to him the supreme command. The said tribunes did so willingly (as Livy declares), 'nor did they believe that their own dignity was in any way diminished by what they had done for his'.* Hence, Camillus, taking this obedience literally, commanded that three armies be enrolled. He wanted to be the commander of the first in order to go against the Etruscans. He made Quinctius Servilius commander of the second, wanting him to stay close to Rome to face the Latins and the Hernici if they moved. He placed Lucius Quinctius at the head of the third army, which he enrolled to keep the city guarded and to defend its gates and the curia in whatever situation might arise. Besides this, he ordered Horatius, one of his colleagues, to provide the arms and grain and other things required in wartime. He placed Cornelius, another of his colleagues, in charge of the senate and the public council, so that he could recommend actions that would be undertaken and executed on a daily basis; in this way, the tribunes of those times were willing to command and to obey for the well-being of the city.

This text takes note of what a good and wise man should do, of how much good it can bring about, and how great a benefit such actions can bestow upon his native city when, through his goodness and exceptional ability, he has extinguished envy, which is on many occasions the cause of men's inability to do good deeds, since it does not permit them to enjoy the authority necessary in important matters. This envy is extinguished in two ways: either through some serious and difficult incident, where someone, seeing himself lost, defers every ambition and willingly races to obey the man he believes may, with his exceptional ability, deliver him; this happened to Camillus, who, having given so many indications of being a most excellent man, having been dictator three times, and having always conducted that office for the benefit of the public rather than for his own, had acted in such a way that men did not fear his greatness; and since he was so great and so renowned, they did not deem it shameful to be inferior to him (and for that reason, Livy wisely declares in these words: 'nor did they believe, etc.').* Such envy is extinguished in another way when, either through violence or the natural course of events, those men die who have been your competitors in attaining a certain reputation and a certain level of greatness; such men will never be able to acquiesce or remain patient, seeing you are more highly esteemed than they. Furthermore, when they are men accustomed to living in a corrupt city, where education has produced no good in them whatsoever, in order to fulfil their wishes and to satisfy their perversity of mind, they will be happy to see the ruin of their native city.

To conquer such envy, there is no other remedy than the death of those who feel it, and when fortune is so favourable to a man of exceptional ability that he dies in a normal fashion, he becomes illustrious without scandal from the moment that, without any obstacle or harm, he can demonstrate his exceptional skill. But when he does not have such good fortune, he must think about every means of removing the envious from his path, and before he does anything else, he needs to adopt methods that will overcome this difficulty. Anyone who reads the Bible intelligently will see that, in order to advance his laws and his institutions, Moses was forced to kill countless men, who were moved to oppose his plans by nothing more than envy.* Brother Girolamo Savonarola recognized this necessity very clearly; Piero Soderini, the standard-bearer of Florence, also recognized it. The former (that is, the priest) could not overcome envy, because he lacked sufficient authority to do so, and because he was not well understood by those who followed him and who might have possessed such authority. Nevertheless, he did what he could, and his sermons are full of accusations and invectives against the wise men of the world: for this is what he called such envious men as well as those who opposed his institutions. The latter believed he could extinguish that envy in the passing of time through kindness, his own good fortune, and favours to some; he saw himself to be rather young and with the great new popularity his mode of conduct brought him, he believed he could overcome those many who opposed him out of envy without any unusual acts, violence, or disorder, and he did not know that time does not wait, kindness is insufficient, fortune varies, and malice receives no gift that placates her. In this way both of these two men came to ruin, and their downfall was caused by not knowing how or not being able to overcome this envy.

The other noteworthy thing is the organization that Camillus dictated inside and outside Rome for its well-being. Truly, not without reason do good historians, like our own, set forth certain cases in great detail and quite clearly so that those who come afterwards may learn how they might defend themselves in similar circumstances. It must be noted in this text that there is no more dangerous nor more useless defence than one created in the midst of commotion and without order. This can be seen in the third army that Camillus had raised to leave behind in Rome for the purpose of guarding the city: many would have thought and would still think that this element was superfluous, since that people was normally armed and combative, and that, for this reason, it was not necessary to raise another army, since it was enough to arm the people when the need arose. But Camillus, and any other man who was as wise as he, thought otherwise, because he never permitted a multitude to take up arms except with a fixed order and by a fixed method. Following this example, anyone who is placed in charge of guarding a city must, therefore, avoid like a reef the arming of men in the midst of great confusion; rather, he must first have enrolled and selected those men he wishes to take up arms and who must obey him, and he must have decided where to meet and how to proceed, while ordering those who are not enrolled, each and every one, to stay in their homes to guard them. Those who will hold to such order in a city under siege will easily be able to defend themselves; anyone who will do otherwise will fail to imitate Camillus and will fail to defend himself.

CHAPTER 31
Strong Republics and Excellent Men Retain in Every Kind of Fortune the Same Spirit and Dignity

Among the other magnificent things that our historian has Camillus say and do, to show how an excellent man must be made, he puts these words into his mouth: 'My resolution has never gained anything from dictatorship, any more than it lost anything through exile.'* His words show that great men always remain the same in every kind of fortune, and if it varies, now by elevating them, now by oppressing them, they themselves never change but always keep a firm resolve, joined in such a manner to their way of life that anyone can easily recognize that fortune has no power over them. Weak men govern themselves differently: they become vain and intoxicated with good fortune, attributing all the good they receive to an exceptional ability they have never known. As a result, they become insufferable and hateful to all those around them. This situation then brings about some sudden change in their luck, and upon looking such a change in the face, they immediately fall into the opposite fault and become vile and abject. From this arises the fact that princes of this type, in times of adversity, think more about fleeing than about defending themselves, like men who, having badly used their good fortune, are unprepared for any defence.

This ability and this flaw, which I say can be found in a single man, can also be found in a republic, and as an example, there are the Romans and the Venetians. No bad luck ever made the former abject, nor did good fortune ever make them insolent, as became evident after their defeat at Cannae or their victory over Antiochus, for after their defeat, even though it was extremely serious in being the third, they never became frightened and still sent forth their armies; they refused to pay ransom for their prisoners contrary to their practices, nor did they send envoys either to Hannibal or to Carthage to sue for peace but, leaving all such abject behaviour aside, they thought only of war, arming the old men and their servants for lack of soldiers. This fact, recognized by Hanno the Carthaginian, as was mentioned above,* demonstrated to that senate how little account should be taken of the defeat at Cannae. Thus, it was seen that in difficult times the Romans were never afraid nor were they humbled. On the other hand, prosperous times never made them insolent; for, when Antiochus sent ambassadors to Scipio to ask for an agreement before they engaged in the battle in which Antiochus was defeated, Scipio dictated to him certain conditions for the peace;

these were that he should withdraw into Syria and leave the rest up to the will of the Roman people. Antiochus rejected this agreement and after engaging in battle and losing, he again sent ambassadors to Scipio with the charge of accepting all the conditions imposed upon them by the victor; to them, Scipio proposed no new pacts other than those he had offered before his victory, adding these words: 'When Romans are defeated, they do not become discouraged; nor, when they win, do they become insolent.'*

It is evident that the Venetians have done exactly the contrary of this, because in times of good fortune, thinking that they earned it with an exceptional ability they do not possess, they had become so insolent that they called the king of France a son of St Mark; they did not respect the church; they could never gain enough territory in Italy; and they had it in mind to create a universal empire like the Romans. Later, when good fortune abandoned them and they suffered a semi-defeat at Vailà* at the hands of the king of France, they lost not only all their territory through rebellion but a good part was given over to the pope and to the king of Spain because of their cowardice and baseness of heart; they debased themselves to such an extent that they sent ambassadors to the emperor to become his tributary, and they wrote the pope letters full of cowardice and submission to move him to compassion. In four days, and after no more than a semi-defeat, they came to this state of unhappiness, because once their army had fought a battle, during its retreat only about half of it actually fought and was defeated, so that one of the quartermasters who saved himself arrived in Verona with more than 25,000 soldiers on foot or on horseback. Thus, if in Venice or in their institutions any measure of exceptional skill had existed, they could easily have regrouped, faced their fortune once again, and have been in time either to conquer or to lose more gloriously, or even to gain a more favourable accord. But their cowardice of spirit, caused by the quality of their institutions, which were not good in matters of war,* caused them to lose, all at once, their state and their courage. This will always happen to anyone who acts as they did. For this matter of becoming insolent in good fortune and abject in bad fortune arises out of your mode of conduct and the education with which you have nourished yourself; when it is weak and vain, it makes you similar to itself; when it is otherwise, it also brings you a different destiny and, making you more knowledgeable about the world, it causes you to rejoice less in the good and grieve less over the bad. Whatever one says about a single person can also be said of many people who live in a republic and who reflect the state of perfection of its own way of life.

Although it has been said elsewhere* that the foundation of all states is a good militia, and that where this is not a reality, neither good laws nor any other good thing can exist, I do not feel it is superfluous to repeat this, because at every point, in the reading of this history, this necessity is everywhere evident, and it is evident that a militia cannot be good if it is not trained, and that it cannot be trained if it is not composed of your own subjects. For no one is always at war, nor is that possible, but it is necessary to train the militia in times of peace, and it is impossible to carry out such exercises with others rather than with one's own subjects because of the expense. Camillus, as we said above, had gone with his army against the Etruscans, and once his soldiers had seen the size of the enemy army all of them were terrified, since they felt themselves to be so inferior to the Etruscans that they could not withstand their attack. When news of this bad attitude in the field reached Camillus' ears, he came out and went through the camp speaking now to these soldiers and now to those, drawing that notion out of their heads, and finally, without organizing the battlefield in any other manner, he declared: 'everyone will act in accordance with his training and habit.'* Anyone who will carefully consider this expedient and the words he said to them to fill them with enough courage to confront the enemy will realize that he could neither say nor do any of these things to an army that had not first been organized and trained both in peace and in war, because a commander cannot trust soldiers who have not learned to do anything, nor believe that they will do anything good: even if a new Hannibal were to command them, he would be brought to ruin. Thus, since a commander cannot be everywhere while a battle is raging, if he has not first organized things so that in every location he can have men who share his spirit and even his rules and modes of conduct, then he must of necessity come to ruin. If a city is, therefore, armed and organized like Rome, and every day its citizens, in private and in public, have the opportunity to test their ability and the power of their fortune, it will always happen that they will act with the same spirit on all occasions, and they will maintain the same dignity. But when they are unarmed and depend only upon the throws of fortune rather than upon their own ability, they will change with fortune and will always give the same account of themselves that the Venetians have given.

CHAPTER 32

What Methods Some Have Used to Disturb a Peace

Circei and Velitre, two of their colonies, had rebelled against the Roman people in the hope of being defended by the Latins, but when the Latins were later conquered and their hopes were no longer alive, many of their citizens advised that they should send ambassadors to Rome to make a plea to the senate: this decision was overturned by those who had been the authors of the rebellion, who feared that all the punishment would come down upon their heads. In order to eliminate any discussion of peace, they incited the crowd to arm itself and to race across the Roman borders. Truly, when anyone wants either a people or a prince to abandon their inclination to an agreement, there is no truer remedy nor one more lasting than to make them carry out some seriously wicked act against the person with whom you do not wish to conclude the agreement, since the fear of the punishment they think they deserve for the wrong they have committed will always keep such an accord at a distance. After the first war the Carthaginians fought with the Romans, those soldiers employed by the Carthaginians for that war in Sicily and Sardinia went off to Africa once the peace was concluded, where, dissatisfied with their salary, they took up arms against the Carthaginians, and having appointed two of their number as leaders, Matho and Spendius, they seized many Carthaginian cities and sacked many others. Attempting at first every means other than military engagement, the Carthaginians sent them

Hasdrubal,* a citizen of theirs, as an ambassador, who they thought might have some authority over them since he had been their commander in the past. When Hasdrubal arrived, wishing to force all those soldiers to lose hope of ever having peace with the Carthaginians, and, in this way, to force them to wage war, Spendius and Matho persuaded the soldiers that it was better to murder Hasdrubal along with all the Carthaginian citizens who were prisoners in their hands. Whereupon they not only killed them but first tortured them with a thousand torments, adding to this wickedness an edict that all Carthaginians captured in the future would be killed in a similar fashion. This decision and its execution made that army cruel and obstinate against the Carthaginians.

CHAPTER 33

To Win a Battle, It Is Necessary to Make an Army Confident, Both in Itself and in Its Commander

In order for an army to win a battle, it is necessary to make it confident, so that it will believe that it must win in any event. The things that make an army confident are that it be well armed and organized, and that the soldiers know each other. Nor can this confidence or this organization come about except among those soldiers who have been born and raised together. The commander must be admired in such a way that the soldiers trust in his prudence and will always trust him when they see him to be organized, attentive, and courageous, and to uphold well and reputably the dignity of his rank. He will always maintain this dignity when he punishes mistakes and avoids making the soldiers work at useless tasks, when he keeps his promises to them and shows them the easy path to victory, concealing or making light of those things that from a distance can appear to be dangerous. These rules, when effectively observed, give an army strong reason to trust him, and, trusting him, to win.

The Romans used to instil this confidence in their armies by means of religion. Hence, it came about that they created the consuls, drafted soldiers, marched off with their armies, and joined in battle with auguries and omens. And without having done any of these things, a good and wise commander would never have attempted any military action, realizing that he could easily lose if his troops had not first understood that the gods were on their side. If any consul or any of their other commanders fought contrary to the omens, they would have punished him as they punished Claudius Pulcher.* Although this point can be found in all the Roman histories, none the less, it proves itself more certainly through the words that Livy places in the mouth of Appius Claudius, who, in complaining to the plebeians about the arrogance of the tribunes of the plebeians and demonstrating that they were allowing the omens and other matters relating to religion to become corrupted, spoke in this manner: ' "What does it matter," they say, "if the sacred chickens will not feed and are slow to come out of the coop or a bird gives an ill-omened squawk?" These are trivial matters, but it was because they did not scorn those trivial matters that your forefathers could build up this republic to be so great.'* For in these small things there is the power to keep the soldiers united and confident, which is the primary reason for every victory. Nevertheless, such things must be accompanied by exceptional ability, otherwise they are worth nothing. The Praenestines, having their army in the field against the Romans, went off to set up camp by the Allia River, the place where the Romans were defeated by the Gauls. They did this to inspire confidence in their soldiers and to frighten the Romans by the ill fortune of the place. Although this decision of theirs was appropriate for the reasons discussed above, the outcome of the affair demonstrated, none the less, that true ability does not fear every minor circumstance. The historian expresses this very well with these words placed in the mouth of the dictator, who speaks in this way to his master of horse: 'Do you see how they have taken their stand at the Allia, trusting to the ill fortune of the place? . . . put your trust in arms and morale, and charge their centre at the gallop.'*

Thus, true ability, good organization, and security gained from so many victories cannot be extinguished by things of such little moment, nor can some empty thing frighten them, nor some disorder harm them. This is made clear by the example of the two Manlii who were consuls against the Volscians; they recklessly sent part of the camp out to plunder, with the result that at the same time both those who had gone off and those who had remained found themselves under attack; it was not the prudence of the consuls but the exceptional skill of their own soldiers which saved them from the danger. Here Livy says these words: 'what survived of the good fortune of the Roman people was saved by the soldiers' courage, which did not waver even when they had no leader to direct it.'* I do not want to leave out a device employed by Fabius to make his army confident when he first led it into Etruria, in the belief that such confidence was all the more necessary since he was leading it into a new territory against new enemies: that is, in speaking to the soldiers before the battle, and claiming that he had many reasons for thinking they could expect victory, he said that he could indeed tell them certain good things from which they would see that victory was certain, if it were not dangerous to reveal them. This method, as it was wisely employed, thus deserves to be imitated.

CHAPTER 34

What Kind of Fame, Rumour, or Opinion Makes the People Begin to Favour One Citizen; and Whether the People Assign Magistracies With Greater Prudence Than a Prince

We have spoken on another occasion* about how Titus Manlius, who was later called Torquatus, saved Lucius Manlius, his father, from an accusation that was made against him by Marcus Pomponius, tribune of the plebeians. Although the method of saving him was rather violent and extraordinary,* none the less this filial compassion toward his father was so pleasing to the multitude that not only was he not reproached for it, but when they came to select the tribunes for the legions, Titus Manlius was chosen second. Because of his success, I think it would be good to consider the method that the people employ to judge men in assigning offices, and whether, so far as we can see, it is true as was concluded above, that the people make better assignments than a prince.

Let me say, therefore, that in its assignments the people follow what public rumour and reputation says about someone, when they do not know him in a different way through his actions, either on the grounds of presumption or on the grounds of the opinion that it has of him. These two things are caused either by the fact that the fathers of such men have been great men and worthy ones in the city and everyone believes that their sons must be similar to them, until through their actions everyone understands the contrary; or it is caused by the methods used by the one the people are speaking about. The best method that can be employed is to keep the company of serious men of good habits who are considered wise by everyone. Since there can be no clearer indication about a man than the company he keeps, it is only fitting that a man who keeps the company of honest companions acquires a good name, because it is impossible for him not to share some similarities with them. Or this public recognition is truly acquired through some extraordinary and noteworthy deed, even though private, that has met with honourable success. Of all three of these things, which from the beginning give one a good reputation, none bestows a better reputation than this last one. The first method, acquiring a reputation from relatives and fathers, is so prone to error that men are cautious about it, and it vanishes in a short time when the actual ability of the man to be judged does not match his reputation. The second method, in which you become recognized by means of your companions, is better than the first, but much inferior to the third, because as long as you yourself give no indication of ability, your reputation is based upon opinion, which is extremely easy to cancel out. But the third method, being initiated by and founded upon fact and upon your actions, gives you at the outset such a reputation that you must later do many things in contrast to your achievements in order to annul them.

Men who are born in a republic must therefore choose this third method and must strive to begin to distinguish themselves through some extraordinary deed. Many men did this in Rome during their youth, either with the promulgation of a law that worked for the common benefit or by accusing some powerful citizen as a transgressor of the laws, or by doing similar notable and innovative things about which people talked. Nor are such things necessary only in beginning to earn oneself a reputation, but they are also necessary in order to maintain it and to make it grow. And to do this, one needs to renew one's reputation, as Titus Manlius did throughout his entire lifetime; for, a number of years after he had defended his father so ably and extraordinarily and through this action earned his early reputation, he fought with that Gaul, and once he was dead, removed the collar of gold that won him the name Torquatus.* Even this was insufficient, and later, when already a mature man, he executed his son for having gone into combat without permission, even though he had overcome his enemy. These three actions, then, gave him greater reputation and made him more celebrated through the centuries than any triumph or any other victory, for which he was as decorated as any other Roman. And the reason for this is that in those victories there were a great many men like Manlius, but in these particular actions there were either very few or none at all.

Scipio the Elder did not gain as much glory from all his triumphs as that which he gained when, still a young man, he defended his father on the Ticinus River,* and later after the rout of Cannae, when with sword drawn, he courageously forced the young Romans to swear they would not abandon Italy, as they had already decided among themselves to do;* these two actions were the basis of his reputation, and they served as the stepping-stone to his triumphs in Spain and Africa. His fame was further increased when he sent back the daughter to her father and the wife to her husband in Spain.* This mode of conduct is not only necessary for those citizens who want to acquire fame in order to obtain the honours of their republic, but it is also necessary for a prince to maintain his reputation in his own principate, because nothing earns him more esteem than giving striking examples of himself through some excellent deed or saying that conforms to the common good, which shows a lord to be either magnanimous or generous or just, and which is such that it becomes, as it were, a proverb among his subjects.

But to return to where we began this discourse, let me say that when a people begins to grant some rank to one of its citizens, basing its decision on the three reasons given above, it does not have a poor basis for doing so; but later, when many examples of the good behaviour of one of its citizens makes him better known, it has a better basis for doing so, because in such a case the people can almost never be deceived. I am speaking only of those ranks that are given to men in the beginning, before they are known through steady experience, or before they pass from one sphere of action to a different one; in such a matter and as far as false opinions and corruption are concerned, the people will always commit fewer errors than princes. Since it can come about that the people will be deceived by the fame, judgement, and deeds of a man, deeming them greater than they really are (something which does not happen to a prince, because he will be told and warned by whoever advises him), in order that the people, too, will not lack such advice, the good organizers of republics have established things in such a way that, given the need to appoint men to the supreme ranks in the cities, where it would be dangerous to place unfit men, and seeing popular desire directed to appointing someone unfit, any citizen has the right to make public speeches about that man's defects—and he will be honoured for doing this—so that the people, with some knowledge of him, can make better judgements. That this was the custom in Rome is attested to by the oration Fabius Maximus delivered to the people during the Second Punic War, when, in the process of appointing consuls, popular favour was turning toward Titus Otacilius; judging him unfit to hold the consulate at that time, Fabius spoke against him, demonstrating his lack of qualifications, to such a degree that the people took away his rank and turned its approval toward a man more meritorious than he was.* In the election of magistrates, therefore, the people judge according to those indications about men they believe most accurate; and when they can be counselled as princes are, they commit fewer errors than princes; and any citizen who wishes to begin to gain the favour of the people must, as Titus Manlius did, gain it for himself with some noteworthy deed.

CHAPTER 35

What Risks Are Run in Making Oneself the Leader by Counselling an Undertaking; and How Much Greater the Risks Are When the Undertaking Is an Extraordinary One

How dangerous it is to make oneself the leader of a new undertaking in the service of many people, and how difficult it is to direct and execute it and, once it is carried out, to maintain it, would be too long and too lofty a topic for discussion here; reserving it for a more convenient place, therefore, I shall speak only of those dangers incurred by citizens or those who advise a prince when they make themselves the leader in a serious and important deliberation, so that all of the suggestions on the matter will be ascribed to them. Since men judge things by their results,* all the evil that comes about is blamed upon the one who gave the advice, and if things turn out well, he is commended for it; but the reward is far from counterbalancing the blame. When the present Sultan Salì, called the Grand Turk, was making preparations (according to what those who come from his lands have related to us) for the enterprise in Syria and Egypt, he was encouraged by one of his pashas, whom he kept on the borders of Persia, to attack the Shah.* Prompted by this advice, he went with his enormous army to engage in this enterprise, and arriving in a vast country where there were numerous deserts and few rivers, he encountered so many of the obstacles that had already ruined many Roman armies and was so overwhelmed by them that, even though he was victorious in the war, he lost a large part of his forces from famine and plague; thus, enraged against the author of this advice, he killed him. We also read how many citizens, having been supporters of some enterprise, were sent into exile when it came to a sorry conclusion. Certain Roman citizens made themselves leaders when they selected the plebeian consul in Rome. It happened that the first consul who went out with his armies was defeated, as a result of which these advisers would have suffered some harm, if the faction on whose behalf the decision was made had not been so courageous.

It is, therefore, quite certain that those who give advice to a republic and those who give advice to a prince find themselves amidst these difficulties: that is, if they do not recommend without reservation the policies they believe to be useful, either to the city or the prince, they fail in their duties; and if they give such advice, they place their lives and their position at risk, because all men are blind in the sense that they judge good and bad advice by the results. After considering how to avoid either this infamy or this danger, I see no other path to follow than that of choosing moderate undertakings and never seizing upon any of them as your own, and that of speaking your mind without passion and, without passion, defending it with modesty; so that, if the city or the prince follows this advice, they follow it willingly, without it appearing that they are pulled along by your insistence. When you act in this fashion, it is not reasonable for a prince or a people to wish you ill because of your advice, since it was not followed against the will of many others; in fact, the danger arises where many have opposed you, who later, after an unhappy result, rush to destroy you. If in this case there is a lack of the glory that can be acquired by being one against many in recommending something when it produces a good result, there are, on the other hand, two benefits: first, you are in less danger; second, if you counsel a thing with modesty and, through opposition, your advice is not taken, while through the advice of someone else some disaster results from it, in this way you will achieve even greater glory. Although glory that is acquired through evils suffered by either your city or your prince cannot be enjoyed, it is, nevertheless, something to take into account.

I do not believe it possible to give men any other advice on this matter, because if I were to advise them to remain silent and to refrain from speaking their opinion, it would be useless to a republic or to their prince, and it would not avoid danger, since in a very short time, they would become suspect, and what happened to the friends of Persius, king of the Macedonians, could happen to them. After having been defeated by Paulus Emilius and fleeing with a few friends, it happened that, in going over past events, one of them began to tell Persius about the many errors he committed that were the reasons for his downfall; to this person Persius turned and exclaimed: 'Traitor, so you have

put off telling me until now when I have no other remedy!"*
With these words, he killed him with his own hand. Thus, the
man suffered the punishment for keeping silent when he should
have spoken out, and for having spoken when he should have
remained silent; he did not avoid danger by refusing to give
advice. I still believe that it is best to observe and respect the
limits described above.

CHAPTER 36

The Reasons Why the French Have Been and Are Still Considered More Than Men at the Outset of a Battle and, Later on, Less Than Women

The ferocity of that Gaul who provoked some Roman, near the
River Anio, to engage him in combat, and then the struggle
between him and Titus Manlius, reminds me of what Livy says
on many occasions: that is, at the beginning of a battle the
French* are more than men, and then as the fighting continues,
they turn out to be less than women. In considering the reason
for this, many believe that their nature is constituted in this way,
something which I believe to be true; but it is not, therefore, true
that their nature, which makes them ferocious at the beginning,
could not be regulated through some art in such a way that
would keep them ferocious up to the end.

To prove this, let me say that armies are of three kinds: the
first possesses both fury and order,* because fury and exceptional skill arise from order, as it did with the Romans; it is evident in all the histories that their army displayed good
organization, which military discipline had introduced over a
long period of time. In a well-organized army, no one should
engage in any action except in accordance with the rules, and for
this reason, in the Roman army—which, having conquered the
world, should serve as an example to all other armies—they did
not eat, sleep, frequent whores, or undertake any action either
military or domestic without orders from the consul. For armies
that do otherwise are not true armies, and if they do make a
showing of themselves in some way, they do it out of fury and

impetuosity and not through exceptional skill. But where well-organized skill employs its fury in the right way and at the right time, no difficulty will make it cowardly or lacking in courage, because good institutions renew it in its courage and its fury, nourished by the hope of victory, which is never lacking as long as institutions are sound. The opposite occurs in those armies where there is fury and not order, like those of the French, who usually failed in battle, because when they did not succeed in winning on the first charge, and the fury in which they placed so much hope was not sustained by any well-organized skill, so that they had nothing other than fury upon which to rely, they failed as soon as that cooled.* On the contrary, the Romans, fearing dangers less because of their good organization and having no doubt about victory, fought firmly and stubbornly with the same courage and skill at the conclusion as at the beginning; more than that, spurred on by the fight, they always grew more ardent. The third kind of army possesses neither natural fury nor acquired order, like the Italian armies in our times, which are completely useless, and if they do not happen to meet an army that for some reason runs away, they will never emerge victorious. Without citing other examples, they can be seen every day giving proof that they possess no skill whatsoever.

Since, through Livy's testimony, everyone can understand how a good militia must be created and how a bad one is created, I would like to cite the words spoken by Papirius Cursor when he wanted to punish Fabius (his master of horse); he said: 'No one would have respect either for men or for the gods; neither edicts of generals nor auspices would be regarded; without leave of absence soldiers would roam around in peaceful or hostile territory alike; with no thought of their oath they would discharge themselves by their own permission when they liked; the standards would be abandoned through lack of numbers to guard them; the army would not muster to order, and would fight regardless of day or night, good or bad position, order or prohibition of their general, keeping neither to ranks nor formation, so that army life would become a blind and casual kind of brigandage instead of a long-established and dedicated service.'* Through this text, it is possible, therefore, to see quite easily if the militia of our times is blind and haphazard or sworn to duty through solemn oaths; the degree to which it lacks any similarity to what can be called a militia, and how far it is from being full of fury and well organized, like the Roman army, or even simply full of fury, like the French.

CHAPTER 37

Whether Small Skirmishes Before the Battle Are Necessary; and What Must Be Done to Understand a New Enemy in Order To Avoid Them

It appears that in human actions, as we previously discussed,* one finds, among other difficulties, that in the desire to bring something to a perfect conclusion, there is always some evil very near this good which arises so easily along with it that it seems impossible to avoid the one while wanting the other. This is observed in all the things that men undertake. And so this good is acquired with difficulty, if you are not assisted by fortune in such a way that with her strength she overcomes this ordinary and natural drawback. The skirmish between Manlius and the Gaul made me think about this, in the passage where Livy declares: 'This combat had indeed great influence on the outcome of the whole war, so much so that next night the army of the Gauls left their camp in alarm and went over to the territory of Tibur. There they made a military alliance, and after being generously supplied with provisions by the Tiburtines, soon moved on to Campania.'* Thus, I believe, on the one hand, that a good commander must avoid at all costs undertaking anything of little importance that can have bad effects on his army, because initiating a skirmish in which all your forces are not brought into play and in which you risk your entire fortune is a completely reckless thing to do, as I said above when I condemned the guarding of passes.*

On the other hand, I believe that, upon encountering a new enemy of repute, wise commanders are compelled, before engaging in battle, to show their troops, through small skirmishes, what the enemy is like, so that by beginning to know and to deal with the enemy, the troops will lose the terror that their fame and reputation have provoked in them. It is extremely important for a commander to do this. In fact, there is almost a necessity within it that constrains you to do this, since you seem to be moving toward certain defeat unless first, through small trials, you have eliminated the terror among your troops that the enemy's reputation had placed in their hearts.

Valerius Corvinus was sent by the Romans with his armies against the Samnites, new enemies, and in the past they had never tested each other in arms; Livy writes that Valerius had the Romans engage in some light skirmishes with them, 'bidding them have no fear of a strange war or strange enemy'.* Nevertheless, there is very grave danger that if your soldiers are defeated in such skirmishes, their fear and cowardice will increase and the results will prove contrary to your plans—that is, that you frighten them when you had planned to reassure them. Hence, this is one of those matters in which the evil is so close to the good, and they are so closely joined together that it is an easy thing to acquire one in the belief that you are gaining the other. I have said above that a good commander must take every care to ensure that nothing ever arises that, through some unforeseen event, can deprive his army of courage. Beginning to lose is what can take away courage, and it is, therefore, necessary to guard against small skirmishes and never to permit them unless you have an enormous advantage and the hope of certain victory; a commander should not undertake to guard passes where he cannot maintain his entire army; he should not garrison cities unless they are the ones whose loss would necessarily bring about his downfall; and those he garrisons should be organized both with the garrison troops and with his army in such a way that, if there is an attempt to capture them, he can utilize all his forces; other cities he should leave undefended. Thus, every time something is lost that is abandoned and the army is still intact, your reputation in war is not lost nor is the hope of winning. But when something is lost that you have planned to defend and everyone believes that you are defending it, then there is damage and loss, and like the Gauls,* through a matter of little importance, you have almost lost the war.

Philip of Macedonia, father of Persius, was a military man of great renown in his times, and upon being attacked by the

Romans, he abandoned and destroyed many of his towns which he judged he could not defend, just like one who, in order to be prudent, believed it more harmful to lose his reputation by being unable to defend what he had set out to defend than to leave it as spoils for the enemy, losing it as something indifferent. After the rout of Cannae the Romans were in a sorry state, and they denied assistance to many of their dependants and subjects, ordering them to defend themselves as best they could. Such policies are much better than to establish lines of defence and, subsequently, fail to defend them, because with such a policy one loses friends and forces, whereas in the latter one only loses friends.

But returning to the matter of small skirmishes, let me say that even if a commander is forced to undertake some skirmish because the enemy is a new one, he must do so with so much advantage that there is no danger of losing it; or, indeed, he should do as Marius did (which is the best policy), who marched against the Cimbri, extremely ferocious peoples who had come to plunder Italy; their invasion had caused great terror by reason of their ferocity and their great number as well as the fact that they had already defeated one Roman army, which made Marius decide that, prior to engaging in battle, it was necessary to undertake some action through which his army could put aside the terror that the fear of the enemy had created in them; and as an extremely prudent commander, on more than one occasion, he placed his army in a spot where the Cimbri would have to pass by. Thus, from the fortifications of their camp, he wanted his troops to see the Cimbri and to accustom their eyes to the sight of this enemy, so that, when they saw a disorganized multitude, loaded down with baggage, some with arms idle and others with no arms at all, they were reassured and became eager for battle. Just as this decision was wisely taken by Marius, so must it be carefully imitated by others to avoid running the dangerous risks I have described above and to avoid having to act like the Gauls, 'who in fear of a matter of little account, crossed into Tiburtine territory and on to Campania'.* And since we have referred to Valerius Corvinus in this discourse, I would like to demonstrate through his own words, in the following chapter, what a commander should be like.

CHAPTER 38

What a Commander Should Be Like to Gain the Trust of the Army

As we said above, Valerius Corvinus was with his army fighting the Samnites, new enemies of the Roman people, and in order to reassure his soldiers and to make them acquainted with their enemies, he had his troops engage in certain light skirmishes, but since for him this was insufficient, he wanted to speak to them before the battle, and he showed them with great effectiveness how little they should esteem such enemies, citing their own exceptional skill as well as his own. Here it is possible to note, through the words Livy has him speak, what a commander should be like to gain the trust of an army; these words are as follows: 'Each one of them must go into battle with confidence in such a glorious record in war as well as in his own valour, and still more should he keep in mind under whose leadership and auspices he must enter battle—was it a man who commanded attention only as a superb orator, warlike in words but ignorant of military operations, or one who knew from his own experience how to handle arms, advance in front of the standards, and take his place in the thick of the fray? "It is my deeds, not my words, soldiers," he said, "which I want you to follow, and you should look to me not only for training but for an example as well. Not by means of political factions nor through the conspiracies beloved of the nobility have I won for myself three consulships and the highest praise, but by this right hand of mine".'* These words, carefully examined, will teach anyone how a man must conduct himself if he wishes to hold the rank of commander, and anyone who is not like this will discover in the passing of time that this rank, when it is held through fortune or through ambition, will have the effect of stripping him of any reputation, not of bestowing it upon him; because it is not titles that make men illustrious, but men who make titles illustrious. It must also be considered, as was noted at the beginning of this discourse, that if great commanders have employed extraordinary expedients to strengthen the courage of a veteran army when they are to confront unfamiliar enemies, how much more shrewdness must be employed in commanding a new army which has never before looked the enemy in the face, because if a new enemy terrifies the experienced army, every enemy will terrify an inexperienced army that much more. Still, we have seen on many occasions how good commanders have overcome all these difficulties with the utmost prudence, as did Gracchus the Roman and Epaminondas the Theban, about whom we have spoken elsewhere,* who with new armies vanquished well-trained armies of veterans.

The methods they employed were the following: they trained them for several months in mock battles and made them accustomed to obedience and discipline, and later on, they used these men with the greatest confidence in actual battle. No military man should, therefore, be discouraged about his capability to create good armies when he does not lack for men, because the prince with an abundance of men who lacks soldiers must not complain about the cowardice of his men but only about his own laziness and lack of prudence.

CHAPTER 39

A Commander Must Be Knowledgeable About Localities

Among the other things necessary to a commander of armies is the knowledge of localities and countries, because without such general and particular knowledge, a commander of armies cannot undertake any action. In fact, all the sciences require experience in order to master them completely, and this is one that requires enormous experience. This experience, or rather this particular knowledge, is acquired more through hunting than through any other exercise. Accordingly, ancient writers say that those heroes who ruled the world in their time were brought up in the woods and in the hunt, because hunting, besides providing that kind of knowledge, teaches us countless things necessary in warfare. In his life of Cyrus, Xenophon shows that when Cyrus went to attack the king of Armenia, he reminded his men, in planning that undertaking, that this was nothing more than one of those hunting expeditions they had gone on many times with him. He reminded those he sent in ambush on the mountain-tops that it was similar to the times they had gone to set up nets on the mountain ridges, and those who went to scour the countryside would be like men who went to rouse the wild beast from its lair, so as to drive it into the nets.

This is said to show that hunting, according to what Xenophon confirms, is a simulation of a war, and for this reason great men consider such an exercise honourable and necessary. Nor can this knowledge of different countries be learned through any more convenient means than by way of hunting, because the man who engages in hunting becomes acquainted with the lay of the land in the place where he hunts. When one is well acquainted with one region, he later on will easily comprehend all the new territories, because each country and each part of it, taken together, have some similarity, so that from knowledge of one part one can easily pass to knowledge of another. But anyone who remains unfamiliar with one country can never, or only over a long period of time, come to know another; and anyone who has this experience knows, in the blink of an eye, how that plain lies, how that mountain rises, where that valley goes, and all other similar things, of which in the past he has gained a solid understanding. That this is true is demonstrated to us by Livy through the example of Publius Decius, who was tribune of the soldiers in the army led by Cornelius the consul against the Samnites, for when the consul had led the Roman army into a valley where they could be trapped by the Samnites, and seeing it in so much danger, Publius said to the consul: ' "Do you see, sir," he said, "that hilltop rising above the enemy? There lies the bulwark of our hope and safety, if we are quick to capture it, as the Samnites have been so blind as to neglect it." '* Just before these words spoken by Decius, Livy declares: 'a military tribune, Publius Decius, espied an isolated hill which rose above the wood and dominated the enemy's camp. It was difficult of access for an encumbered army, but easy for lightly equipped men.' Hence, after being sent to the top of the hill by the consul with 3,000 men and saving the Roman army, as he is planning, once night comes, to leave and to save himself and his soldiers as well, Livy has him speak these words: ' "Come on now, follow me, and while there is still some daylight let us see if we can find out where they put their guard-posts, and where there's a way out of here." All this he then investigated, wrapped in a common soldier's cloak and taking with him the centurions, also dressed like men from the ranks, so that the enemy should not see that the commander was in the reconnaissance party.'

Anyone, therefore, who examines this text will see how useful and necessary it is for a commander to know the nature of different lands, because if Decius had not known and recognized these things, he would not have been able to judge how useful it would be for the Roman army to take that hill, nor would he have been able to recognize from afar if the hill was accessible or not; and once he had brought his men to the summit, then, wishing to leave to return to the consul with the enemy surrounding him, he could not have searched out from afar the paths of escape and the places guarded by the enemy. Thus, out of necessity Decius had to have such perfect knowledge: it enabled him to save the Roman army by taking the hill; later on when he was besieged, he knew how to find a path to safety for himself and for those who had been with him.

CHAPTER 40

Why Employing Deceit in Waging a War Is a Glorious Thing

Although employing deceit in every action is detestable, in waging a war it is, nevertheless, a laudable and glorious thing, and the man who employs deceit to overcome the enemy is to be praised, just like the man who overcomes him by force. This is evident in the judgement those who write the lives of great men make in praising Hannibal and others who have been very well known for similar methods of conduct. Since there are many examples to be read, I shall not repeat any of them. I shall say only that I do not mean that deceit is glorious when it causes you to break your word and your agreements, because this kind of deceit, even though it may on occasion gain state and kingdom for you, as was discussed above, will never bring you glory.

But I am speaking of the kind of deceit that is employed with an enemy who does not trust you, and that especially involves waging war, as was the deceit of Hannibal, when on the lake of Perugia* he simulated a retreat to trap the consul and the Roman army, and when to escape from the hands of Fabius Maximus he lit the horns of his cattle.*

Similar to this kind of deceit was that employed by Pontius, commander of the Samnites, to encircle the Roman army at the Caudine Forks: having stationed his army behind the mountains, he sent out some of his soldiers in the disguise of shepherds with a large flock on the plain; once they were captured by the Romans and asked where the Samnites' army was, they all agreed in saying, according to Pontius' orders, that it was at the siege of Nocera. This story, believed by the consuls, caused them to enclose themselves within the Caudine gorge, where they were immediately surrounded by the Samnites. This victory, obtained by deceit, would have been most glorious for Pontius if he had followed the advice of his father, who wanted the Romans either to be allowed to survive in liberty or all of them to be massacred and to avoid choosing a middle path, 'which neither wins friends nor removes enemies'.* Such a path is always pernicious in matters of state, as I have already discussed above, in another place.*

CHAPTER 41

That One's Native Land Must Be Defended Either With Shame or With Glory, and Is Well Defended in Either Way

As was said above, the consul and the Roman army were surrounded by the Samnites, who imposed upon the Romans the most shameful conditions (that is, to put them under the yoke and to send them, disarmed, back to Rome), and for this reason, the consuls seemed dazed and the entire army was in despair. Lucius Lentulus, the Roman legate, declared that he did not believe they should avoid any opportunity to save their city; that Rome's survival depended upon the survival of that army, and he felt it should to be saved at all costs; that one's country is well defended in whatever way one defends it, either with shame or with glory; and that by saving this army, Rome would still have time to erase its shame, though by failing to save it, even if it perished gloriously, Rome and its liberty would be lost. Thus, his advice was followed. This approach deserves to be noted and imitated by any citizen who finds himself giving advice to his native city, because where the ultimate decision concerning the safety of one's country is to be taken, no consideration of what is just or unjust, merciful or cruel, praiseworthy or shameful, should be permitted; on the contrary, putting aside every other reservation, one should follow in its entirety the policy that saves its life and preserves its liberty. This approach is imitated in word and deed by the French when they defend the majesty of their king and the power of their kingdom; for this reason, they hear no voice with more impatience than one which declares: 'This policy is disgraceful for the king'; for they say that their king cannot suffer shame in any of his decisions, either in good or in adverse fortune, because if he wins or if he loses, everyone agrees it is entirely a king's affair.

CHAPTER 42

That Promises Exacted by Force Need Not Be Kept

After the consuls returned to Rome with their army disarmed and themselves in disgrace, the first man in the senate who said that the peace made at Caudium should not be kept was the consul Spurius Postumius, who declared that the Roman people were not obligated to do so, but that he was clearly obligated to do so, along with the others who had promised peace; and that if the people, however, wished to free themselves of such an obligation, they had to give himself and all the others who had made such a promise to the Samnites as prisoners. He affirmed this conclusion with such obstinacy that the senate was happy to do so, and sending him and the others back to Samnium as prisoners, they protested to the Samnites that the peace was not valid. Fortune was so favourable to Postumius in this instance that the

Samnites did not detain him, and once he had returned to Rome, Postumius enjoyed more glory among the Romans for having lost than Pontius enjoyed among the Samnites for having triumphed. Here two things are to be noted: first, glory can be acquired from any action; it is ordinarily acquired through victory, but in defeat it is acquired either by demonstrating that such a defeat did not occur through any fault of yours, or by immediately executing some worthy action that cancels it; the other is that it is not shameful to avoid keeping those promises you were constrained to make by force; for promises exacted by force that regard the state are always broken when the force is removed, and they are broken without shame on the part of the one who breaks them. Various examples of this can be read in all the histories, and at the present more of them are seen every day. Not only are promises exacted by force never kept between princes, when the force is removed, but no other promises are observed when the causes for them are removed. Whether or not this is a praiseworthy thing, and whether or not similar methods should be observed by a prince, is examined by us at length in our treatise *De Principe;** I shall therefore remain silent at the present.

CHAPTER 43

That Men Born in One Province Display Almost the Same Nature in Every Age

Prudent men are in the habit of saying, neither by chance nor without reason, that anyone wishing to see what is to be must consider what has been: all the things of this world in every era have their counterparts in ancient times. This occurs since these actions are carried out by men who have and have always had the same passions, which, of necessity, must give rise to the same results. It is true that their actions are more effective at one time in this province than in that, and at another, in that rather than this one, according to the form of the education from which these peoples have derived their way of living. Understanding future affairs through past ones is also facilitated by observing how a nation over a lengthy period of time keeps the same customs, being either continuously avaricious or continuously deceitful, or having some other similar vice or virtue. Anyone who reads about the past affairs of our city of Florence and examines what has occurred recently will discover the German and French peoples to be full of greed, pride, ferocity, and faithlessness, because all these four qualities have, at different times, harmed our city. As for breach of faith, everyone knows how many times King Charles VIII was given money and how he promised to return the fortresses of Pisa and never did so. In this the king demonstrated his perfidiousness and extreme greed. But let us leave aside such fresh examples. Everyone has probably heard about what happened in the war that the Florentine people waged against the Visconti dukes of Milan; deprived of all other expedients, Florence thought about bringing the emperor with his reputation and forces into Italy to attack Lombardy. The emperor promised to come with many soldiers and to wage war against the Visconti and to defend Florence from their power, if the Florentines gave him 100,000 ducats to move his troops and another 100,000 when he arrived in Italy. The Florentines agreed to these conditions and gave him the first payment and then the second, but after he reached Verona he turned back without engaging in any action, claiming he remained behind because the Florentines had not kept the agreements between them. Thus, if Florence had not been constrained by necessity or overcome by passion, and if it had read about and understood the ancient customs of the barbarians, it would never have been, either on this occasion or on many others, deceived by them, since they have always acted in the same way and have always employed the same methods in every instance and with everyone. This is evident from what they did in ancient times to the Etruscans; oppressed by the Romans by virtue of having been put to flight and defeated by them many times, and seeing that with their own forces alone they could not resist the Roman onslaught, the Etruscans made an agreement with the Gauls who lived in Italy on this side of the Alps to give them a sum of money, so that they would be obligated to bring their armies to join with the Etruscans in the march against the Romans; and it came about that the Gauls, having taken the money, did not then want to take up arms on their behalf, claiming that they had not received the money to wage war with their enemies but rather to abstain from pillaging the Etruscan countryside. Thus, because of the greed and treachery of the Gauls, the Etruscan peoples were left in a single stroke deprived both of their money and the assistance they expected from the Gauls. So, this example of the ancient Etruscans and that of the Florentines make it clear that the French have always employed the same expedients, and for this reason, it is easy to speculate on how much faith princes can have in them.

CHAPTER 44

That One Often Obtains Through Impetuosity and Audacity What Would Never Be Obtained Through Ordinary Methods

Attacked by Rome's army and unable to remain in the field with their own army facing up to the Romans, the Samnites decided to leave the towns in Samnium guarded and to pass with their entire army into Etruria, which was in a state of truce with the Romans; and to see, with this movement, whether they might be able, with the presence of their army, to induce the Etruscans once again to take up arms, something they had refused to do for the Samnite ambassadors. In the speeches the Samnites delivered to the Etruscans, especially in demonstrating to them what had induced them to take up arms, they used a noteworthy expression in declaring that 'peace with servitude was harder to bear than war with liberty'.* And so, partly by their arguments and partly by the presence of their army, they persuaded the Etruscans once again to take up arms. Here, it is to be noted that when a prince desires to obtain something from someone else, he must, if the occasion permits, avoid giving him time to think it over and act in such a way that he will see the necessity of a prompt decision, which occurs when the person asked realizes that refusing or deferring will result in an immediate and dangerous provocation.

It can be seen that this expedient was well used in our own

times by Pope Julius II with the French and by Monsieur de Foix, general of the king of France, with the marquis of Mantua: Pope Julius wished to drive the Bentivogli family out of Bologna and decided that to do this, it would be necessary for French and Venetian forces to remain neutral, and having approached both of them, receiving from both an ambiguous and vacillating response, he decided to force them both to join in his decision by not giving them any time. Once he left Rome with as many troops as he could scrape together, he marched toward Bologna; he sent a message to the Venetians telling them to remain neutral, and one to the French telling them to send troops. In this way, both were constrained by the small period of time, and seeing that deferring or negating his request would result in a very obvious provocation of the pope, they both gave in to his wishes; the king sent reinforcements and the Venetians remained neutral.

Again, Monsieur de Foix, who was with his army in Bologna when he learned about the rebellion in Brescia and decided to go and retake the city, had two paths, one through the territory of the king, which was long and tedious, and the other short but through the territory of Mantua; not only did he need to pass through that marquis's territory, but he was obliged to go through certain passages between swamps and lakes, of which that region is full, which were blocked off by fortresses and other devices and guarded by the marquis. As a result, once de Foix decided to go by the shortest path and to overcome every difficulty, without giving the marquis the time to deliberate, in an instant, he set his troops down that path and again asked the marquis to send him his permission to pass through. Thus, constrained by this sudden decision, the marquis sent him the permission, which he would never have done had de Foix acted more cautiously, since the marquis was in league with the pope and the Venetians, and since one of his sons was in the hands of the pope, all matters which gave him many honest excuses to refuse the request. But assailed by this sudden decision, for the reasons explained above, he conceded. The Etruscans dealt with the Samnites in the same way when, in the presence of the Samnite army, they took up arms, which they had refused to do on other occasions.

CHAPTER 45

Whether It Is a Better Policy in Battles to Sustain the Enemy's Attack and Then to Counter-attack After Doing So; or to Assault Him Violently from the First

Decius and Fabius* were Roman consuls with two armies facing the armies of the Samnites and the Etruscans, and since they happened to be engaged in a skirmish and a battle at the same time, it is to be noted which of two different methods of proceeding followed by these two consuls in this action was best. Decius, with all possible impact and effort, attacked the enemy; Fabius only sustained the enemy attack, judging a slow attack to be more useful and saving his onslaught for last, when the enemy would have lost their initial fervour for combat and, as we say, their intensity. It is evident from the outcome of the affair that Fabius' plan had greater success than that of Decius: the latter became worn out in his first onslaughts, so that when he saw that more of his troops were turning back than standing fast, he sacrificed himself for the Roman legions, in imitation of his father, to acquire the glory in death he was unable to achieve with victory. When Fabius learned of this, to acquire no less honour in life than his colleague had won in death, he thrust forward all those forces he had reserved for such a necessity; whence, he brought home a most happy victory. Thus, it is evident that Fabius' method of proceeding is more secure and imitable.

CHAPTER 46

How It Happens That a Family Maintains the Same Customs in a City Over a Long Period of Time

It seems that not only does one city have different methods and forms of education than another, and bears men who are either tougher or more effeminate, but within the same city, it is clear that such differences can exist between one family and another. This is found to be true in every city, and we can read of many such examples in the city of Rome. We can see that the Manlius family was tough and stubborn, the Publicola family was kind and friendly to the people, the Appius family ambitious and hostile to the plebeians, and likewise many other families, in turn, have each had qualities distinct from the others. Such a thing cannot arise solely from blood-lines, since these must change through the diversity of marriages, but it necessarily derives from the differences in education between one family and another. Consequently, it is much more important for a young man of tender years to begin by hearing good or bad of something, because it necessarily makes an impression on him according to which he will then regulate his mode of conduct at all periods of his life. If this were not the case, it would be impossible for the entire Appius family to have possessed the same ambition and to have been stirred by the same passions, as Livy notes in many of them. In one last example, when one member of the family was made censor and his colleague had, at the end of eighteen months, as the law provided, left the magistracy, he did not wish to do so, declaring that he was able to hold the office for five years, according to the first law established by the censors. Although there were many speeches about this matter and it caused many disturbances, there was, nevertheless, no way to make him leave office, even though he acted against the will of the people and the majority of the senate. Anyone who reads the speech he made against Publius Sempronius, tribune of the plebeians, will note there all the usual Appian insolence and all the goodness and humanity exercised by countless citizens to obey the laws and auspices of their native city.

CHAPTER 47

That a Good Citizen Ought to Forget Private Injuries for Love of His Country

Marcius the consul was with the army against the Samnites, and when he was wounded in a skirmish and constituted a danger to his troops, the senate decided it was necessary to send Papirius Cursor as dictator to make up for the weakness of the consul.

Since it was necessary for a dictator to be nominated by Fabius, who was consul with the armies in Etruria, the senators, fearing that Fabius would not be willing to nominate Papirius, who was his enemy, sent two ambassadors to beg him to put aside private hatreds and to name him for the public good. This Fabius did, moved by love for his native city, even though, through his silence and in many other ways, he indicated that such a nomination weighed heavily upon him. All those who seek to be considered good citizens should follow this example.*

CHAPTER 48

When an Enemy Is Seen Committing a Gross Error, It Should Be Assumed that There Is a Trick Behind It

When Fulvius was left as legate in the army that the Romans had in Etruria, and the consul had gone to Rome for some ceremonies, the Etruscans, to see if they might catch him, set up a trap near the Roman fortifications, and sending some soldiers disguised as shepherds with a large flock, they had them move into view of the Roman army; disguised in this fashion, they drew near to the stockades of the camp whereupon the legate, amazed at their presumption, which did not appear reasonable to him, managed to discover their treachery, and in this way the plan of the Etruscans was thwarted. Here it is easy to note that a commander of armies must not trust an error that is committed by the enemy in an obvious way; there will always be some form of deceit behind it, since it is not reasonable for men to be so incautious. But the desire to win often blinds the minds of men, so that they see nothing but what seems to suit their purposes.

The Gauls, having defeated the Romans at the Allia River, came to Rome and found the gates open and unguarded, and they all remained there that day and night without entering, fearing deceit, unable to believe that there might be so much cowardice and so little counsel in Roman hearts that they would abandon their native city. When in 1508* the Florentines were besieging Pisa, Alfonso del Mutolo, a Pisan citizen, found himself a prisoner of the Florentines, and he promised that if he were freed, he would deliver one of Pisa's gates over to the Florentine army. He was released; then, to work out the plan, he came many times to speak with the commissioners' legates, arriving not in secret but openly and accompanied by Pisans, whom he left to one side when he spoke with the Florentines. Thus, they could have assumed his two-faced nature, because it was not reasonable, if the planning were real, for him to carry it out so much in the open. But their desire to take Pisa blinded the Florentines in such a way that, after they had reached the Lucca gate, according to their agreement with him, they left behind a number of their leaders and other soldiers, to their great dishonour, because of the double-dealing of this Alfonso.

CHAPTER 49

If a Republic Is to Be Kept Free, Each Day It Requires New Measures; and the Good Qualities for Which Quinctius Fabius Was Called Maximus

Every day in a great city, as has been said many times, accidents necessarily arise that require a physician, and the more important such accidents are, the more necessary it is to find the wisest physician. If such accidents ever arose in any city, they arose in Rome, both strange and unexpected ones; as, for instance, when it looked as if all Roman women had conspired against their husbands to murder them, and many were discovered who had poisoned them, and many who had prepared the poison to do so. Another such event discovered during the time of the Macedonian war was the conspiracy of the Bacchanals, which involved many thousands of men and women, and it would have been dangerous for that city, had it not been discovered, or had the Romans not been accustomed to punishing great numbers of wrong-doers, because if the greatness of that republic and the power of its executive actions are not seen in countless other ways, they are evident in the severity of the punishments that the Romans imposed upon those who erred. Rome never hesitated to put to death in the interest of justice an entire legion at a time or an entire city, or to banish eight or ten thousand men under extraordinary conditions to be endured not just by one man but by many; this happened to those soldiers who had fought unsuccessfully at Cannae and who were banished to Sicily, for they were forbidden to take lodgings in towns and were required to eat standing up.

But of all the forms of executive action, decimating the armies was most terrifying; in this instance, one of every ten men in an entire army was chosen to be executed by lot. Nor could one find a more frightening punishment than this one to bring a multitude under control, for when a multitude errs, and there is no certain instigator, all cannot be punished since they are too numerous, and to punish only a part, leaving others unpunished, would be doing a wrong to those who are punished, while the unpunished would have the courage to err once again. But by killing the tenth part by lot, when all deserve execution, whoever is punished mourns his fate; whoever is not punished is afraid that on another occasion it will be his turn and takes care not to go astray.

The poisoners and the Bacchanals, therefore, were punished according to the nature of their sins. Although such diseases in a republic have evil effects, they are not deadly, for there is almost always time to correct them; but for those which concern the state, there is no time, and unless they are cured by a prudent man, they will cause the downfall of the city. Because of the generosity the Romans displayed in giving citizenship to foreigners, so many new people were born in Rome that they began to possess a large percentage of the vote, so that the government began to change, departing from those policies and those men it was accustomed to employ. Aware of this, Quinctius Fabius, who was the censor, placed all these new people, who were the source of this disorder, within four tribes, so that they could not, reduced to such small spaces, corrupt all of Rome. This matter was well understood by Fabius, and he provided a suitable remedy for it without changing the government; it was so widely accepted by that civic body that he deserved to be called Maximus.

EXPLANATORY NOTES

13 *to Zanobi Buondelmonti*: Machiavelli also dedicated his *Life of Castruccio Castracani of Lucca* to Buondelmonti (1491–1527), who was a member of the Florentine republican circle identified with the Orti Oricellari, the garden belonging to the Rucellai family at which Machiavelli apparently discussed his commentary on Livy with other humanists; he is also one of the interlocutors in Machiavelli's humanist dialogue, *The Art of War*. Buondelmonti was forced to flee Florence in 1522 when an anti-Medici conspiracy in which he was involved was uncovered; he returned during the short-lived restoration of the republic in 1527, only to die shortly thereafter.

and Cosimo Rucellai: like Buondelmonti, one of the interlocutors of Machiavelli's dialogue on warfare, Cosimo was the host of the political discussions at the Orti Oricellari (1495–1519). His grandfather Bernardo (1448–1514), a staunch supporter of Lorenzo de' Medici, who first laid out the gardens of the Orti Oricellari, was the author of a history of the invasion of Italy by Charles V in 1494–5, *De bello italico*, in which the concept of the 'balance of power' is first discussed.

14 *Hiero of Syracuse*: king of Syracuse (306–215 BC).

Perseus of Macedonia: last king of Macedonia (213–162 BC), defeated in 168 by Paulus Aemilius at Pydna and led in chains back to Rome for the victor's triumph.

in the beginning: that is, in the Preface to Book I; the dedication was originally placed after the end of Book III in some editions and manuscript copies of *The Discourses*.

15 *Preface to Autograph Manuscript*: as Giorgio Inglese notes in a discussion of the manuscript tradition of Machiavelli's *Discorsi* (Niccolò Machiavelli, *Discorsi sopra la prima deca di Tito Livio* (Milan: Rizzoli, 1984), 31–42), most modern editions of this work depart from Mazzoni's 1929 edition, which accepts the version of the preface in the autograph manuscript rather than the revised preface that appeared in the first (1531) printed edition. Inglese believes, on the contrary, that the printed edition reflects Machiavelli's final version. In this translation we have reprinted both the traditional preface, generally employed in other current translations, as well as the briefer version from the 1531 book. The

differences between the two versions are subtle but extremely significant.

new methods and institutions: while *virtù* (ability, skill, merit, ingenuity, strength, sometimes even virtue) is the key intellectual concept underlying *The Prince*, Machiavelli focuses upon methods and institutions (*modi e ordini nuovi*) in the *Discourses on Livy*. His emphasis thus shifts from the personal characteristics of an individual hero toward the political effects of state-building and a government's key institutions. This distinction holds true in spite of the fact that Machiavelli omits this important passage in the revised preface published in the first 1531 edition.

unknown lands and seas: Machiavelli implicitly compares his new direction in republican political theory to the courageous explorations of Italian navigators such as Columbus, Vespucci, and Verrazzano. This metaphor was removed from the published preface.

16 *today's religion*: in the autograph manuscript, Machiavelli blames religion for the decadence of contemporary civil society, but the first printed edition points the finger at a more generalized defective education, training, or upbringing; in short, a cultural shortcoming rather than a religious one.

all the books by Livy: of the original 142 books in Livy's history of Rome, books 1–10 and 21–45 survived, but books 41–5 came to light only in 1527, too late to influence Machiavelli's thinking before his death.

17 *today's education*: the change from religion to education (in the broadest sense of training, good habits, or sound upbringing) in the printed version represents the most significant revision of the original manuscript.

20 *in Ragusa*: now Dubrovnik in the former Yugoslavia, Ragusa was a maritime republic once in the Venetian sphere of influence but controlled, after 1526, by the Ottoman Turks.

21 *the Mamelukes*: rulers of Egypt from 1252 until 1517, when Cairo was captured by the Ottoman Turks.

Dinocrates: the architect who designed Alexandria for Alexander; this anecdote concerning his proposal to reshape Mount Athos can be found in a number of ancient authors, including Strabo, Lucian, and especially Vitruvius (*The Ten Books of Architecture*, ii., Introduction).

23 *were destroyed*: between June and September of 1502, after the rebellion of Arezzo and the Valdichiana against Florentine

dominion, as well as the capture of Urbino by Cesare Borgia, the Florentine government decided to create the post of *gonfaloniere* or standard-bearer for life, a post that was occupied by Machiavelli's patron, Piero Soderini. Exactly a decade later (29 August 1512), Spanish troops sacked Prato, causing the downfall of Soderini's republic and the eventual return of the Medici family to govern Florence, an event that brought Machiavelli's career in the Florentine Chancery to an abrupt halt.

23 *come to be pernicious*: this important chapter of the *Discourses on Livy* reflects Machiavelli's reliance upon the Greek historian Polybius' discussion of Roman history and government in his *Histories* (2nd century BC). The political theory of Polybius was revived in Florence in the fifteenth century, and Books I–V were rendered from Greek into Latin as early as 1450 by Niccolò Perotti for Pope Nicholas V; an Italian translation of Polybius appeared in 1546 some years after Machiavelli's death. Since most scholars believe Machiavelli read little or no Greek and the important Book VI had not been translated into Latin during Machiavelli's lifetime, there has been a great deal of scholarly debate about exactly how Machiavelli might have had access to the ideas in Book VI. The most likely answer is that Machiavelli's republican friends in the Orti Oricellari discussed with him the material not yet available in Latin or Italian. Bernardo Rucellai, the founder of the gardens where these discussions took place, apparently used Book VI of Polybius in a work he wrote around 1505. See Polybius, *The Rise of the Roman Empire*, trans. Ian Scott-Kilvert (New York: Penguin, 1979), for an English translation.

26 *And this is the cycle*: here Machiavelli accepts the analysis of a political cycle put forward by Polybius, a circular sequence to which Polybius gives the name *anacyclosis*. Apparently, in a now-lost section of Book VI of his *Histories*, Polybius maintained that the Romans fortunately converted their oligarchy not into a democracy (as his theory requires) but into the mixed constitution where the three elements of the state (the consuls representing the monarchy, the senate representing the aristocracy, and the popular element) were perfectly balanced.

    in tranquillity for that city: Machiavelli arrives at this total of 800 years of tranquillity under the constitution of Lycurgus by considering Sparta free until the city was absorbed into the Roman empire in 27 BC.

28 *the discord between the plebeians and the senate*: classical and medieval political theory generally criticized a republican form of

government because of the social conflict often attributed by traditional political theorists to this form of government; with his emphasis on the fact that Rome's republican government achieved unparalleled stability through social conflict, Machiavelli introduced one of his most original contributions to republican thinking.

30 *as Cicero declares*: *De Amicitia* (On Friendship), 25–6.

32 *two of them*: two plebeian consuls were elected for the first time in 172 BC.

the censorship: the first plebeian censor was Gaius Marcius Rutulus, elected to the office in 351 BC.

the praetorship: the first plebeian praetor, elected in 337 BC, was Quintus Publilius Philo.

Marius and the ruin of Rome: Gaius Marius (157–86 BC), head of the popular party in Rome, whose biography Machiavelli consulted in Plutarch's *Lives*. Machiavelli considered Marius, the Gracchi, and Julius Caesar responsible for the destruction of republican liberty in Rome.

Marcus Menenius and Marcus Fulvius: while Machiavelli's edition of Livy gave these two names in its description of the events which took place in 314 BC, current critical editions of Livy cite two different individuals: Gaius Maenius and Marcus Folius. The master of horse served as an assistant to the dictator.

34 *a king with a small senate*: actually two kings and twenty-eight senators.

they closed the avenue to participation: Machiavelli refers here to the momentous *serrata* or closing of the Maggior Consiglio in 1297, an act calculated to reinforce the control of a small circle of patrician families in Venice and to eliminate the influence of a larger, more popular assembly.

35 *and those who are governed*: Machiavelli badly miscalculates the proportions of the governors and the governed in Venice; between the fourteenth and the sixteenth centuries, some 1,200 to 2,500 nobles had access to the government out of a population that ranged from 120,000 to 160,000 inhabitants.

37 *the complete ruin of the republic*: the rebellion broke out in 379 BC, and eight years later, under the leadership of Pelopidas, the Spartans were defeated by the Thebans and their hegemony in Greece was destroyed for ever.

in a single day: at the disastrous battle of Agnadello (1509), Venice was opposed by the League of Cambrai (France, the Holy Roman

Empire, and the papacy) and lost almost all of the possessions it had gained on *terra firma*. Machiavelli does not add that by 1517, however, most of these territories had been regained by the Serenissima.

38 *humours*: in his political works, Machiavelli constantly draws parallels between the human body and the body politic. Renaissance scientific theory relied upon the works of Galen, Hippocrates, and their learned commentators to explain the behaviour of the human body by various mixtures of four different humours: blood, phlegm, yellow bile, and black bile. Anthony J. Parel's *The Machiavellian Cosmos* (New Haven: Yale University Press, 1992) persuasively argues that Machiavelli's original view of the body politic as a dynamic organism achieving unity through the conflict of opposing institutions reflects this Renaissance theory of the humours accepted in Machiavelli's times.

39 *to plead his case*: the incident cited by Machiavelli from Livy's history concerning Gaius Marcius Coriolanus took place in 491 BC.

Francesco Valori: one of the Florentine aristocrats who engineered the ouster of Piero de' Medici from the Florentine government in 1494 and a staunch supporter of Savonarola, Valori was murdered by Medici supporters shortly before Savonarola's execution in 1498.

40 *except by a sect*: here Machiavelli uses the religious term (*sètta*) that underlines heresy or divergence from orthodoxy rather than *parte* ('faction').

Piero Soderini: see note to p. 23.

before eight judges: Machiavelli's reference to this number arises from the institution of the *Otto di guardia*, eight Florentine magistrates who were entrusted with the administration of justice in the republic and who examined Soderini on the charge of public corruption before pronouncing him innocent.

41 *in his history*: Livy, v. 33.

the barbarian forces: this incident occurred in 391 BC, a year before the Gauls (called by Machiavelli here and elsewhere *franciosi* or 'French' rather than *galli* or 'Gauls') sacked Rome; Clausium is known today as Chiusi.

not inferior to him: awakened by the famous geese of the Capitol, Manlius turned back a night attack of the Gauls against the citadel on the Capitol in 386 BC, thereby gaining the name Capitolinus; in 390 BC, Furius Camillus lifted the Gauls' siege of Rome with troops brought from the city of Veii.

42 *a dictator*: Aulus Cornelius Cossus, created dictator in 385 BC.

43 *and from sects to ruin*: Machiavelli again employs the religious term 'sects' (*sètte*) to mean factions, parties, or interest groups; he views any such group negatively if it does not pursue the common good and operates only in the defence of narrowly defined political interests.

Giovanni Guicciardini, its commissioner: Guicciardini commanded this army in 1430; Machiavelli discusses this incident in his *Florentine Histories* (iv. 25).

44 *Captain [of the People]*: a magistracy of the judiciary; although Messer Giovanni was cited by this office, his patrician connections managed to quash the indictment (see Machiavelli's *Florentine Histories*, iv. 25).

to make changes in Florence: these unnamed partisans of the popular faction in Florence were led by the Medici family; Cosimo de' Medici eventually returned from exile to Florence in 1434 and immediately established a republic controlled by his family and their partisans.

the ruin of that republic: that is, the downfall of the republic characterized as a *governo stretto*, or a government with limited popular participation. Controlled by the Degli Albizzi family and its supporters, this government managed Florentine affairs between 1393 and 1433 until the return of Cosimo de' Medici from foreign exile.

as his companion in the kingdom: Livy (i. 14) actually declares that Titus Tatius was killed in a riot in Lavinium, but that Romulus was unconcerned by his death, perhaps thinking the man received what he deserved.

45 *in order to set them aright*: this statement about the relationship of means and ends should be compared with the remarks Machiavelli makes in *The Prince* (XVIII). Conventional wisdom identifies Machiavelli with an unsophisticated notion that the 'ends justify the means', but in fact, Machiavelli only suggests such an idea in the most serious of circumstances—here, Romulus' establishment of the most important republican form of government in world history.

46 *absolutist and tyrannical*: according to Giorgo Inglese's commentary on *Discourses on Livy* (p. 215), the original Italian terms ('*uno vivere civile e libero . . . uno assoluto e tirannico*') form an equation treating the theme of laws and the government's goal. A government is either free or absolutist, depending upon whether it has the

proper laws or lacks them; it is either free or tyrannical, depending
upon whether it operates in the interests of the common good or
for some particular, private interest.

46 *establish a tyranny*: the Spartan Ephors were five magistrates
elected annually to oversee the city's affairs of state. Agis IV was
king of Sparta between 250 and 241 BC, and in his desire to reinsti-
tute Lycurgus' laws he was opposed by Leonidas. Machiavelli
takes this example, interpreted rather loosely, from Plutarch's
Lives.

48 *extravagantly praised*: unlike Dante, Machiavelli considered
P. Cornelius Scipio Africanus (235–183 BC), the conqueror of
Hannibal and Carthage, as the supreme Roman republican hero,
and he viewed Julius Caesar (c.100–44 BC), following the Florentine humanist tradition, as the destroyer of republican liberty. The
other three pairs of good rulers and tyrants come from Greek
history: Agesilaus II, king of Sparta (444–360 BC); Timoleon
(c.411–c.337 BC), ruler of Syracuse; Dion of Syracuse (408–354 BC),
who freed Syracuse from the tyranny of Dionysius II in 356, who
returned in 354, when he was expelled again by Timoleon; Nabis,
tyrant of Sparta (d. 192 BC); and Phalaris, tyrant of Agrigentum
between 570 and 555 BC. The reference to an evil Dionysius may
mean either Dionysius the Elder, tyrant of Syracuse between 406
and 367 BC, or his son Dionysius II, tyrant of Syracuse between 367
and 343 BC. Machiavelli's sources for these examples are primarily
Plutarch's *Lives*, but mention of Nabis occurs in Polybius and
Livy, while Phalaris is noted in Aristotle's *Politics* and *Rhetoric*.

freely about him: after Caesar's death Roman emperors used his
name as an honorific title, a practice that continued into the twen-
tieth century with the German 'kaiser' and the Russian 'czar'.

what they say about Catiline: Lucius Sergius Catiline (108–62 BC),
a conspirator against the Roman republic who was successfully
opposed by Cicero (106–43 BC); accounts of Catiline occur in the
works of Plutarch, Sallust, and, most importantly, Cicero.

they celebrate his enemy: Marcus Junius Brutus (85–42 BC), the
assassin of Julius Caesar (not Lucius Junius Brutus of the sixth century BC, one of the legendary founders of the republic after the
expulsion of the Tarquin tyrants and the rape of Lucretia).

49 *his very great fortune and ability*: in *The Prince* (XIX: On Avoiding Being Despised and Hated), Machiavelli also singles out
Severus (emperor, AD 193–211) as a special case in a discussion
of a large group of other emperors, including Marcus Aurelius

(121–80), Commodus (180–93), Pertinax (193), Julianus (193), Caracalla (211–17), Macrinus (217–18), Heliogabalus (218–22), Alexander (222–35), and Maximinus (235–38). Machiavelli admires the combination of fortune and ability (*virtù*), the special quality he praises in *The Prince* and that he discerns in the life of Severus. The emperors who were assassinated, and therefore considered as evil rulers by Machiavelli, were: Caesar (d. 44 BC), Caligula (d. AD 41), Claudius (d. 54), Nero (d. 68), Galba (d. 69), Otho (d. 69, a suicide), Vitellius (d. 69), Domitian (d. 96), Commodus, Pertinax, Julianus, Caracalla, Macrinus, Heliogabalus, Alexander, and Maximinus. The emperors who died natural deaths were: Augustus (d. 14), Tiberius (d. 37), Vespasian (d. 79), Titus (d. 81), Nerva (d. 98), Trajan (d. 117), Hadrian (d. 138), Antonius Pius (d. 161), Marcus Aurelius (d. 180), and Severus. To arrive at a total of twenty-six emperors during the period under discussion, Machiavelli omits from his list the following individuals who were emperors or co-emperors, if only briefly: Lucius Verus (d. 169), Decimus Clodius Albinus (d. 194), Gaius Pescennius Niger (d. 194), and Geta (d. 212). While Machiavelli's sources for the Roman emperors of the first century AD were the obvious ones (Tacitus, Suetonius), other, lesser-known works served as his sources in studying the emperors during the second and third centuries from the time of Marcus Aurelius to Maximinus. He certainly knew Herodian's *History of the Empire from the Time of Marcus*, originally written in Greek but available in a Latin translation by Angelo Poliziano published in 1493; and he might also have used the Latin collection of emperors' biographies known as the *Augustan History*, a work that had become popular by the late Middle Ages.

like to be put in charge: Machiavelli foreshadows Edward Gibbon's similar opinion of the reigns of Nerva, Trajan, Hadrian, Antoninus Pius, and Marcus Aurelius (96–185). In *The Decline and Fall of the Roman Empire*, Gibbon remarks: 'If a man were called to fix the period in the history of the world during which the condition of the human race was most happy and prosperous, he would, without hesitation, name that which elapsed from the death of Domitian to the accession of Commodus' (*The Portable Gibbon* (New York: Viking Penguin, 1952), 107).

full of new disasters: from this line to the penultimate sentence in the paragraph, Machiavelli paraphrases the famous description of the calamities striking Rome in the year AD 69 that he found in Tacitus' *Histories* (i. 2). For the English text, see Tacitus, *The Histories*, trans. Kenneth Wellesley (New York: Penguin, 1975), 3.

50 *Numa Pompilius as his successor*: Numa was reputed to have died in 673 BC. In many ways, his contribution to the Roman republic—the conscious invention of a civic religion as the ethical basis for the political and social fabric of Rome—was even more crucial and lasting than the foundations laid by Romulus.

51 *of the Romans at Cannae*: 216 BC.

   a close relationship with a nymph: the nymph Egeria, discussed in Livy (i. 19).

52 *any new form whatsoever*: here, as he so often does in *The Prince*, Machiavelli implies that the statesman is an artist, giving form to a shapeless and amorphous political mass, a metaphor that is explained at greater length in the next sentence at the end of this paragraph.

   that He bestow it: Dante, *The Divine Comedy: Purgatory*, trans. and ed. Mark Musa (New York: Penguin, 1985), vii. 121–3. Machiavelli actually misquotes the original Italian (which we modify in English translation), using the verb 'descend' rather than 'rise'. Apparently, he was thinking of a genealogical tree, where branches descend, rather than a real tree, such as Dante had in mind, where the branches rise up.

53 *that he spoke with God*: a Dominican preacher born in Ferrara in 1452, Savonarola became Prior of San Marco in Florence in 1491, and was a major force in Florentine politics after the expulsion of the Medici in 1494. He was the author of an important political treatise, *Treatise on the Organization and Government of Florence* (1498), which proposed a republican government for the city and an enlarged grand council based on his interpretation of that branch of the Venetian government. A fierce republican opposed to the Medici family under whose patronage he was first brought to Florence, Savonarola was excommunicated by Pope Alexander VI and executed in 1498 in the Piazza della Signoria. Some contemporary scholars believe Machiavelli's election to the Florentine chancery came about as a result of his opposition to Savonarola's policies, and the sarcastic tone of his description of Savonarola's discourse with God certainly shows his dislike of the friar. A letter dated 9 March 1498 from Machiavelli to Ricciardo Becchi, the Florentine envoy at the papal court sent by Piero Soderini's government, describes in detail several of Savonarola's sermons, and in the letter Machiavelli describes the friar's preaching as 'lies' (see *The Portable Machiavelli*, 56–8, for a complete translation of the letter). Machiavelli's most important remark about Savonarola, of

course, comes from the famous discussion of armed prophets (who always succeed) and unarmed prophets like Savonarola (who always fail) in chapter VI of *The Prince*.

the existence of the pagan religion: in the original Italian, Machiavelli actually employs the word *gentile* ('gentile') rather than *pagana* ('pagan'), employing the point of view of the ancient Jews and Christians.

55 *or punishment*: it should not be forgotten that Machiavelli was in the process of writing the *Discourses on Livy*, when Martin Luther's conflict with the papacy was beginning (his famous ninety-five theses appeared in Wittemberg on 31 October 1517). Luther was often referred to as the 'punishment' or 'scourge' (*il flagello*) of the church. The fact that Machiavelli underlines the physical location of Rome as the key to the corruption produced by such geographical proximity shows that he was criticizing the court at Rome and not the Christian religion in this famous passage. The comical paradox arising from the juxtaposition of physical proximity to Rome, the headquarters of the Holy See and, presumably, proximity to God, with moral corruption and great distance from religion's moral teachings is not original with Machiavelli. It was apparently a proverbial popular belief and is brilliantly exploited for comic effect in Giovanni Boccaccio's tale of how a Jew was miraculously converted to Christianity when he visited Rome and witnessed the same corruption at the papal court that Machiavelli notes here (*The Decameron*, i. 2). This chapter also contains an implicit criticism of Pope Leo X (Giovanni de' Medici), who held the papacy between 1513 and 1521 and who was the leader of the Medici faction then ruling Florence. In *The Prince*, in spite of his republican leanings, Machiavelli had seen the conjunction of Medici power in Florence with the Medici papacy in Rome as an expedient means of driving foreigners out of Italy. Now, in this openly republican commentary, there is no beneficial result that can emerge from a corrupt Roman court.

to bring in someone powerful: Machiavelli assumes that such a powerful man will be a foreigner.

with the aid of the Swiss: here Machiavelli alludes to the League of Cambrai (1508–9) against Venice and to the Holy League (1511–12) against the French, both organized by Pope Julius II.

56 *powerful barbarians*: Machiavelli also calls foreign invaders of Italy barbarians at the conclusion of *The Prince* (XXVI: An Exhortation to Liberate Italy From the Barbarians).

56 *the Romans discovered that Apollo*: in 398 BC, according to Livy (v. 15–16), the unusual level of the waters at Lake Albanus caused the Romans to send a delegation to Delphi (the oracle of Apollo) for an interpretation of its significance; meanwhile, an aged sooth-sayer from Veii informed the Romans that they would not take the city until the water was drained off. When the delegation returned from Delphi and confirmed the old man's prediction, the Roman soldiers regained their confidence. Although it is not so clearly stated in the Latin original, Machiavelli obviously believes that every form of oracular prediction in Rome was employed and manipulated by its political leaders: recourse to oracles and prophecy is synonymous with fraud and political manipulation in his view of ancient Rome.

57 *because of Terentillus the tribune*: according to Livy (iii. 9–10), in 462 BC the consul Gaius Terentillus Arsa proposed that a commis-sion of five men be set up to define and limit the powers of the consuls.

a certain Appius Herdonius: see Livy, iii. 15–18. Appius Herdonius was a Sabine, and the army under his control took the Capitol in 460 BC. Livy mentions an army of 2,500 men, but Machiavelli adds a substantial number to his figure.

a certain Publius Ruberius: Livy (iii. 15) refers not to Publius Ruberius but to Publius Valerius Publicola.

Titus Quinctius was immediately re-elected consul: not Titus Quinctius but Lucius Quinctius Cincinnatus, the man who would later became one of Roman political mythology's most celebrated characters when, as Roman dictator, he would save the republic after being called away from his farm. Machiavelli also errs in say-ing that this election was a re-election (he presumably confuses this election with a first re-election that Livy mentions shortly there-after (iii. 21); the election in question here was his first as consul.

58 *'to suit its own convenience'*: cited in Latin from Livy, iii. 20. For the English text which we cite throughout, see Livy, *The Early History of Rome*, trans. Aubrey De Selincourt (New York: Pen-guin, 1971), 206–7.

they called pullarii: this technical term might be rendered as 'chicken-keepers' or 'poultry-diviners', neither possibility repre-senting a felicitous phrase in English.

59 *the consul Papirius*: Lucius Papirius Cursor the Younger, consul in 293 and 272 BC, defeated the Samnites at the battle of Aquilonia in 293 BC during the third Samnite War (see Livy, x. 40–1).

60 *into the ocean*: Machiavelli could not have found this anecdote in Livy, since the complete account in Book XIX is not extant; Livy's account is mentioned in passing in the extant summary of Book XIX and is also discussed in Polybius (i. 49–51; vi. 52); Machiavelli probably found the story either in Valerius Maximus (i. 4; or v. 3), or in Cicero (*De Natura Deorum* ii. 3 and 7). Valerius Maximus (vii. 2 and 5) also recounts the story of Papirius Cursor. Machiavelli fails to mention the fact that this battle, fought near modern Trapani in 249 BC, was a naval, not a land, battle.

'*to try for victory*': Machiavelli cites Livy (x. 31) in Latin. For the English text which we cite throughout, see Livy, *Rome and Italy*, trans. Betty Radice (New York: Penguin, 1982), 333.

61 '*painted and gilded*': Livy (x. 39), cited in Latin. For the English text see Livy, *Rome and Italy*, 344. The Roman general in question is the previously mentioned Lucius Papirius Cursor (*Discourses on Livy*, i. 14).

for Roman ability: in this sentence and the next, Machiavelli again employs the most important term of *The Prince* (*virtù*, meaning exceptional ability, ingenuity, strength, or valour) three times, but the term here is not applied to an individual but to a people and its institutions.

through religion when it is properly used: here, as elsewhere, Machiavelli always considers religion as an *instrumentum regni*, as a means of bolstering a government's power; while he personally may believe in the ethical and moral message of the Christian religion, he never hesitates to describe it in the same utilitarian terms that he employs to deal with the pagan religions of classical times.

in the discussion of foreign affairs: that is, in Book II.

62 *who seeks to put it back into chains*: Machiavelli was apparently inspired to employ this metaphor of a wild beast for a newly freed people by his readings of Polybius (vi. 9).

its substance is not corrupted: Machiavelli employs the word *materia* for 'substance' or 'material' here, a term related to his concept of the political leader or founder who moulds or gives form to the 'substance' of the society he organizes.

enemies rather than friends: In his later *Florentine Histories* (iii. 1), Machiavelli clarifies the difference between the relatively uncorrupted Roman republican period (the 300-year period between the expulsion of the Tarquins to the advent of the Gracchi) and the corrupted city of Florence. Rome's conflicts were carried on between the plebeians and the aristocrats without factions, sects, or partisans, which arise when private citizens acquire excessive power, influence, or wealth through private means and employ them for private ends. Factions produce partisans rather than citizens and promote the concentration of power and wealth, two major sources of political corruption. While Machiavelli admired the republican period of Rome, it is difficult to say from his works whether he sincerely believed that republican Florence was sufficiently free of civic corruption to follow the Roman example.

63 *against their native city*: while the original Italian, *patria*, can be rendered as 'homeland' or 'fatherland', 'native city' or 'native land' may more accurately reflect Machiavelli's belief that a citizen's first loyalty was owed to his or her native city. The negative connotation the term 'fatherland' has acquired in this century argues against its usage here.

the people friendly to him: Machiavelli gives his same advice on numerous occasions in *The Prince* (III, V, VII, VIII, IX, X, XIX).

64 *an appropriate example*: Machiavelli found the historical information that follows on Clearchus in Justin's *Histories* (xvi. 4–5). Heraclea was a Greek city on the Black Sea, where Clearchus ruled for twelve years until his assassination in 353 BC. Several Renaissance editions of Justin's work existed: after the first Venetian edition of 1470, at least eight more appeared in that city, as well as four in Milan and two each in Rome and Florence (where the first edition saw the light in 1510). In Machiavelli's time Justin was an early history text for children, and we know from Bernardo Machiavelli's *Ricordi* or memoirs that Niccolò's father borrowed a copy when he was 12 years old. While little read today, and certainly less important than Livy or Tacitus, Justin is cited on several occasions in the *Discourses on Livy*: i. 16; 26; ii. 10; 28; iii. 6 (twice); and 31.

the greatest satisfaction of the people: the reader should bear in mind how Machiavelli's discussion of Clearchus parallels a similar action by Cesare Borgia in a celebrated passage in *The Prince* (VII): 'And having found the occasion to do this, one morning at Cesena he had Messer Remirro placed on the piazza in two pieces with a block of wood and a bloody sword beside him. The ferocity of such a spectacle left those people satisfied and amazed at the same time' (*The Prince*, trans. Peter Bondanella and Mark Musa (The World's Classics, Oxford, 1984), 26).

66 *to its long-standing tyranny*: Machiavelli has once before (i. 10) referred to this pair of good rulers from Greek history (see note to p. 48 above).

Caesar's race was extinguished: after the death of Nero in AD 68 the family of Augustus became extinct.

he, like the first Brutus: like all republican thinkers, Machiavelli makes much of the contrast in Rome between the 'first Brutus', who helped drive out the Tarquin tyrants after the rape of Lucretia, and the 'second Brutus', who failed to stop civic corruption within Rome's republican institutions even though he assassinated Julius Caesar (see note to p. 48). For a consideration of the role of Brutus in Roman mythology, see M. L. Clarke, *The Noblest Roman: Marcus Brutus and His Reputation* (Ithaca: Cornell University Press, 1981); Ian Donaldson, *The Rapes of Lucretia: A Myth and Its Transformation* (Oxford: Clarendon Press, 1982); William Everdell, *The End of Kings: A History of Republics and Republicans* (New York: The Free Press, 1983); and Peter Bondanella, *The Eternal City: Roman Images in the Modern World* (Chapel Hill: University of North Carolina Press, 1987).

the death of Filippo Visconti: Filippo Maria Visconti (1392–1447; ruler of Milan from 1412 until his death). The short-lived (1447–50) Ambrosian Republic of Milan was unable to maintain freedom in the city after Visconti's death, and after leading Venetian forces against this republic, Francesco Sforza (1401–66) became the duke of Milan. Machiavelli treats the death of Visconti in his *Florentine Histories* (vi).

67 *to its former disorders*: Epaminondas, the famous Theban general, defeated Spartan troops at two great battles—Leuctra (371 BC) and Mantinea (362), although he lost his life in the latter struggle. Here Machiavelli seems to be following Polybius (vi. 43), who remarks: 'And indeed, Fortune soon proved that the successes which the Thebans gained at the time were due to the heroism of her leading men, not to the form of her constitution. It is well-known that the predominance of Thebes took its rise, attained its height and ceased with the lives of Pelopidas and Epaminondas, and we must conclude that the hegemony which she enjoyed at that time was the work of her citizens and not of her system of government' (*The Rise of The Roman Empire*, 338–9).

in greater detail: see i. 18.

70 *into a body politic*: Machiavelli employs the phrase *vivere politico*.

concerning what Cleomenes did: see i. 9, for Machiavelli's discussion of Cleomenes, Remus, and Titus.

72 *only with great effort*: Machiavelli follows the history of the succession after kings David and Solomon in 2 Chronicles 10, where

eleven of the twelve tribes of Israel revolt against Rehoboam to
rally to Jeroboam, leaving Rehoboam with a single tribe—
one-twelfth rather than one-sixth of the population if we count by
tribes.

72 *Bajazet, sultan of the Turks*: Bajazet II (1482–1512), conqueror of
Croatia, who defeated the Venetians several times at sea and caused
Pope Alexander VI in 1500 to urge Christian princes to band
together to face the Turkish menace.

his father Mahomet's labours: Mahomet II (1451–81), known as
'the Conqueror', who conquered Constantinople in 1453 as well as
Asia Minor, Serbia, Bosnia, Albania, and the Crimea and even
landed at Otranto in Italy before turning back from an Italian
invasion.

his son Selim: Selim II (1512–20), alive while Machiavelli began
writing *Discourses on Livy*, was the conqueror of the Persians, Kur-
distan, Egypt, and Syria; Machiavelli's predictions about the genius
of the Ottoman Turks were accurate, for Selim's son, Suleiman I
(1520–66), reached the outskirts of Budapest in Hungary with his
armies before turning back from further European adventures.

after him came Ancus: Ancus Marcius (640–616 BC), Rome's fourth
king, who eventually conquered the Latins when they invaded
Roman territory, misled by his peaceful manner.

73 *under the rule of the kings*: according to Livy, Rome lived under
kings for 244 years (i. 40), roughly equivalent to the period of time
it took the republic to reach its zenith of power after its victory
over the Carthaginians at the battle of Zama in 202 BC.

to conquer the world: Philip (382–336 BC) was followed by his son
Alexander the Great (356–323): the father conquered Greece and
the son subsequently conquered most of the known world.

74 *Tullus' example*: Tullus Hostilius, Rome's third king (673–642 BC).

during the Italian wars: Machiavelli's 'recent example' refers to
Henry VII's invasion of France in 1513; Machiavelli derives the
period of roughly thirty years in England by considering the end of
the Wars of the Roses (1485) as the last great English military
campaign.

the historian who writes about this feat: the historian is Plutarch,
who discusses the two rulers Pelopidas (403–364 BC) and
Epaminondas (d. 362 BC) in his *Lives*. See note to p. 67 above.

75 *his shiftless men to arms*: a reference to *Aeneid*, vi. 813–14, cited in
Latin (with a variation from Virgil's text). For a complete English

translation see Virgil, *The Aeneid*, trans. Robert Fitzgerald (New York: Vintage, 1983), 188.

became subjected to the Romans: the famous duel of the two sets of triplets from Rome and Alba is described by Livy (i. 24–6); Mettius was dictator, not king, of Alba.

the decision he took: Livy (i. 27–30) describes the indignation of the Albans and the treachery of Mettius, who was obligated to support Roman troops against the citizens of Fidenae but who held back his troops; after the Roman victory over the Fidenates, Mettius was killed by being torn between two chariots driven in opposite directions. Interestingly enough, Livy expresses his disgust at such inhuman punishment at the end of his account, while Machiavelli passes no such judgement on it.

77 *another unknown route*: after the defeat of the French at the battle of Novara in 1513, the French returned to Lombardy in 1515 through the Argentera pass, which was considered too small to be used by a large army and left unguarded by the Swiss troops defending Milan. The reference by Machiavelli to this particular battle indicates that this portion of *Discourses on Livy* was written no earlier than 1515.

80 *the rich away empty*: here Machiavelli confuses a reference from the Magnificat (Luke 1: 53), verses that refer to the Lord and not to David.

81 *Pope Julius II*: Giuliano della Rovere, who ruled as Pope Julius II from 1503 to 1513; Machiavelli's date is in error, since the pope entered Bologna in 1506; the Bentivogli family ruled Bologna from 1401 to that time, with brief interruptions.

Giovampagolo Baglioni: Baglioni (1470–1520) was a soldier of fortune who ruled Perugia from 1500 to 1506 and again from 1513 until his death.

The prudent men: among this group Machiavelli apparently numbered himself, since he was present at this memorable event in the company of the pope and describes it in some detail in his diplomatic correspondence. Julius II entered Perugia on 13 September 1506.

83 *the former*: the rape of Lucretia, the wife of L. Tarquinius Collatinus, was the immediate cause of the expulsion of the Tarquin kings and the establishment of a republic in Rome in 509 BC; Collatinus and L. Junius Brutus (the 'first' Brutus) became the republic's first consuls, but Collatinus was eventually forced to go into exile because of the hatred the people felt for the tyrants' name he bore

(Livy i. 2). For a discussion of the history of this myth, see Donaldson, *The Rapes of Lucretia: A Myth and Its Transformation* or Bondanella, *The Eternal City: Roman Images in the Modern World*.

83 *on the Caelian hill*: after the exile of Collatinus, Publius Valerius joined Brutus as consul, and when Brutus was killed in battle, Valerius remained sole consul. Livy does not mention any actual exile suffered by Publius Valerius but says, rather, that Valerius wanted to build his home on the Velia, a ridge linking the Palatine to the Esquiline hill. This massive edifice aroused popular suspicion, so Valerius pulled it down and eventually earned such popular support that he became known as Publius Valerius Publicola ('friend of the people').

84 *'is accounted gain'*: Tacitus, *The Histories* (iv. 3), cited in Latin. For the English text see *The Histories*, 204.

93 *without this open opposition*: Cosimo was exiled in 1433 but returned to Florence the following year; although he ruled Florence as if he were a prince, Cosimo never actually held such an official title. Machiavelli discusses Cosimo's rise to power in his *Florentine Histories* (especially Books IV and VII).

    began to fear Caesar too late: Cicero's *Letters To His Friends* (xvi. 11).

96 *'takes no harm'*: Machiavelli cites this formulaic pronouncement in the original Latin. It is found in Livy, iii. 4 (for this English translation, see Livy, *The Early History of Rome*, 187).

    deprived Rome of its liberty: the decemvirate, as this rule by ten citizens was called in Livy (iii. 32–44) lasted a very short time (451–450 BC); the ten citizens were dominated by Appius Claudius. Livy considers the delegation of power by the consuls to the decemvirs to be a constitutional upheaval equal to the expulsion of the Tarquin kings from Rome.

97 *material that is not corrupt*: see note to p. 62.

98 *creates friends and partisans*: see note to p. 62.

    these previously mentioned decemvirs: Machiavelli will examine the decemvirate in detail in i. 40–5.

99 *a saying of ancient writers*: if Machiavelli is citing specific authors (which is doubtful here), no modern editors have found his classical sources. It is more likely that he is strengthening the pedigree of his argument here by attributing the theory he is about to present to a classical tradition.

and the exaltation of another: in only a few brief lines, Machiavelli outlines a number of key theoretical ideas concerning political psychology, political economy, and political conflict. Human desire is limitless (a product of nature and a given in human psychology), but the object of such desire is limited (economics teaches that resources and wealth are scarce); given the conflict of human nature and human economics, political conflict is the natural and inevitable result.

100 *two principal provisions*: Machiavelli's historical explanations here are somewhat confusing. The first agrarian law mentioned by Livy (ii. 41) is that passed in 486 BC by the consul Spurius Cassius, who intended to assign captured lands to the plebeians; patrician objections to this plan were so strenuous that when the consul's term of office expired, he was indicted for seeking to become king and was subsequently executed. Machiavelli's description of the agrarian laws here seems closer to the laws proposed by C. Licinius and L. Sextius in 367 BC, which prohibited any citizen from holding more than 500 *jugera* of such public land (a *juger* being the amount of land a yoke (*juger*) of oxen could plough in a day). This issue would be capable of arousing political passions in Rome for many years to come: one of the controversial reforms proposed by the tribunes Tiberius Sempronius Gracchus and Caius Gracchus in 133 BC was the revival of the Licinian law of 367 BC. Gracchus modified the law, allowing a father with one son to hold an extra 250 *jugera* and an additional 250 *jugera* if he had a second son, for a total of 1,000. All families holding more than 1,000 *jugera* or individuals with more than 500 were to lose the surplus without compensation if they had purchased the extra land. The legislation was thus too 'retroactive', in Machiavelli's view, because it failed to adapt an old law to new and different circumstances: the proof of this lay in the fact that when Gracchus was nominated for the tribune the year afterwards, a riot ensued in which he and several hundred citizens were killed. Machiavelli takes most of these details from Plutarch's account of the Gracchi in his *Lives*.

in Antium: Antium (modern Anzio) was captured in 467 BC. See Livy, iii. 1.

101 *on three other occasions*: Marius was first elected consul in 107 BC, then five times in a row from 104 to 100; the final occasion was in 88, in opposition to Sulla.

turned to favour Sulla: L. Cornelius Sulla (138–78 BC), head of the aristocratic faction in Rome; after overcoming Marius and Cinna,

Sulla remained in control of Rome until he stepped down from power in 79, a year before his death.

101 *came out the winner*: Pompey was defeated at the battle of Pharsalus and killed in Egypt in 48 BC.

103 *Duke Valentino*: Cesare Borgia (1475–1507), son of Pope Alessandro VI, who was named duke of Valentinois in 1498 by the French king, and who held Romagna and much of central Italy until the pope's death in 1503. For Machiavelli's judgement of this historical figure, see *The Prince* (VII), an evaluation based upon his earlier diplomatic letters and several minor political treatises, in particular *A Description of the Method Used by Duke Valentino in Killing Vitellozzo Vitelli, Oliverotto da Fermo, and Others* (1503), or *On the Method of Dealing with the Rebellious Peoples of the Valdichiana* (1503). Borgia is always held up by Machiavelli as the most useful model of the 'new' prince who gains power with the assistance of others (in this case, the help of his father). For a consideration of the figure of Cesare Borgia in Machiavelli's writings, see Peter Bondanella, *Machiavelli and the Art of Renaissance History* (Detroit: Wayne State University Press, 1974).

had taken Faenza: Faenza fell to Borgia on 26 April 1501.

to come to terms with him: Bologna's ruler, Giovanni Bentivogli, was forced to cede to Borgia troops and fortified positions on 29 April 1501.

104 *and left in disgrace*: on 30 June the French troops tried to breach the city walls but withdrew when they began to take casualties; after the Swiss mercenaries in their ranks rebelled over a pay dispute, the French lifted the siege on 10 July.

106 *Signoria*: the Signoria was Florence's most important city-state governmental body and was controlled by the wealthy members of the major city guilds. Its members were elected for brief terms and were eventually housed together in one of the city's most famous landmarks—the Palazzo della Signoria, better known after the sixteenth century as the Palazzo Vecchio—in the centre of Florence.

the magistracy of the Ten: Machiavelli knew a great deal about this particular Florentine institution, since he served as its secretary.

Terentillus, a tribune: Gaius Terentillus Arsa in 462 BC (Livy, iii. 9).

they re-created the consuls: from 448 to 368 BC, consuls generally were substituted by tribunes with consular powers; such tribunes with consular power were abolished by the Licinian law of 367 BC, which opened the consulate to the plebeians.

107 *base Roman laws upon them*: Livy (iii. 31) says the Romans sent
Spurius Postumius Albus, Aulus Manlius, and Publius Sulpicius
Camerinus to Athens.

a shrewd but restless man: Appius Claudius and the other
decemvirs were appointed in 451 BC.

108 *lictors . . . as their leader*: lictors were attendants who carried the
fasces (a bundle of wooden rods and a single-headed axe), the symbol of magisterial authority. Roman consuls had twelve of these
lictors who announced their approach, cleared a path for them, and
carried out their orders to summon, arrest, and even to execute.

'without some ulterior motive': cited in Latin from Livy, iii. 35. For
this and the following quotations, see Livy, *The Early History of
Rome*, 222–4.

109 *'to liberty for all'*: Livy, iii. 37, cited in Latin; Livy's text is actually
somewhat different from the text Machiavelli cites, and in the English translation reads: 'The decemvirs' young toadies were easily
corrupted by such pay, and, far from making any attempt to check
their masters' brutal conduct, openly rejoiced in it; for them, personal immunity in crime was a more agreeable thing than national
liberty.' *The Early History of Rome*, 224.

the Sabines and the Volscians: Machiavelli's memory fails him here,
for Livy says that the Sabines and the Aequi attacked Rome (iii. 38).

in particular Valerius and Horatius: Lucius Valerius Potitus and
Marcus Horatius Barbatus (Livy, iii. 39).

110 *Mons Sacer*: a hill near Rome, just beyond the Anio River.

111 *Nabis, tyrant of Sparta*: Nabis was king of Sparta from 206 to
192 BC. Machiavelli underlines the importance of the support of
the people in a prince's defence of his rule in *The Prince* (IX).

112 *King Ferdinand*: either Ferdinand the Catholic (Ferdinand II of
Aragon, 1474–1516), or Ferdinand I of Aragon, ruler of Naples
from 1458 until 1494.

115 *'so bitterly to hate'*: Livy, iii. 53, cited in Latin. See *The Early History of Rome*, 242. A more literal translation would be: 'In con-
demning cruelty, you rush to act cruelly.'

116 *After 1494*: in 1494 the Florentines sent the Medici family into
exile and restored a broader republican form of government, which
in its initial stages was heavily influenced by Girolamo
Savonarola's followers and the friar's political ideas.

five citizens: Bernardo del Nero, Niccolò Ridolfi, Lorenzo
Tornabuoni, Giannozzo Pucci, and Giovanni Cambi were

arrested for plotting to bring Piero de' Medici back to power and were executed in 1497.

117 *an edict*: Livy (iii. 59) discusses this edict issued in 449 BC.

his precise words: Machiavelli's entire discussion in this chapter refers to Livy's remarks in iii. 56: 'True moderation in the defense of political liberties is indeed a difficult thing: pretending to want fair shares for all, every man raises himself by depressing his neighbor; our anxiety to avoid oppression leads us to practice it ourselves; the injustice we repel, we visit in turn upon others, as if there were no choice except either to do it or to suffer it' (*The Early History of Rome*, 257).

118 *'good beginnings'*: See Sallust, *The Conspiracy of Catiline*, 51.

119 *'when the fight is over'*: Machiavelli cites Livy's text (iv. 6) in Latin, with some variations. See *The Early History of Rome*, 276–7.

'in one single man': cited in Latin from Livy, iv. 6. See *The Early History of Rome*, 277.

120 *inside the palace*: the Curia in the Roman Forum.

121 *'find in them'*: unlike most of the quotations that are taken directly from Livy in the original Latin, in this case Machiavelli creates his own Italian speech from material he found in Livy's original (xiii. 2–4). Livy criticizes Pacuvius as a demagogue and a manipulator intent upon building his own personal power, however, and does not recount the story as a positive example. Machiavelli, incidentally, calls the character Pacuvius Calanus, whereas his true name was Pacuvius Calavius Campanus.

123 *when they created the censors*: in 443 BC.

the dictator: Manlius Aemilius Mamercus, military tribune and dictator in 433 BC.

either the historian was incomplete: this criticism of Livy's reliability as a historian is unusual in Machiavelli and demonstrates that, unlike some of his humanist predecessors, he could cast a critical eye on his source. Contrast, in *Inferno*, xxviii. 12, Dante's remark: 'as Livy's history tells, that does not err' (Dante, *The Divine Comedy: Inferno*, trans. Mark Musa (New York: Penguin, 1984), 325).

124 *by the powerful citizens*: in his *Florentine Histories* (i. 5), Machiavelli recounts that in 1250 Florence created two foreign judges: one called the 'Captain of the People', the other the 'Podestà'. In fact, the second office was in existence before 1250.

125 *ten citizens*: this occurred in 1310.

the Council of Forty: the Quarantìa functioned as a kind of supreme court and was first established in 1179 and therefore predates the Council of the Ten. After the closing of the Great Council in 1296, which limited participation in the government, the Quarantìa was assigned the crucial task of determining which of the Venetian inhabitants by right belonged to this oligarchic establishment and could be considered citizens.

Council of the Pregadi: the Council of the Pregadi or the Pregai was a senate of sixty members which served as an advisory body when 'requested' (*pregadi*) by the Doge to render judgements for the Grand Council.

were consuls: 431 BC.

128 *served him best*: for a detailed discussion about the various ways patrician opponents reacted to Cosimo's power and Machiavelli's critique of Cosimo's enforced exile in 1433, see *Florentine Histories*, iv. 27–8.

came to ruin: see note to p. 23.

129 *Hirtius and Pansa*: after the murder of Julius Caesar in 44 BC, Mark Antony was declared a public enemy and the two consuls, C. Vibius Pansa and A. Hirtius, waged war upon his army, defeating him at the battle of Mutina in 43 BC but dying in the struggle. Cicero urged the senate to give command of the army to Octavian, but when Octavian fell out with the senate and came to a reconciliation with Mark Antony through the mediation of Lepidus, the three men formed the triumvirate that was to govern for the next five years. One of Mark Antony's demands for this agreement was the execution of Cicero, whose head and hands were displayed in the Roman Forum.

130 *to their life*: Machiavelli confuses *On Monarchy* with Dante's *Convivio* (The Banquet), i. 11.

before their downfall: Machiavelli refers to the League of Cambrai, formed on 10 December 1508 by the pope, the emperor, the king of France, the duke of Savoy, the duke of Ferrara, and the marquis of Mantua against the Venetians, who had refused to return territory taken from the duke of Ferrara at the request of Pope Julius II; the Venetians were excommunicated and suffered a major military defeat at the battle of Agnadello on 14 May 1509 (see note to p. 37 above), which curtailed their power on the Italian mainland for an entire decade until the league members began to quarrel among themselves.

131 *the fall of Rome*: Quintus Fabius Maximus was made consul in 217 BC, and his master of the horse was Marcus Minucius Rufus.

'Fabian' or delaying tactics have ever since described the Roman consul's cautious but successful policy of refusing to give Hannibal the opportunity of a victory in the field by wearing him down on foreign soil. When the Romans preferred to act with their usual impetuosity and failed to follow the advice of Fabius, disaster ensued: in 216 BC Varro and his army were routed at the battle of Cannae, with enormous casualties on the Roman side.

131 *were routed and killed*: in 212 BC, in an attempt to lift the siege of Capua, a foolhardy centurion named Marcus Centennius Paenula offered to attack Hannibal with volunteers but was immediately destroyed by Carthaginian forces (Livy, xxv. 19).

Nicias: an Athenian general (470–413 BC) described in Plutarch's *Lives*, where he is compared to the unlucky Roman general Crassus, who perished in Parthia in 53 BC.

132 *please the people*: the arguments of Fabius Maximus and Scipio Africanus (the latter of whom prevailed in this instance) may be found outlined in lengthy speeches in Livy, xxviii. It is important to note that Machiavelli praises both Fabius Maximus and Scipio Africanus because their personality traits (temporizing in the first case and bold impetuosity in the second) were successful when the times in question required them. The obvious difficulty lies in discerning exactly when a particular character trait is in tune with the times.

of the commander: after taking Torre a San Vincenzo in the Maremma on 17 August 1505, Florentine troops besieged Pisa unsuccessfully.

among the people: for a detailed account of this incident, see Francesco Guicciardini, *The History of Florence*, Book XXVI.

133 *'Willing to stop and listen'*: Virgil, *Aeneid*, i. 151–2 (p. 8 of the Fitzgerald translation).

the Arrabbiati: the *Frateschi* or *Piagnoni* ('Weepers') were the followers of Savonarola, while the *Arrabbiati* ('Enraged') opposed the friar's policies.

Francesco: 1453–1524; one of the staunch supporters of Savonarola.

to go to Veii: a proposed immigration to Veii was discussed in *Discourses on Livy*, i. 53; Machiavelli originally found mention of this in Livy, v. 51–5.

138 *into Italy*: in his Lenten sermons in 1492 Savonarola warned the Florentines of a 'new Cyrus' who would march through Italy

without any opposition; Charles VIII, king of France from 1483 to 1498, invaded Italy in 1494 and rapidly became master of Naples by May 1494; returning to France, he was blocked by the Holy League, an alliance of Italian states (principally Venice with Milanese troops) at Fornovo (6 July 1495), a battle from which Charles emerged victorious and continued his march back to France. At Fornovo the Italians lost their best opportunity to keep foreigners out of their territory during the early sixteenth century.

Lorenzo de' Medici the elder: therefore not Lorenzo the Duke of Urbino (d. 1519), to whom *The Prince* was eventually dedicated, but the more famous Lorenzo il Magnifico (d. 1492).

by lightning: according to contemporary chronicles, this occurred on 4 November 1511.

139 *coming to Rome*: this story may be found in Livy, v. 32.

'for himself': Livy, vi. 4, cited in Latin but from an edition that is substantially different from the modern critical edition in this passage. See Livy, *Rome and Italy*, 42.

140 *to save themselves*: see Livy, i. 50-1; earlier (*Discourses on Livy*, i. 44) Machiavelli cites the example of Virginia in discussing how a crowd is useless without a leader.

141 *'regretted their loss'*: Livy, vi. 20, cited in Latin. See *Rome and Italy*, 64.

'a cruel master': Livy, xxiv. 25, cited in Latin. For the English text which we cite throughout, see Livy, *The War With Hannibal: Books XXI–XXX of 'The History of Rome from its Foundation'*, trans. Aubrey De Selincourt (New York: Penguin, 1965), 262.

142 *as Herod did with Mariamne*: Cleitus, some twenty years older than Alexander, and whose sister had been the young ruler's wet-nurse, saved Alexander's life at the battle of Granicus in 334 BC, but some years later at a banquet he expressed the Macedonians' dissatisfaction with what they felt was an endless series of wars fought only for Alexander's glory. This incensed Alexander who killed him with a spear in a fit of anger but was immediately so sorry for his deed that his own men had to prevent him from committing suicide. See Plutarch's *Lives* for the details. Mariamne (or Marianne, as Machiavelli actually writes her name) was the wife of Herod the Great, king of Judea from 40 to 4 BC, who put his wife to death in 29 BC in a fit of anger but later repented his hasty deed. Machiavelli probably found this story in Josephus' *The Jewish War* (Book I).

143 *less ungrateful than princes*: see *Discourses on Livy*, i. 29.

146 *his entire army*: Demetrius (337–283 BC), called Poliorecetes or
     Conqueror of Cities, was king of Macedonia between 294 and
     283 BC. For details, see Plutarch, *Lives*.

     he was killed by him: after the defeat of Pompey (106–48 BC) at the
     battle of Pharsalus, Pompey took refuge with Ptolemy XII, whose
     father he had been instrumental in restoring to the throne of Egypt,
     but Romans in the king's employ murdered Pompey as he pre-
     pared to speak to the king.

     Saguntum in Spain: Saguntum was faithful to its alliance with
     Rome but was captured in 218 BC by Hannibal (see Livy, xxi).

147 *completely rejected it for that reason*: this incident is recounted in
     Plutarch's *Lives*, but some scholars believe that Machiavelli may
     have read of it in Cicero's *De officiis* (On duties) (iii. 49).

     'not of birth': Machiavelli's version of this speech (given in Latin) is
     briefer but more dramatic than the original in Livy (vii. 32). The
     complete text in English translation is: 'But today the consulship is
     open to all, to us patricians and to you plebeians, and is the reward
     not of birth, as before, but of merit' (Livy, *Rome and Italy*, 141).

     on another occasion: *Discourses on Livy*, i. 6.

148 *argued elsewhere*: in *Discourses on Livy*, i. 6.

150 *entered Italy and Rome*: in tracing the evolution of exceptional abil-
     ity (*virtù*) through the ancient world, Machiavelli skips over Greece.

     the Roman empire of the east: in this passage Machiavelli refers to
     the people commanded by Charlemagne, the Mameluks of Egypt,
     and the Swiss as well as the Germans (Germany in Machiavelli's
     works always includes the free cities of Switzerland). The Saracen
     'sect' is, of course, Islam, but it was the Ottoman Turks who finally
     destroyed the Byzantine Empire.

151 *human appetites are insatiable*: Machiavelli's political theory rests
     upon a fundamental chain of logic: a psychological principle
     (human nature cannot be satiated) conflicts with an economic fact
     (scarce resources), resulting in a political situation (conflict is uni-
     versal and inevitable). Nowhere in his various political writings
     does this association of human psychology and political economy
     emerge more clearly than in this passage.

152 *the expansion of their empire*: the reader is reminded that Machi-
     avelli understands the Roman republic's establishment of an
     empire as one of its most positive attributes and that republicanism
     (not democracy) is his preferred political credo.

Ability or Fortune?: in *The Prince*, Machiavelli discussed the relationship of *virtù* and *fortuna* in the character of the individual political leader; now he turns to consider the relationship of the two concepts in the operation of a model political system from the ancient world.

Plutarch, a most authoritative writer: in his *Moralia* Plutarch discusses several arguments to support the idea that Rome rose to power because of fortune's favours rather than through ability.

155 *on principalities*: see Machiavelli, *The Prince*, chapters III–V, for a discussion of the conditions under which various occupations of foreign territory by the Romans and other modern rulers occurred.

of the Capuans: Livy (vii. 29–32) discusses how the Sidicini, attacked by the Samnites, appealed to the Capuans, who in turn appealed to Rome when they found themselves in military difficulty around 340 BC.

of the Camertines: the alliance of the Romans and the Camertines against the Etruscans took place around 310 BC (Livy, ix. 36).

of the Mamertines: originally mercenary troops employed by Agathocles in Sicily, the Mamertines seized Messina in 289 BC; after being threatened by the Carthaginians in 264 BC, they asked Rome for help, thereby bringing about the First Punic War (264–241 BC), which Livy treated in a section of his history of Rome, Books XVI–XIX, subsequently lost to posterity. Machiavelli, however, would have found the cause of this war discussed in Polybius (i. 8).

of the Saguntines: see Livy, xxi. 6, for a discussion of how Saguntum, attacked by Hannibal in 219 BC, appealed to Rome before being captured by the Carthaginians; the city was recovered in 212 BC by Gnaeus, brother of Publius Cornelius Scipio, the father of Scipio Africanus (Livy, xxiv. 42).

with that of Masinissa: Masinissa, the king of Numidia, deserted Carthage and joined the Romans in 204 BC when they invaded Africa, recovering his kingdom in 203 BC after the defeat of Syphax.

of the Aetolians: in 211 BC (Livy, xxvi. 24; see also *The Prince*, III). The Romans formed an alliance with the Aetolian League against Philip of Macedonia, an act that eventually led to Roman occupation of the Greek peninsula.

and other Asian princes: in 193 BC Eumenes II, king of Pergamum, encouraged the Romans to wage war upon Antiochus and was eventually given vast dominions in Asia as his reward (Livy, xxxvii. 37-45).

155 *the Massilienses and the Aedui*: the Massilienses, natives of Massilia (modern Marseilles) were Greeks living in southern France who aided the Romans in the Second Punic War, and subsequently appealed to Rome for assistance in both 154 and 125 BC. The Aedui, a Gallic tribe, were Julius Caesar's closest ally during his Gallic campaigns.

156 *throughout the provinces*: Machiavelli believed that truly free cities like those he discerned in antiquity existed only outside of Italy in Germany (which, for Machiavelli, also included Switzerland). Note that his use of the word 'province' refers to Roman provinces.

157 *from the tyranny of Pisistratus*: roughly from 510 BC until Athens fell under Spartan domination in 404 BC.

Xenophon's treatise entitled 'On Tyranny': the *Hiero*, a Socratic dialogue on tyranny, featured Hiero of Syracuse, a historical figure frequently mentioned by Machiavelli, as one of its interlocutors. The work was translated into Latin during the Quattrocento by Leonardo Bruni.

158 *under the debris*: this occurred around 425 BC on the island of Corfu.

to take away from you: here, as elsewhere in Machiavelli's theoretical works, the writer shifts from the abstract consideration of political events to an intimate, more personal address to his reader.

the pagans: see note to p. 53.

160 *by Roman skill*: Livy (x. 31) arrives at the figure of forty-six years by counting the forty-eight years from 343 to 295 BC minus two years of truce. After the First (343–341), Second (326–304), and Third Samnite Wars (298–293), which concluded with the decisive Roman victories at Sentinum (295) and Aquilonia (293), the Samnites became part of Rome.

'in the size of Rome': cited in Latin from Livy, i. 30. See Livy, *The Early History of Rome*, 67. Some of Machiavelli's modern commentators believe that the location of such a Latin quotation from Livy at the beginning of a chapter may reflect a remnant of the early purpose of his *Discourses on Livy*, a strict commentary upon the Latin text, rather than the more complicated political treatise the intended commentary eventually became.

162 *its sixth king*: Servius Tullius (Livy, i. 44).

so that the sap: here Machiavelli employs the word *virtù* to refer to the sap within a healthy plant. Normally, this key concept in Machiavelli's political theory must be translated as ingenuity, strength, exceptional ability, and only rarely (if ever) as 'virtue'.

use only leather money: Seneca (*De Beneficiis*, v. 14) states that the Spartans were obliged to pay their debts either in gold or in leather bearing an official stamp. In the biography of Lycurgus in Plutarch's *Lives*, the historian claims that the ruler introduced a large iron coin too bulky to carry off in any great quantity.

163 *'in the size of Rome'*: here Machiavelli repeats the original Latin sentence found in Livy, i. 30 (see note to p. 161 above). Such a repetition in the body of a chapter implies that this particular section of the work was probably never extensively revised in Machiavelli's transition from a strict commentary on Livy to a political treatise on republics only occasioned, in part, by Livy's history.

168 *Diodorus Siculus*: the author of a universal history in Greek, covering mythological times to 60 BC. In spite of its fragmentary condition, the *Bibliotheke* ('Library') is the most extensively preserved of all classical historical works by a Greek author. Diodorus settled in Rome *c.*56 BC and had completed his history by 30 BC.

172 *in our system, of . . .*: in Livy (v. 30), the text reads *septena iugera*, but a variant text (apparently employed by Machiavelli) also reads *terna iugera et septunces*. Machiavelli left this passage unfinished, meaning to return to it eventually, filling in the modern equivalents in Italian measurements. According to some estimates, the amount is roughly 1 hectare or 2.471 acres.

173 *for their safety*: the closing paragraph of Sallust's *Jugurthine War* (xiv) discusses how Rome's terrified reaction to the military defeats of two Roman consuls at the battle of Arausio produced this special fear of the Gauls (actually Sallust incorrectly identifies as 'Gauls' two other tribes, the Cimbri and the Teutones).

against Rome: this siege of Rome took place in 390 BC.

200,000 Gauls: Livy's record of the second Gallic War (226–222 BC) is lost. While the casualties were enormous in this war, Machiavelli may be confusing these figures with estimates associated with casualties from the invasion of the Teutonian and Cimbric tribes that the Roman general Marius annihilated at the battle of Aquae Sextiae in 102 BC, which Machiavelli mentions in the next sentence.

174 *from Syria*: the exploits of Belisarius, the Byzantine warrior who defeated the Vandals in AD 534 are described in the *Gothic Wars* by

his secretary, the Greek historian Procopius. Machiavelli cites in Latin from the translation *De bello italico adversus Gothos* (iv. 10).

175   *which they had come*: According to Livy (i. 1), Aeneas was welcomed by the Latin king in Italy; Procopius and Justinian (xviii. 5) describe how Dido founded Carthage with the consent of her African neighbours. The Massilienses were Greeks settlers who reportedly founded the ancient city which eventually became Marseilles in France. According to popular legend, they were welcomed by the area's original inhabitants.

177   *inhabitants of Capua*: that is, the Campanians mentioned earlier.

      who was attacking them: after their defeat at the battle of Altopascio in 1325 by Castruccio Castracani, lord of Lucca, the Guelph government in Florence gave the duke of Calabria (the son of King Robert of Naples) the *signoria* of the city for a period of ten years, although he died in 1328. For Machiavelli's biography of Castruccio Castracani, shaped by both stylistic means and changes in historical facts to make him the archetypal Renaissance prince, see *The Life of Castruccio Castracani* in *The Portable Machiavelli*, 518–47.

      without fighting: we know very little about Quintus Curtius Rufus except that he was the author of a life of Alexander the Great, several editions of which existed in Renaissance Italy after its initial discovery in 1470. The available critical edition of this text, however, lacks precisely the episode in question, the rebellion of Agis III, king of Sparta, against Antipater, one of Alexander's generals, whose death in 331 BC occurred not a few days before the news of Alexander's death reached Greece, as Machiavelli claims, but some eight years before. Machiavelli may have been reading a now-lost Renaissance manuscript in which this lacuna did not exist.

178   *in the war over Urbino*: in 1476 Charles the Bold, duke of Burgundy, was defeated by the Swiss and killed; the pope in question is Leo X (1513–21), a member of the Medici family. This particular passage is important for the dating of the composition of the *Discourses on Livy*, since we know that Francesco Maria della Rovere had regained control of Urbino in September 1517 after that duchy had been given in August 1516 by Pope Leo X to his nephew, Lorenzo de' Medici, the duke of Urbino (1491–1519), the same person to whom Machiavelli dedicated the final edition of *The Prince* between 1516 and 1519.

      in their defence: the Venetians lost many of their possessions on the mainland after the battle of Agnadello in 1509 (see notes to pp. 37, 130).

179 *that Spartan king*: Machiavelli returns to his previous example of Agis III, king of Sparta (see note to p. 177 above).

as happened to Hasdrubal: in 207 BC, according to Livy (xxvii. 48), Hasdrubal, Hannibal's brother, made this fateful decision, which cost him his life, when he engaged the troops of the two Roman consuls on the Metaurus River.

180 *without ever mentioning money*: Livy's famous discussion of Alexander the Great and the Romans may be found in ix. 17–18. His conclusion is that Rome would have triumphed over Alexander the Great.

if they wished to save themselves: see Livy, vii. 30.

'to protect their allies': cited in Latin from Livy, vii. 29, this remark is also paraphrased by Machiavelli in Latin two additional times in this chapter. See Livy, *Rome and Italy*, 135.

'than actual strength': in 1478 Pope Sixtus IV placed Florence under an interdict following the repression by the Medici of the Pazzi Conspiracy; papal forces commanded by Alfonso, eldest son of Ferdinand of Aragon, king of Naples, and Federico da Montefeltro, lord of Urbino, invaded Tuscany before Lorenzo de' Medici sued for peace by going to Rome. Machiavelli discusses this war in *Florentine Histories*, viii. 10–18.

Maximilian the emperor: the Habsburg ruler reigned from 1493 until his death on 12 January 1519, and since Machiavelli speaks of him as if he were alive in this passage, this internal evidence suggests that this part of the *Discourses on Livy* was composed before 1519.

181 *the Capuans offered to the Sidicini*: since Capua was the major city of Campania, the Capuans are the same Campanians mentioned by Machiavelli in the first sentence of this chapter.

182 *also cite the example of Agathocles*: this tyrant ruled Syracuse from 316 to 289 BC, and is cited by Machiavelli in his famous discussion in *The Prince* (IX) as the perfect example of a ruler who came to power through wickedness, in the ancient world.

and lost their liberty: according to Thucydides (vii. 82–7), the Athenian army invaded Sicily in 415 BC during the seventeenth year of the Peloponnesian War, and was either destroyed in the field or made prisoner in several campaigns it lost to Syracuse, resulting in the decline of Athens as a major power in the Greek world.

from the earth: the Labours of Hercules (discussed in Apollodorus, ii. 5 and Diodorus Siculus, iv), include Hercules's wrestling match with Antaeus, the Libyan giant who was the son of Poseidon and Ge. The image of Hercules wrestling with Antaeus became well known in the Renaissance, particularly on medals. 'Hercules the Egyptian' (*Ercole Egizio*) might refer to the fact that this encounter took place while he was crossing North Africa (in the legend his next act is the slaying of Busiris, king of Egypt), and could be taken to mean 'Hercules *in* Egypt'.

183 *along with his state*: Naples had five kings between 1494 and 1496: Ferdinando I, who ruled from 1458 until his death in 1494; his son Alfonso II, who succeeded his father in 1494 and abdicated in 1495, dying at the end of that year; Alfonso's son, Ferdinando II, who ruled for several months in 1495 and again for several months in 1496, when he died; Charles VIII of Anjou, the king of France, who captured Naples in February of 1495 and held it until July of the same year (he died in 1498); and finally Frederick, the son of Ferdinando I, who ruled Naples from 1496 until 1501, when he was deposed and succeeded by Louis XII of France.

184 *in those nearby*: Castruccio Castracani waged war on Florence in 1325 (see *Florentine Histories*, ii. 29–30), forcing the Florentines to seek the support of King Robert of Naples and the protection of his son Charles, duke of Calabria, who came to the city with troops to defend it against Castruccio. Florence waged war against Giangaleazzo Visconti, lord of Milan from 1385 until 1402, but never succeeded in deposing him from power in Milan (see *Florentine Histories*, iii. 25).

1,800,000 armed men: this figure may be an error; 800,000 armed men would be more likely a total, even though it, too, seems exaggerated.

185 *they destroyed the Cimbri*: the Romans annihilated the Cimbri at the battle of Campi Raudii in 101 BC (the battle took place on a field between the modern cities of Turin and Milan).

186 *Messer Bernarbò*: Giangaleazzo Visconti seized control of Milan in 1385 and was made first duke of Milan.

forced to come to terms: according to Livy (vii. 33–7), the Romans defeated the Samnites at Mount Gaurus and Suessela in 343 BC during the First Samnite War (343–341).

187 *'a fair treaty, etc.'*: Livy, viii. 4, cited in Latin. See Livy, *Rome and Italy*, 161.

'with their own?': Livy, viii. 4, cited in Latin but abbreviated somewhat. See *Rome and Italy*, 161.

189 *'our plans in order'*: Livy, viii. 4, cited in Latin. See *Rome and Italy*, 161.

190 *to result from it*: Hieronymus was murdered in 215 BC; although Apollonides advised the Syracusans to continue their half-century alliance with Rome, they decided to throw their lot in with Carthage in 214 BC (see Livy, xxiv. 28). The result was the famous siege of Syracuse by Marcellus, in which Livy describes the invaluable assistance of the scientist Archimedes to the Syracusan cause. Syracuse finally fell to Rome in 212 BC.

'with the Roman people': Machiavelli cites this passage from Livy (viii. 11), but translates it himself into Italian rather than quoting the original Latin as he so often does elsewhere in the *Discourses on Livy*. This suggests that he may have ultimately intended to translate all the Latin passages he includes in his text before a final draft was completed.

against Ludovico, duke of Milan: after Louis XII became king of France in 1498, he also assumed the title of duke of Milan, and with the support of the Venetians and Pope Alexander VI he invaded Italy in 1499, seizing Milan in September of that year from Ludovico Sforza, Il Moro. Ludovico attempted to retake the city from the French in 1500 but was captured at the battle of Novara and died in captivity in 1508. He is best known for his patronage of Leonardo da Vinci as well as for having been the instigator of the disastrous foreign invasions of Italy that destroyed its independence at the beginning of the sixteenth century. The causes of these invasions and their calamitous results provide Machiavelli with a primary motivation for writing about politics, not only in the *Discourses on Livy* but also in *The Prince*, *The Art of War*, and the *Florentine Histories*.

for a similar reason: besides losing the goodwill of their French ally, Florence was obliged to pay the French a large sum (25,000 gold florins) that they had owed to the Duchy of Milan. Machiavelli refers here to the fall of the Florentine republic in 1512, which he and others attributed to the vacillation of its executive officer, Piero Soderini, for whom Machiavelli served as an assistant.

191 *in another chapter*: *Discourses on Livy*, i. 38.

the other killed his son: as reported by Livy (viii. 3–10), the two consuls Titus Manlius Torquatus and Publius Decius Mus decided that, because the two armies engaged in battle were so similar, no private combat without specific orders was permitted on pain of death, and that if either flank commanded by a consul were to give way, that consul would sacrifice himself to restore discipline. The flank commanded by Publius Decius did give way and he threw himself into the battle to meet his death. Titus Manlius Torquatus ordered his own son to be executed for disobeying the orders against single combat even though he had emerged victorious. The second example of stern Roman discipline became famous after Livy's report of it and found expression in many works of Renaissance art of republican inspiration. See Bondanella, *The Eternal City: Roman Images in the Modern World*, for a discussion of this tradition.

192 *had its own cavalry*: Leslie J. Walker's commentary on the *Discourses on Livy* suggests that these terms are of Etruscan origin and can be rendered by the contemporary terms 'vanguard', 'second line', and 'rear guard'. For his discussion, see Leslie J. Walker (ed.), *The Discourses of Niccolò Machiavelli* (London: Routledge & Kegan Paul, 1950), ii. 118.

193 *'our last card'*: see Livy, viii. 8.

194 *than in depth*: at the battle of Ravenna, fought on 11 April 1512, French forces led by Gaston de Foix emerged victorious against the armies of the Holy League (Spain, the pope, Venice), but the bloody cost of the victory and the loss of the French general soon led Louis XII to abandon Italy.

195 *called giornate*: a gallicism, *journées* or days.

and fatti d'arme: feats of arms.

199 *from sword wounds and not from cannon shot*: Count Ludovico died in 1509; Louis d'Armagnac, the duke de Nemours and French viceroy of Naples, was killed in 1503 at the battle of Cerignola, where Spanish troops defeated the French and took possession of Neapolitan territory.

200 *against Sophy and the Sultan*: the 'Turk' refers to Selim I (Sultan of Turkey from 1512 to 1520), who defeated the Shah of Persia (Sophy), Ismail I, in 1514, and the Mameluk sultan (the 'Sultan') of Egypt and Syria in 1516.

201 *near Lake Regillus*: this battle of 496 BC is described in Livy, ii. 20.

'in chains': Livy, xxii. 49; this is an unusual passage, since Machiavelli both cites the Latin original (albeit in a slightly altered form) and then provides an Italian translation in the text itself. The battle of Cannae took place in 216 BC.

202 *some twenty-five years ago*: it is possible that the text of the *Dis-*

courses on Livy is corrupted at this point, since elsewhere (*The Prince*, XII; *Florentine Histories*, v) Machiavelli dates the origins of mercenary soldiers in Italy as far earlier than a mere two-and-one-half decades before the composition of this work (see Giorgio Inglese's note in *Discorsi*, 430).

204 *north of Milan*: the battle of Novara took place on 6 June 1513; this battle of Marignano took place on 13 September 1515. Machiavelli fails to mention a crucial fact about the lack of Swiss cavalry: after their defeat of the French at Novara, because the Swiss lacked cavalry to pursue the routed French forces the French army escaped complete destruction.

205 *remained alive*: Filippo Visconti, duke of Milan from 1402 until 1447, employed Count Francesco Bussone, known as Il Carmignuola, as his mercenary commander until 1424; the battle in question is that of Arbedo, fought in 1422. After passing from service with the Visconti to that of his Venetian enemy, Bussone was eventually executed in 1432 by the Venetians, who suspected him of double dealing. In the nineteenth century a famous tragedy based upon this mercenary soldier's life was written by Alessandro Manzoni.

may bring him strength and prestige: here the Italian uses 'him' rather than 'them'; it is not uncommon for Machiavelli to shift from the plural to the singular and vice versa; indeed, such sudden grammatical shifts, such as moving from an abstract statement ('one must . . .') to a direct address to the reader ('you must . . .'), are typical of the rhetorical style of his greatest prose works. In general, we have translated such passages so as to read correctly in English.

206 *how Lucullus*: Machiavelli relies on Plutarch's *Lives* for this description of a battle fought against Tigranes, king of Armenia, in 69 BC near Tigranocerta. Plutarch says, however, that Tigranes lost 150,000 infantry and 55,000 mounted soldiers, not 150,000 cavalry.

207 *called the Swiss*: the first Swiss confederation was formed in 1291 by the cantons of Uri, Schwytz, and Unterwalden.

208 *'forgot their homeland'*: Livy, vii. 38, cited in Latin. See Livy, *Rome and Italy*, 149.

209 *'avenging the conquered world'*: from Juvenal's *Satires*, vi. 291–2, cited in Latin, although Machiavelli adds 'gluttony' to the original. For the complete English text, see *The Satires of Juvenal*, trans. Rolfe Humphries (Bloomington: Indiana University Press, 1958), 74.

another work of mine: Machiavelli treats this question not only in *The Prince* (XII, XIII), but also in *The Art of War*, a work published in 1521 and one of only a few of his writings that appeared in print during his lifetime.

210 *we deal with conspiracies*: see *Discourses on Livy*, iii. 6.

as a garrison: Polybius (i. 7) describes how the people of Rhegium (today Reggio in Calabria) lost control to a Roman garrison between 279 and 271 BC, when Roman troops retook the city and sent many of the rebels to Rome for execution.

212 *'to be widely felt'*: cited in Latin from Livy (ii. 20). See *Rome and Italy*, 246.

213 *amply discussed in the appropriate place*: see *Discourses on Livy*, iii. 16.

defeated by the Romans: according to Livy (viii. 11), after suffering one defeat by the Romans, the Latins were persuaded by Numisius to offer battle to the Romans again and were defeated by Manlius Torquatus at the battle of Trifanum in 340 BC.

214 *after Louis XII died*: the French monarch died on 31 December 1514.

an agreement with the church: this occurred following the battle of Marignano in September 1515.

215 *'equally intolerable'*: Livy, viii. 13, cited in Latin. See *Rome and Italy*, 176. The fact that Machiavelli opens a chapter with a sentence from Livy once again points to the fact that the *Discourses on Livy* was initially conceived of as a simple commentary on Livy but developed into a more complex work of republican theory.

216 *as we said above*: *Discourses on Livy*, ii. 10.

later by Camillus: Lucius Furius Camillus was consul in 338 BC.

217 *'or generous treatment'*: Livy, viii. 13, cited in Latin, shortening slightly the last sentence. See *Rome and Italy*, 177.

the entire Valdichiana rebelled in 1502: in 1503 Machiavelli wrote one of his earliest works in which he combines such historical examples from both the ancient and modern world with political analysis, a brief treatise entitled *On the Method of Dealing with the Rebellious Peoples of the Valdichiana*. It dealt with the rebellion in the Valdichiana and contrasted Florentine policy with that of the Romans in a similar situation.

218 *'the Privernates deserved'*: Machiavelli constructs this conversation out of the Latin text of Livy (viii. 21). See *Rome and Italy*, 187. The events described here took place between 330 and 329 BC.

219 *in the proper place*: *Discourses on Livy*, iii. 40–1.

220 *by our own wise men*: here, as elsewhere when he discusses the usefulness of fortresses, Machiavelli treats this Florentine belief with contempt (see *The Prince*, XX).

221 *'arms remain'*: cited in Latin from Juvenal, *Satires*, viii. 124. For a translation of the complete text, see *The Satires of Juvenal*, trans. Humphries, 105.

'*anger supplies weapons*': cited in Latin from Virgil, *Aeneid*, i. 150. See Fitzgerald (trans.), *Aeneid*, 8 for a complete translation of the passage.

Count Francesco Sforza: ruler of Milan, 1450–66.

to his heirs: upon his father's death, Galeazzo Maria Sforza ruled Milan tyrannically until his death in 1476; his son, Giangaleazzo Sforza, lost control of Milan to his uncle, Ludovico Sforza (called Il Moro or the Moor) in 1480; Ludovico, in turn, lost the city to the French in 1499–1500, and when he was captured by the French at the battle of Novara he remained in captivity until his death; in 1512 the French left Milan; but the Sforza family once again lost control of the city after the battle of Marignano in 1515 as a result of their failure to hold the fortress, the Castello Sforzesco, which remains largely intact in the centre of the city today.

222 *he chose to destroy them*: Guidobaldo, duke of Urbino between 1482 and 1508, lost Urbino to Cesare Borgia in 1502 but regained it almost immediately, then lost it, regaining it again in 1503 after the death of Pope Alexander VI. Federico da Montefeltro was the most famous duke of Urbino, ruling between 1444 and 1482. The 'unforeseen incident' Machiavelli mentions is the rebellion against Cesare Borgia by his former allies that assisted the ruler of Urbino in regaining his territories, and which was suppressed by Borgia in the violent manner described in both *The Prince* (VII) and in *A Description of the Method Used By Duke Valentino in Killing Vitellozzo Vitelli, Oliverotto da Fermo, and Others*, written in 1503. For a discussion of the treatment of this episode in these two works, see Bondanella, *Machiavelli and the Art of Renaissance History*.

useful to him: the administration of the papal governor, Francesco Alidosi, who ruled the city after 1508, was so disastrous that the city rebelled in 1511 and restored its former rulers from the Bentivoglio family.

223 *in that state*: Niccolò Vitelli from the town of Città di Castello was able to regain control of that city in 1482 with the assistance of Lorenzo de' Medici. Pope Sixtus IV was Francesco della Rovere, pontiff between 1471 and 1484.

224 *the example of Tarentum*: Tarentum was captured by Hannibal in 212 BC, but the Roman citadel held out until Romans liberated the city in 209 (see Livy, xxvii. 15–16).

the example of Capua: occupied by Hannibal in 216 BC, it was reconquered by Rome after a lengthy siege in 211 (see Livy, xxvi. 14).

turn to Brescia: as Machiavelli has already noted in the *Discourses on Livy*, ii. 17, the town of Brescia was occupied by the Venetians and rebellious townspeople in 1512, but it was retaken by the French and suffered a disastrous sacking by de Foix's troops.

225 '*only women living there*': in the *Moralia* by Plutarch there are several references to remarks by Spartan kings (Agesilaus, Agis, Theopompus) to the effect that walls are less useful than armed citizens, but these do not refer to Athens. For this and other related texts, see the section 'Sayings of Spartans' in Plutarch, *Plutarch on Sparta*, trans. Richard J. A. Talbert (New York: Penguin, 1988), 106–63.

226 *the actions of Francesco Maria*: according to Francesco Guicciardini's *History of Italy* (xiii), Francesco Maria della Rovere marched upon Urbino in 1516, ignoring enemy towns controlled by his adversaries, and forced Urbino to surrender to him on 6 February 1517.

written previously: *Discourses on Livy*, ii. 22.

227 *a different subject*: *Discourses on Livy*, ii. 21.

229 *the appropriate place*: *Discourses on Livy*, iii. 6.

'*they rankle*': cited in Latin from Tacitus, *Annals* (xv). See Tacitus, *The Annals of Imperial Rome* trans. Michael Grant (New York: Penguin, 1971), 378.

231 *the ruin of the Florentine state*: the downfall of the republic also ended Machiavelli's political career.

Hasdrubal: not Hannibal's brother but another general by the same name.

235 '*meet no check!*': Livy, v. 37, cited in Latin. See *The Early History of Rome*, 382.

237 '*to a cash payment*': Livy, v. 49, cited in Latin. See *The Early History of Rome*, 395.

238 *a few years ago*: 1509, a reference to the Venetian defeat at Agnadello (see note to p. 37).

239 *that kingdom in 1513*: allied with the emperor, the English invaded Picardy in this year.

'*as it was before*': in this instance, Machiavelli provides an Italian paraphrase of the original Latin in Livy (ii. 13). See Livy, *The War with Hannibal*, 182.

240 *if they murdered him*: see Livy (viii. 23) in *Rome and Italy*.

for fear of retribution: for the complete account, see Plutarch's *Lives*.

241 '*a crown around the city*': Machiavelli cites a Latin expression here which is not literally taken from Livy's history (x. 43). For the complete English text of the passage to which Machiavelli's expression refers, see *Rome and Italy*, 349–51.

New Carthage in Spain: in 209 BC.

243 *Aratus of Sicyon*: 275–213 BC, leader of the Achaean League.

245 *at present*: Machiavelli's assessment of the condition of the two most important republican governments in Italy (Venice and Florence) at the time the *Discourses on Livy* was composed is gloomy. Florence had been returned to the control of the Medici, and soon after Machiavelli's death the city would fall under the hereditary rule of that family. Venice had lost much of its power through disastrous military defeats on the Italian mainland. Moreover, throughout the sixteenth and seventeenth centuries European politics would be characterized by the rise of nation states dominated by monarchies, not republics, until the republican resurgence in the eighteenth century to which Machiavelli's *Discourses on Livy* and *The Art of War* made important intellectual contributions.

246 '*from time to time*': this aphorism (cited by Machiavelli in Latin) is the kind of maxim associated with popular versions of Galen's teachings on medicine.

247 '*in opposition to the law of nations*': cited by Machiavelli in Latin, this phrase refers to the unwritten codes of conduct Romans and other Italian peoples followed in their dealings with each other and sometimes with other states. The most obvious example of such practices would be a prohibition against harming ambassadors and emissaries.

248 *the deaths of the decemvirs*: the decemvirs were actually exiled, not executed, although two committed suicide in prison (see Livy, iii. 58).

249 *the laws and institutions*: for a discussion of the lengthy tradition of exemplary republican heros, see Bondanella, *The Eternal City: Roman Images in the Modern World*.

249 *the two Catos*: Marcus Porcius Cato the Censor (234–149 BC), and his great-grandson Marcus Porcius Cato the Younger (94–46 BC), immortalized by Plutarch's biography and his appearance in Dante's *Commedia* as a republican hero who preferred suicide to living under the tyranny of Julius Caesar.

still maintains this religion: Machiavelli's view that ecclesiastical reforms by Franciscans and Dominicans actually increased corruption in the church represents one of his most shocking and cynical historical judgements.

250 *father of Roman liberty*: Machiavelli refers to the first Brutus, the man who established the first republic after the rape of Lucretia by a Tarquin aristocrat, not the second Brutus, the assassin of Julius Caesar (see note to p. 48).

251 *any king ruling in Rome*: in i. 56–60, the Roman historian recounts the single most important story in Roman historical mythology, that of the 'first' Brutus. Livy reports that Brutus 'deliberately assumed a mask to hide his true character' (Livy, *The Early History of Rome*, 86), and that when he and two friends went to Delphi and asked who would be the next king of Rome, the oracle replied that it would be the man who was the first to kiss his mother. Brutus interpreted the reference to a mother to be a reference to Mother Earth, and he immediately pretended to fall, kissing the earth in the process. Later, in a dramatic change of personality, Brutus would provide the catalyst to the indignant reaction to Lucretia's rape and subsequent suicide, which resulted in the overthrow of the Tarquins and the establishment of a republic in Rome.

252 *at length above*: see *Discourses on Livy*, i. 16.

in this matter: for Soderini see note to p. 23 above. His extraordinary election to a lifetime position as *gonfaloniere* was intended to counterbalance the power of certain aristocratic groups in Florence who wished to destroy the pro-French and popularly based republic for which Machiavelli worked. Machiavelli owed his political career to his patron Soderini, but Machiavelli did not allow the personal gratitude he felt for his superior to influence the negative judgement he makes on Soderini's career.

253 *over with some reward*: see Livy, i. 40 and 48.

256 *Conspiracies*: Machiavelli's treatment of conspiracies is by far the longest chapter in the *Discourses on Livy*, and although classical political theorists (especially Aristotle) discuss them, no major work in the history of political theory before Machiavelli devotes so much space and intellectual energy to the analysis of conspiracies.

should tolerate them: see Tacitus, *Histories*, iv. 8. For the English text see Wellesley (trans.), *The Histories*, 208. In giving this kind of advice to the reader, Machiavelli anticipates the popular image of Tacitus that emerged after his death, which relegated Livy's republicanism to the background and preferred Tacitus as the classical historian who had anticipated an age of absolute monarchs and who offered sage advice to the private citizen about how to avoid dangerous entanglements in such a political system. For a treatment of Tacitus in the late Renaissance and the seventeenth century, see Kenneth C. Schellhase, *Tacitus in Renaissance Political Thought* (Chicago: University of Chicago Press, 1976), or Bondanella, *The Eternal City: Roman Images in the Modern World*.

257 *discussed at sufficient length above*: *Discourses on Livy*, ii. 32.

   with this matter elsewhere: in *The Prince* (XIX).

258 *die a dry death*: cited from Juvenal's *Satires*, x. 112–13, in Latin. See *The Satires of Juvenal*, 125.

259 *the opportunity to do so*: 'the present Turk' is Selim I (1467–1520), the Ottoman ruler who succeeded his father Bajazet II (1446–1512), the target of an attempted assassination after he had failed to take Belgrade in 1492.

260 *and Sejanus against Tiberius*: it is significant that Machiavelli shifts from republican Rome to imperial Rome to find many of his examples of Roman conspiracies. With the support of the Praetorian guard, Perennius retained power until his execution by Commodus in AD 184; Plautianus, another prefect of the Praetorian guard under the emperor Septimus Severus, even had the promise of succeeding to the throne but was denounced and executed in AD 205; Sejanus practically controlled the empire in the absence of Tiberius but was finally denounced and executed in AD 31. Machiavelli relies on several sources for these examples: Herodian, *On the Roman Empire* for Perennius (i. 9) and Plautianus (iii. 12); and either Tacitus, *Annals* (v. 1–5) or Suetonius' biography of Tiberius.

   then took away his state: after both men had been driven into exile by Giangaleazzo Visconti, upon their return to Pisa Gambacorti made Jacopo his chancellor, but after a dispute over whether to ally the city with Florence (Gambacorti's position) or Milan (Jacopo's preference), Gambacorti was killed by his minister in 1392 and Jacopo ruled over Pisa until his death in 1398.

   to acquire that as well: Francesco Coppola (1420–87), a rich merchant who became the count of Sarno, attained the highest offices in the kingdom of Naples before being involved in the plot of that kingdom's barons against the king. The revolt supposedly ended with the signing of an agreement in 1485, when Ferdinand promised to pardon Coppola and other ringleaders. Only two years later, in May 1487, Ferdinand had Coppola and others executed and their property confiscated. Machiavelli makes a very brief reference to Coppola in *The Florentine Histories* (viii. 32).

262 *it was to be carried out*: the *Annals* of Tacitus (xv. 49–54) lists some twenty conspirators in this particular plot against Nero and also expresses the historian's astonishment that it was not discovered sooner, given the number of people involved. In *The Florentine Histories* (viii. 3–7), Machiavelli lists the main conspirators involved in the 1478 plot that ended in the assassination of Giuliano de' Medici, including not only the Pazzi family and their associates in Florence but also numerous anti-Medici exiles, who all enjoyed the tacit support of the pope. The Pazzi conspiracy is described in some detail in *The Florentine Histories*, viii. 1–10.

and Cebalinus to the king: Machiavelli's source is the life of Alexander the Great by Quintus Curtius Rufus (vi. 7). The event took place in 330 BC.

the ruin of all the conspirators: see Tacitus, *Annals*, xv. 54. This event took place in AD 65.

263 *showed any sign of fear*: see Livy, xxiv. 5. Machiavelli mistakes Theodorus for Theodotus, the name mentioned in Livy's account. This occurred in 215 BC.

Nelematus' plan: 'Nelematus' is a corrupted form of the correct name Hellanicus, mentioned both in Justin (xxvi. 1) and in Plutarch's *Of Virtuous Wives*, 253 A–B. The event occurred in 272 BC.

264 *'accuse you all'*: unlike so many of the speeches and remarks cited by Machiavelli from classical history, this remark is apparently his own invention, not a cited source.

executed their plans: Machiavelli mistakes Ortanes for Otanes, the figure Herodotus (iii. 70–8) credits as the leader of the successful conspiracy against a Magus, or Zoroastrian priest, named Smerdis. The event took place in 521 BC.

succeeded in killing Nabis: Livy's account of this event (xxxv. 35), which took place in 192 BC, gives the number of foot-soldiers as 1,000.

could not fail to succeed: Machiavelli does not mention the fact that, according to Tacitus (*Annals*, xv. 52), Piso refused to carry out the assassination of Nero in his gardens because it would have represented a breach of hospitality.

266 *they killed Commodus*: this occurred in AD 192, according to the account Machiavelli follows in Herodian, i. 16-17.

267 *Martial carried out successfully*: Machiavelli's source for this event, which took place in AD 217, is Herodian (iv. 12-13).

268 *the cardinal of San Giorgio*: Raffaele Riario (1451/60-1521) was part of the Pazzi Conspiracy, which included not only Jacopo and Francesco Pazzi but also the archbishop of Pisa (Salviati). The conspirators enjoyed the tacit approval of Pope Sixtus IV. In Machiavelli's works he generally refers to cardinals by the church to which their rank is attached, not by their family names.

while carrying out their plan: the men assigned to murder the Medici brothers in the church lost their nerve at the last minute, bungled the job (killing only Giuliano), and left Lorenzo alive to rally his followers and eventually to take revenge upon everyone connected with the conspiracy.

to kill him: see the biography of Marius in Plutarch's *Lives* for the complete story.

Sitalces, king of Thrace: it seems that Machiavelli has taken an episode from Herodotus' account of Cypselus, tyrant of Corinth (v. 92) and added it to Herodotus' account of Sitalces (ii. 95-101). No failed conspiracy can be found concerning Sitalces in Herodotus or in any other historical source.

269 *the duke's cantor*: Ferdinando and Giulio d'Este in 1506 plotted against Duke Alfonso I, who ruled from 1505 until 1534. The duke's cantor, their accomplice, was Giovanni or Jean d'Artignanova, a Gascon. The plot failed and the two illegitimate brothers were imprisoned for life. See Francesco Guicciardini's *History of Italy*, vii. 4, for details.

'*the great task that faced him*': Livy, xxxv. 35, cited in Latin. See *Rome and the Mediterranean*, 221.

270 *could ever make me believe it*: Giorgio Inglese (*Discorsi*, 593) notes that the Latin translation of Herodian (iii. 12) by Angelo Poliziano, which Machiavelli probably read, specified that the two men were to be struck down in two different rooms of the same palace, not really in two different geographical locations.

and avenged him: Machiavelli's source is Justin, ii. 9, but it was Hipparchus, not Diocles, who was killed.

avenged him: see Justin, xvi. 5, for more details on this plot, which occurred in 353 BC.

271 *a rare and almost unparalleled event*: Machiavelli finds a description of this conspiracy in the biography of Pelopidas in Plutarch's
Lives, but makes some factual errors. The conspirators met in
Charon's home, but it was Phillidas, not Charon, who was their
advisor. Plutarch does not mention ten tyrants but a lesser number
of individuals. The conspiracy took place in 379 BC.

272 *to flee from Siena*: Giorgio Inglese (*Discorsi*, 594) notes that an earlier editor had corrected the MS to read 'Luzio Bellanti', confusing
this conspiracy of 1508 against Pandolfo by Giulio with an earlier
conspiracy led by Lucio Bellanti in 1495. Pandolfo Petrucci ruled
Siena from 1498 until 1512.

they in time avenged the dead man: as Machiavelli notes in *The
Florentine Histories* (vii. 34), Galeazzo Maria Sforza was assassinated in 1476 by three men (Giovanni, Carlo Visconti, and Girolamo Oligato), all of whom were ultimately executed for their
crimes. The conspirators failed because they left Giangaleazzo,
Ludovico il Moro, and Ascanio Sforza alive.

273 *at various times and places*: Machiavelli bases his remarks on the
biographies of Caesar and Brutus he read in Plutarch's *Lives*.

which clearly implicated them: Machiavelli's sources are the biography of Cicero in Plutarch's *Lives* and Sallust's *The Conspiracy
of Catiline*, xxxi.

274 *of banquets and weddings*: Machiavelli's source is Justin, xxi. 4,
which describes this event taking place around 350 BC.

tyrant of Athens: the biography of Solon in Plutarch's *Lives*
describes the stratagem Pisistratus employed to gain power.

the ruler of the city: Petrucci came back from exile in 1487 and
received the command of the mercenary troops of the city government in 1496. See *The Florentine Histories*, viii. 35.

a tyranny in that city: Machiavelli's source is Plutarch's *Lives*,
although the incident is also mentioned in Justin (iii. 6).

275 *as we said elsewhere*: *Discourses on Livy*, ii. 26. Machiavelli takes
this example from Livy, vii. 38–41.

276 *into operation*: see Livy, vii. 38–41, for a fuller description of the
actions of C. Marcius Rutulus in 342 BC.

to take the state away from him: some of most inspired pages in
Machiavelli's *Florentine Histories* (ii. 33–7) are devoted to the rapid
rise and sudden downfall of Walter de Brienne, duke of Athens. He
was first appointed as executive officer in Florence in 1325 and
then again in 1342. During his second stay in Florence the duke

attempted to set up a tyranny in the city, and not one but three different conspiracies were organized against him. The arrest of Antonio Adimari caused riots in the streets, which forced the duke to withdraw from Florence.

from being a commissioner to being a prisoner: this occurred in 1502, not 1501, but Machiavelli's account in other respects generally agrees with that in Francesco Guicciardini's *History of Italy* (v. 8) or *History of Florence* (xxii).

277 *of his state and his life*: see the biography of Dion in Plutarch's *Lives*.

278 *the examples of Spurius Cassius*: see Livy, ii. 41; the date is 485 BC.

and Manlius Capitolinus: see Livy, vi. 14–20. Manlius was executed in 384 BC. For a discussion of how these particular examples inspired not only Machiavelli but republican art in Renaissance Italy, see Bondanella, *The Eternal City: Roman Images in the Modern World*.

279 *'not been born in a free state'*: cited in Latin from Livy, vi. 20. See *Rome and Italy*, 64.

280 *as was discussed above*: see *Discourses on Livy*, iii. 1.

281 *on many occasions*: Machiavelli deals with the role of fortune and how men's characters suit or fail to suit their times in a number of places, including the famous discussion in *The Prince* (XXV); a letter written in 1506 to Giambattista Soderini (see *The Portable Machiavelli*, 60–4); and a poem in *terza rima*, 'Tercets on Fortune' (see *Machiavelli: The Chief Works and Others*, trans. Allan Gilbert (Durham, NC: Duke University Press, 1989), ii. 745–9).

with the times: Livy discusses the successful delaying tactics of Quintus Fabius Maximus against Hannibal, as well as his bad counsel in advising Scipio not to cross over into Africa to conclude the war against Carthage, in several books (xxii, xxiii, xxviii).

283 *'in an unfriendly country'*: Livy, vii. 12, cited in Latin. See *Rome and Italy*, 112. The dictator in question is Gaius Sulpicius in the year 358 BC. Machiavelli's Latin text differs somewhat from the modern critical edition employed by the English translation cited here, and mentions Gneus (not Gaius) Sulpicius, an error.

284 *the father of Perseus*: this is Philip V of Macedonia (not the father of Alexander the Great), who was finally defeated by the Romans at the battle of Cynoscephalae in Thessaly in 197 BC (see Livy, xxxii. 11–12).

285 *Gneus Sulpicius*: as mentioned above, the correct name is 'Gaius'.

285 *'in an unfriendly country'*: Machiavelli here repeats in Latin the
    quotation from Livy that opens the chapter with a slight variation,
    omitting a few words. See note to p. 283 above.

286 *likewise routed by the Swiss*: in 1476 Charles was defeated by the
    Swiss at both Granson and Morat. The battle of Novara took place
    in 1513, when French troops sent by King Louis XII to conquer
    Milan were routed by Swiss troops engaged by Duke Massimiliano
    Sforza.

287 *after the peace*: the alliance against Venice consisted of Pope Sixtus
    IV, Naples, Milan, and Florence, and was formed in 1482 to guar-
    antee the territories owned by the duke of Ferrara; when Venice
    refused to give back some of this territory, the pope placed the
    Venetian republic under an interdict in 1483. These anti-Venetian
    forces were joined by the Gonzaga rulers of Mantua and the Ben-
    tivoglio rulers of Bologna. When it seemed that the Venetians were
    completely defeated and at the mercy of their enemies, Ludovico il
    Moro of Milan made a separate peace with the Venetians, and his
    partners were obliged to accept this *fait accompli*. The conflict was
    settled by the Treaty of Bagnolo in 1484. Not surprisingly, given
    the machinations of the parties involved, it was the duke of Ferrara
    who emerged with fewer territories than he had expected to pro-
    tect through this alliance, while the duke of Milan was reported to
    have received a large payment from the Venetians for breaking
    ranks with his allies.

    to come to terms themselves: commentators differ on the interpre-
    tation of the league formed 'a few years ago': Walker (*The Dis-
    courses*, ii. 173) interprets this remark to refer to the League of
    Venice, formed in 1495 by the Emperor Maximilian, Ferdinand
    and Isabella of Spain, Pope Alexander VI, and Ludovico il Moro of
    Milan with Venice against France. When Ludovico signed a sep-
    arate accord with France, Spain followed suit in 1497, resulting in
    the breakup of the league. On the other hand, Giorgio Inglese (*Dis-
    corsi*, 605) believes the alliance to which Machiavelli refers is the
    Holy League of 1511, sponsored by Pope Julius II, which broke up
    in 1513 when Spain signed a separate peace treaty with France.
    Given the similarity of the two historical situations, Machiavelli's
    point would remain the same with either example in mind.

290 *the life of this commander*: Machiavelli refers to the biography of
    Marcus Crassus in Plutarch's *Lives*. The promises of the Parthian
    general Surenas lulled the Romans into believing they could retreat,
    and in the resulting battle in 53 BC Crassus was killed, along with
    some 20,000 Roman soldiers, while another 10,000 were enslaved.

298 *or even equal to him*: Machiavelli modifies this account to suit his purpose. For a more accurate account of how the invasion of Sicily began, see Thucydides, vi. 8–24.

299 *as we have said elsewhere*: *Discourses on Livy*, i. 1.

　　the office to him: Lucius Paulus Aemilius, surnamed 'Macedonicus' because of his victory over the Macedonians at Pydna in 168 BC, is discussed in Plutarch's *Lives*.

301 *shamelessly insulted him*: the Spanish campaign of Gaius Claudius Nero (211 BC) and his subsequent defeat of Hasdrubal (207) is discussed by Livy in xxvi. 17 and xxvii. 43. The battle of the Metaurus River resulted in the largest number of Carthaginian casualties in the entire war—Livy says 57,000, including Hasdrubal, Hannibal's brother—thereby avenging the bloody Roman defeat at Cannae.

302 *he killed himself*: Machiavelli finds the description of the battle of Philippi (42 BC), where Mark Antony and Octavius Caesar defeated Brutus and Cassius, in the biography of Brutus in Plutarch's *Lives*.

　　the French who were victorious: the battle of Marignano took place on 13–14 September 1515; Machiavelli mentions it in *Discourses on Livy*, ii. 18 and 22.

　　of the Aequi: Machiavelli slips here, meaning to say the Volscians (see Livy, iv. 37–41, for the correct details).

303 *and won the war*: Guicciardini's version of this event, which took place in 1498, is in his *History of Florence* (xvii) and his *History of Italy* (iv. 3), although the detail about the old woman is not reported.

304 *with their armies*: see Livy, ii. 55–60, for events occurring in 472–471 BC involving Titus Quinctius Capitolinus and Claudius Appius (not to be confused with the notorious decemvir whose attempted rape of Virginia sparked a reform of the republican regime).

　　'punishment is more valuable than indulgence': Tacitus, *Annals*, iii. 55, cited in Latin. As both Walker (*The Discourses*, ii. 183) and Giorgio Inglese (*Discorsi*, 617–18) note, there is a discrepancy between the text cited by Machiavelli and the text as it has been transmitted to our day. The modern translation of Tacitus reads as follows: 'For deference to the emperor and the wish to imitate him were more effective than legal penalties and threats' (trans. Grant, *Annals*, 145–56). In effect, Machiavelli claims that Tacitus said

exactly the opposite of what we believe today the historian wrote.
Inglese explains this discrepancy in the following manner. The first
six books of the *Annals* were originally published in March 1515
for Pope Leo X, who owned the only original manuscript
(Mediceo Laur. 68). Inglese believes that the first Italian to consult
the codex was Cardinal Francesco Soderini, who mentions receiving it in 1509. Machiavelli himself was in the Tyrol from January to
June of 1508 and received a letter from a friend in Cologne inform-
ing Machiavelli that he was searching for such classical manu-
scripts. Inglese concludes that Machiavelli probably encountered
friends who knew the text before it was printed and who probably
heard some of Tacitus' ideas expressed as maxims without being
able to consult the critical edition until 1515. For the treatment of
Tacitus in the Renaissance, see Schellhase, *Tacitus in Renaissance
Political Thought*.

305 *another treatise on this subject*: in *The Prince* (XVII).

of Falerii than arms: this famous incident took place in 394 BC,
when Marcus Furius Camillus was besieging the town of Falerii
(see Livy, v. 27).

306 *the generosity of Fabricius*: Machiavelli here follows the story contained in the biography of Pyrrhus in Plutarch's *Lives*. Since the
war continued for several years, it is probable that Pyrrhus did not
abandon his 'Pyrrhic' victories in Italy because of this act of generosity but, rather, because he was significantly weakened by his
costly military successes against the Romans.

the friendship of all of Spain: for these two events that took place in
210 BC, see Livy, xxvi. 46 and 50.

307 *on another occasion*: *Discourses on Livy*, i. 37.

anyone who makes himself loved: Machiavelli's most important
discussion of this topic is chapter XVII of *The Prince*.

308 *both of them were glorified as well*: the comparison of Scipio and
Hannibal and the paradoxical success of each man through completely different methods were questions that intrigued Machiavelli early on, even before the composition of either *The Prince* or
the *Discourses on Livy*. This is clear from an important letter written to Giovanbattista Soderini in 1506 which contains an earlier
formulation of this comparison (see *The Portable Machiavelli*,
61–4, for an English translation). Giorgio Inglese's commentary
(*Discorsi*, 619–20) provides an illuminating discussion of the development in Machiavelli's thought from this early letter to this section of his commentary on Livy.

309 *'Manlian commands'*: cited in Latin from Livy, viii. 7. See *Rome and Italy*, 167.

310 *'certain of victory'*: cited in Latin from Livy, vii. 10. See *Rome and Italy*, 108.

  A prudent man: possibly a reference to Aristotle's *Politics*, III. xv. 1286b.

312 *'greater popularity than this'*: cited in Latin from Livy, vii. 33. See *Rome and Italy*, 141.

313 *with Publicola*: as Giorgio Inglese notes (*Discorsi*, 624), the family of Valerius Corvus (called Corvinus by Machiavelli) was traditionally associated with the name Publicola or 'friend of the people'. Thus, this reference is probably not to P. Valerius Publicola who, with Brutus, served as one of Rome's two first consuls in 509 BC (Livy, ii. 2).

  bring him love: Xenophon's works were published in Latin in 1490. Machiavelli certainly read his biography of Cyrus (the *Cyropaedia*) as well as the *Hiero*, a work on tyranny.

  a gentleman appeared: many commentators identify this figure with Vettore Pisani (1324–80), who was first defeated by the Genoese in 1379, incarcerated by the Venetians, and then released when the Genoese fleet threatened to attack the city of Venice itself. His subsequent victory over the enemy fleet saved the city. Both Giorgio Inglese (*Discorsi*, 624) and Walker (*The Discourses*, ii. 188) note, however, that Machiavelli's description is extremely confused and far removed from the historical facts about Pisani as they are accepted by contemporary historians of the Venetian republic.

314 *'but admired his exceptional ability'*: cited by Machiavelli incompletely in the original Latin from Livy, v. 26 (editors' translation). The complete text (see *The Early History of Rome*, 371) is somewhat longer: 'this the troops violently resented, but discipline was good and they could not but admire the strict honesty of their commander however much they might disapprove of it.'

315 *Lucius Quinctius*: Lucius Quinctius Cincinnatus, military tribune and dictator, celebrated in republican mythology for relinquishing military power and returning to his simple farm (see *Discourses on Livy*, iii. 25).

316 *Publilius Philo*: Q. Publilius Philo, consul in 339 BC and the first plebeian praetor in 337; Livy (viii. 26) describes how his military command at the siege of Palaeopolis (Naples) in 326 BC

was extended, remarking: 'He was the first to enjoy these two distinctions: an extension of his command, which was unprecedented; and a triumph after his term of office had ended' (Livy, *Rome and Italy*, 195).

316 *explained elsewhere*: *Discourses on Livy*, i. 37.

317 *'inseparable from wealth'*: cited in Latin from Livy, iii. 26. See *The Early History of Rome*, 213. Cincinnatus became dictator in 458 BC.

'know how to be consul': contrary to his usual practice of citing Livy in the original Latin, in this instance Machiavelli uses Italian translations in his text to convey the speeches of Cincinnatus to the besieged army and to Minucius (see Livy, iv. 29).

ruined by his workers: Marcus Atilius Regulus is more famous for the fact that, after being captured by the Carthaginians in the First Punic War, he was sent to Rome to arrange peace terms. Once at home, he urged the Romans to fight on, then returned (as he had sworn to do) to Carthage to face a terrible punishment and death. Valerius Maximus (iv. 4) mentions his request to return home to his farm in 256 BC, before his capture by the Carthaginians in the following year.

318 *preferred the nobleman*: Livy (iv. 9) refers only to the woman's beauty, not her wealth.

320 *fifteen years ago*: the disturbances in Pistoia took place between 1501 and 1502. Machiavelli, in Pistoia as a commissioner from the Florentine government, wrote a brief report on these events in 1502 entitled *De rebus pistoriensibus*. Some commentators see this passage as proof that the *Discourses on Livy*, at least in part, were composed during the year 1516.

at the beginning: in the introduction to Book I of the *Discourses on Livy*.

at length above: see *Discourses on Livy*, ii. 24.

321 *you possess divided*: a typical example of Machiavelli's stylistic shift between an impersonal reflexive verb and a direct address to the reader, employing the familiar *tu* form.

'they divided themselves': see the *Decades* (ii. 9) of Flavio Biondo (1392–1463), which Machiavelli cites in Italian rather than the original Latin. Biondo's history was first printed in 1559, years after the publication of the first edition of the *Discourses on Livy*, but MS copies circulated widely long before that date.

a certain Monsieur de Lant: Monsieur de Langres.

the Marzocco faction: the symbol of the city of Florence, a rampant lion, was called the Marzocco.

322 *had him put to death*: around 439 BC (see Livy, iv. 13–14).

324 *'which always resembles its leader'*: see Livy, v. 28 (editors' translation). A less literal translation of this line is found in *The Early History of Rome*, 373.

fixed on their lord: cited from Lorenzo de' Medici's *Rappresen-
tazione di SS Giovanni e Paolo* (ii. 100). Giorgio Inglese (*Discorsi*,
631) notes that only Dante and Lorenzo de' Medici receive the
honour of being cited in the vernacular in the *Discourses on Livy*.
Only a few sentences before this citation, Machiavelli cites Flavio
Biondo in Italian, but he is translating material from a history originally composed in Latin.

325 *'what they had done for his'*: cited in Latin from Livy, vi. 6. See
Rome and Italy, 44.

326 *'nor did they believe, etc.'*: see note to p. 325.

by nothing more than envy: Machiavelli greatly simplifies the
account in Exodus 32, which describes how Moses and the sons of
Levi slew numerous Israelites who failed to worship the one true
god. Thus, Machiavelli overlooks the religious reasons for this
event, attributing more 'Machiavellian' motives to Moses than can
be found in the text itself.

328 *'lost anything through exile'*: cited in Latin from Livy, vi. 7. See
Rome and Italy, 46.

as was mentioned above: see *Discourses on Livy*, ii. 30.

329 *'do they become insolent'*: unlike most of the Latin passages cited
by Machiavelli in the *Discourses on Livy* from Livy's history, this
text is not a direct quotation, although Livy makes a similar remark
in discussing Antiochus (xxxvii. 45): 'But our feelings are subject to
our own minds; and we have kept them unchanged and still keep
them unchanged in every kind of fortune; success has never exalted
them nor has adversity depressed them' (*Rome and the Mediterranean*, 323). Machiavelli must have had this passage in mind when
he employed a much shortened and more effective sentence to
replace Livy's more complicated explanation.

at Vailà: at Vailate or Agnadello (14 May 1509). This battle and its
disastrous effects on the Venetians are also described in Francesco
Guicciardini's *History of Italy* (viii).

in matters of war: Machiavelli distrusts Venetian military policy,
which usually employed mercenary soldiers on *terra firma*,
whereas their splendid fleets were commanded by citizen-sailors
and included many Venetians in their crews.

330 *it has been said elsewhere*: a possible reference to *The Prince* (XII), but the *Discourses on Livy* (ii. 4 and 21) also contains a similar argument.

'*with his training and habit*': cited in Latin from Livy, vi. 7. See *Rome and Italy*, 47.

332 *sent them Hasdrubal*: the account of this event Machiavelli finds in Polybius (i. 65–88) says the ambassador was Gesco, not Hasdrubal. Machiavelli also refers to this event in *The Prince* (XII) and *The Art of War* (I). The Hasdrubal in question is not the brother of the Carthaginian general Hannibal.

333 *punished Claudius Pulcher*: see *Discourses on Livy*, i. 14.

'*to be so great*': cited in Latin from Livy, vi. 41. See *Rome and Italy*, 94.

'*at the gallop*': cited in Latin from Livy, vi. 29. The dictator is Titus Quinctius Cincinnatus, and his master of horse is Aulus Sempronius Atratinus. See *Rome and Italy*, 75.

334 '*no leader to direct it*': the Latin phrase Machiavelli cites from Livy, vi. 30 is somewhat shorter than the quotation in the English edition from which we cite (see *Rome and Italy*, 77).

on another occasion: see *Discourses on Livy*, i. 11.

rather violent and extraordinary: an understatement—according to Livy (vii. 5), the tribune was threatened with instant death by the son if he did not swear an oath to forgo any action against the father.

336 *that won him the name Torquatus*: according to Livy (vii. 12), Titus Manlius killed an enormous Gaul who challenged the Romans to single combat and despoiled him of his torque or collar.

on the Ticinus River: Livy (xxi. 46) describes this act of filial loyalty during the first major battle against Hannibal.

decided among themselves to do: see Livy, xxii. 53.

to her husband in Spain: this noble act, known in the classical tradition as 'the continence of Scipio', inspired numerous paintings, frescos, and works of literature (Livy, xxvi. 50). For a consideration of this tradition in Western culture, see Bondanella, *The Eternal City: Roman Images in the Modern World*.

337 *a man more meritorious than he was*: see Livy, xxiv. 8. Machiavelli does not mention that Quintus Fabius Maximus was the man who replaced Otacilius as consul.

338 *by their results*: the original Italian text ('giudicando gli uomini le cose dal fine') recalls the even more famous and often mistranslated

line in *The Prince* (XVIII) concerning ends and means: 'si guarda al fine' or 'one must consider the final result'.

to attack the Shah: Selim I, Ottoman ruler from 1515 to 1520, who captured Syria in 1515 and Egypt in 1516.

340 *'when I have no other remedy!'*: Machiavelli found the biography of Paulus Aemilius in Plutarch's *Lives*, but unlike his many quotations from Livy, which he customarily takes from the original Latin text, Machiavelli has invented this remark.

the French: the reader should remember that Machiavelli employs the word *Franciosi* for both ancient Gauls and modern Frenchmen. In most cases an English translation is able to distinguish his usage because of the context. In this particular instance Machiavelli links the ancient Gauls to the sixteenth-century inhabitants of France.

both fury and order: this classical term 'fury' refers to the specific quality of being belligerent or to ferociousness in war.

341 *they failed as soon as that cooled*: it is a commonplace of Machiavelli scholarship that *The Prince* concentrates upon a personalized and exceptional ability, skill, or ingenuity (*virtù*) in a single individual, whereas his *Discourses on Livy* emphasizes an institutionalized ability in *ordini* (organization, institutions, sometimes military discipline). Few passages in the *Discourses on Livy* show how closely these two terms may be related in Machiavelli's thought as does this one discussing the French and their military virtues and vices.

'and dedicated service': these words, in Livy, viii. 34, are not the actual words spoken by Papinius Cursor but represent Livy's summation of his oration, which Machiavelli cites in the original Latin. See *Rome and Italy*, 206–7.

342 *as we previously discussed*: see *Discourses on Livy*, i. 2.

'on to Campania': cited in Latin from Livy, vii. 11. See *Rome and Italy*, 108.

the guarding of passes: see *Discourses on Livy*, i. 23.

343 *'or strange enemy'*: cited in Latin from Livy, vii. 32. See *Rome and Italy*, 140.

and like the Gauls: in the case of Manlius Torquatus (see *Discourses on Livy*, iii. 22).

344 *'on to Campania'*: in this citation, Machiavelli has modified this previously cited passage from Livy's Latin (see note to p. 342 above).

345 *'but by this right hand of mine'*: cited in Latin from Livy, vii. 32. See *Rome and Italy*, 140.

346 *spoken elsewhere*: see *Discourses on Livy*, ii. 13.

347 *'so blind as to neglect it'*: this and the two following quotations are cited in Latin from Livy, vii. 34. See *Rome and Italy*, 143–4.

349 *on the lake of Perugia*: at the battle of Lake Trasimeno in 217 BC (see Livy, xxii. 4).

    the horns of his cattle: Hannibal escaped entrapment by Fabius Maximus in central Italy in 217 BC with just such a stratagem (see Livy, xxii. 17).

    'nor removes enemies': cited in Latin from Livy, ix. 3. See *Rome and Italy*, 219.

    in another place: see *Discourses on Livy*, ii. 23.

351 *in our treatise 'De Principe'*: see *The Prince*, ch. XVIII.

353 *'than war with liberty'*: cited in Latin from Livy, x. 16. See *Rome and Italy*, 310.

355 *Decius and Fabius*: this occurred in 295 BC (Livy, x. 27–9).

357 *should follow this example*: Livy discusses Gaius Marcius Rutulus, Papirius Cursor, and Q. Fabius Maximus Rullianus, consuls in 310 BC, in ix. 38.

    in 1508: the Florentines calculated dates from the Annunciation or the Incarnation of Christ (25 March). Thus, the event in question actually occurred in 1509.

DATE DUE

	APR 1 9 2004		